GLENCOE

INTRODUCTION TO
Multimedia

- Project-Based Learning
- Supports Perkins and NCLB Requirements
- Standards-Based
- Real-World Applications

Ana Weston Solomon

Hayward Adult Career and
Education Center
Hayward, California

 **Glencoe**

 **Glencoe**

The *McGraw·Hill* Companies

Send all inquiries to:
Glencoe/McGraw-Hill
4400 Easton Commons
Easton, OH 43219

ISBN: 978-0-07-894271-6   (Student Edition)
MHID: 0-07-894271-3   (Student Edition)

1 2 3 4 5 6 7 8 9   DOW/LEH   15 14 13 12 11 10

About the Author

Ana Weston Solomon is the principal of Hayward Adult Career and Education Center, within the Hayward Unified School District, California. As an instructional leader, Ana's focus is academic literacy, workforce development in the 21st century, and support of lifelong learning.

Her experience includes developing, implementing, and teaching curriculum for technology students and English language learners (ELL) in the Oakland Unified School District and other local institutions. She has instructed teachers through the University of California Berkeley Extension Program where she taught courses including Integrating Technology into Curriculum; Software Evaluation;

and Access, Equity, and Ethics in Technology. Ms. Solomon is a guest instructor at Holy Names University where she teaches Web Page Design.

Ms. Solomon earned her BA in English Literature from Holy Names University, her MA Ed in Instructional Technologies from San Francisco State University, and her Leadership Administrative Credential from California State East Bay. She is also the founder of MediaTech Consulting, a Technology Training and Resource Consulting Company which provides in-service training for educators and industry. She lives in the San Francisco Bay area with her family and three standard poodles.

Creative Media Advisory Board

Janet Bremer
Cincinnati Hills Christian Academy
Cincinnati, OH

Cathy DeSimone
Academy for the Arts, Science, and
    Technology
Myrtle Beach, SC

Christianne Disser
Montgomery High School
Montgomery, TX

Alan Penner
Moorpark High School
Moorpark, CA

Stacy Sherman, ACA
Atlantic Technical Center
Coconut Creek, FL

Lucinda Wright
Instructional Technology Specialist
Columbus, OH

Academic and Technical Review Board

Marsha Bass, M.S., ED.
Instructor, Kaplan University, College of
    Arts and Sciences
Elkhart, IN

Doug Bergman
Porter Gaud School
Charleston, SC

Matt Bracher
Cascade Christian Junior/
    Senior High School
Payallup, WA

James Capra
Coronado High School
Henderson, NV

Trudy Davis
West Visual Arts and Technology Magnet
    of RISD
Richardson, TX

Steve Franklin
Dartmouth
Nova Scotia, Canada

Deborah Gore
Douglas County High School
Douglasville, GA

Lee Geary Grafton
Director of Educational Technology
Palm Springs Unified School District
Palm Springs, CA

Lorraine Grice
Mid Florida Tech Center
Orlando, FL

Denise Harmon
Dale Jackson Career Center Media Arts
    Department
Lewisville, TX

Kay Hennighan
The Career Center
Winston-Salem, NC

Billy Hix
Professor, Business Information
    Technology
NASA Faculty Fellow
Motlow State Community College
Lynchburg, TN

Lorna Jacobs
Deer Park High School
Deer Park, TX

Stephen London
Reseda High School Digital Arts Academy
Los Angeles, CA

Nancy Mack
Technology Education Chairperson
Booker T. Washington High School for the
    Performing and Visual Arts
Dallas, TX

Audrey Marshall
Auburn High School
Auburn, AL

Kevin Niemeyer
Technical Writer
Houston, TX

Charles Robert Paige
St. Paul Technical College
St. Paul, MN

Patti Pawlowski
Oak Park High School
Oak Park, CA

Michael Perry
East Paulding High School
Dallas, GA
Kennesaw State University, Adjunct
    Business Professor

Keith Ruthledge
Travis High School
Austin, TX

Angie Schuman
Dumas High School
Dumas, TX

Mark Sheinberg
Santa Susana High School
Simi Valley, CA

Tom Vogelgesang
Technology Coordinator
Lincoln High School
Tallahassee, FL

Polly White
Wawasee High School
Syracuse, IN

Take the Multimedia Challenge!

Many features in this text—such as color headings, illustrations with captions, tables, and charts—have been carefully created to help you read, understand, and remember key ideas and concepts. Taking advantage of these features can help you improve your reading and study skills.

Get Started
The scavenger hunt on this page highlights features that will help you get the most out of your textbook.

1 How many **chapters** are in this book? How many **units**? *(Hint: Look in this book's Table of Contents.)*

2 What is the title of the **Portfolio Project** previewed on page 2?

3 What is the purpose of the **Graphic Organizer** on page 6?

4 In which **Appendix** can you learn more about career skills?

5 How many steps will it take you to complete **You Try It Activity 7A**?

6 What **Ethics & Technology** topic is discussed on page 58?

7 What **online tool** will help you check the project you create in **Projects Across the Curriculum**, Chapter 1?

8 How many **Reading Checks** are in Chapter 1?

9 What types of skills are needed to complete an **Academic Connections** activity, such as the one on page 125?

10 Where can you find activities that will allow you to build **21st Century Skills**?

For answers to the Scavenger Hunt, go to this book's Online Learning Center at **glencoe.com**.

Table of Contents

FOCUS ON **Reading Strategies**
Look for these reading strategies
in each chapter:

- Before You Read
- Graphic Organizer
- Reading Check
- After You Read

Table of Contents

FOCUS ON Academic Success

To help you succeed in your classes and on tests, look for these academic skills:
- **Reading Guides**
- **Quick Write Activities**
- **English Language Arts Features**
- **Mathematics Features**
- **Practice Academic Skills**
- **Academic Connections**

FOCUS ON **Project-Based Learning**

Projects throughout this book can help you use your skills in real-life situations:
- Step-by-step You Try It Activities
- Portfolio Projects
- Projects Across the Curriculum

Table of Contents

FOCUS ON **Online Resources**
Look for the online icon and go to the book's Online Learning Center at glencoe.com for:
- Online Student Manuals
- Graphic Organizers
- Practice Quizzes
- Evaluation Rubrics
- Additional Enrichment Activities

Prepare for Academic Success!

Do you know why it is important to proofread an essay? Do you know how to calculate a file's download time? Use these academic features to succeed in school, on tests, and with life!

Academic Focus **English Language Arts**

Academic Focus  **Mathematics**

Quick Write Activity

Develop Real World Career Skills

Do you know what career opportunities are available in multimedia production? Do you know what ethics means? These activities will help you develop your job skills.

Learn About Careers Online

Visit this book's Online Learning Center at **glencoe.com** to find additional career information.

Real World — Why It's Important

Build 21st Century Skills

Do you know why you should use online resources ethically? Do you know how to prioritize and set realistic goals? These features will help you develop skills that you can use at school and in the workplace.

21st CENTURY SKILLS

PLAN AHEAD

Ethics & Technology

Go Online ACTIVITY
glencoe.com

Apply Multimedia Skills

Do you know how to create a multimedia production? Do you know how to chart a navigation scheme? These step-by-step activities allow you to apply your multimedia skills.

YOU TRY IT > Activities

Program Overview

The *Introduction to Multimedia* program seamlessly integrates academic concepts, college readiness skills, 21st Century Skills, and project-based learning with core multimedia concepts.

Academic Rigor

READING HANDBOOK
Use this handbook to learn reading and note-taking tips.

 READING GUIDE
Preview main ideas, key concepts, and vocabulary terms.

ACADEMIC STANDARDS
Standards are integrated into each chapter.

Quick Write Activity
Master essential writing skills.

 English Language Arts
Connect English language arts concepts to multimedia skills.

Mathematics
Connect mathematics concepts to multimedia skills.

STANDARDIZED TEST PRACTICE
Prepare for standardized tests or certification exams.

MATH HANDBOOK
Learn more about core mathematical skills and concepts.

Career Readiness

CAREERS & TECHNOLOGY
Explore multimedia career opportunities.

CAREER SKILLS HANDBOOK
Learn more about the skills and behaviors needed for career success.

CAREER RESOURCES
Find multimedia career resources.

Real World Technology
Learn how to apply work skills to real-life situations.

21st Century Skills

STANDARDS AT WORK
Practice skills needed to succeed in today's workforce.

Ethics & Technology
Explore ethical issues related to multimedia.

21st CENTURY SKILLS
Apply these essential workplace skills.

Project-Based Learning

YOU TRY IT Activities
Step-by-step activities allow you to apply essential multimedia skills and concepts.

PROJECTS ACROSS THE CURRICULUM
Plan, research, and create your own multimedia projects in a real-world context.

UNIT PORTFOLIO PROJECTS
Demonstrate mastery of multimedia skills. Use your portfolio to display your progress in this course.

 ONLINE STUDENT MANUAL
Apply and extend your multimedia skills with these application-specific, step-by-step activities.

ONLINE STUDENT MANUAL PORTFOLIO PROJECTS
Showcase your multimedia skills.

Begin the Unit

Apply Multimedia Skills to Real Life

Multimedia is a part of your everyday life. *Introduction to Multimedia* teaches skills you need to plan and create multimedia projects. Consider how you can use what you learn in this book to create attractive, user-friendly multimedia components and presentations.

Read the Chapter Titles to find out what topics will be covered.

Use the Photo to Predict what the unit will be about. Answer questions to help focus on unit topics.

Preview the Project at the end of the unit. Use the preview to think about how what you are learning applies to the project.

Review the Unit

Build Career Skills with Portfolio Projects

Each unit ends with a Portfolio Project that allows you to apply the skills you have learned in a real-world project. To complete each project, you will make decisions, do research, develop content, and share what you have learned.

Read the Project Assignment to learn what you will need to do. Follow the numbered steps to complete the project.

Follow the Project Checklist to make sure that you have done everything you need to complete your project.

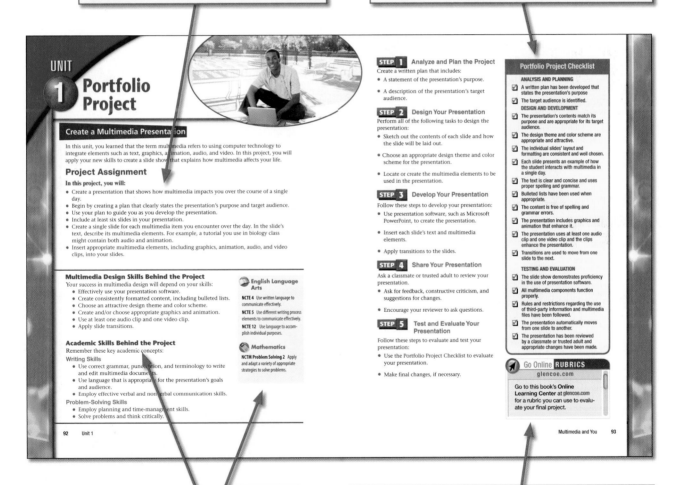

Integrate Academics throughout the portfolio projects.

Evaluate Your Work A rubric is a scoring tool that lists the project criteria. You can find the rubric at the book's **Online Learning Center** at **glencoe.com**.

Program Overview

Begin the Chapter

Develop Essential 21st Century Skills

Use the activities in the opener to help you connect what you already know to chapter topics. Think about different multimedia tools that you have used, such as cell phones, Web sites, DVDs, and videos. How are they similar with those in the textbook?

Read the Chapter Objectives to preview the key ideas you will learn. Keep these in mind as you read the chapter.

Explore the Photo to jump-start your thinking about the chapter's main topics.

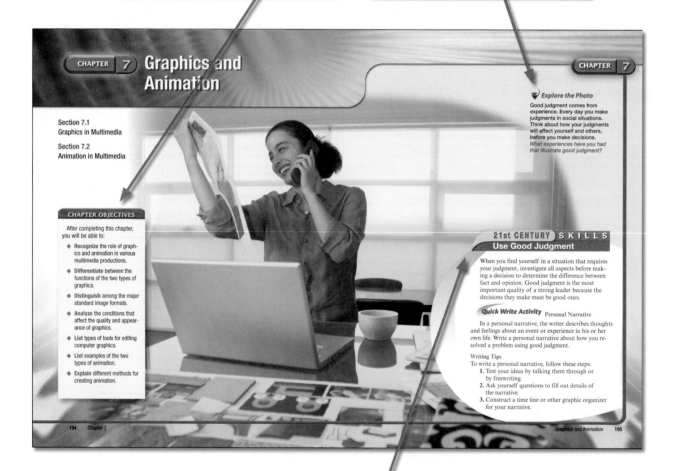

CHAPTER 7 Graphics and Animation

Section 7.1
Graphics in Multimedia

Section 7.2
Animation in Multimedia

CHAPTER 7

🌿 *Explore the Photo*
Good judgment comes from experience. Every day you make judgments in social situations. Think about how your judgments will affect yourself and others, before you make decisions. *What experiences have you had that illustrate good judgment?*

CHAPTER OBJECTIVES

After completing this chapter, you will be able to:
* Recognize the role of graphics and animation in various multimedia productions.
* Differentiate between the functions of the two types of graphics.
* Distinguish among the major standard image formats.
* Analyze the conditions that affect the quality and appearance of graphics.
* List types of tools for editing computer graphics.
* List examples of the two types of animation.
* Explain different methods for creating animation.

21st CENTURY SKILLS
Use Good Judgment

When you find yourself in a situation that requires your judgment, investigate all aspects before making a decision to determine the difference between fact and opinion. Good judgment is the most important quality of a strong leader because the decisions they make must be good ones.

Quick Write Activity Personal Narrative

In a personal narrative, the writer describes thoughts and feelings about an event or experience in his or her own life. Write a personal narrative about how you resolved a problem using good judgment.

Writing Tips
To write a personal narrative, follow these steps:
1. Test your ideas by talking them through or by freewriting.
2. Ask yourself questions to fill out details of the narrative.
3. Construct a time line or other graphic organizer for your narrative.

194 Chapter 7

Graphics and Animation 195

Practice Academic and 21st Century Skills. Use the writing tips to develop your writing skills.

Review the Chapter

Review and Assess Core Concepts

Review what you learned in the chapter and see how you can apply it to other subject areas.

> **Review Vocabulary and Key Concepts** to check your recall of important ideas.

> **Critical Thinking** takes your knowledge of the chapter further.

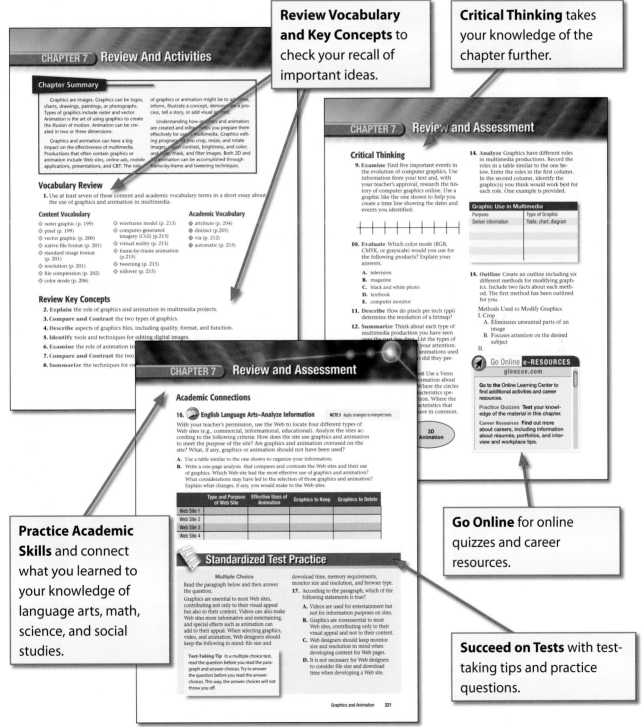

> **Practice Academic Skills** and connect what you learned to your knowledge of language arts, math, science, and social studies.

> **Go Online** for online quizzes and career resources.

> **Succeed on Tests** with test-taking tips and practice questions.

Program Overview

Review the Chapter

Apply Multimedia and Career Skills

Activities at the end of each chapter provide opportunities to develop essential workplace and 21st century skills.

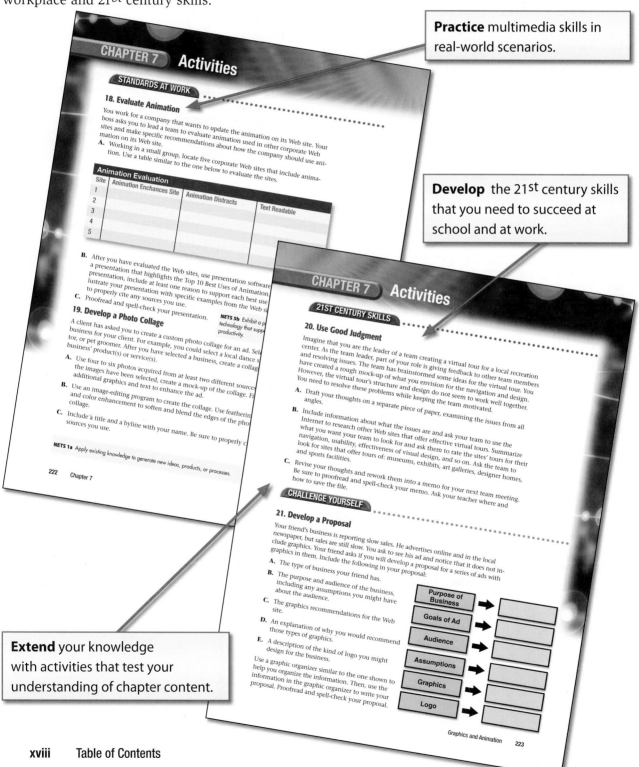

Practice multimedia skills in real-world scenarios.

Develop the 21st century skills that you need to succeed at school and at work.

Extend your knowledge with activities that test your understanding of chapter content.

Review the Chapter

Integrate Academics and Multimedia Skills

Every chapter ends with projects that allow you to integrate the multimedia concepts and skills you have learned with academic concepts.

Projects give you the opportunity to practice and develop your multimedia skills in real-life scenarios.

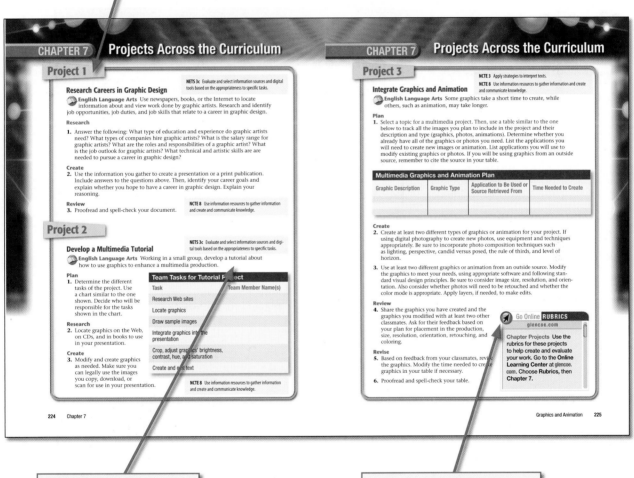

Apply Academic Skills that are behind the project.

Evaluate your project by using the rubrics available at the book's Online Learning Center.

Begin the Section

Prepare with Reading Guides and Study Tools

Use the reading guide at the beginning of each section to preview what you will learn in the section. See if you can predict events or outcomes by using clues and information that you already know.

Before You Read the main text, predict what the section will be about.

Preview key concepts and the main idea before you read.

Check Vocabulary lists for words you do not know. You can look them up in the glossary before you read the section.

Look for Academic Standards throughout the text. You can apply what you learn to other subjects.

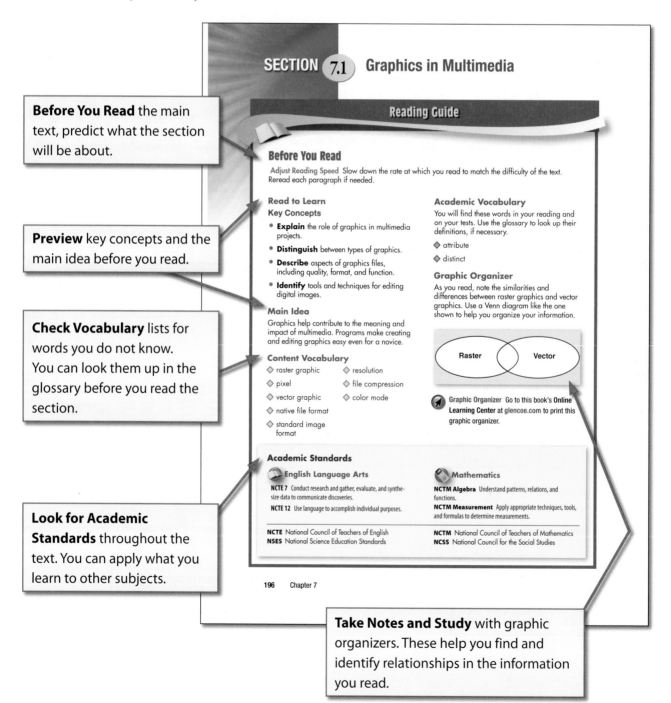

SECTION 7.1 Graphics in Multimedia

Reading Guide

Before You Read

Adjust Reading Speed Slow down the rate at which you read to match the difficulty of the text. Reread each paragraph if needed.

Read to Learn
Key Concepts
- **Explain** the role of graphics in multimedia projects.
- **Distinguish** between types of graphics.
- **Describe** aspects of graphics files, including quality, format, and function.
- **Identify** tools and techniques for editing digital images.

Main Idea
Graphics help contribute to the meaning and impact of multimedia. Programs make creating and editing graphics easy even for a novice.

Content Vocabulary
◇ raster graphic   ◇ resolution
◇ pixel   ◇ file compression
◇ vector graphic   ◇ color mode
◇ native file format
◇ standard image format

Academic Vocabulary
You will find these words in your reading and on your tests. Use the glossary to look up their definitions, if necessary.
◇ attribute
◇ distinct

Graphic Organizer
As you read, note the similarities and differences between raster graphics and vector graphics. Use a Venn diagram like the one shown to help you organize your information.

Raster   Vector

Graphic Organizer Go to this book's **Online Learning Center** at glencoe.com to print this graphic organizer.

Academic Standards

English Language Arts
NCTE 7 Conduct research and gather, evaluate, and synthesize data to communicate discoveries.
NCTE 12 Use language to accomplish individual purposes.

NCTE National Council of Teachers of English
NSES National Science Education Standards

Mathematics
NCTM Algebra Understand patterns, relations, and functions.
NCTM Measurement Apply appropriate techniques, tools, and formulas to determine measurements.

NCTM National Council of Teachers of Mathematics
NCSS National Council for the Social Studies

196   Chapter 7

Take Notes and Study with graphic organizers. These help you find and identify relationships in the information you read.

Review the Section

Practice and Assess Essential Skills and Concepts

Use the You Try It Activities to apply core multimedia concepts. The section review allows you to check your understanding. Make sure you can answer the questions in your own words before moving on in the text.

Follow the guided step-by-steps to complete the activity.

Practice with cross-curricular activities.

Visuals allow you to check your work.

Verify Your Understanding of key concepts in the section.

Check Your Answers online at this book's Online Learning Center at **glencoe. com**.

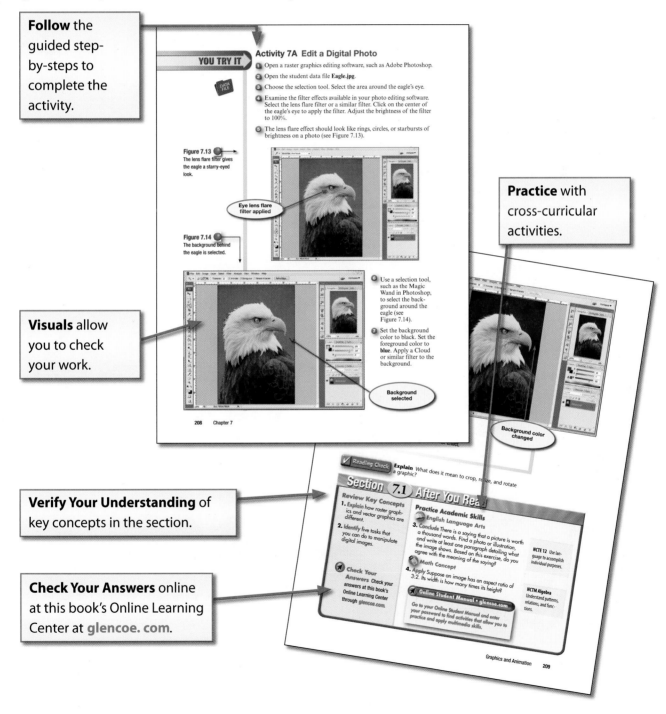

YOU TRY IT

DATA FILE

Activity 7A Edit a Digital Photo

1. Open a raster graphics editing software, such as Adobe Photoshop.
2. Open the student data file **Eagle.jpg**.
3. Choose the selection tool. Select the area around the eagle's eye.
4. Examine the filter effects available in your photo editing software. Select the lens flare filter or a similar filter. Click on the center of the eagle's eye to apply the filter. Adjust the brightness of the filter to 100%.
5. The lens flare effect should look like rings, circles, or starbursts of brightness on a photo (see Figure 7.13).

Figure 7.13
The lens flare filter gives the eagle a starry-eyed look.

Eye lens flare filter applied

Figure 7.14
The background behind the eagle is selected.

6. Use a selection tool, such as the Magic Wand in Photoshop, to select the background around the eagle (see Figure 7.14).
7. Set the background color to black. Set the foreground color to **blue**. Apply a Cloud or similar filter to the background.

Background selected

Background color changed

208   Chapter 7

Reading Check **Explain** What does it mean to crop, resize, and rotate a graphic?

Section 7.1 After You Read

Review Key Concepts

1. Explain how raster graphics and vector graphics are different.

2. Identify five tasks that you can do to manipulate digital images.

Check Your Answers Check your answers at this book's Online Learning Center through glencoe.com.

Practice Academic Skills

English Language Arts

3. **Conclude** There is a saying that a picture is worth a thousand words. Find a photo or illustration, and write at least one paragraph detailing what the image shows. Based on this exercise, do you agree with the meaning of the saying?

Math Concept

4. **Apply** Suppose an image has an aspect ratio of 3:2. Its width is how many times its height?

NCTE 12 Use language to accomplish individual purposes.

NCTM Algebra Understand patterns, relations, and functions.

Online Student Manual • glencoe.com
Go to your Online Student Manual and enter your password to find activities that allow you to practice and apply multimedia skills.

Graphics and Animation   209

Program Overview

How to Use the Introduction to Multimedia Program

The *Introduction to Multimedia* Student Edition introduces key multimedia concepts. The Online Student Manual allows you to extend and apply your multimedia skills with application-specific, step-by-step activities.

Use the Student Edition to learn about core multimedia concepts.

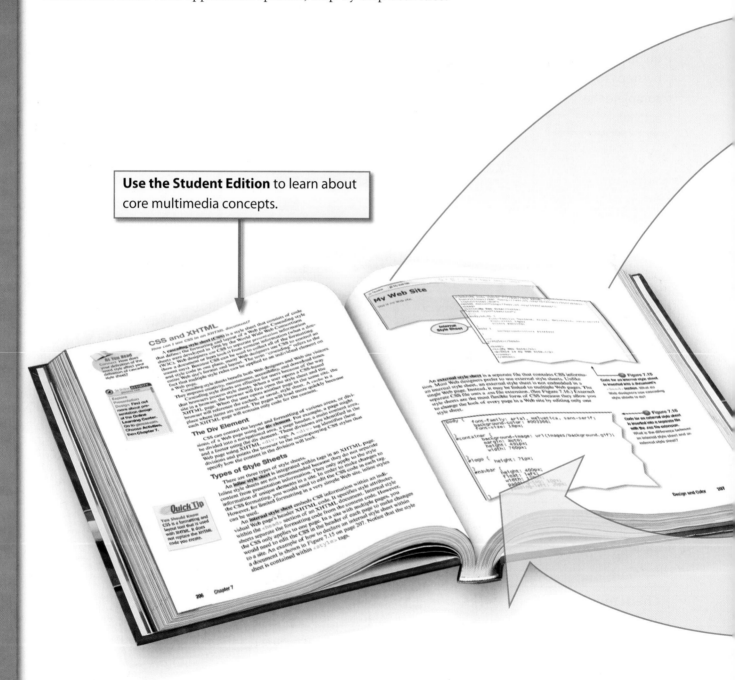

Program Overview

Use the Online Student Manual with your software to apply the concepts learned in the Student Edition.

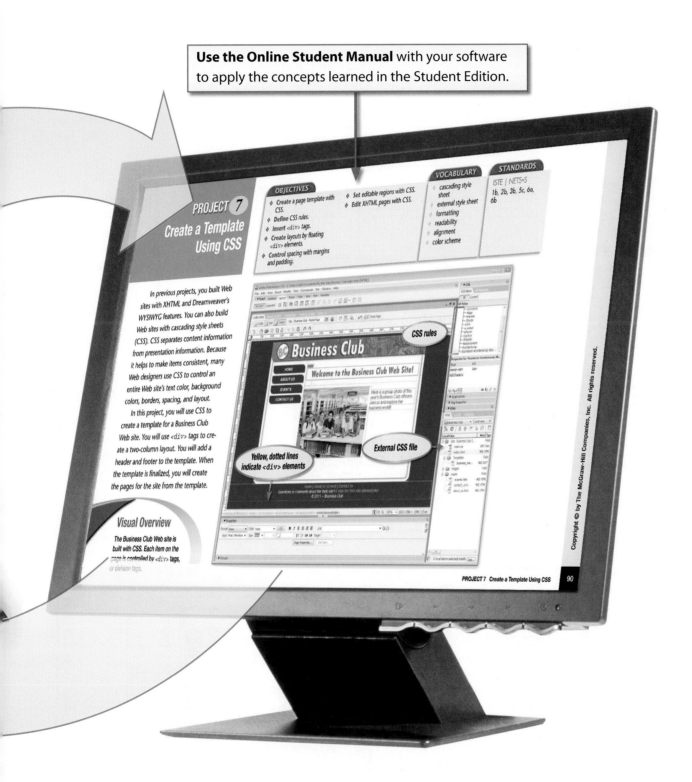

PROJECT 7
Create a Template Using CSS

OBJECTIVES
- Create a page template with CSS.
- Define CSS rules.
- Insert <div> tags.
- Create layouts by floating <div> elements.
- Control spacing with margins and padding.
- Set editable regions with CSS.
- Edit XHTML pages with CSS.

VOCABULARY
- cascading style sheet
- external style sheet
- formatting
- readability
- alignment
- color scheme

STANDARDS
ISTE | NETS•S
1b, 2b, 3b, 5c, 6a, 6b

In previous projects, you built Web sites with XHTML and Dreamweaver's WYSIWYG features. You can also build Web sites with cascading style sheets (CSS). CSS separates content information from presentation information. Because it helps to make items consistent, many Web designers use CSS to control an entire Web site's text color, background colors, borders, spacing, and layout.

In this project, you will use CSS to create a template for a Business Club Web site. You will use <div> tags to create a two-column layout. You will add a header and footer to the template. When the template is finalized, you will create the pages for the site from the template.

Visual Overview

The Business Club Web site is built with CSS. Each item on the page is controlled by <div> tags, or division tags.

CSS rules

External CSS file

Yellow, dotted lines indicate <div> elements

PROJECT 7 Create a Template Using CSS **90**

Online Student Manual

Step-by-Step Projects Focus Skills

Projects begin with a Visual Overview. Then, step-by-step instructions let you break down complex multimedia concepts. Visual Checks allow you to confirm your multimedia skills.

Prepare for what you will learn.

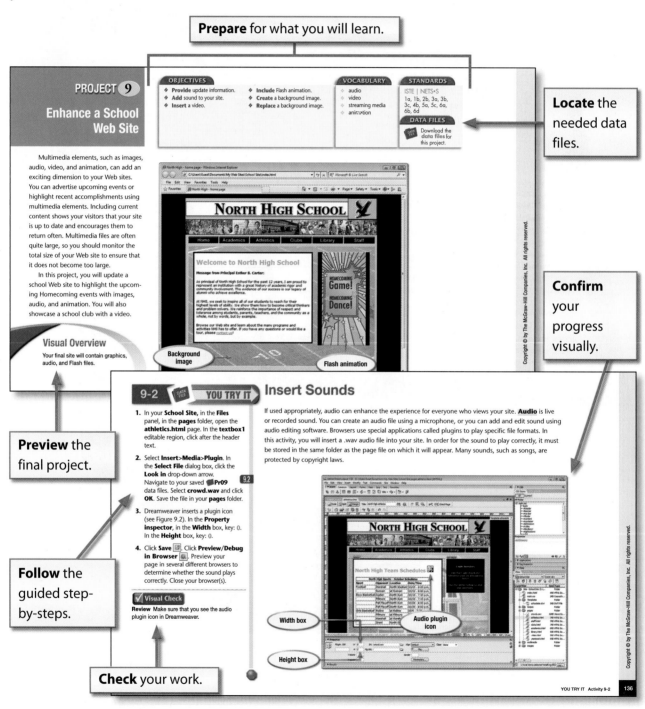

Locate the needed data files.

Confirm your progress visually.

Preview the final project.

Follow the guided step-by-steps.

Check your work.

Program Overview

Online Student Manual

Use Portfolio Projects to Extend Multimedia Skills

Portfolio Projects allow you to integrate multimedia skills and academic skills in real-world projects.

Build Your Portfolio through real-world projects.

Integrate Academics throughout Portfolio Projects.

Complete projects using checklists.

Integrate real-world skills.

Evaluate projects with rubrics.

Portfolio Project 15

Create an Online Portfolio

You have decided that you want to pursue a career as a Web site designer. To begin planning for this career, you are developing an online portfolio that showcases your Web design skills. You will begin this process by creating a one-page Web site that will eventually link to your résumé and samples of your work, as well as to any certifications you may have received. This home page should include general information about yourself and your career goals. It also should contain an unordered list stating at least three Web design skills you have mastered. You should leave blank space at the bottom of the home page. Later, this space will contain links to Web sites you have developed. Be sure to avoid sharing personal information when posting items online.

Project Assignment
- Create a one-page Web site.
- Insert formatted text, including general information about yourself, into the page.
- Insert a graphic that you have created or edited for a Web site.
- Create an unordered list that explains three Web design skills you have mastered.
- Insert a block quotation about Web design. Make certain that the quotation is properly cited.

Web Design Skills Behind the Project
Skills you will use in this project include:
- Define a Web site in Dreamweaver.
- Format text and insert an image.
- Create an unordered list and format a block quotation.

Academic Skills Behind the Project
Research Skills
- Locate and edit the image or photograph to be used on the site.
- Conduct research to locate and cite a quotation.

Writing Skills
- Use correct grammar, punctuation, and spelling.
- Write clearly and concisely.
- Determine appropriate content based on the site's purpose and audience.

English Language Arts
NCTE 5 Use different writing process elements to communicate effectively.
NCTE 7 Conduct research and gather, evaluate, and synthesize data to communicate discoveries.
NCTE 12 Use language to accomplish individual purposes.

Portfolio Project 15

Real World

Professionalism
Because an online portfolio will be viewed by potential employers, it should show you at your best. All of the information should focus on your job-related experiences and skills.

Why It's Important
Why is it important to think of an online portfolio as a "first impression" you give to potential employers?

STEP 4 Share Your Site

Present your Web site to a classmate:
- Ask a classmate to play the role of a potential employer who is interested in your Web design skills and offer suggested improvements.
- Make any changes based on your classmate's feedback.

STEP 5 Evaluate Your Work

Evaluate your site:
- Make certain you have completed the items on the checklist.
- Complete the rubric to evaluate the project.
- Use a Web browser to test your site to make certain its contents work and display correctly.
- For your portfolio, include screen captures and an electronic copy of your finished product.
- Turn in the project.

Go Online RUBRICS

Access a rubric to plan and evaluate your portfolio project.

Portfolio Project Checklist

INFORMATION AND FUNCTIONAL DESIGN
- ☑ Name and general information are present.
- ☑ The unordered list contains at least three items that explain your Web design skills.
- ☑ A quotation on Web design has been inserted and has been correctly cited.
- ☑ The content is free of grammar, punctuation, and spelling errors.

PRESENTATION DESIGN
- ☑ The design is attractive, consistent, and uncluttered.
- ☑ Room has been left for links and descriptions of Web sites to be added at a later time.
- ☑ Name and general information are formatted for visibility and attractiveness.
- ☑ The unordered list is used effectively.
- ☑ The block quotation and its citation are properly formatted.
- ☑ At least one graphic or photograph has been inserted.

IMPLEMENTATION
- ☑ The site has been properly created using Dreamweaver and has been given a meaningful name.
- ☑ The site demonstrates proper use of folder structure hierarchy.

PORTFOLIO PROJECT 15 | 214

Copyright © by The McGraw-Hill Companies, Inc. All rights reserved.

Online Learning Center

Build Skills and Extend Your Learning

The *Introduction to Multimedia* Online Learning Center provides activities to extend your learning. Follow these steps to access the textbook resources on the Online Learning Center.

Step 1
Go to **glencoe.com**.

Step 2
Select **your state** from the pull-down menu.

Step 3
Select **Student/Parent**.

Step 4
Select **Computer Education**.

Step 5
Click **Enter**.

Step6
Select Introduction Series, then select *Introduction to Multimedia* © 2011.

Step 7
Click **Student Center** to access student resources.

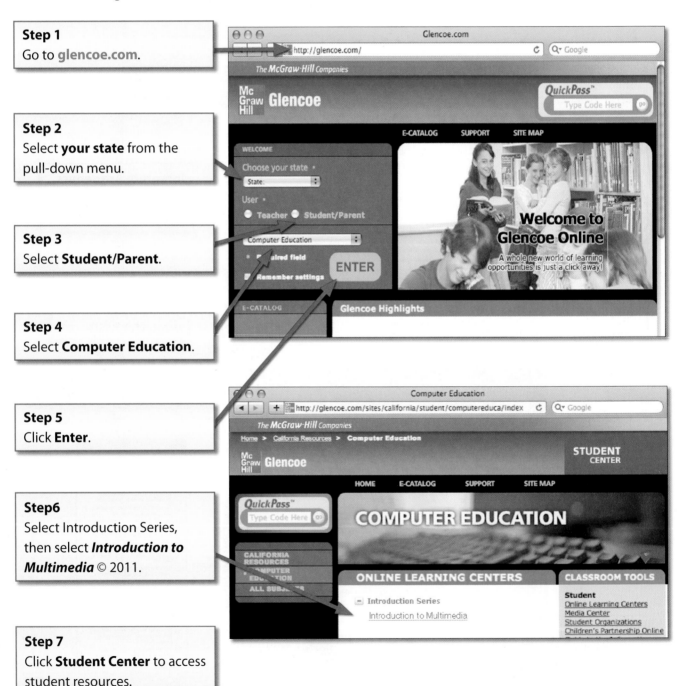

Prepare for 21st Century Success

ISTE and NETS

The International Society for Technology in Education (ISTE) has developed National Educational Technology Standards to define educational technology standards for students (NETS•S). The activities in this book are designed to meet the ISTE standards.

NETS·S Standards

To live, learn, and work successfully in an increasingly complex and information rich society, students must be able to use technology effectively. ISTE standards identify skills that students can practice and master in school, at home, and at work. For more information about ISTE and the NETS, please visit www.iste.org.

National Educational Technology Standards and Performance Indicators for Students

The NETS are divided into the six broad categories that are listed below. Activities in the book meet the standards within each category.

❶ Creativity and Innovation

Students demonstrate creative thinking, construct knowledge, and develop innovative products and processes using technology. Students:
  a. apply existing knowledge to generate new ideas, products, or processes.
  b. create original works as a means of personal or group expression.
  c. use models and simulations to explore complex systems and issues.
  d. identify trends and forecast possibilities.

❷ Communication and Collaboration

Students use digital media and environments to communicate and work collaboratively, including at a distance, to support individual learning and contribute to the learning of others. Students:
  a. interact, collaborate, and publish with peers, experts or others employing a variety of digital environments and media.
  b. communicate information and ideas effectively to multiple audiences using a variety of media and formats.
  c. develop cultural understanding and global awareness by engaging with learners of other cultures.
  d. contribute to project teams to produce original works or solve problems.

Technology Standards

③ Research and Information Fluency

Students apply digital tools to gather, evaluate, and use information. Students:

   a. plan strategies to guide inquiry.
   b. locate, organize, analyze, evaluate, synthesize, and ethically use information from a variety of sources and media.
   c. evaluate and select information sources and digital tools based on the appropriateness to specific tasks.
   d. process data and report results.

④ Critical Thinking, Problem-Solving, and Decision-Making

Students use critical thinking skills to plan and conduct research, manage projects, solve problems, and make informed decisions using appropriate digital tools and resources. Students:

   a. identify and define authentic problems and significant questions for investigation.
   b. plan and manage activities to develop a solution or complete a project.
   c. collect and analyze data to identify solutions and/or make informed decisions.
   d. use multiple processes and diverse perspectives to explore alternative solutions.

⑤ Digital Citizenship

Students understand human, cultural, and societal issues related to technology and practice legal and ethical behavior. Students:

   a. advocate and practice safe, legal, and responsible use of information and technology.
   b. exhibit a positive attitude toward using technology that supports collaboration, learning, and productivity.
   c. demonstrate personal responsibility for lifelong learning.
   d. exhibit leadership for digital citizenship.

⑥ Technology Operations and Concepts

Students demonstrate a sound understanding of technology concepts, systems, and operations. Students:

   a. understand and use technology systems.
   b. select and use applications effectively and productively.
   c. troubleshoot systems and applications.
   d. transfer current knowledge to learning of new technologies.

Prepare *for* Academic Success!

National Language Arts Standards

To help incorporate literacy skills (reading, writing, listening, and speaking) into *Glencoe's Introduction to Multimedia*, each project includes opportunities to reinforce language arts skills. These skills have been developed into standards by the *National Council of Teachers of English* and *International Reading Association*.*

- Read texts to acquire new information.
- Read literature to build an understanding of the human experience.
- Apply strategies to interpret texts.
- Use written language to communicate effectively.
- Use different writing process elements to communicate effectively.
- Apply knowledge of language structure and conventions to discuss texts.
- Conduct research and gather, evaluate, and synthesize data to communicate discoveries.
- Use information resources to gather information and create and communicate knowledge.
- Develop an understanding of diversity in language used across cultures.
- Use first language to develop competency in English language arts and develop an understanding of content across the curriculum.
- Participate as members of literacy communities.
- Use language to accomplish individual purposes.

Principles and Standards for School Mathematics

Glencoe's Introduction to Multimedia textbook provides students with opportunities to practice the math skills indicated in the national math standards developed by the *National Council of Teachers of Mathematics*. The basic skills are:

- Number and Operations
- Algebra
- Geometry
- Measurement
- Data Analysis and Probability
- Problem Solving
- Communication
- Connections
- Representation

*Standards for the English Language Arts, by the International Reading Association and the National Council of Teachers of English, Copyright 1996 by the International Reading Association and the National Council of Teachers of English. Reprinted with permission. For more information, visit http://www.ncte.org/standards.

Reading Skills Handbook

▶ Reading: What's in It for You?

What role does reading play in your life? The possibilities are countless. Are you on a sports team? Perhaps you like to read about the latest news and statistics in sports or find out about new training techniques. Are you looking for a new dish to serve your family? You might be looking for advice about nutrition, cooking techniques, or information about ingredients. Are you enrolled in an English class, an algebra class, or a business class? Then your assignments require a lot of reading.

Improving or Fine-Tuning Your Reading Skills Will:

- ◆ Improve your grades.
- ◆ Allow you to read faster and more efficiently.
- ◆ Improve your study skills.
- ◆ Help you remember more information accurately.
- ◆ Improve your writing.

▶ The Reading Process

Good reading skills build on one another, overlap, and spiral around in much the same way that a winding staircase goes around and around while leading you to a higher place. This handbook is designed to help you find and use the tools you will need **before, during,** and **after** reading.

Strategies You Can Use

- ◆ Identify, understand, and learn new words.
- ◆ Understand why you read.
- ◆ Take a quick look at the whole text.
- ◆ Try to predict what you are about to read.

- ◆ Take breaks while you read and ask yourself questions about the text.
- ◆ Take notes.
- ◆ Keep thinking about what will come next.
- ◆ Summarize.

▶ Vocabulary Development

Word identification and vocabulary skills are the building blocks of the reading and writing processes. By learning to use a variety of strategies to build your word skills and vocabulary, you will become a stronger reader.

Use Context to Determine Meaning

The best way to expand and extend your vocabulary is to read widely, listen carefully, and participate in a rich variety of discussions. When reading on your own, though, you can often figure out the meanings of new words by looking at their **context,** or the other words and sentences that surround them.

Tips for Using Context

Look for clues like these:

◆ A synonym or an explanation of the unknown word in the sentence:
Elise's shop specialized in millinery, or hats for women.
◆ A reference to what the word is or is not like:
An archaeologist, like a historian, deals with the past.
◆ A general topic associated with the word:
The cooking teacher discussed the best way to braise meat.
◆ A description or action associated with the word:
He used the shovel to dig up the garden.

Predict a Possible Meaning

Another way to determine the meaning of a word is to take the word apart. If you understand the meaning of the **base,** or **root,** part of a word, and also know the meanings of key syllables added either to the beginning or end of the base word, you can usually figure out what the word means.

Word Origins Since Latin, Greek, and Anglo-Saxon roots are the basis for much of our English vocabulary, having some background in languages can be a useful vocabulary tool. For example, *astronomy* comes from the Greek root *astro,* which means relating to the stars. *Stellar* also has a meaning referring to stars, but its origin is Latin. Knowing root words in other languages can help you determine meanings, derivations, and spellings in English.

Prefixes and Suffixes A prefix is a word part that can be added to the beginning of a word. For example, the prefix *semi* means half or partial, so *semicircle* means half a circle. A suffix is a word part that can be added to the end of a word. Adding a suffix often changes a word from one part of speech to another.

Using Dictionaries A dictionary provides the meaning or meanings of a word. Look at the sample dictionary entry on the next page to see what other information it provides.

Thesauruses and Specialized Reference Books A thesaurus provides synonyms and often antonyms. It is a useful tool to expand your vocabulary. Remember to check the exact definition of the listed words in a dictionary before you use a thesaurus. Specialized dictionaries such as *Barron's Dictionary of Business Terms* or *Black's Law Dictionary* list terms and expressions that are not commonly included in a general dictionary. You can also use online dictionaries.

Glossaries Many textbooks and technical works contain condensed dictionaries that provide an alphabetical listing of words used in the text and their specific definitions.

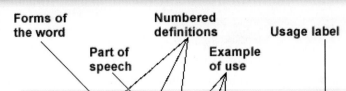
Dictionary Entry

Forms of
the word

Part of
speech

Numbered
definitions

Example
of use

Usage label

help (help) **helped** or *(archaic)* **holp**, **helped** or *(archaic)* **hol-pen**, **help-ing**. *v.t.* **1.** to provide with support, as in the performance of a task; be of service to: *He helped his brother paint the room.* ▲ also used elliptically with a preposition or adverb: *He helped the old woman up the stairs.* **2.** to enable (someone or something) to accomplish a goal or achieve a desired effect: *The coach's advice helped the team to win.* **3.** to provide with sustenance or relief, as in time of need or distress; succor: *The Red Cross helped the flood victims.* **4.** to promote or contribute to; further. *The medication helped his recovery.* **5.** to be useful or profitable to; be of advantage to: *It might help you if you read the book.* **6.** to improve or remedy: *Nothing really helped his sinus condition.* **7.** to prevent; stop: *I can't help his rudeness.* **8.** to refrain from; avoid: *I couldn't help smiling when I heard the story.* **9.** to wait on or serve (often with to): *The clerk helped us. The hostess helped him to the dessert.* **10.** **cannot help but.** *Informal* cannot but. **11. so help me (God).** oath of affirmation. **12. to help oneself to.** to take or appropriate: *The thief helped himself to all the jewels.*—*v.i.* to provide support, as in the performance of a task; be of service.—*n.* **1.** act of providing support, service, or sustenance. **2.** source of support, service, or sustenance. **3.** person or group of persons hired to work for another or others. **4.** means of improving, remedying, or preventing. [Old English *helpan* to aid, succor, benefit.] **Syn.** *v.t.* **1. Help, aid, assist** mean to support in a useful way. Help is the most common word and means to give support in response to a known or expressed need or for a definite purpose: *Everyone helped to make the school fair a success.* **Aid** means to give relief in times of distress or difficulty: *It is the duty of rich nations to aid the poor.* **Assist** means to serve another person in the performance of his task in a secondary capacity: *The secretary assists the officer by taking care of his corresponding.*

Idioms

Origin
(etymology)

Synonyms

Recognize Word Meanings Across Subjects Have you learned a new word in one class and then noticed it in your reading for other subjects? The word might not mean exactly the same thing in each class, but you can use the meaning you already know to help you understand what it means in another subject area. For example:

Math Each digit represents a different place **value**.

Health Your **values** can guide you in making healthful decisions.

Economics The **value** of a product is measured in its cost.

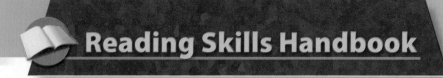
▶ Understanding What You Read

Reading comprehension means understanding—deriving meaning from—what you have read. Using a variety of strategies can help you improve your comprehension and make reading more interesting and more fun.

Read for a Reason

To get the greatest benefit from your reading, **establish a purpose for reading.** In school, you have many reasons for reading, such as:

- to learn and understand new information.
- to find specific information.
- to review before a test.
- to complete an assignment.
- to prepare (research) before you write.

As your reading skills improve, you will notice that you apply different strategies to fit the different purposes for reading. For example, if you are reading for entertainment, you might read quickly, but if you are reading to gather information or follow directions, you might read more slowly, take notes, construct a graphic organizer, or reread sections of text.

Draw on Personal Background

Drawing on personal background may also be called activating prior knowledge. Before you start reading a text, ask yourself questions like these:

- What have I heard or read about this topic?
- Do I have any personal experience relating to this topic?

Using a KWL Chart A KWL chart is a good device for organizing information you gather before, during, and after reading. In the first column, list what you already **know,** then list what you **want** to know in the middle column. Use the third column when you review and assess what you **learned.** You can also add more columns to record places where you found information and places where you can look for more information.

K (What I already know)	W (What I want to know)	L (What I have learned)

Adjust Your Reading Speed Your reading speed is a key factor in how well you understand what you are reading. You will need to adjust your speed depending on your reading purpose.

Scanning means running your eyes quickly over the material to look for words or phrases. Scan when you need a specific piece of information.

Skimming means reading a passage quickly to find its main idea or to get an overview. Skim a text when you preview to determine what the material is about.

Reading for detail involves careful reading while paying attention to text structure and monitoring your understanding. Read for detail when you are learning concepts, following complicated directions, or preparing to analyze a text.

▶ Techniques to Understand and Remember What You Read

Preview

Before beginning a selection, it is helpful to **preview** what you are about to read.

> ### Previewing Strategies
>
> ◆ Read the title, headings, and subheadings of the selection.
> ◆ Look at the illustrations and notice how the text is organized.
> ◆ Skim the selection: Take a glance at the whole thing.
> ◆ Decide what the main idea might be.
> ◆ Predict what a selection will be about.

Predict

Have you ever read a mystery, decided who committed the crime, and then changed your mind as more clues were revealed? You were adjusting your predictions. Did you smile when you found out that you guessed who committed the crime? You were verifying your predictions.

As you read, make educated guesses about story events and outcomes; that is, **make predictions** before and during reading. This will help you focus your attention on the text and will improve your understanding.

Determine the Main Idea

When you look for the **main idea**, you are looking for the most important statement in a text. Depending on what kind of text you are reading, the main idea can be located at the very beginning (news stories in a newspaper or a magazine) or at the end (scientific research document). Ask yourself the following questions:

- What is each sentence about?
- Is there one sentence that is more important than all the others?
- What idea do details support or point out?

Take Notes

Cornell Note-Taking System There are many methods for note taking. The **Cornell Note-Taking System** is a well-known method that can help you organize what you read. To the right is a note-taking activity based on the Cornell Note-Taking System.

Graphic Organizers Using a graphic organizer to retell content in a visual representation will help you remember and retain content. You might make a **chart** or **diagram,** organizing what you have read. Here are some examples of graphic organizers:

Venn Diagrams When mapping out a compare-and-contrast text structure, you can use a Venn diagram. The outer portions of the circles will show how two characters, ideas, or items contrast, or are different, and the overlapping part will compare two things, or show how they are similar.

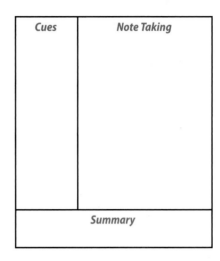

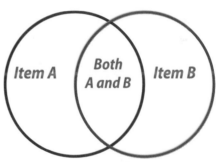

Flow Charts To help you track the sequence of events, or cause and effect, use a flow chart. Arrange ideas or events in their logical, sequential order. Then, draw arrows between your ideas to indicate how one idea or event flows into another.

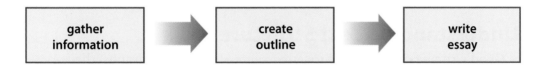

Visualize

Try to form a mental picture of scenes, characters, and events as you read. Use the details and descriptions the author gives you. If you can **visualize** what you read, it will be more interesting and you will remember it better.

Question

Ask yourself questions about the text while you read. Ask yourself about the importance of the sentences, how they relate to one another, if you understand what you just read, and what you think is going to come next.

Clarify

If you feel you do not understand meaning (through questioning), try these techniques:

> **What to Do When You Do Not Understand**
>
> ◆ Reread confusing parts of the text.
> ◆ Diagram (chart) relationships between chunks of text, ideas, and sentences.
> ◆ Look up unfamiliar words.
> ◆ Talk out the text to yourself.
> ◆ Read the passage once more.

Review

Take time to stop and review what you have read. Use your note-taking tools (graphic organizers or Cornell notes charts). Also, review and consider your KWL chart.

Monitor Your Comprehension

Continue to check your understanding by using the following two strategies:

Summarize Pause and tell yourself the main ideas of the text and the key supporting details. Try to answer the following questions: Who? What? When? Where? Why? How?

Paraphrase Pause, close the book, and try to retell what you have just read in your own words. It might help to pretend you are explaining the text to someone who has not read it and does not know the material.

▶ Understanding Text Structure

Good writers do not just put together sentences and paragraphs, they organize their writing with a specific purpose in mind. That organization is called text structure. When you understand and follow the structure of a text, it is easier to remember the information you are reading. There are many ways text may be structured. Watch for **signal words**. They will help you follow the text's organization. (Also, remember to use these techniques when you write.)

Compare and Contrast

This structure shows similarities and differences between people, things, and ideas. This is often used to demonstrate that things that seem alike are really different, or vice versa.

Signal words: similarly, more, less, on the one hand/on the other hand, in contrast, but, however

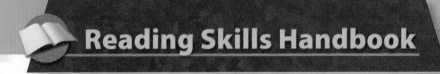

Cause and Effect

Writers use the cause-and-effect structure to explore the reasons for something happening and to examine the results or consequences of events.

Signal words: so, because, as a result, therefore, for the following reasons

Problem and Solution

When they organize text around the question how?, writers state a problem and suggest solutions.

Signal words: how, help, problem, obstruction, overcome, difficulty, need, attempt, have to, must

Sequence

Sequencing tells you in which order to consider thoughts or facts. Examples of sequencing are:

Chronological order refers to the order in which events take place.

Signal words: first, next, then, finally

Spatial order describes the organization of things in space (to describe a room, for example).

Signal words: above, below, behind, next to

Order of importance lists things or thoughts from the most important to the least important (or the other way around).

Signal words: principal, central, main, important, fundamental

▶ Reading for Meaning

It is important to think about what you are reading to get the most information out of a text, to understand the consequences of what the text says, to remember the content, and to form your own opinion about what the content means.

Interpret

Interpreting is asking yourself, "What is the writer really saying?" and then using what you already know to answer that question.

Infer

Writers do not always state exactly everything they want you to understand. By providing clues and details, they sometimes imply certain information. To **infer** involves using your reason and experience to develop the idea on your own, based on what an author implies, or suggests. What is most important when drawing inferences is to be sure that you have accurately based your guesses on supporting details from the text. If you cannot point to a place in the selection to help back up your inference, you may need to rethink your guess.

Draw Conclusions

A conclusion is a general statement you can make and explain with reasoning, or with supporting details from a text. If you read a story describing a sport where five players bounce a ball and throw it through a high hoop, you may conclude that the sport is basketball.

Analyze

To understand persuasive nonfiction (a text that discusses facts and opinions to arrive at a conclusion), you need to analyze statements and examples to see if they support the main idea. To understand an informational text (a text, such as a textbook, that gives you information, not opinions), you need to keep track of how the ideas are organized to find the main points.

Hint: Use your graphic organizers and notes charts.

Distinguish Facts from Opinions

This is one of the most important reading skills you can learn. A fact is a statement that can be proven. An opinion is what the writer believes. A writer may support opinions with facts, but an opinion cannot be proven. For example:

Fact: California produces fruit and other agricultural products.

Opinion: California produces the best fruit and other agricultural products.

Evaluate

Would you take seriously an article on nuclear fission if you knew it was written by a comedic actor? If you need to rely on accurate information, you need to find out who wrote what you are reading and why. Where did the writer get information? Is the information one-sided? Can you verify the information?

▶ Reading for Research

You will need to **read actively** to research a topic. You might also need to generate an interesting, relevant, and researchable **question** on your own and locate appropriate print and nonprint information from a wide variety of sources. Then, you will need to **categorize** that information, evaluate it, and **organize** it in a new way to produce a research project for a specific audience. Finally, **draw conclusions** about your original research question. These conclusions may lead you to other areas for further inquiry.

Locate Appropriate Print and Nonprint Information

In your research, try to use a variety of sources. Because different sources present information in different ways, your research project will be more interesting and balanced when you read a variety of sources.

Literature and Textbooks These texts include any book used as a basis for instruction or a source of information.

Book Indices A book index, or a bibliography, is an alphabetical listing of books. Some book indices list books on specific subjects; others are more general. Other indices list a variety of topics or resources.

Periodicals Magazines and journals are issued at regular intervals, such as weekly or monthly. One way to locate information in magazines is to use the *Readers' Guide to Periodical Literature*. This guide is available in print form in most libraries.

Technical Manuals A manual is a guide or handbook intended to give instruction on how to perform a task or operate something. A vehicle owner's manual might give information on how to operate and service a car.

Reference Books Reference books include encyclopedias and almanacs, and are used to locate specific pieces of information.

Electronic Encyclopedias, Databases, and the Internet There are many ways to locate extensive information using your computer. Infotrac, for instance, acts as an online readers' guide. CD encyclopedias can provide easy access to all subjects.

Organize and Convert Information

As you gather information from different sources, taking careful notes, you will need to think about how to **synthesize** the information—that is, convert it into a unified whole, as well as how to change it into a form your audience will easily understand and that will meet your assignment guidelines.

1. First, ask yourself what you want your audience to know.
2. Then, think about a pattern of organization, a structure that will best show your main ideas. You might ask yourself the following questions:

   - When comparing items or ideas, what graphic aids can I use?
   - When showing the reasons something happened and the effects of certain actions, what text structure would be best?
   - How can I briefly and clearly show important information to my audience?
   - Would an illustration or even a cartoon help to make a certain point?

Student Organizations

What Is a Student Organization?

A student organization is a group or association of students that is formed around activities, such as:

- Technology education
- Visual and performing arts
- Professional career development
- Community service
- Student government
- Multicultural alliances
- Honor societies
- Sports teams
- Politics
- Social clubs

A student organization is usually required to follow a set of rules and regulations that apply equally to all student organizations at a particular school.

Why Should You Get Involved?

Being an active part of a student organization opens a variety of experiences to you. Many student clubs are part of a national network of students and professionals, which provides the chance to connect to a wider variety of students and opportunities.

What's in It for You?

Participation in student organizations can contribute to a more enriching learning experience. Here are some ways you can benefit:

- Demonstrate leadership qualities and skills that make you more marketable to employers and universities.
- Demonstrate the ability to work as a team member.
- Interact with professionals to learn about education, job skills, and experience required to enter into a technology profession.
- Demonstrate positive personal qualities, such as listening attentively to speakers, flexibility, and a willingness to learn new knowledge and skills.
- Learn valuable skills such as verbal and nonverbal communication, problem solving, and critical thinking.
- Make a difference in your life and the lives of those around you. Learn the importance of civic responsibility and involvement.
- Build relationships with instructors, advisors, students, and other members of the community who share similar backgrounds and world views.

Find and Join a Student Organization!

Take a close look at the organizations offered at your school or within your community. Are there any organizations that interest you? Talk to your teachers, guidance counselors, or a parent or guardian. Usually, posters or flyers for a variety of clubs and groups can be found on your school's message board or Web site. Try to locate more information about the organizations that meet your needs. Then, think about how these organizations can help you gain valuable skills you can use at school, at work, and in your community.

What Is Future Business Leaders of America?

Future Business Leaders of America (FBLA) is a national organization preparing students for career-related fields. FBLA offers students the opportunity to develop their leadership potential by participating in real-world activities through local, state, and national conferences.

These conferences allow students to participate in workshops, share their leadership experiences, and compete in business-related events. Students may participate in many events, including:

* Web Site Development
* Digital Video Production
* Electronic Career Portfolio
* E-Business

Students may participate individually, as a team, or with a chapter.

What Is Business Professionals of America?

Business Professionals of America (BPA) is a leading Career Technical Student Organization (CTSO) for students pursuing a career in business, information technology, and other career fields. The mission of BPA is to prepare students for the workforce by providing opportunities to demonstrate leadership, citizenship, and academic and technological skills.

One of the most visible programs of BPA is the annual Workplace Skills Assessment Program. Students from around the country compete in technology events to prove their skills in the following areas:

* Web Site Design Team
* Web Application Team
* Fundamentals of XHTML
* Video Production Team
* Digital Media Production
* Computer Animation Team

Regardless of competition outcome, participation in these events allows students to develop leadership skills and to develop job contacts.

1

Multimedia and You

Chapter 1 — Multimedia Fundamentals
Chapter 2 — Multimedia Online
Chapter 3 — Computers and Networks

UNIT Portfolio Project Preview

Create a Multimedia Presentation

After completing this unit, you will recognize and understand multimedia software and hardware. You will also use multimedia resources ethically. In the Unit Portfolio Project, you will create a presentation that describes multimedia's impact on your life. You will incorporate multimedia elements in your presentation.

 Go Online PREVIEW

glencoe.com

Go to the **Online Learning Center** and select your book. Click **Unit 1>Portfolio Project Preview** to learn more about multimedia project software and hardware.

Section 1.1
What Is Multimedia?

Section 1.2
Types of Multimedia Projects

Section 1.3
Multimedia Careers and Skills

CHAPTER OBJECTIVES

After completing this chapter, you will be able to:

❖ **Define** multimedia.

❖ **Summarize** the role of multimedia presentations.

❖ **List** the components of multimedia.

❖ **Describe** the importance of text, graphics, animation, audio, and video in multimedia presentations.

❖ **Identify** the types of multimedia presentations.

❖ **Describe** the role of multimedia in society.

❖ **Analyze** how extended learning experiences relate to multimedia careers and skills.

Explore the Photo

Multimedia tools can be used to create a variety of presentations and projects.
What types of multimedia presentations do you find most interesting and why?

21st CENTURY SKILLS
Set Realistic Goals

Goals help you focus on the things that are important now. Set realistic goals, create a plan to meet the goals, and work steadily to achieve the goals.

Quick Write Activity Freewriting

Freewrite about a time when you achieved a specific goal, such as completing a big project for a class. How did you begin your work? What steps did you take to meet your goal? How did you feel when you finished? What did you learn about setting goals?

Writing Tips
To freewrite effectively, follow these steps:
1. Let your thoughts run free, and simply begin writing whatever comes to mind.
2. Write without stopping to re-read, rephrase, or rethink what you are saying.
3. Set a definite time limit.

Reading Guide

Before You Read

Survey Look at the figures in this section and read their captions. Write one or two sentences predicting what you think the section will be about.

Read to Learn
Key Concepts

- **Define** multimedia.
- **List** multimedia elements.
- **Summarize** how multimedia elements convey information.

Main Idea

Multimedia is a combination of digital elements. The role of multimedia presentations is to convey information effectively.

Content Vocabulary

◇ multimedia   ◇ text
◇ medium   ◇ graphic
◇ media   ◇ animation
◇ interactive media ◇ audio
◇ rich media   ◇ video

Academic Vocabulary

You will find these words in your reading and on your tests. Use the glossary to look up their definitions, if necessary.

◆ element

◆ ensure

Graphic Organizer

As you read the section, identify five multimedia elements. Use a Web diagram like the one shown below to organize your notes.

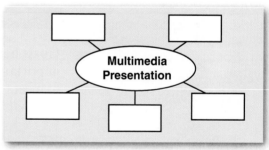

 Graphic Organizer Go to this book's **Online Learning Center** at **glencoe.com** to print this graphic organizer.

Academic Standards

 English Language Arts

NCTE 3 Apply strategies to interpret texts.
NCTE 4 Use written language to communicate effectively.

NCTE 12 Use language to accomplish individual purposes.

NCTE National Council of Teachers of English
NSES National Science Education Standards

NCTM National Council of Teachers of Mathematics
NCSS National Council for the Social Studies

Multimedia Elements

How does multimedia affect your life?

Have you visited a Web site, listened to music on a portable music player, read an advertisement on the Internet or in a magazine, or watched a video today? If so, you have experienced how multimedia affects our lives.

Multimedia is the integration of interactive elements such as text, graphics, animation, audio, and video using computer technology. Each **element**, or component, of multimedia contributes to the user's experience. Any means of conveying information is called a **medium**. The plural form of medium is **media**. The term *multimedia* literally means using more than one type of media. Not all multimedia projects will contain all of the possible elements. For example, a multimedia educational program that includes text and graphics might not include audio, but it still qualifies as multimedia because it includes multiple elements and computers are used to create it.

The term **interactive media** refers to media that allows active participation by the user, or viewer. For example, if you have purchased tickets online for a movie or participated in an online survey or poll, you were using interactive media. You were required to input information in order for the application to run. **Rich media** applications are interactive multimedia productions that use technology such as Flash, Java applets, and streaming video. You will learn more about these types of technologies in Chapter 2.

Text

Text, which consists of written words, numbers, or symbols, is an element of multimedia. Virtually all multimedia productions include text. The text might be in the form of paragraphs, as in books or newsletters, or it might be a tagline on a display screen.

Text is enhanced when used with other multimedia elements such as graphics, animation, audio, or video. For example, a company newsletter might show text combined with graphics to attract attention and to explain concepts, as shown in Figure 1.1.

What the text says, of course, will depend on the purpose and goals of your multimedia project. The individual or team creating the multimedia must **ensure**, or guarantee, how the text looks in its finished format. Text attributes, such as font, size, and color, must be chosen carefully to convey the necessary information or message of the multimedia project and its text to the viewer.

As You Read

Connect In what ways is multimedia a part of your life each day?

Figure 1.1
Text is often combined with graphics to communicate messages. How does the text in this document attract attention?

PedalCo Employee Newsletter

Bike Sales Rising
Bike sales increased steadily over the course of the year.

Mountain bikes continue to be our top seller, selling well in the Southeast, in the Northeast, and in the West.

Road and hybrid bike sales increased dramatically in the Northeast in the second half of the year.

Although the overall sale of hybrid bikes decreased in the third quarter, this market will likely continue to grow over

Use Your Head!
May Is Bike Safety Month
Safety is essential! PedalCo proudly designates May as Bike Safety Month.

Responsible bike riders wear protective gear. To help promote responsible bike riding, PedalCo will give all its customers a free helmet when they buy a bike from our stores during the month of May.

PedalCo employees are eligible for this offer as well.

Expand Your Knowledge!

Visit the PedalCo Web site to learn more about helmet safety.

New Market Prompts Reorganization
A growing interest in hybrid bikes has led to increased sales in the coastal regions. This increase in sales has prompted PedalCo to reorganize its current sales force.

A new sales team will serve customers who live in the coastal regions. This sales team will be divided into West Coast and East Coast representatives.

Leaders of both coasts will be supervised by a Coastal Manager.

Joyce Adams
Coastal Manager

Travis Bright
West Coast Leader

Lee Jones
East Coast Leader

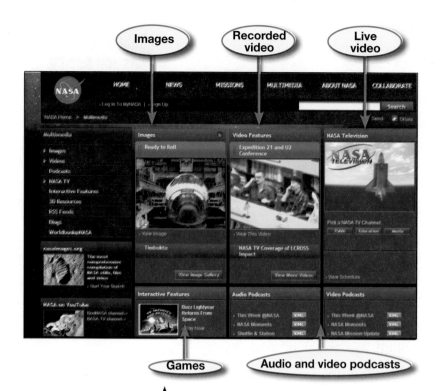

Images

Recorded video

Live video

Games

Audio and video podcasts

Figure 1.2
Web sites may use many multimedia elements. **What elements are included in this Web page?**

Graphics and Animation

Multimedia projects nearly always include a **graphic**, which can be a drawing, chart, diagram, painting, picture, or photograph. Graphics, also called images, can be used to provide visual interest, attract attention, or convey information. Multimedia graphics are sometimes animated. **Animation** is the representation of motion in graphics or text. For example, text can be animated so that it seems to roll or bounce across a screen. A drawing of a bird might be animated so that the bird's wings flap, making it look like the bird is in motion. Animation is frequently used in games to attract the user's attention.

Audio

In multimedia development, live or recorded sound is referred to as **audio**. Using audio can help to both engage users and provide information. Audio is embedded in television programs, motion pictures, animated media, and computer games, as shown in Figure 1.2. Audio can include:

- **Voice-over or Narration** Speech can be pre-recorded and played along with the presentation, or a presenter may talk during the presentation.
- **Audio Effects** Sounds can add a sense of realism or help emphasize information, such as hearing a cash register when talking about money.
- **Music** Music can play in the background during a presentation or be a central element of the project. It is often used to establish moods. For example, think of the way music is used in a movie to build suspense and excitement.

Video

Video consists of live or recorded moving images and is found in many multimedia projects. Video can be used to convey information, teach new skills or provide directions, and entertain. You can play the latest online music video from your favorite band, you can see video clips of recent stories on news sites like CNN.com, and you can even watch original content made just for the Internet.

Go Online **ACTIVITY**
glencoe.com

History of Multimedia **Find out more about the development of multimedia at the Online Learning Center. Go to** glencoe.com. **Choose Activities, then Chapter 1.**

 **Reading Check** **Identify** What elements are used in multimedia productions?

Using Multimedia Elements

How do multimedia presentations help you convey information?

It is important to know the best way to share different types of information with a variety of people. You should carefully consider the purpose of a presentation and the audience before deciding which elements will best help you accomplish your purpose. For example, if you are creating a presentation to teach someone how to fold paper into shapes for origami, a short video of the action might be easier to follow than a series of pictures or a text description. Animated video might be the best option if you are demonstrating proper first aid techniques.

Some general questions to consider are:

- What is the purpose of this presentation? Do I want to entertain or to inform? Am I trying to teach or persuade my viewers?
- What is the expected age of my audience? (Remember, your project may be seen by viewers of all ages.)

Each multimedia element is used to meet the purpose and goals of the multimedia project and to meet the needs of the audience. For example, imagine you are creating a presentation about an after-school program in which you tutor children in reading. Your presentation will use text to provide information about the program. Graphics will illustrate the program in action and attract viewers' attention. Animation, video, and audio may be used to illustrate how tutors and students work together. All of these elements used together will engage the audience about the topic. At the end of the presentation, you might include a text sign-up sheet so that your audience can volunteer to be tutors.

 **Reading Check** **Recall** List two guidelines for deciding which multimedia elements will best help you convey information.

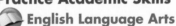

Section 1.1 After You Read

Review Key Concepts

1. **Summarize** the five types of multimedia elements.

2. **Explain** the different purposes for each type of multimedia element.

 Check Your Answers Check your answers at this book's **Online Learning Center** through glencoe.com.

Practice Academic Skills

English Language Arts

3. **Predict** Write a paragraph describing how multimedia elements might be used to advertise a product, such as athletic shoes.

4. **Draw Conclusions** Write a paragraph exploring why it is important to consider carefully how multimedia elements are integrated into a project.

 **Online Student Manual • glencoe.com**

Go to your Online Student Manual and enter your password to find projects that allow you to practice and apply multimedia skills.

NCTE 4 Use written language to communicate effectively.

NCTE 3 Apply strategies to interpret texts.

Reading Guide

Before You Read

Preview Read the Key Concepts listed in each section's Reading Guide. Write one or two sentences predicting what the section will cover.

Read to Learn

Key Concepts

- **List** six multimedia project formats.
- **Describe** common uses of each type of multimedia project format.
- **Summarize** guidelines for choosing a multimedia format.

Main Idea

There are many different types of multimedia project formats. Which kind of format you choose to create depends on the information being conveyed and the intended audience.

Content Vocabulary

◇ print publication   ◇ simulation

◇ presentation   ◇ video game

◇ tutorial

Academic Vocabulary

You will find these words in your reading and on your tests. Use the glossary to look up their definitions, if necessary.

◆ demonstrate

◆ interact

Graphic Organizer

As you read this section, identify six multimedia project formats. Use a tree diagram like the one below to organize your notes.

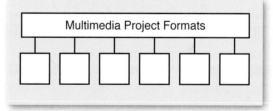

Multimedia Project Formats

 Graphic Organizer Go to this book's **Online Learning Center** at glencoe.com to print this graphic organizer.

Academic Standards

 English Language Arts

NCTE 3 Apply strategies to interpret texts.
NCTE 5 Use different writing process elements to communicate effectively.

NCTE 12 Use language to accomplish individual purposes.

NCTE National Council of Teachers of English
NSES National Science Education Standards

NCTM National Council of Teachers of Mathematics
NCSS National Council for the Social Studies

Multimedia Project Formats

How can I categorize multimedia projects?

There are many options to consider for multimedia project formats and delivery methods. Multimedia project formats include:

- print publications.
- presentations.
- tutorials.
- simulations.
- games.
- Web sites.

As You Read

Connect What types of multimedia products do you use most frequently?

Most multimedia projects can be delivered on a CD or DVD. A CD is a compact disc used to store data. A DVD is a high-density compact disc, also used for data storage. CDs and DVDs are popular delivery methods because of their portability. Another popular delivery method for multimedia projects is the Web. While a Web site is itself a project format, it can also be used to deliver another multimedia project, such as a presentation or tutorial.

Print Publications

A **print publication** is a document that can be printed. Flyers, brochures, magazines, cards, banners, posters, coupons, and invitations are all examples of multimedia print publications. They are multimedia because they are generally created using computer software to combine text and graphics. Figure 1.3 shows a printable template for an invitation.

Presentations

A **presentation** is a sequence of slides that usually incorporates multimedia elements. Each slide can be printed as a handout or seen on a viewing screen. Viewing screens are most often a computer monitor, television screen, or a large projection screen.

The term *presentation* can be used generically in the multimedia industry to refer to all types of multimedia projects. However, the term is used in this text to refer to a specific kind of multimedia project: a digital slide show presentation, or slide show.

Slide show presentations can be shared via the Internet or saved in an e-mail, on a network, or on a CD or DVD.

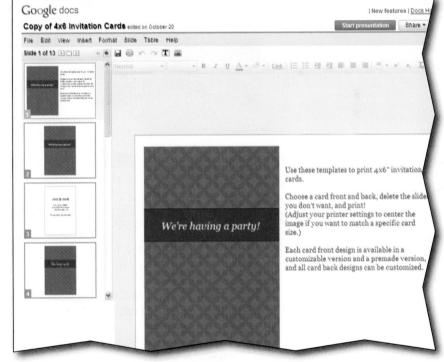

● **Figure 1.3**
Cards and invitations are common print publications. What are some other examples of multimedia print publications?

In the following You Try It activity, you will create a brief presentation about media literacy.

YOU TRY IT

Activity 1A Create a Multimedia Presentation

1. Browse to your data files for Chapter 1. The **Media Literacy** folder contains several files.

2. If necessary, copy the files to the folder specified by your teacher.

3. Examine the files before you open them. Notice that each file has a different file format.

Figure 1.4
Choose colors and graphics that support or match the purpose of your presentation.

READING REACH

Literacy Program

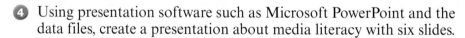

4. Using presentation software such as Microsoft PowerPoint and the data files, create a presentation about media literacy with six slides.

5. Identify the audience and add content that highlights the purpose and goals of the presentation.

6. Be sure to include fonts, colors, graphics, and other objects, such as audio and video, that are appropriate for your audience.

7. Choose a color scheme and design theme that is appropriate for your audience (see Figure 1.3).

8. Insert audio and video and use effects and slide transitions on at least one slide in your presentation.

9. Proofread and spell-check your presentation. Save your work.

10. When you are finished with the presentation, evaluate your presentation. Does the presentation meet the needs of your target audience? Does the presentation support the purpose and goals?

Quick Tip

You Should Know Be aware of your audience. The design of a presentation might need to be different for each audience.

11 Open a new word processing document or take out a piece of paper. Write or key an explanation for why you think the presentation is effective. Is the information presented in an easy-to-read and consistent format? Is it appealing? Is it accurate and grammatically correct?

12 Explain how you have met the presentation's purpose and goals and the reasons for your design choices. Save and close your files.

PLAN AHEAD

Design Organize your thoughts when designing a multimedia presentation. A presentation should be organized around a central thesis statement or purpose.

Tutorials

A **tutorial** is a computer application that trains or teaches content or skills. Tutorials generally use a combination of several elements of multimedia. Tutorials usually **demonstrate**, or illustrate and explain, new information. Businesses often use tutorials to train people who want to improve their workplace skills or who need to learn about an organization's systems, products, or procedures. Educational tutorials like the one shown in Figure 1.5 can be used in school or at home to teach subjects like keyboarding, math, foreign languages, and computer software.

Users move around in tutorials by choosing paths preset by the developer. For example, in an English grammar tutorial, you could select nouns or verbs. Within the tutorial, the user answers questions or completes activities. Generally, if the question is answered correctly, or the activity correctly completed, the user will be taken to a new concept. An incorrect answer will refer the user to the previous information for review. Interactive tutorials thus allow the level of training each user needs, and at the speed that best works for the user.

Figure 1.5
Tutorials may use a combination of multimedia elements to demonstrate a skill or process. How do users move through tutorials?

Simulations

A **simulation** is a computer-based model of a real-life situation. Simulations are used to educate, train, entertain, or inform. As with other tutorials and games, simulations are usually interactive. This means that the user's choices will affect the outcome of the experience. Users **interact**, or act together, with the simulation to control the end result.

Simulations use multimedia elements such as animation, video, and audio to reproduce the environment or situation that the simulation is imitating. For example, training simulations can be used to show a help desk trainee how to deal with customers, to provide practice for a medic's emergency responses, or to train a surgeon on the hand-eye coordination needed to perform surgeries. Simulations are often used when the "real thing" is dangerous or requires access to locations or materials that are not easily accessible to the user. For instance, the armed services often use multimedia simulations to train and test fighter pilots under challenging conditions.

Games

A **video game** is a software program combining multimedia elements designed primarily for the entertainment of the participant or participants (see Figure 1.6). Games generally use all of the elements of multimedia, relying strongly on audio, graphics, animation, and video for prompts, feedback, and setting. Video games are an excellent example of the powerful use of multimedia.

There are thousands of games that can be accessed on the Web, via gaming consoles, and on handheld gaming devices. Cell phones, smartphones such as the BlackBerry®, and other mobile communication devices provide even more choices for on-the-go gaming.

Figure 1.6 Video games are a popular form of entertainment. **What multimedia components are typically used in video games?**

Games can include realistic interactive simulations. For example, an interactive game that simulates car racing might show the car's steering wheel and dashboard, duplicate the sounds of a speeding car, and show the track moving past as you control the car's speed and direction.

Although games are often used for entertainment, they are sometimes designed to be used to reinforce concepts or teach new skills. Corporations may use video games to train new employees and teach new skills. Games add an element of fun that can help keep the user's attention. For example, a game designed to teach employees the correct procedures for a fire drill might require the user to guide his or her character through the correct evacuation route. A correct response would allow the employee to complete his or her training.

Games allow users to win points for each correct step. They also allow users to compete with each other in real time. Some games encourage teams of people to work together even if they are in different physical locations. Games on social networking sites such as Facebook encourage interaction within a network of associates.

Web Sites

Multimedia is frequently used on the Internet. In addition to hosting other multimedia projects, such as presentations, a Web site can itself be a multimedia project. With proper planning and knowledge, your Web site can be a wonderful use of multimedia, combining text, graphics, video, and audio while allowing for unlimited interaction.

A Web site is a versatile multimedia tool. As with video games, Web sites can also overlap other multimedia project formats. A Web site can be designed as a tutorial application or as a video game. Web sites can also include links to tutorials or simulations.

You may build a Web site to inform people about different hiking trails in your area. In addition to the text describing the locations, you might include photos of the trails, a video clip of the scenery on the trail, or even an audio clip of nature sounds.

Go Online **ACTIVITY**
glencoe.com

View Professional Multimedia Presentations **View presentations that integrate multimedia elements at the Online Learning Center. Go to glencoe.com. Choose Activities, then Chapter 1.**

- Multimedia only benefits a Web site when it helps meet its purpose and goals. Think about each type of multimedia element and decide how you can use it to enhance the user's experience.

- Most people like to visit Web sites that contain multimedia. Too much multimedia in a site, however, can make the site distracting and unmanageable.

It is important that if you include a lot of multimedia elements, your Web sites users should have fast Internet connections. It is also important to use technologies such as streaming media that make multimedia easier to access and download. These technologies are sometimes called content delivery enablers because they make it easier for users to access large multimedia files using Internet software. You will read more about the Internet and Web sites in Chapter 2.

 **Reading Check** **Identify** What is a simulation?

Choosing Multimedia Project Formats

Why is it important to consider how a multimedia project will be used?

With many different types of multimedia project formats and delivery methods to choose from, it is important for developers to understand exactly what information is being conveyed and the intended audience. Whether you want to teach, inform, train, entertain, or report, you must decide what will be the best way to present the content.

Consider these questions when deciding your project's format and delivery method:

- What information do you want to convey? A slide show presentation might be a good option for sharing knowledge, while a tutorial or game might be better to teach a skill.

- How do you want users to interact with the project? Will they answer questions, as in a tutorial? Will the users control the outcome as in a simulation or game?

- What multimedia elements do you plan to include in your project? If you are including video and audio, consider whether all Web sites can handle the size of the files or if a DVD would be a better delivery method.

 **Reading Check** **Explain** What guidelines should you consider when choosing a multimedia project format?

Academic Focus

English Language Arts

Determine a Presentation's Purpose Locate a multimedia presentation that is designed to present information to elementary school students. For example, it might teach math. Write a paragraph that explains the presentation's purpose to fourth- to sixth-grade students. Keep your language at an appropriate level.

NCTE 5 Use different writing process elements to communicate effectively.

Section 1.2 After You Read

Review Key Concepts

1. **Explain** why a magazine is a multimedia project.

2. **Summarize** how the elements in a multimedia project might affect your choice of delivery method.

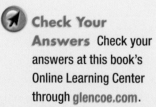 **Check Your Answers** Check your answers at this book's Online Learning Center through glencoe.com.

Practice Academic Skills
English Language Arts

3. **Compare and Contrast** Write a one-page essay describing how multimedia tutorials and simulations are similar and different.

4. **Draw Conclusions** You are creating a multimedia project to show your classmates how to perform a specific task, such as cooking a dish or playing the guitar. Determine which elements would work best and explain your choices in a brief essay.

NCTE 3 Apply strategies to interpret texts.

NCTE 12 Use language to accomplish individual purposes.

Online Student Manual • glencoe.com

Go to your Online Student Manual and enter your password to find projects that allow you to practice and apply multimedia skills.

SECTION (1.3) Multimedia Careers and Skills

Reading Guide

Before You Read

Adjust Reading Speed Slow down your reading speed to match the difficulty of the text. Reread each paragraph, if needed.

Read to Learn
Key Concepts

- **List** ways that multimedia is frequently used in society.
- **Explain** how you can develop a career plan while in school.
- **Describe** how extended learning experiences contribute to career preparation.

Main Idea

Today's multimedia-driven society offers many career opportunities. Extended learning experiences can help determine and prepare for a career pathway.

Content Vocabulary

- ◆ extended learning opportunity
- ◆ curricular experience
- ◆ job shadowing
- ◆ internship
- ◆ cooperative
- ◆ extracurricular
- ◆ service learning

Academic Vocabulary

You will find these words in your reading and on your tests. Use the glossary to look up their definitions, if necessary.

- ◆ significant
- ◆ focus

Graphic Organizer

As you read, identify five types of learning experiences and summarize how they can help you prepare for a career. Use a graphic organizer like the one below to organize your ideas.

Educational Experience	How It Helps

 Graphic Organizer Go to this book's **Online Learning Center** at **glencoe.com** to print this graphic organizer.

Academic Standards

 English Language Arts

NCTE 7 Conduct research and gather, evaluate, and synthesize data to communicate discoveries.
NCTE 8 Use information resources to gather information and create and communicate knowledge.

 Mathematics

NCTM Problem Solving Apply and adapt a variety of appropriate strategies to solve problems.

NCTE National Council of Teachers of English
NSES National Science Education Standards

NCTM National Council of Teachers of Mathematics
NCSS National Council for the Social Studies

As You Read

Connect Why do you think multimedia jobs have become so popular?

Multimedia and Society

How has multimedia affected society?

We rely on multimedia in many aspects of our everyday lives—to stay in touch with contacts, watch movies or videos, listen to music, manage photo albums, and play games. This increasing use of multimedia in our lives means there are many career opportunities that will use the multimedia skills you are learning. For example, all the advertising on the Web is created by people with multimedia skills. Eye-catching e-commerce sites are designed by talented graphic designers. Even teachers often use multimedia to help get their students' attention and convey information.

In addition to career opportunities, multimedia is also an important resource in education, business, and recreation. Many colleges now offer online courses. Today's businesses use multimedia for distributing information, training, and even communication. We use multimedia Web sites to help plan our vacations. When we are at home, our leisure time is often filled with watching DVDs, playing video games, chatting online with friends or family, or surfing the Internet.

Figure 1.7 lists a few of the ways that multimedia is used in different areas of our lives.

Figure 1.7 ●──▶
Multimedia is emerging as a basic skill because of its significant role in society. In addition to personal use, how have you used multimedia in these areas of your life?

Real World

Job Skills An important challenge in life is finding the right job.

Why It's Important

Why is it important to know what job skills you already have?

Multimedia and Society	
Area of Life	**How Multimedia Is Used**
Business	• E-commerce Web sites • Advertising • Presentations for meetings and conferences • Employee training and tutorials • Employee collaboration
Publishing, News, and Entertainment	• Online news and Webzines • Blogs • E-books • Music, animations, and video distribution • Social networking
Education	• Distance learning, online schools, and virtual classroom experiences • Web-based training • Classroom presentations
Health Care	• Medical training • Medical information for the public • Telemedicine

 **Reading Check** **Recall** What are four areas of life in which multimedia is used?

Career Planning Starts Now

What steps can you take now to explore careers?

Multimedia skills are key to many job opportunities and career paths such as design, engineering, desktop publishing, Web design, and game design. The first step to making a career decision is to ask yourself some basic questions. What kinds of activities do you like to do? What kind of work do you enjoy? For example, if you enjoy editing digital photos, research career paths that use this skill. The U.S. Department of Education has organized careers into 16 groups of related occupations called career clusters (see Figure 1.8). Multimedia-related careers have experienced **significant**, or considerable, growth. You can help your career prospects by exploring career paths now and taking classes that will help you gain the skills you will need.

 **Reading Check** **Identify** What questions should you ask yourself to begin developing a career plan?

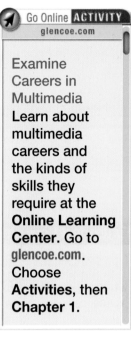

Go Online **ACTIVITY**
glencoe.com

Examine Careers in Multimedia **Learn about multimedia careers and the kinds of skills they require at the Online Learning Center.** Go to **glencoe.com. Choose Activities,** then **Chapter 1.**

The U.S. Department of Education Career Clusters

Career Cluster	Job Examples
Agriculture, Food, and Natural Resources	Farmer, ecologist, veterinarian
Architecture and Construction	Contractor, architect, building inspector
Arts, Audio/Video Technology, and Communications	Graphic desinger, musician, filmmaker
Business Management and Administration	Executive assistant, bookkeeper, business owner
Education and Training	Teacher, counselor, librarian
Finance	Bank teller, financial planner, stockbroker
Government and Public Administration	Soldier, postal worker, nonprofit director
Health Science	Pediatrician, registered nurse, physical therapist
Hospitality and Tourism	Chef, hotel manager, tour guide
Human Services	Social worker, psychologist, child care worker
Information Technology	Web designer, software engineer, technical writer
Law, Public Safety, Corrections, and Security	Attorney, police officer, paralegal
Manufacturing	Production supervisor, manufacturing engineer
Marketing, Sales, and Service	Sales associate, retail buyer, customer service
Science, Technology, Engineering, and Math	Lab technician, marine biologist, electrical engineer
Transportation, Distribution, and Logistics	Pilot, railroad contractor, automotive mechanic

◄——— ● **Figure 1.8**
The U.S. Department of Education groups careers into 16 career clusters based on similar job characteristics. **What career clusters list job examples in multimedia?**

Extended Learning Opportunities

Why are extended learning opportunities an important part of career preparation?

How you spend your time right now can help you **focus,** or concentrate your attention or effort, on your career course. As you begin exploring career options, extended learning opportunities can give you insight in choosing a career path. An **extended learning opportunity** is a program that allows you to connect what you learn in school today to possible future careers. Figure 1.9 describes four types of extended learning opportunities.

Extended Learning Opportunities

Type of Experience	Description	Examples
Curricular Experience	Experiences that are available to you within the high school curriculum	• Multimedia courses
Career-Based Learning Experience	Job-related experiences that are available to you while still in school	• Job shadowing • Internship • School-work cooperative experience • Work-based learning
Extracurricular Experience	Experiences outside of high school coursework	• Future Business Leaders of America (FBLA) • Yearbook • School newspaper
Service Learning Experience	Opportunities to give your time to the community	• Community organizations • Community service volunteer • Church youth groups or music groups • Tutoring/mentoring programs

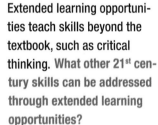

Figure 1.9
Extended learning opportunities teach skills beyond the textbook, such as critical thinking. **What other 21ˢᵗ century skills can be addressed through extended learning opportunities?**

Curricular Experiences

A **curricular experience** is one that teaches real-world skills through class content. For example, the multimedia skills you learn in this class can be applied in a real-world business context. Other classes also teach useful skills for future careers, such as:

- Business classes
- Keyboarding classes
- Art classes

In addition to the topics taught in your classes, you can also take this time to learn other 21ˢᵗ century skills, such as teamwork, leadership, and communication. Consider as you prepare your next oral report how the speaking practice will help you better present yourself in an interview. Working with your classmates on a science project allows you to improve your teamwork skills. Even completing your homework each week shows your accountability and responsibility skills.

Career-Based Learning Experiences

The best way to learn about a career is to work. There are several options available to help you explore possible careers. A **job shadowing** experience involves following a worker on the job for a short time, sometimes a few days. An **internship** is a temporary paid or unpaid position that involves direct work experience in a career field.

Work–school **cooperative** experiences are agreements with local businesses to hire students to perform jobs that use knowledge and skills taught in their classes. Such work experiences can offer real-world opportunities to use multimedia skills such as developing Web site content for a small business or editing photos for a photographer.

Extracurricular Activities

Extracurricular activities are school activities that you do outside the classroom such as working on the online school newspaper or participating in organizations and clubs. For example, adding video to the school Web site requires multimedia skills. Membership in organizations such as the Future Business Leaders of America shows teamwork skills and helps develop leadership ability.

Service Learning

Service learning is an extended learning opportunity in which you do volunteer work in the community. Service learning can be personally rewarding, providing opportunities to help others while learning about careers. Developing presentations for the humane society or writing newsletters for hospital patients are examples of service learning.

Academic Focus

Mathematics

Determine Savings
A company purchases a tutorial for $4,000 to help its designers learn a new graphics package. Using the tutorial saves designers 8 hours a week. Designers make $35.00 an hour. If there are three designers, approximately how many weeks will it take to earn back the tutorial's cost? Begin by calculating the amount saved each week.

NCTM Problem Solving Apply and adapt a variety of appropriate strategies to solve problems.

 **Reading Check** **List** Identify types of extended learning experiences.

Section 1.3 After You Read

Review Key Concepts

1. **Summarize** how multimedia is used in business today.

2. **Explain** how extended learning opportunities can help prepare you for a future career.

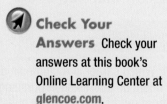 **Check Your Answers** Check your answers at this book's Online Learning Center at glencoe.com.

Practice Academic Skills

English Language Arts

3. **Examine** Research a career that interests you and write a paragraph describing how multimedia skills are used in that career.

4. **Predict** Locate a service learning opportunity in your community. Create a graphic organizer showing how you might use multimedia skills by participating in this opportunity.

 **Online Student Manual • glencoe.com**

Go to your Online Student Manual and enter your password to find projects that allow you to practice and apply multimedia skills.

NCTE 8 Use information resources to gather information and create and communicate knowledge.

NCTE 7 Conduct research and gather, evaluate, and synthesize data to communicate discoveries.

Careers & Technology

Internet-Related Multimedia Careers

The Internet is the source for many multimedia career pathways. These multimedia career opportunities use different types of skills to develop new multimedia and to ensure that multimedia can be accessed and used corectly.

There are many career opportunities for developing multimedia projects for the Internet.

Producers/Project Managers

Producers and project managers for online multimedia need great organizational skills and the ability to problem-solve, budget, prioritize, and negotiate. They should also have creative design experience, including storyboarding, interactive scripting, animation, video, compression techniques, and product delivery vehicles.

Programmers

Programmers design and create software that runs an online multimedia program. It requires knowing programming languages, but it can be very exciting because, on the Web, programmers can immediately see results of work.

Webmasters

Companies with Web sites need a Webmaster to develop and maintain the site, ensure user accessibility to the site, monitor site traffic, and meet traffic demands. Webmasters can also design the look and feel of the site.

Interactive Writers and Designers

Multimedia designers and writers combine project content with various media and forms of interactivity. Online games are often created by individuals who have strong programming skills as well as other creative skills, such as skills in graphic design, animation, and interactive design. Game designers might specialize in action games, card games, fantasy games, or strategy games. Game designers must be able to turn abstract ideas into graphic images and creative formats that can be enjoyed by one or many players.

Video and Audio Specialists

Artists not only have the opportunity to create new types of graphics and animation, but also to lay out and design the appearance of multimedia projects. Video specialists use technology to produce original videos and display video from other sources over the Internet. Audio specialists create sounds and make sure that they interact correctly with other media.

Skill Builder

1. Research Careers Conduct online research and evaluate three multimedia careers that interest you. Create a presentation that compares and contrasts careers based on job descriptions, skill requirements, and salaries.

2. Write a Report Which career in multimedia do you think you might be interested in pursuing and why? Write a brief report to answer the question.

Chapter Summary

Multimedia is the integration of elements such as text, graphics, animation, audio, and video using computer technology.

Multimedia projects can be used to teach, inform, train, entertain, and report. There are many different types of multimedia projects including print publications, presentations, tutorials, simulations, video games, and Web sites.

There are many job opportunities in multimedia. Extended learning opportunities, which connect what you learn in school to your future career, will give you insight in choosing a career path.

Vocabulary Review

1. Arrange the vocabulary terms below into groups of related words. Explain why you grouped the words together.

Content Vocabulary

◇ multimedia (p. 7)
◇ medium (p. 7)
◇ media (p. 7)
◇ interactive media (p. 7)
◇ rich media (p. 7)
◇ text (p. 7)
◇ graphic (p. 8)
◇ animation (p. 8)
◇ audio (p. 8)
◇ video (p. 8)
◇ print publication (p. 11)
◇ presentation (p. 11)

◇ tutorial (p. 13)
◇ simulation (p. 14)
◇ video game (p. 14)
◇ extended learning opportunity (p. 20)
◇ curricular experience (p. 20)
◇ job shadowing (p. 21)
◇ internship (p. 21)
◇ cooperative (p. 21)
◇ extracurricular (p. 21)
◇ service learning (p. 21)

Academic Vocabulary

◇ element (p. 7)
◇ ensure (p. 7)
◇ demonstrate (p. 13)
◇ interact (p. 14)
◇ significant (p. 19)
◇ focus (p. 20)

Review Key Concepts

2. **Define** multimedia.

3. **List** multimedia elements.

4. **Summarize** how multimedia elements convey information.

5. **List** six multimedia project formats.

6. **Describe** common uses of each type of multimedia project format.

7. **Summarize** guidelines for choosing a multimedia format.

8. **List** ways that multimedia is frequently used in society.

9. **Explain** how you can develop a career plan while in school.

10. **Describe** how extended learning experiences contribute to career preparation.

Critical Thinking

11. Describe Summarize the five multimedia elements. Use a web diagram like the one below to organize your ideas.

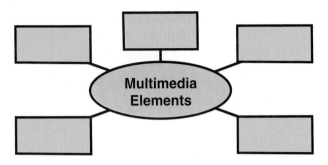

12. Analyze With your teacher's approval, find a Web site that incorporates these multimedia elements: text, graphics, animation, audio, and video. Analyze the Web site and write a paragraph that discusses the effectiveness of the use of these elements.

13. List Identify the seven types of multimedia project formats and provide an example of each. Use a table like the one below to help organize your thoughts.

Project Format	Example
1.	
2.	
3.	
4.	
5.	
6.	
7.	

14. Draw Conclusions Multimedia is more common today than in previous years. Explain why it was not as widespread 25 years ago as it is today.

15. Predict Imagine that you have the opportunity to shadow people who have careers in multimedia. Choose three multimedia careers and list them in a graphic organizer similar to the one below. Then list the skills you would like to learn from shadowing these people.

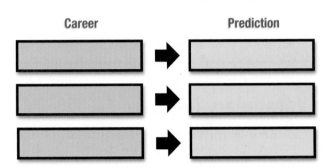

16. Analyze With your teacher's approval, select a multimedia Web site to analyze. Determine the purpose. Is it used for education, business, recreation, entertainment, or another purpose? Also evaluate what other kinds of multimedia project formats and multimedia elements are used on the site. How easy was it for you to see the purpose of the site? Why do you think that is?

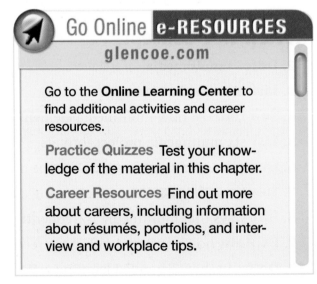

Go Online e-RESOURCES

glencoe.com

Go to the **Online Learning Center** to find additional activities and career resources.

Practice Quizzes Test your knowledge of the material in this chapter.

Career Resources Find out more about careers, including information about résumés, portfolios, and interview and workplace tips.

Academic Connections

17. **English Language Arts–Plan a Project**

Think of an activity that you enjoy participating in and would like to teach to other people. Perhaps you enjoy playing soccer, drawing, jogging, or cooking. Decide whether you would want to use a tutorial, simulation, or game to train other people in this activity. Answer the questions below, using a tree diagram to organize your answers. Then create a one-page plan of your project.

A. What kind of text will you include?

B. How will you use graphics in your project?

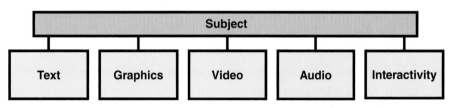

C. Will you include video? If so, what will the video include?

D. If audio is part of your production, what type of audio will you use?

E. What types of interactivity will your project contain?

NSES 1 Develop an understanding of concepts and processes.

Standardized Test Practice

Multiple Choice

Read the paragraph below and then answer the question.

When dealing with information from a Web site, the first and most important question to ask is "Who wrote this information?" Once you have found the name of the author (usually located near the top or bottom of the page), do a quick Web search to see what else that author has written. Keying the author's name into a search engine will often return not only pages by the author, but also pages about that author, such as reviews of his or her work. Check to see if the author has published in print. Search online for books that he or she has written. All this information will help you decide whether you should consider the person's information trustworthy.

18. According to the paragraph, which of the following statements is true?

A. All Web sites provide the name of the person who wrote the information for the Web page.

B. Information about Web page authors can often be found by keying the author's name into a search engine.

C. All Web sites must give reliable information.

D. If an author's name is included in a Web site, it is safe to assume the information is true.

Test-Taking Tip When answering multiple-choice questions, ask yourself if each option is true or false. This may help you find the best answer if you are unsure.

STANDARDS AT WORK •

19. Conduct Research for a Presentation

You have been asked to conduct research to determine how multimedia is used in business today and how it can be used to help market a business. The information you gather will help the media company you work for, JMT Media, develop an advertising campaign to promote its services. You will present your findings at the next board meeting. Your research should include:

NETS 3b Locate, organize, analyze, evaluate, synthesize, and ethically use information from a variety of sources and media.

A. An outline for the presentation, which includes your research results.

B. Charts and graphs based on your research, showing different ways businesses use multimedia, and other visual materials that will enhance the presentation outline.

Adapt your language and use of graphics to your planned audience: the JMT Media board. Share your presentation outline and graphics with two classmates. Ask them to evaluate the completeness of your research and your organization and use of graphics for the specific audience. Make improvements based on their feedback.

20. Analyze the Effective Use of Multimedia

With your teacher's approval, choose two Web sites about the same subject. Subjects might include sports, entertainers, movies, cooking, cars, music, or the arts. Web sites should contain a variety of multimedia elements: text, graphics, animation, audio, and video. Analyze the purpose of each Web site, and compare and contrast the sites' use of multimedia elements. Then analyze which multimedia team did the best job conveying its message.

NETS 3d Process data and report results.

NETS 4c Collect and analyze data to identify solutions and/or make informed decisions.

A. Compare the use of text on the Web sites. Is it sized correctly for emphasis and readability? Do the color and font enhance or detract from the content?

B. Compare the graphics on the two sites. Do they make the site more interesting? How do they affect your ability to find other content on the site?

C. How is animation used on the sites? Is it eye-catching or does it make things difficult to read?

D. Is there audio on the site? Does it help you understand the site better? Does the site have video? If so, does it enhance the site? What kind of interactivity is included?

E. After you have compared and contrasted the Web sites, determine which site is most effective in its use of multimedia. Use a table like the one shown to organize your findings. Then, write a one-page summary that explains your results and identifies which multimedia team you would hire to design a Web site and why.

USE OF	SITE #1	SITE #2
Text		
Graphics		
Animation		
Audio		
Video		
Interactivity		

21. Set Realistic Goals

You are applying for a position in development at a large multimedia design and development company. You decide to create a new multimedia project for your portfolio. Before you can achieve that goal, you need to decide what steps you must take to reach that goal. Draft a plan to help you identify the tasks you will need to complete in order to create the project for your portfolio. Your multimedia project can be a print publication, presentation, or Web site. You have an hour to complete a draft of your plan. You need to decide:

A. Which project format will you use for your multimedia portfolio?

B. What are the purpose and goals for your multimedia portfolio? What information will you include? How will you use the project to identify the career skills you already have?

C. Who is the target audience for your multimedia portfolio? Who will see your portfolio? What is expected or required of you?

D. What multimedia elements will the project include (text, graphics, animation, audio, video)?

E. What color scheme or design theme will the project include?

Set realistic goals for your multimedia portfolio. Draft tasks and timeframes for completing the task in three weeks. In your plan, write a summary that lists your decisions. Write a paragraph that describes the goals you set. Are your goals realistic? What would you change?

22. Create an Educational Presentation

You have been asked to teach your class how to play a game that you enjoy. You might want to teach how to play a video game, a board game, or a sports game. Use presentation software such as Microsoft® PowerPoint®, Apple® Keynote®, Freelance Graphics®, or Harvard Graphics® to create your presentation.

To develop your presentation, you will need to:

A. Choose a topic to teach to your class. Research the topic so you have all the information you need to answer questions that might be asked.

B. Decide on a design for your presentation, including layout and colors.

C. Determine the steps in which you will teach the topic. Use a chain of events diagram like the one shown to help organize your information. Use appropriate software to create the presentation. Give your presentation to your class.

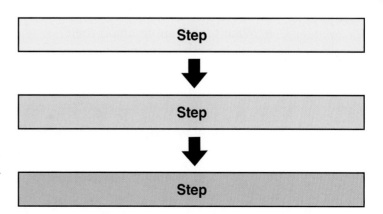

Projects Across the Curriculum

Project 1

NCTE 4 Use written language to communicate effectively.

Create a Multimedia Project

English Language Arts You work for a travel agency. Create a multimedia project to share important information with a client who is visiting your home town for the first time.

Plan

1. Decide which type of multimedia project will best meet your needs.

Research

2. Gather all of the information your client will need to know such as the locations of the hotel, your office, restaurants, and movie theaters.

3. Develop a schedule of the tours and activities planned for the client.

Create

4. Use appropriate materials to create your project. If creating a print publication, use word processing or desktop publishing software. If creating a presentation, use presentation software.

5. Include graphics that might add interest or enhance the finished product.

6. Edit your presentation. Proofread and spell-check the document.

Project 2

NCTE 4 Use written language to communicate effectively.

NCTE 5 Use different writing process elements to communication effectively.

Develop an Employee Orientation

Social Studies You work for a company that is going to open an office in a different country. You have been asked to create a presentation that will help inform your coworkers about the country.

Research

1. Choose a country to research for your presentation.

2. Research the country online. Gather information such as the following:

   - What are the social customs of the country?
   - What is the primary language spoken in the country?
   - What t foods are common there?

Create

3. Based on your research, create your presentation. Add graphics such as maps and charts to enhance the presentation.

4. Develop a script (audio) to be read during the presentation. Edit your final presentation. Proofread and spell-check your documents.

Project 3

Recognize Multimedia Productions

English Language Arts The different types of multimedia project formats discussed in this chapter can be found in various and numerous places. Find an example of each of the different types of multimedia project formats.

NCTE 7 Conduct research and gather, evaluate, and synthesize data to communicate discoveries.

NCTE 8 Use information resources to gather information and create and communicate knowledge.

Research

1. Locate an example of each of the six types of multimedia project formats: print publication, presentation, tutorial, simulation, game, and Web site.

Create

2. Based on your research, create a table or spreadsheet to contain the information you collect. The table may look similar to the one below.

	Title of Production	Purpose	Text	Graphics	Animation	Audio	Video
Print publication							
Presentation							
Tutorial							
Simulation							
Game							
Web page							

For each type of multimedia project format, collect the following information:

- Title and purpose of the production.
- Is text used? If so, analyze the effectiveness of its use.
- Are graphics used? Analyze their effectiveness.
- Is animation used? Analyze their effectiveness.
- Is audio used? Analyze its effectiveness.
- Is video used? Analyze its effectiveness.

Review

3. Work with a small group of classmates to evaluate and critique one another's tables.

4. Make changes to your table based on feedback from your classmates' reviews and critiques.

5. Proofread and spell-check the document.

Go Online **RUBRICS**
glencoe.com

Chapter Projects Use the rubrics for these projects to help create and evaluate your work. Go to the **Online Learning Center** at glencoe.com. Choose **Rubrics, then Chapter 1.**

CHAPTER 2 Multimedia Online

Section 2.1
The Internet and the World Wide Web

Section 2.2
Introduction to the Web

Section 2.3
Web Resources and Guidelines

CHAPTER OBJECTIVES

After completing this chapter, you will be able to:

- ❖ **Compare** the Internet and the Web.
- ❖ **Explain** how the Internet works.
- ❖ **Describe** Internet resources.
- ❖ **Explain** how browsers work.
- ❖ **Identify** URL components.
- ❖ **Describe** types of Web sites.
- ❖ **Use** search engines.
- ❖ **Describe** Web resources.
- ❖ **Summarize** how to stay safe using online resources.
- ❖ **Describe** how to use protected information.

Explore the Photo

Multimedia tools are all around you.
Which tools do you think would be most helpful to create a slide show presentation with photos?

21st CENTURY SKILLS
Understand Your Audience

When you build multimedia projects, it is important to consider your audience at every stage. Understanding your audience will help ensure that your multimedia projects are focused and interesting.

Quick Write Activity Prewriting

Write about a time when you had to perform or present information to an audience. Do a prewriting activity to help you develop ideas and explore why it is important to know your audience before you do a presentation.

Writing Tips
To prewrite effectively, follow these steps:
1. Freewrite or collect ideas from other sources.
2. List ideas and see how they relate to each other.
3. Create a web diagram or word cluster to organize your thoughts.

Reading Guide

Before You Read

Preview Choose a content or academic vocabulary term that is new to you. When you find it in the text, write down the definition.

Read to Learn

Key Concepts

- **Compare and Contrast** the Internet and the Web.
- **Explain** how the Internet and the Web work.
- **Describe** types of Internet resources.

Main Idea

The Internet and the World Wide Web work together, but they are not the same thing. Ethical guidelines must be followed to stay safe online.

Content Vocabulary

- Internet
- network
- hardware
- World Wide Web
- Internet service provider (ISP)
- protocol

Academic Vocabulary

You will find these words in your reading and on your tests. Use the glossary to look up their definitions, if necessary.

- access
- communicate

Graphic Organizer

As you read the section, identify and describe eight multimedia Internet resources. Use an organizer like the one shown below to organize your notes.

Resource	Description

 Graphic Organizer Go to this book's **Online Learning Center** at **glencoe.com** to print this graphic organizer.

Academic Standards

 English Language Arts

NCTE 4 Use written language to communicate effectively.
NCTE 9 Develop an understanding of diversity in language use across cultures.

NCTE 12 Use language to accomplish individual purposes.

NCTE National Council of Teachers of English
NSES National Science Education Standards

NCTM National Council of Teachers of Mathematics
NCSS National Council for the Social Studies

The Internet Versus the Web

How is the World Wide Web different from the Internet?

The Internet and the World Wide Web are not the same thing. The World Wide Web is just one of the main resources on the Internet. The more you know about the Internet, the better you will be able to **access**, or find and retrieve, its wealth of multimedia resources.

The Internet Is Hardware

The **Internet** (also called the Net) is a huge network that connects computers all over the world. A **network** is a group of computers that can **communicate**, or transmit information, with one another. The Internet consists of components, called **hardware**, that you can physically touch. Some examples of hardware are computers and communication lines.

The Web Is Software

The Web is not the same as the Internet. The **World Wide Web**, or Web, is a system of linked files that may also contain text, graphics, audio, video, or animation. The Web is a complicated software system that is used on the Internet's network, as shown in Figure 2.1.

- The Internet provides the equipment, tools, and hardware that allow users to access the World Wide Web.

- The Web is a system that visually displays information in a user-friendly way.

 **Reading Check** **Compare and Contrast** How are the Internet and the Web different?

As You Read

Connect What do you already know about the Internet and the World Wide Web?

Go Online ACTIVITY
glencoe.com

The History of the Internet Find out more about the history of the Internet at the **Online Learning Center**. Go to **glencoe.com**. Choose **Activities**, then **Chapter 2.**

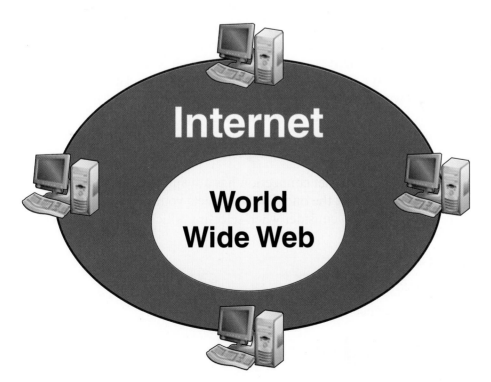

Figure 2.1
The Internet connects computers globally, and the Web is one software application on the Internet. **How do you use the Internet each day?**

How the Internet Works

How can I connect to the Internet?

You must be connected to the Internet to use its resources. To connect to the Internet, most people use a computer with a communication line, such as a telephone line or a cable connection. Communication lines connect to the high-speed telecommunications networks. These networks are owned by telecommunications companies such as AT&T® and Sprint®. Files are stored on servers that send the files to individual computers. A server is a computer that manages files and other resources for a network.

Before you can use the Internet, your computer or mobile device must be set up to access an Internet service provider. An **Internet service provider (ISP)** is a business that allows users to to access the Internet through the provided network. Some examples of ISPs include EarthLink®, AT&T®, and Time-Warner®. Three common types of Internet connections include dial-up, broadband, and wireless.

- **Dial-up** A dial-up connection requires a modem and a standard telephone line. Dial-up connections are generally inexpensive but they have slow transmission speeds and often disconnect suddenly.

- **Broadband** Broadband connections require hardware that is provided by the ISP, along with cable television equipment, a satellite dish, or a dedicated digital subscriber line (DSL). With a broadband connection, your computer is always connected to the Internet, so access is instantaneous. In addition, the transmission rates are faster than dial-up connections. However, broadband connections also tend to be more expensive than dial-up and the continuous Internet connection makes your computer more vulnerable to viruses, spyware, and hackers.

- **Wireless** You can connect to the Internet using infrared waves, radio waves, or microwaves. This is called a wireless connection. A popular wireless choice is Wi-Fi, which is short for wireless fidelity. Wi-Fi uses high-frequency radio waves. The advantage of a wireless connection is that it makes the Internet portable because no cables or cords are needed to connect. Unfortunately, not every location has wireless accessibility, and the connections are not as reliable as other types of connections.

Each type of Internet connection has advantages and disadvantages. You must select the one that best meets your needs. There are three basic factors to consider when selecting which type of Internet connection to use:

- Cost
- Speed
- Convenience

 **Reading Check** **List** What are three types of Internet connections?

Internet Resources

How do computers communicate with one another to share resources?

The Internet provides a host of resources such as the Web, e-mail, chat rooms, and instant messaging. Figure 2.2 lists some popular Internet resources.

Computers on the Internet must communicate in order to share information. A **protocol** is a set of rules and procedures specifying how data needs to be formatted and transmitted between computer systems. Computers must follow the same protocol in order to "talk" to one another. Transmission Control Protocol (TCP) and Internet Protocol (IP) communicate data over the Internet. Another protocol, the File Transfer Protocol (FTP), provides a standardized method of uploading and downloading files on the Internet. This functionality is especially helpful when handling files for a multimedia project. Files for FTP sites are stored on FTP servers. To access Internet resources, IP requires that every device that is connected to the Internet have a unique IP address. This address identifies the computer or mobile communication device.

E-mail is a key Internet resource and is important for both business and personal communications. Using multimedia elements in an e-mail can make it more engaging. To receive e-mail, you need a unique e-mail address that routes your messages directly to you. In order to send and receive e-mail messages, you need an e-mail application such as Microsoft® Outlook®, Lotus Notes®, or Microsoft® Entourage®.

Figure 2.2
The Internet is commonly used for communication.
What is a protocol?

Types of Internet Resources

Resource	Function
Chat Rooms	Users talk in a group in real time about particular subjects such as hobbies. No special software is required to access a chat room.
Electronic Mail (E-mail)	Users send messages directly to one or more people via the Internet.
FTP Site	Users share large files, often in business, via a site. Can also be used to upload Web site files to a Web server.
Instant Messaging (IM)	Users talk person-to-person, or in group chats. Works like IRC communication. Unlike IRC, many private companies have developed IM applications. With IM, you must know the user name of the person you want to talk to.
Internet Relay Chat (IRC)	Users communicate with one another in real time by keying messages back and forth. Conversations may be public or private. Mostly used for group chatting.
Listserv	Users post group messages; can access and respond to messages at their convenience.
Newsgroups or Forums	Users post articles on a topic that other subscribers to the newsgroups can read. Many newsgroups reside on USENET, a worldwide bulletin board system.
Online Gaming	Users play games in real time with people in other locations. Multiuser domain games (MUDs) and MUD object-oriented games (MOOs) let users experience a virtual universe where they interact with other users.

Activity 2A Explore the Multimedia Elements in an Internet Resource

1 With your teacher's permission, open an Internet resource, such as an e-mail newsletter or instant message window. For example, Figure 2.3 shows an instant message chat window.

2 Explore the Internet resource by clicking menus and buttons.

3 Identify text, graphics, animation, audio, and video elements included in this resource.

Figure 2.3
Internet resources feature multimedia to engage users.

4 Following your teacher's instructions, create a list of the elements used. Close the Internet resource.

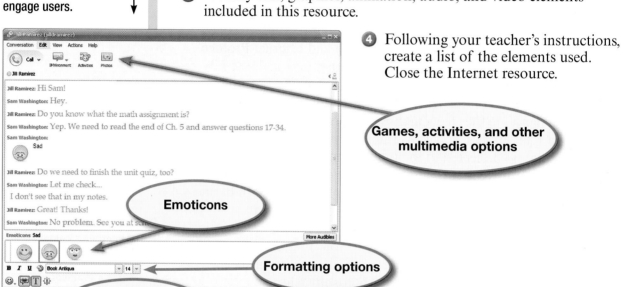

Games, activities, and other multimedia options

Emoticons

Formatting options

Text entry box

Reading Check **List** What are two examples of Internet resources?

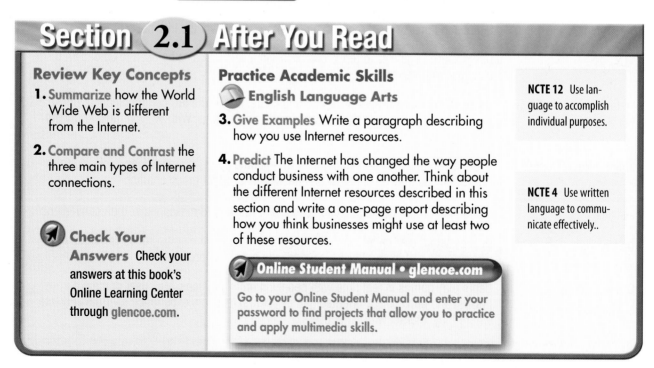

Section 2.1 After You Read

Review Key Concepts

1. **Summarize** how the World Wide Web is different from the Internet.

2. **Compare and Contrast** the three main types of Internet connections.

Check Your Answers Check your answers at this book's Online Learning Center through glencoe.com.

Practice Academic Skills

English Language Arts

3. **Give Examples** Write a paragraph describing how you use Internet resources.

4. **Predict** The Internet has changed the way people conduct business with one another. Think about the different Internet resources described in this section and write a one-page report describing how you think businesses might use at least two of these resources.

Online Student Manual • glencoe.com

Go to your Online Student Manual and enter your password to find projects that allow you to practice and apply multimedia skills.

NCTE 12 Use language to accomplish individual purposes.

NCTE 4 Use written language to communicate effectively..

Reading Guide

Before You Read

Predict Before starting this section, browse the headings, bold terms, and figure captions to predict what this section is about.

Read to Learn

Key Concepts

- **Describe** the role of Web browsers.
- **Identify** URL components and types of Web sites.
- **Explain** how to search the Web by keywords and Boolean operators.

Main Idea

Browsers are used to navigate the Web. URLs identify the unique locations of Web pages and types of Web sites. Search tools can be utilized to find information on the Web.

Content Vocabulary

◇ Web site
◇ Web page
◇ Web browser
◇ Hypertext Transfer Protocol (HTTP)
◇ plug-in
◇ streaming media
◇ uniform resource locator (URL)
◇ domain name
◇ search engine
◇ keyword
◇ Boolean search

Academic Vocabulary

You will find these words in your reading and on your tests. Use the glossary to look up their definitions, if necessary.

◇ retrieve
◇ unique

Graphic Organizer

As you read the section, identify five types of Web sites. Use a diagram like the one shown to help organize your information.

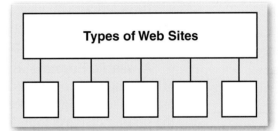

Types of Web Sites

 Graphic Organizer Go to this book's **Online Learning Center** at glencoe.com to print this graphic organizer.

Academic Standards

 English Language Arts

NCTE 8 Use information resources to gather information and create and communicate knowledge.
NCTE 12 Use language to accomplish individual purposes.

NCTE National Council of Teachers of English
NSES National Science Education Standards

 Mathematics

NCTM Reasoning and Proof Select and use various types of reasoning and methods of proof.

NCTM National Council of Teachers of Mathematics
NCSS National Council for the Social Studies

As You Read

Connect What browsers have you used to access information on the Web?

PLAN AHEAD

Accessibility It is important to plan your projects so that they are as consistent as possible across multiple platforms and browsers.

Web Basics

What are the functions of a Web browser?

The World Wide Web, or Web, is perhaps the Internet's most widely used resource. A **Web site** is a group of linked pages of related files, organized around a common topic. Each of these pages is called a Web page. A **Web page** is a file with a unique name and is the basic component of the Web. Web pages can include text, graphics, audio, video, and animation.

The main Web page on a site is called the home page. This is the first page a user sees when visiting a Web site. It usually contains general information about the Web site, as well as links to other Web pages or Web sites. The Web address for the home page will end in *index.html* or *default.html*.

Web Browsers

Special software called a **Web browser** allows you to locate and display Web pages on a computer screen. Designing multimedia elements requires an understanding of Web browsers. The two basic, and important, functions of a Web browser are:

- translating the text-based code used to create Web pages into a graphical Web page. This code is called Extensible Hypertext Markup Language (XHTML).

- letting the user move from one page to another.

Browsers let you view Web pages (see Figure 2.5 on page 39) and other multimedia productions, such as Web-based slide show presentations that display graphics and other elements in an interactive format.

Available Formats Browsers are available on cell phones and other handheld communication devices in smaller formats. Mobile browsers are designed specially to display Web content effectively on the smaller displays found in these handheld mobile devices, as shown in Figure 2.4.

Web browsing is also available for televisions through special Internet-connected devices. Browsing the Web on a television is more limited than browsing on a computer monitor.

Figure 2.4
The Web is published in smaller formats on handheld devices. What types of handheld devices can you name?

Choosing a Browser There are many browsers from which to choose. Some popular choices include Microsoft® Internet Explorer®, Apple® Safari®, Mozilla® Firefox®, and Google Chrome™.

Multimedia files often require more time to load onto computers or handheld communication devices because of the large size of the files. You should keep this in mind when designing multimedia elements and build them so that they can be accessed with ease on any platform or browser. Remember that your users may use personal computers or Macintosh computers.

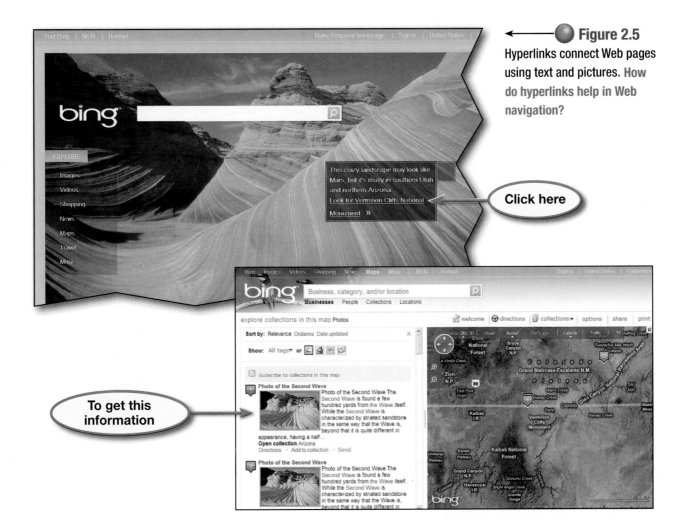

Figure 2.5
Hyperlinks connect Web pages using text and pictures. How do hyperlinks help in Web navigation?

Click here

To get this information

Hyperlinks

A Web page is connected to other Web pages through a hyperlink, which allows you to "surf," or navigate, from one online page to another. As seen in Figure 2.5, a hyperlink can be a word, phrase, or graphic. The Web uses **Hypertext Transfer Protocol** or **HTTP**, which interlinks Web pages by interpreting a hyperlink and jumping to the specified location.

There are two basic types of hyperlinks: hypertext and hypermedia. As the name implies, hypertext is text that acts as a link. This link can be to another location on the same Web page, or it can link to a new Web page. For example, on a Web page for a sports league, you might click on a specific team's name to go to a different Web page with information about that team, or to that team's Web site.

Hypermedia is similar to hypertext and uses pictures or other media files to link Web pages. Through hypertext links and hypermedia links, individual Web files are joined together like a giant spider web. In the above example, the league's Web page could include a graphic of each team's logo that would also link you to that team's information.

Some Web pages include links to different locations on the same Web page so the user does not have to scroll and search for specific information.

Figure 2.6

Plug-ins can help make your
computer more useful. **Which
type of plug-in can help you
view videos online?**

Web Browser Plug-Ins		
Name	**Manufacturer**	**Function**
Acrobat® Reader®	Adobe	Open and read Adobe Portable Document Format (PDF) files
Shockwave® Player	Adobe	View rich multimedia content
Flash® Player	Adobe	View animations and videos and interact with games
Real Player®	RealNetworks	Stream audio and video on the Web
Crescendo™	LiveUpdate	Listen to music while on the Web
QuickTime®	Apple	Stream audio and video on the Web

Plug-Ins

Browsers let you **retrieve**, or locate and bring back, information over the Internet. To retrieve some kinds of information, however, browsers need help from programs called plug-ins. A **plug-in** is software that works with a browser to play a particular file format. Figure 2.6 lists popular browser plug-ins. For example, plug-ins might work with a Web browser to offer the ability to play audio or video, view animation or 3D graphics, or access interactive media. When a plug-in is needed, the browser generally shows a message telling you how to get the plug-in. Most plug-ins are free to download and install (see Figure 2.7).

Some plug-ins enable browsers to use **streaming media**, a technique for transmitting audio and video files so they can begin playing sound or video files as soon as the computer begins receiving them. Without streaming media, the computer must download the entire file before it begins to play back. Because sound and video files can often be too large to download quickly, streaming media is important to multimedia Web sites.

✓ **Reading Check** **Describe** How can browser plug-ins help you play multimedia files?

Figure 2.7

Browsers like Mozilla Firefox
supply information about
media plugins that can be
downloaded for free. **What is
a plug-in?**

Uniform Resource Locators (URLs)

What are URLs and how do they work with Web browsers?

Every Web page has a **unique**, or one-of-a-kind, address known as a **uniform resource locator**, or **URL**. Like IP (Internet Protocol) addresses, URLs enable a browser to retrieve specific page files on the World Wide Web.

Parts of a URL

Web page URLs must be in a standard format so browsers will know how to interpret them. Most URLs are made up of four main parts: **protocol://address/directory path/retrieved file**.

- **Protocol** indicates the type of server where the file is stored.

- **Address** is the server's address, including the domain name and the domain name extension. A **domain name** identifies the entity (such as a university, individual, or business) that sponsors the site.

- **Directory path** is the file's location within the file structure of that particular server.

- **Retrieved file** is the name of the specific Web page file being accessed.

Each URL specifies a single Web page. This means that each Web page within a Web site has its own address. In a very similar way, every page in a book has its own page number.

- In the URL in Figure 2.8, the protocol is shown as "http." This protocol indicates that the Web page is stored on an HTTP, or Web, server.
- The address begins with "www" to show that the server is part of the World Wide Web.
- The domain name tells users that the Web site belongs to McGraw-Hill, while the domain name extension (".com") indicates that it is a commercial site.
- The address is followed by the directory path for the specific page and the name of the retrieved file that contains the Web page being viewed. The "html" in the file name indicates that the page is written in XHTML code. The "s" means it is a secure page.

Figure 2.8

Each component of a URL has a specific meaning. How can you tell that this URL specifies a file on the World Wide Web?

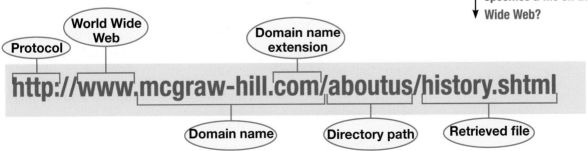

Domain Name Extensions

The domain name included in the address portion of a URL generally ends with a dot followed by three or four letters. These letters are known as the domain name extension. A domain name extension tells users what type of organization uses the address. For example, the familiar extension ".com" indicates a commercial site. Figure 2.9 lists the most commonly used domain name extensions.

Figure 2.9
URLs contain domain name extensions. **What information can you learn from a domain name extension?**

Common Domain Name Extensions		
Extension	Type of Site	Example
.com	Commercial or for-profit business	www.hp.com
.edu	Educational	www.getty.edu
.gov	U.S. or state government organization	www.loc.gov
.org	Professional or nonprofit organization	www.specialolympics.org
.mil	Military	www.army.mil
.net	Network	http://eelink.net
.biz	Commercial business	www.dart.biz
.info	Information	www.eclipses.info

How a Browser Accesses a URL

As you learned in Section 2.1, a network is a system in which communication lines or wireless connections are used to connect computers together. The Web is part of the Internet. It uses the same hardware resources.

In fact, accessing information on the Web is similar to accessing information in a client/server network. A client is an individual computer or browser. A server is a powerful computer on a network that is the center of activity on that network. When you key a URL into your browser and press the Enter key, a specific Web page is retrieved from a Web server by following a standard process.

- First, your browser (the client) sends the URL to an Internet domain name server (DNS).

- Then, the DNS determines the Internet protocol (IP) address of the Web server that maintains the requested page.

- Your browser uses the IP address to find the needed Web server and request the specific page that you want. The Web server then sends that page to your computer.

- The XHTML code is interpreted by your computer and the page is displayed in your browser window.

 **Reading Check** **List** What are the four main parts of a URL?

Types of Web Sites

What are the categories of Web sites?

Multimedia Web sites influence the way we communicate, learn, do business, and lead our daily lives. Most Web sites can be categorized based on their main purpose, as described in Figure 2.10.

Categories of Web Sites		
Type of Site	**Purpose**	**Web Site Examples**
Commercial Sites	Sell or promote a company's products or services	Home Depot, Dell
Informational Sites	Provide people with useful information	Consumer Reports, U.S Bureau of Labor Statistics
Educational Sites	Provide information about a school, university, or museum	University of Michigan, Smithsonian
Personal Sites/ Social Networking	Used by individuals to share information	Facebook, individually owned sites
Portal Sites	Provide a variety of services that people use every day	Excite, Bing

Figure 2.10
Different types of Web sites have different purposes. What is the purpose of an educational site?

Commercial Sites

A commercial site is designed to sell or promote a company's products or services. The two main types of commercial sites are e-commerce and corporate presence sites.

E-commerce Sites Shopping online is called electronic commerce, or e-commerce. Mobile electronic commerce, or m-commerce, refers to purchases made on Internet-connected handheld communication devices. For example, when you download and purchase a song using your cell phone, you are using m-commerce.

Corporate Presence Sites Some commercial Web sites, known as corporate presence sites, do not sell anything. For example, a pharmaceutical (drug) company would probably not sell any medications on its Web site. This site differs from an information site because it seeks to promote the company's image.

Informational Sites

Informational sites provide people with useful information. Web sites are gaining popularity as information sources because they are relatively easy to update. Types of information sites include:

- news sites, such as FoxNews and CNN Web sites.
- government sites, such as The Library of Congress Web site.
- public interest sites, such as Make-A-Wish-Foundation® and Red Cross Web sites.

Educational Sites

Educational sites, such as the one shown in Figure 2.11, provide information about a school, university, or museum. School and university sites can provide general information such as class schedules and courses offered. Distance learning sites offer Web-based interactive tutorials. Some educational sites are sponsored by museums to provide information about exhibits and events.

Figure 2.11

Web sites for museums are considered educational sites. What type of information is generally included on a museum's Web site?

Personal and Social Networking Sites

Personal Web sites allow people to share their interests or news with others. They are a great way to display a portfolio. However, all individuals should be very careful when posting personal information on the Internet. Keep in mind that online information is available to anyone with an Internet connection, and posting personal information can be dangerous. Remember that many of the people viewing your information are strangers. Follow these guidelines when creating a personal site.

- Do not post personal contact information.
- Do not describe how you look or where you live.
- Do not post personal information about other people.

Portal Sites

A Web site that provides a variety of services that people use every day is called a portal. Most portals provide general news and business information. Many also provide e-mail services, stock prices, and links to entertainment information.

Reading Check **Identify** What are two types of commercial sites?

Finding Information on the Web

How can search tools help users locate online information?

The vast number of pages on the Web can make it hard to find the specific information or services that you need. Search engines can help you locate online information easier.

Search Engines

A **search engine** is an application that locates information about Web pages and then stores this information in searchable databases that you can access from your browser. If you enter one or more words related to your topic into the search engine, it will look for the information you want. The search engine then shows a list of the Web pages that are relevant to the entered words. For example, if you wanted to find information about multimedia, you could key the word "multimedia" in the search box. The search engine would then go through its indexes to find matches for the word, and the number of results, or "hits," is displayed, as seen in Figure 2.12. Some popular search engines include Google™, Yahoo!®, Bing™, Ask.com™, AltaVista™, and Excite®.

Search engines catalog individual Web pages. Sometimes, in addition to receiving a list of Web pages about your topic, you may also get a link to a Web directory. A Web directory catalogs Web sites, rather than single Web pages, by topic or category. After you choose a category, the directory will then compile and display a list of sites related to that category. Since databases tend to contain different information, it can be a good idea to use at least two search tools when attempting to locate online information.

Go Online **ACTIVITY**
glencoe.com

Online Searches **Find out more about searching online at the Online Learning Center. Go to glencoe.com. Choose Activities, then Chapter 2.**

Figure 2.12
Google is just one of many search engines on the Web. **Why is it important to become familiar with multiple search engines?**

Conditional Logic
When you enter the Boolean search "water AND ocean", results will be returned only if both terms are present. You can write the conditional logic like this: water AND ocean = true. Write the conditional logic for a search for water but not ocean.

NCTM Reasoning and Proof Select and use various types of reasoning and methods of proof.

Using Search Engines Effectively

When you use a search engine to find information, you are making a search query. Two main types of queries are keyword searches and Boolean searches.

Keyword Searches A keyword search consists of one or more keywords that you enter into the search engine. A **keyword** is an important word related to the topic you are trying to locate. For example, if you are looking for a Web site that contains information on multimedia, you would enter the keyword "multimedia." The engine would then search Web sites for possible matches and return the results, or hits, to you. You need to be careful when selecting a keyword. A keyword that is too general can return too many results.

Boolean Searches To search for a more focused topic, you may want to use a Boolean search. A **Boolean search** specifies how the search engine should use keywords to locate specific pages. You perform a Boolean search by entering multiple keywords that are separated by Boolean operators. See Figure 2.13 for a description of the most commonly used Boolean operators.

Figure 2.13
Using Boolean operators will help you perform a more precise search. **What are three commonly used Boolean operators?**

Boolean Operators	
Common Operator	**Function**
AND	The search engine locates only those pages containing both keywords. Many search engines use the plus sign (+) in place of AND.
OR	The search engine locates pages containing one or both of the keywords. An OR search generally produces more "hits" than an AND search.
NOT	The search engine locates pages that contain the first keyword but not the keyword after the NOT operator. Many search engines use the minus sign (−) in place of NOT.

YOU TRY IT

Activity 2B Practice Using a Search Engine

❶ Open your Web browser. With your teacher's permission, key the following URL into the address box at the top of the browser window: www.google.com. Press **Enter**. The Google search engine appears.

❷ Suppose you want to research information about dog training. Start with a simple keyword search. Key: dog into the search box and press **Enter**. Write down the number of results (displayed on the blue bar near the top of the page).

❸ Perform a Boolean search by keying: dog+training into the search box. (Note: Some search engines require that there be no space between the symbol [+ or −] and the keyword.) Press **Enter**. Write down the number of results you receive.

④ Now suppose you are creating a multimedia presentation about dog training. Key: training video+dog into the search box (see Figure 2.14). Press **Enter**. Write down the number of results you receive. Close your browser.

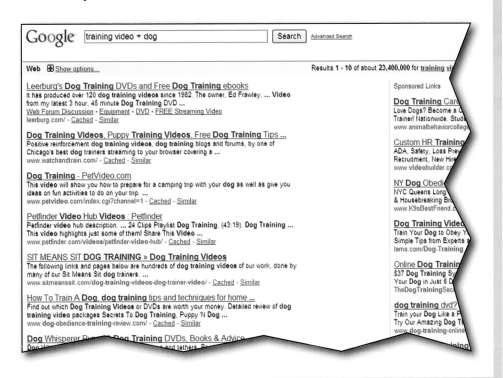

Figure 2.14 Boolean searches are often more helpful than simple keyword searches to find specific information.

Reading Check **Recall** What are three common Boolean operators?

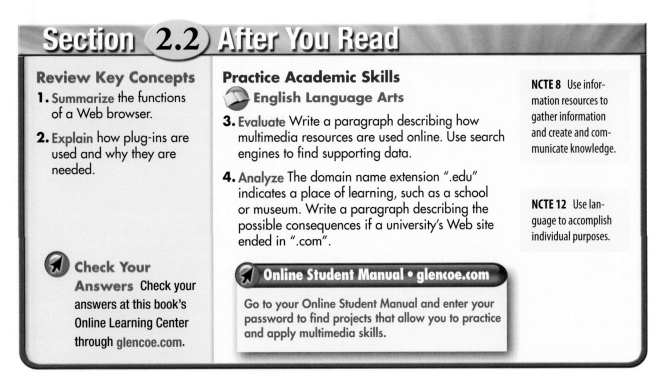

Section 2.2 After You Read

Review Key Concepts

1. **Summarize** the functions of a Web browser.

2. **Explain** how plug-ins are used and why they are needed.

Check Your Answers Check your answers at this book's Online Learning Center through glencoe.com.

Practice Academic Skills

English Language Arts

3. **Evaluate** Write a paragraph describing how multimedia resources are used online. Use search engines to find supporting data.

4. **Analyze** The domain name extension ".edu" indicates a place of learning, such as a school or museum. Write a paragraph describing the possible consequences if a university's Web site ended in ".com".

Online Student Manual • glencoe.com

Go to your Online Student Manual and enter your password to find projects that allow you to practice and apply multimedia skills.

NCTE 8 Use information resources to gather information and create and communicate knowledge.

NCTE 12 Use language to accomplish individual purposes.

Reading Guide

Before You Read

Vocabulary To gain a better understanding of vocabulary, create a vocabulary journal. Divide a piece of paper into three columns labeled "Vocabulary", "What is it?", and "What else is it like?". Write down each word and answer the questions as you read the section.

Read to Learn
Key Concepts

- **Describe** types of Web resources.
- **Identify** social, ethical, and legal issues related to using Web online resources.

Main Idea

The Web offers many valuable resources. Ethical, social, and legal guidelines govern the use of online resources. When using online resources for personal or business purposes, copyright and trademark laws must be followed. Resources must be cited properly.

Content Vocabulary

- ◇ podcast
- ◇ ethics
- ◇ acceptable use policy (AUP)
- ◇ netiquette
- ◇ cyberbullying
- ◇ copyright
- ◇ trademark
- ◇ citation

Academic Vocabulary

You will find these words in your reading and on your tests. Use the glossary to look up their definitions, if necessary.

- ◇ collaboration
- ◇ propaganda

Graphic Organizer

As you read the section, identify five ways to protect your privacy online. Use a graphic like the one shown below to organize your notes.

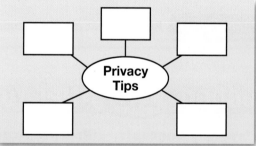

Graphic Organizer Go to this book's **Online Learning Center** at glencoe.com to print this graphic organizer.

Academic Standards

 English Language Arts

NCTE 3 Apply strategies to interpret texts.
NCTE 4 Use written language to communicate effectively.

NCTE 7 Conduct research and gather, evaluate, and synthesize data to communicate discoveries.

NCTE National Council of Teachers of English
NSES National Science Education Standards

NCTM National Council of Teachers of Mathematics
NCSS National Council for the Social Studies

Using Web Resources

How do Web resources affect the way we communicate?

In recent years, multimedia Web resources have been designed that enhance our communication and collaboration. **Collaboration** means working together. Some people refer to this collection of technology resources as *Web 2.0*. These resources allow users to contribute to Web content and interact with it. The Web now makes it easy to create communities of users.

Communication

Multimedia influences the way we communicate. It lets us enhance text with graphics, animation, audio, and video. Web technology offers many different ways to communicate, including resources such as blogs, vlogs, and social networking sites. Wireless technology and mobile communication devices let you communicate from almost anywhere at any time.

A blog, short for Web log, is a Web site in the format of an online journal. The writer of a blog typically offers personal reflections, comments, and links to other Internet resources and users. A vlog, short for video blog, is a type of blog in which the content is video. Typically, readers can write comments in response to blog postings and can connect with others in the "blogosphere." Figure 2.15 shows an example of a free blogging Web site.

As you learned in Section 2.1, e-mail is the most frequently used form of online communication. E-mail can be both an Internet resource and a Web resource. Many Web-based e-mail services are offered free of charge, such as Gmail, Hotmail, and Yahoo!® Mail. Text messaging, or texting, is another popular form of communication. It allows users to send short messages, sometimes combined with multimedia elements, from one cell phone to another.

As You Read

Connect What Web resources do you use on a regular basis?

Figure 2.15
Many Web applications offer free blogging. **What is a blog?**

Collaboration and Socializing

Some very popular Web applications offer the ability to create content and interact with others online. People enjoy using multimedia tools available through social networking sites, wikis, media-sharing sites, and social bookmarking sites. It is important to remember that these tools, discussed below, are intended to promote collaboration. Online collaboration tools allow users to share work with each other, give each other feedback, and learn from each other.

Certain online tools allow users to socialize with one another. A social network is a Web site that allows members to share information about themselves. Members find, meet, and communicate with others in social networks in the same way that they interact within personal social groups. For example, Facebook and MySpace allow users to create Web pages with personal information. Twitter is another social network featuring micro-blogs, known as "tweets." The tweets are delivered to the computers or cell phones of users who have signed up to receive them.

A wiki is a free online forum that is created and edited by multiple authors. Wikis encourage collaboration and interaction, and offer an easy-to-use interface for creating Web pages.

Other Web site services include video, photo, and music sharing. Web sites such as YouTube allow people to post videos and to comment on them. Photos can be shared using Web sites like Flickr®. Media player Web sites, such as Pandora® and iTunes, are services that allow you to listen to music samples and download music for personal use. National network news sites now encourage users to share their own news stories. People can upload videos, photos, and audio to the site, as shown on Figure 2.16.

Figure 2.16
People collaborate online by sharing news and information. **What are some online tools for socializing and sharing information?**

Sharing Multimedia Projects

Web sites have opened up a world of ways to share multimedia projects and presentations. The audio or video recording of a broadcast that is distributed via the Web is called a **podcast**. Podcasts might contain news, information, radio programs, talk shows, and more. They can be played on computers or on portable media players.

You can share multimedia presentations on sites like SlideShare. Feedback from those who view the presentations and the opportunity to explore and discuss presentations on many topics contribute to the popularity of sites for sharing information.

 **Reading Check** **Paraphrase** What is a podcast?

Social and Ethical Issues

How can you be safe online?

Web applications allow us to communicate instantly with almost anyone anywhere (see Figure 2.17). Sharing, collaborating, and interacting globally are important skills that you will use throughout your life, but there are risks in using online tools.

Protecting Your Privacy

People on the Web may not be who they seem. Make sure to follow these tips to keep your personal identity private for your safety and security:

- Do not tell others your name or where you live.

- Do not give out personal information to a stranger.

- Remember that you are not anonymous in newsgroups and chat rooms! Anytime you post a message, a user can track you by your IP address.

- Always read the privacy statement for every Web site that requires you to register online. For example, if you register to make a purchase online, read the site's privacy statement to see how it will handle your information.

- If something makes you uncomfortable for any reason, tell a parent or other trusted adult. This includes personal e-mails you receive and posts that you see on social networking sites or in chat rooms.

Real World

Cookies Cookies are text files that a Web site can place on your computer. A Web bug is a file that gathers information from your system, such as the information contained in cookies.

Why It's Important Why should you delete cookies from your computer on a regular basis?

Figure 2.17
You can use the Web to collaborate with people from around the corner and around the world. **What privacy rules should you follow when using the Web?**

Figure 2.18

Many Web sites have acceptable use policies, or terms of use agreements. Why is it important to read an agreement before you sign it?

Passwords provide access to the world of online communication. Protect yourself by protecting your passwords.

- Never tell anyone your passwords for e-mail, instant messaging, or any online communication use.
- Change your passwords frequently.
- Use passwords that include both letters and at least one number.
- If you write your passwords down, keep them in a private and secure location.

Ethics and Social Responsibility

Responsible Internet users follow ethical behavior online, just as they do in personal relationships. In general, **ethics** applies to what is right and wrong, good and bad.

Acceptable Use Policies Many schools and businesses have an **acceptable use policy**, or **AUP**, which is an agreement that regulates online use, as shown in Figure 2.18. These agreements may have a different name, such as terms of use agreements, but they all contain guidelines for using the Web. Read all the guidelines in an AUP before you sign the agreement. Some common rules include:

- Always check with an authorized individual, such as your teacher, before downloading files.
- Do not abuse an organization's e-mail system.
- Understand which Web sites you are allowed to access. Do not access forbidden sites.
- Do not send spam, or unsolicited e-mail messages.
- Do not use the Internet for personal reasons if the school or organization forbids this practice.

Netiquette Internet etiquette, or **netiquette**, refers to the general rules of social behavior for online users. For example, appropriate conduct includes using acceptable and polite language while online. Netiquette encourages users to respect each other when interacting online. When people are respectful, they treat other online users with courtesy, and they honor their privacy. Avoid communicating online when you are feeling angry. Instead, calm down before responding.

Cyberbullying Repeated harassment of one person by another person using Internet chat rooms, text messages, social networking sites, and other digital technology is called **cyberbullying**. If you receive mild harassment online, you may choose to ignore it. However, if it becomes serious or frequent, or involves multiple participants, you should speak to a trusted adult. You may also be able to report the person to the Web site host. Cyberbullies can be punished for their actions.

 **Reading Check** **Explain** What is the purpose of an AUP?

Legal Issues

What is the purpose of a copyright?

Many Web sites allow you to copy or download text, graphics, multimedia files, or even software to your computer. Some Web sites do not allow this. It is not always legal to copy material from a Web site. Many files can only be used with permission.

Legal Software Use

There are state and federal laws that regulate what files you can legally download and how you can use them. Many Web sites have terms of use (TOU) agreements that you must follow when downloading files. You should always look for these rules and be sure that you have read and understood them before you download or use files from a site. There are three main types of software: commercial, shareware, and freeware. See Figure 2.19 for a description of each.

Types of Software		
Software	**Usage Guidelines**	**Examples**
Commercial software	Copyrighted and intended to be sold for a profit. Cannot be copied or sold to others.	• Microsoft® Office • Adobe® Photoshop® • Most video games
Shareware	Can be downloaded or copied if you pay a small fee to the copyright holder.	• WinZip® • Many online games
Freeware	Can be freely downloaded, copied, and used for any legal purpose.	• Adobe® Reader • Instant messaging software • Yahoo® toolbar

Figure 2.19
Most software can be categorized as one of three types. **What is the difference between shareware and freeware?**

Copyright Laws

Copyrights exist to protect creators of original work. A **copyright** grants ownership of a work and asserts that only the copyright's owner has the right to sell or use the work or to allow someone else to sell or use it. These works are known as intellectual property.

A copyright notice typically contains the copyright symbol (©) followed by the year and the copyright holder's name. Another important type of intellectual property is a trademark (™) or registered trademark (®). A **trademark** is a name, symbol, or other feature that identifies a product with a specific owner. For example, many companies may produce gelatin, but only one company can use the term Jell-O®, because that term is trademarked.

Copyright laws cover work on the Internet as well as other media. You cannot claim a copyrighted or trademarked work as your own or use it without permission on a Web site, any more than you could use it in a printed publication.

- **Intellectual Property** Authors, software developers, and musicians all own their creative works through copyright laws. Intellectual property refers to ideas and concepts and includes books, music, movies, software, inventions, and trademarks.

- **Fair Use** The fair use doctrine allows excerpts from works to be used under specific circumstances. According to fair use, small portions of a work may be used for educational purposes. A "small portion" generally means a few paragraphs from a book or a short excerpt from a song or video.

- **Public Domain** Intellectual property which is not copyrighted or owned by anyone is referred to as public domain material. Though copyright laws differ from country to country, all copyrights are granted for specific periods of time. After that time, works are considered to be in the public domain and available for use by anyone. Public domain works also include those created before copyright laws, as well as any material developed by the U.S. government.

Evaluating Resource Reliability

Unfortunately, both ethical and unethical people use the Internet. Mistakes, deliberate falsehoods, out-of-date information, and personal opinions all make their way into Web resources. Sometimes, facts, ideas, and opinions are used in a misleading way to promote a cause. This is called **propaganda**.

It is important to identify the purpose and audience of an online resource. Also identify any assumptions and propaganda techniques the online resource is making about its audience. By asking important questions about information instead of taking it at face value, you can make sure that information is reliable. If you think information is questionable or inaccurate, use at least one other resource to verify the facts. Figure 2.20 on page 55 provides the criteria for your evaluation of online resources.

Assessing Online Information	
Criteria	**Ask These Questions**
Determine relevance of the information	• What is the site's purpose? • Is it maintained by a company that is trying to sell something? • Is the site sponsored by a particular organization? • Is the site self-published? • Are propaganda techniques, such as misleading statements, used?
Evaluate reliability	• Who are the site's authors? • Are the authors experts in the field? • Do authors make assumptions about the audience?
Examine how recent it is	• Is the Web site current? • How has information changed over time?
Determine whether it is verifiable	• Has the information in the site been reviewed by peers? • If the information on the site has been reviewed, are the reviewers experts on the topic? • What information is known about the reviewers?

Figure 2.20
You should always evaluate the online sources that you use. Why is it important to identify a site's purpose?

Citing Online Sources

It is usually illegal to copy material without providing a **citation**, or a short note that acknowledges the source. You must always cite the source of information obtained online, even when that information comes from a Web site. To use someone's work without giving the appropriate credit is known as plagiarism. Plagiarism is illegal and punishable by law. There are different style guidelines for formatting citations. Figure 2.21 shows the required information and proper format according to the Modern Language Association (MLA). You should include as many of the items shown as you can.

For school projects, you should ask your teacher which guidelines to use for documenting your online sources. Some schools require students to follow guidelines by either the Modern Language Association (MLA) or the American Psychological Association (APA).

Figure 2.21
Citing sources allows your readers to know that your information is reliable. Why do you think it is important to include the date you visited a site?

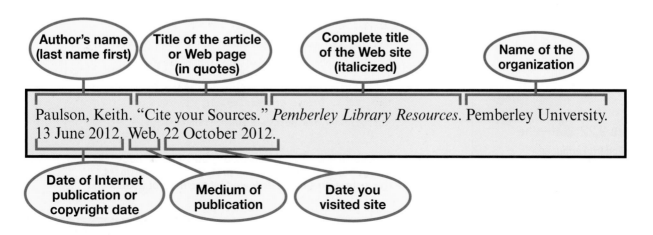

Author's name (last name first) — Title of the article or Web page (in quotes) — Complete title of the Web site (italicized) — Name of the organization

Paulson, Keith. "Cite your Sources." *Pemberley Library Resources*. Pemberley University. 13 June 2012. Web. 22 October 2012.

Date of Internet publication or copyright date — Medium of publication — Date you visited site

In Activity 2C, you will research a reliable site on how to cite electronic sources. Then you will use a search engine to find four types of Web pages. For each page, you will create a citation in a word processing document.

Activity 2C Cite Internet Sources

1. Open a Web browser, such as Microsoft Internet Explorer, Mozilla Firefox, or Apple Safari. With your teacher's permission, in the browser's address window, key: owl.english.purdue.edu. The home page of the Online Writing Lab at Purdue University appears on-screen.

2. On the home page, in the **Search the OWL** search box, key: works cited electronic. Click the search button. A Google page appears with search results. Click the result that includes the phrase **electronic sources**. This result should refer to the MLA citation style.

3. Look for tips for citing online resources. The link you choose should provide information similar to that in Figure 2.22.

Academic Focus

English Language Arts

Citations Different style guides offer different ways of citing sources. All citations include the same basic information, however. Research at least two different styles for citations and create a chart to explain the common information included and why it is important.

NCTE 7 Conduct research and gather, evaluate, and synthesize data to communicate discoveries.

Web Sources

Web sites (in MLA style, the "W" in Web is capitalized, and "Web site" or "Web sites" are written as two words) and Web pages are arguably the most commonly cited form of electronic resource today. Below are a variety of Web sites and pages you might need to cite.

An Entire Web Site

Basic format:

> Name of Site. Date of Posting/Revision. Name of
> institution/organization affiliated with the site
> (sometimes found in copyright statements). Date you
> accessed the site [electronic address].

It is necessary to list your date of access because web postings are often updated, and information available on one date may no longer be available later. Be sure to include the complete address for the site. Here are some examples:

> The Purdue OWL Family of Sites. 26 Aug. 2005. The
> Writing Lab and OWL at Purdue and Purdue University.
> 23 April 2006 <http://owl.english.purdue.edu>.
> Felluga, Dino. Guide to Literary and Critical Theory. 28
> Nov. 2003. Purdue University. 10 May 2006
> <http://www.cla.purdue.edu/english/theory>.

For course or department websites, include "Course home page" or "Dept. home page" after the name of the professor or department and before the institution's name, followed by the date of access and URL.

Figure 2.22
The Modern Language Association (MLA) provides guidelines for citing Web publications.

4️⃣ Use a word processing program to create a table with two columns and four rows. In the first column, key the following scenarios:

- An online article about the future of technology
- A print article about a U.S. President
- A movie or audio clip found on the Web
- An article on Mars exploration

5️⃣ Open your Web browser. Use a search engine to find a Web page for each scenario (see Figure 2.23 for a sample).

6️⃣ Write the citation for each Web page in the second column.

7️⃣ Save the file as **Citation**. With your teacher's permission, print the word processing document and the source Web pages to which you referred.

Figure 2.23
This page provides reliable information.

 **Clarify** What does the term "fair use" mean?

Section 2.3 After You Read

Review Key Concepts

1. **Explain** why it is important to follow the rules of netiquette.

2. **Identify** criteria you should use to identify purposes, assumptions, and propaganda techniques of an online resource.

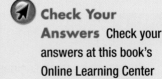 **Check Your Answers** Check your answers at this book's Online Learning Center through glencoe.com.

Practice Academic Skills

📖 English Language Arts

3. **Analyze** With your teacher's permission, visit a Web site of your choice. Write a paragraph that evaluates the site's audience, and any propaganda techniques that are used to mislead the audience.

4. **Evaluate** Research recent court cases on illegal downloading of music. Prepare a presentation to share the outcome.

NCTE 4 Use written language to communicate effectively.

NCTE 3 Apply strategies to interpret texts.

Online Student Manual • glencoe.com

Go to your Online Student Manual and enter your password to find projects that allow you to practice and apply multimedia skills.

Ethics & Technology

Use Internet Resources Ethically

If you were to copy an image from a Web site and use it for noncommercial purposes, such as a school project, you might need to obtain permission. United States copyright laws allow individuals to copy a portion of copyright-protected work for certain purposes, including research and other nonprofit uses. However, always check the terms of use of any site from which you would like to copy material. In addition, you must cite your sources, or give them proper credit.

Academic Citations

You must cite the sources of quotations, images, and even ideas you use that are not your own. Academic organizations, such as the Modern Language Association, have developed formats for citing such sources. Failure to properly cite sources could make you guilty of plagiarism, or presenting someone else's work as if it is your own.

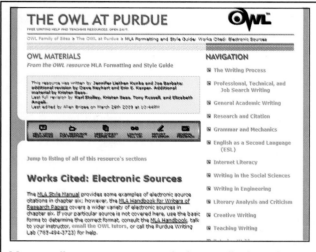

Many online resources can help you find out how to ethically use online content and properly cite it.

Guidelines to Follow

- **Ask for Permission** If you are not sure whether you have the right to use content from a Web page, get permission. Look for contact information for the site or e-mail addresses at the bottom of the site's home page.
- **Cite Your Source** Even if you feel certain that you can legally use content, you must always properly cite the source of any content that you did not create yourself. Your citation should include information about who created the content, when it was created, and where and when you obtained it. Including a citation eliminates questions about how much of the work is yours and gives credit to the people who created any items you have used.

Skill Builder

1. **Practice Ethical Guidelines** Select a Web site that has a multimedia element you would like to use for a project. Locate the contact information on the site. Follow your teacher's instructions to write an e-mail or a letter requesting permission to use the element.

2. **Research Academic Citations** Use search engines to research how to properly cite multimedia and online resources. Your report should properly cite your sources.

Chapter Summary

The Internet is a huge network that connects computers all over the world using communication lines. The World Wide Web is a way of sharing information via the Internet. Internet service providers (ISPs) allow people to connect to the Internet through dial-up, broadband, and wireless connections.

Web browsers allow you to view Web pages. Every Web page has a unique address known as a uniform resource locator, or URL. Many resources such as search engines and Web sites are available on the Web. There are many social, ethical, and legal issues associated with using the World Wide Web.

Vocabulary Review

1. Write your own definition for ten of the content or academic vocabulary terms. Then check your definition with the glossary.

Content Vocabulary

◇ Internet (p. 33)
◇ network (p. 33)
◇ hardware (p. 33)
◇ World Wide Web (p. 33)
◇ Internet service provider (ISP) (p. 34)
◇ protocol (p. 35)
◇ Web site (p. 38)
◇ Web page (p. 38)
◇ Web browser (p. 38)
◇ Hypertext Transfer Protocol (HTTP) (p. 39)
◇ plug-in (p. 40)

◇ streaming media (p. 40)
◇ uniform resource locator (URL) (p. 41)
◇ domain name (p. 41)
◇ search engine (p. 45)
◇ keyword (p. 46)
◇ Boolean search (p. 46)
◇ podcast (p. 50)
◇ ethics (p. 52)
◇ acceptable use policy (AUP) (p. 52)
◇ netiquette (p. 52)
◇ cyberbullying (p. 53)

◇ copyright (p. 54)
◇ trademark (p. 54)
◇ citation (p. 55)

Academic Vocabulary

◇ access (p. 33)
◇ communicate (p. 33)
◇ retrieve (p. 40)
◇ unique (p. 41)
◇ collaboration (p. 49)
◇ propaganda (p. 54)

Review Key Concepts

2. **Compare** the Internet and the Web.

3. **Explain** how the Internet and the Web work.

4. **Describe** types of Internet resources.

5. **Describe** the role of Web browsers.

6. **Identify** URL components and types of Web sites.

7. **Explain** how to search the Web by keywords and Boolean operators.

8. **Describe** types of Web resources.

9. **Identify** social, ethical, and legal issues related to using Web online resources.

Critical Thinking

10. Explain What are three of the factors that many people consider when choosing an ISP? Use a graphic organizer similar to this one to help you.

Choosing an ISP
1.
2.
3.

11. Compare and Contrast What are the similarities and differences for dial-up, broadband, and wireless Internet connections?

12. Distinguish What are the differences between the Internet and the World Wide Web?

13. Apply Read the scenarios below and decide which browser plug-in you would use. Choose from Acrobat Reader, Shockwave Player, Flash Player, Real Player, and Quicktime.

Scenario	Browser Plug-in
a. You are doing research on the Web and would like to listen to an online radio station as you work.	
b. One of the Web sites you find during your research has audio and video components.	
c. You need to access a PDF file to read a report.	
d. You have found a very exciting Web site that contains rich multimedia content.	
e. You take a break from your research to play some interactive games online.	

14. Synthesize Boolean operators allow you to perform a more precise search for information. Provide two examples for when you would use each of these operators: AND, OR, and NOT.

15. Analyze Web-based resources that allow for communication and collaboration are rapidly increasing in number. For each of the resources listed in the table, write a brief description. Then, determine what is unique about that resource and enter it in the table.

Resource	Description	Uniqueness
Blog		
Vlog		
E-mail		
Text messaging		
Social network		
Wiki		

16. Demonstrate Use a graphic organizer similar to the one below to list four risks that come with Internet use and one way each risk can be avoided.

Risk   How to Avoid

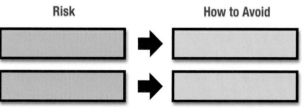
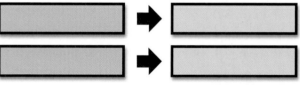

Go Online e-RESOURCES

glencoe.com

Go to the **Online Learning Center** to find additional activities and career resources.

Practice Quizzes Test your knowledge of the material in this chapter.

Career Resources Find out more about careers, including information about résumés, portfolios, and interview and workplace tips.

Academic Connections

NCTE 11 Participate as members of literacy communities.

17. Write Acceptable Use and Netiquette Guidelines

With your teacher's permission, review the acceptable use policy (sometimes called terms of use) of a popular Web site such as Wikipedia. Read the policy and answer these questions.

- What rules does the site have about using content from the site?

- What rules does the site include about netiquette and interacting with other members of the site's community?

- What are the consequences of breaking the AUP and netiquette guidelines?

Using the information you have gathered and your understanding of your own school's rules, write an acceptable use policy and netiquette guidelines for using the school's technology resources, including the school network and the Internet. Use correct grammar and punctuation in your policy.

Standardized Test Practice

Multiple Choice

Read the paragraph below, then answer the question.

IBM decided to make the PC's design details public so that other companies could develop software and peripherals for their PCs, which would increase its usefulness and popularity. It also allowed competitors to develop and sell computers that also ran DOS and worked in much the same way as an IBM PC. Meanwhile, Microsoft had not sold DOS to IBM but had instead only sold IBM the right to use it.

18. Based on the paragraph, which of the following statements is true?

- **A.** Microsoft's wealth came solely from its business dealings with IBM.
- **B.** Microsoft dominated the software market by selling the use of DOS for PCs made both by IBM and IBM's competitors.
- **C.** IBM kept their PC's design details a closely guarded secret.
- **D.** Microsoft sold DOS to IBM.

Test-Taking Tip With questions that rely on information given, read the paragraph very carefully to make sure you understand what it is about. Read the answer choices. Then read the paragraph again before choosing the answer.

• •

19. Make Predictions

E-mail and other forms of digital communication have become commonplace in our world. Suppose that your manager is preparing a presentation for investors about how digital communication is changing the way people do business. Your manager has asked you to conduct online research on the following topics:

A. How is e-mail changing the way we communicate?

B. Does e-mail bring people together or isolate them?

C. Will e-mail ever replace paper mail?

Write a one-page report discussing the answers to these questions. Include both pros and cons for each of these questions. Include answers that you find online as well as your own opinions. Be sure to state reasons for your opinions.

> **NETS 3b** Locate, organize, analyze, evaluate, synthesize, and ethically use information from a variety of sources and media.
> **NETS 3c** Evaluate and select information sources and digital tools based on the appropriateness to specific tasks.
> **NETS 3d** Process and report results.

20. Locate Resources

Your manager was pleased with the report you prepared on digital communication. She now needs additional information about how people use the Web to find information. You will conduct research on Boolean searches and how they work. As part of your research, you will conduct your own Boolean searches and prepare a table that your manager can use as an example in her presentation.

A. Choose a multimedia topic that interests you.

B. Use a Web browser of your choice and Boolean search queries to locate five Web sites that provide information about the selected topic.

C. List the search queries that you used to find the Web sites. Did your queries return useful Web pages? Explain.

D. Explain how you refined your queries to narrow your choices.

E. List the names of the five Web sites and write a brief description of each. Use a table like the one shown to organize your information.

Web Site	Search Queries	Queries Useful?	Refined Queries	Description

> **NETS 4b** Plan and manage activities to develop a solution or complete a project.

21. Understand Your Audience

Select a multimedia project you have seen or created such as a slide show presentation. Following your teacher's instructions, form a team with three other students. Make sure that team members have not seen each other's multimedia projects. As a team, you will review each project and discuss the following:

A. Identify the purpose and audience of the project, as well as assumptions and propaganda techniques that may mislead the audience.

B. Is information easy to see and understand? Does the multimedia project meet the needs of its intended audience?

C. Evaluate the use of text and graphics. Did the author choose form over function?

D. Is the project well developed, logical, and organized?

E. Is the project easy to access, maneuver, and use? Is space used effectively? Is the project appealing?

Repeat this process for each team member's project. Make any needed changes to the project and share the revisions with your team.

22. Research Copyright Laws

Research fair use policies for using copyrighted materials in school projects. Write a one-page report that answers the following questions:

A. How can students use content from other sources in school projects?

B. What portion of copyrighted text, graphics, animation, audio, and video can be used?

C. How must you document the materials you use?

D. How can you create copyrighted materials of your own?

E. How can you get permission to use copyrighted materials for projects outside of the classroom?

Document your information in a report. Be sure to proofread and spell-check your report.

Project 1

NCTE 8 Use information resources to gather information and create and communicate knowledge.

Plan a Multimedia Project

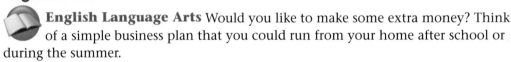

English Language Arts Think of a topic that interests you, such as a hobby, musical group, business organization, club, car, family member, or pet. Then imagine a multimedia production that would inform people about this subject.

Plan

1. Decide whether your multimedia project will be a tutorial, presentation, Web page, or simulation.

Research

2. Conduct online research to locate text, graphics, video, audio, and interactivity to use in your presentation. Note the URLs of the Web sites.

Create

3. Create and fill in a table to outline the project you chose. Include columns to describe text, graphics, video, audio, and interactivity elements. Indicate where you would use animation or interactivity.

Review

4. Edit your table. Proofread and spell-check the table.

Project 2

NCTE 7 Conduct research and gather, evaluate, and synthesize data to communicate discoveries.

Organize Data

English Language Arts Would you like to make some extra money? Think of a simple business plan that you could run from your home after school or during the summer.

Plan

1. Outline a simple plan for using the Internet to create a multimedia presentation about a service that your company would provide, such as dog sitting, lawn care, baby sitting, or car detailing.

Research

2. Conduct Internet research to find the components for your presentation, including graphics, sound, video, and information. Also find tools to use to post the presentation online.

Create and Present

3. Use presentation software to develop your presentation.

4. Show your presentation to your class and ask for feedback in an e-mail format. Make sure students follow netiquette and acceptable use policies.

Review

5. Edit your presentation based on the feedback. Proofread and spell-check the final presentation.

Projects Across the Curriculum

Define a Project's Goal and Purpose

English Language Arts Work in a small group, as determined by your teacher, to create a plan for a multimedia project. This plan will help your group define the goals and purpose of your project.

Research

1. Using what you learned in this chapter and materials available on the Internet, work with your group to research companies that provide the same type of service or project you are creating. For example, if your project is to illustrate a history of your community, you could look at other history Web sites and see how they have delivered similar content. You can use search engines such as the ones listed in the table below or other resources.

Popular Search Engines	
AltaVista	www.altavista.com
Ask	www.ask.com
Bing	www.bing.com
Dogpile	www.dogpile.com
Excite	www.excite.com
Go	www.go.com
Google	www.google.com
Lycos	www.lycos.com
WebCrawler	www.webcrawler.com
Yahoo	www.yahoo.com

NCTE 7 Conduct research and gather, evaluate, and synthesize data to communicate discoveries.

NCTE 8 Use information resources to gather information and create and communicate knowledge.

Create

2. Based on your research, describe the project's goal and purpose on a separate piece of paper. For example, suppose you want to provide a virtual tour of your school so that new students can easily find their way around. The project's goal is to help make new students feel more at ease in a new environment. The project's purpose is to create something (a virtual tour of the school) to achieve the project's goal.

Present

3. Following your teacher's instructions, present your plan to the class. Allow time for other groups to ask questions and provide feedback.

Evaluate

4. Based on the feedback you receive, make any necessary changes to your plan.

5. Proofread and spell-check your document.

Go Online RUBRICS
glencoe.com

Chapter Projects Use the rubrics for these projects to help create and evaluate your work. Go to the **Online Learning Center** at glencoe. com. Choose **Rubrics**, then **Chapter 2.**

CHAPTER 3 Computers and Networks

Section 3.1
Computer Hardware and Software

Section 3.2
Networks

CHAPTER OBJECTIVES

After completing this chapter, you will be able to:

❖ **Describe** computers and computer systems.

❖ **Define** hardware.

❖ **Identify** types of computers.

❖ **List** the processing components of a computer.

❖ **Compare and Contrast** input and output devices.

❖ **Identify** computer storage options.

❖ **Describe** different types of software.

❖ **List** categories of networks.

❖ **Identify** network hardware components and commonly used network operating systems.

Explore the Photo

Many organizations use multimedia and technology tools to encourage participation in important events. *How can you use multimedia skills to get involved?*

21st CENTURY SKILLS

Get Involved

Being involved in your community can be very rewarding. The experience often provides the opportunity to help solve real problems and address real needs. On a personal level, volunteering can give you a feeling of satisfaction. On a social level, you can build bonds with other people in your community.

Quick Write Activity Journal Entry

Write a journal entry about a time you were involved with a charity organization or community effort.

Writing Tips
To write a journal entry, follow these steps:
1. Date your entry.
2. Write about your experiences, reactions, and observations.
3. Let one idea lead to another.

Reading Guide

Before You Read

Understanding Write down any questions you have while reading. Many of them will be answered as you continue. If they are not, you will have a list ready for your teacher when you finish.

Read to Learn

Key Concepts

- **Explain** computers and computer systems.
- **Summarize** how hardware components work in a computer system.
- **Describe** how computer input, output, and storage devices work.
- **Identify** the categories of software, and applications for developing multimedia.

Main Idea

Hardware includes a computer system's input, output, and storage devices. Software gives instructions to the hardware.

Content Vocabulary

- computer
- central processing unit (CPU)
- input device
- graphics tablet
- output device
- software
- operating system (OS)
- graphical user interface (GUI)
- application software

Academic Vocabulary

You will find these words in your reading and on your tests. Use the glossary to look up their definitions, if necessary.

- diverse
- capacity

Graphic Organizer

As you read the section, categorize the four parts of a computer system. Use a diagram like the one below to organize your notes.

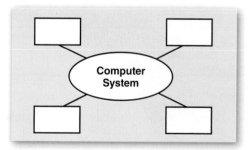

 Graphic Organizer Go to this book's **Online Learning Center** at **glencoe.com** to print this graphic organizer.

Academic Standards

 English Language Arts

NCTE 1 Read texts to acquire new information.
NCTE 7 Conduct research and gather, evaluate, and synthesize data to communicate discoveries.
NCTE 12 Use language to accomplish individual purposes.

NCTE National Council of Teachers of English
NSES National Science Education Standards

Mathematics

NCTM Number and Operations Compute fluently and make reasonable estimates.
NCTM Measurement Understand measurable attributes of objects and the units, systems, and processes of measurement.

NCTM National Council of Teachers of Mathematics
NCSS National Council for the Social Studies

Computers and Computer Systems

What are the four parts of a computer system?

As You Read

Connect What types of computers have you used?

All multimedia programs are developed and viewed using computers. A **computer** is an electronic device that processes data. Computers range in size from huge supercomputers to mobile handheld devices such as smartphones.

A computer designed for use by an individual is a personal computer, or PC. Generally, the term PC is used to distinguish computers used by individuals at home, work, or school from much larger and more powerful computers. Sometimes, the term PC is used to identify a computer that uses the Windows operating system (OS), as opposed to a Macintosh computer, which uses the Macintosh OS.

A computer system is made up of four parts. A system is a group of independent but related parts. Figure 3.1 shows how the four parts of a computer system work together. Each of the four parts is equally important. If any single part is missing, the system will not work.

- **Hardware** Processing components, input and output devices, and storage devices make up the system's hardware.

- **Software** Software gives instructions to the hardware. The computer uses software to perform tasks such as creating, editing, and managing files, and surfing the Internet.

- **Data** Documents, images, and other multimedia elements are saved as bits of information, or data, that must be decoded.

- **User** A person must operate the system's hardware and software to create documents and peform other tasks.

This section focuses on hardware and software. Hardware refers to the physical components of a computer system. The purpose of hardware is to get data into the computer, process the data, and produce results. Hardware includes the parts of a computer system that you can see, such as the monitor, mouse, and keyboard, and parts that are inside the computer, such as the motherboard, hard drive, and memory chips. All of these parts may look very different and even perform very differently depending on the purpose of the computer.

Quick **Tip**

Jargon The term PC is commonly used to refer to a computer that runs the Windows operating system (OS). Computers made by Apple®, which run the Macintosh OS, are called Macs.

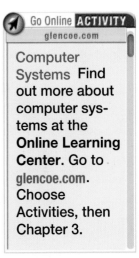

Go Online **ACTIVITY**
glencoe.com

Computer Systems **Find out more about computer systems at the Online Learning Center. Go to** glencoe.com. **Choose Activities, then Chapter 3.**

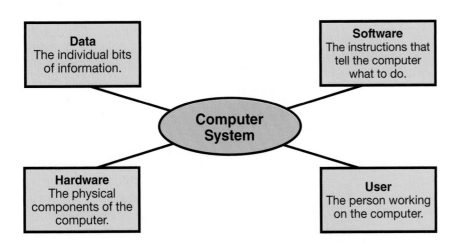

Figure 3.1
A computer system is made up of four parts: the hardware, software, data and user. What is the function of software?

Computers range in size and power to meet **diverse**, or differing, computing needs. Computer technology is constantly producing smaller and more powerful devices. Laptop computers, tablet PCs, and handheld computing devices have given users the option to take their computers with them.

Figure 3.2 identifies and describes different types of computers. For example, people may use desktop or laptop computers for creating and editing many types of files, including those for multimedia projects. Tablet PCs allow users to draw or write directly on a touch-sensitive screen. Tablet PCs are frequently used to edit photos and to create detailed drawings and animations. Smartphones are popular because they combine voice communication with text messaging, music, Web browsing, digital camera features, video clip downloads, and even television programming. Finally, mainframes are large and powerful computers used by businesses and organizations to support multiple users or complex tasks.

 **Reading Check** **Recall** What is a smartphone?

Types of Computers

Computer	Appearance	Function
Desktop		Personal computer designed for use at a desk. The computer may sit on top of or under the desk.
Laptop computer		Portable personal computer.
Tablet PC		Small, portable personal computer with a touch-sensitive display used for writing or drawing.
Smartphone		Handheld computer that includes cell phone capabilities. A smartphone is sometimes called a personal digital assistant (PDA).
Server, mainframe, and supercomputer		Large, powerful computers that are used to perform a single important task, such as powering network and Internet services or managing complex databases.

Figure 3.2
Different types of computers serve different functions.
Which type of computer is a portable version of a desktop PC?

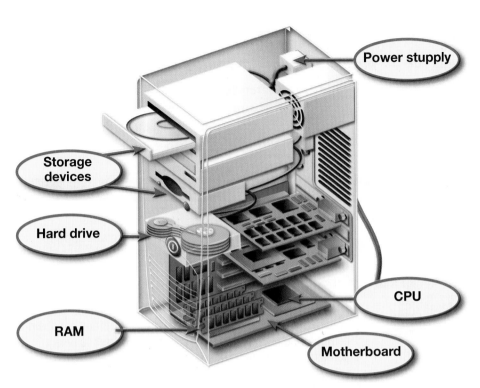

Power stupply

Storage devices

Hard drive

RAM

CPU

Motherboard

Processing Components

What is the difference between RAM and ROM?

The procedure that turns data into useful information is called processing. A computer uses a processor and memory in order to perform this procedure.

Central Processing Unit

All of a computer's internal parts rely on its central processing unit. The **central processing unit (CPU)**, or processor, is the "brain" of the computer. Generally, the CPU is a single chip, called a microprocessor, located on the computer's motherboard. The motherboard is the computer's main circuit board. Figure 3.3 shows the location of the CPU. A faster CPU usually means that a computer can process more data in less time.

Memory

A computer stores data it is currently processing in random-access memory, or RAM. The more RAM a computer has, the faster the computer can process data. RAM is also called primary storage because it is where the computer first processes data. However, RAM only stores data temporarily. The data is lost when the computer is turned off. Read-only memory, or ROM, is permanent information on a computer. ROM holds a computer's built-in instructions and cannot be erased or changed.

 **Reading Check   Explain** Why is RAM also called primary storage?

Academic Focus

English Language Arts

Technical Writing
Use at least two sources to research a currently available microprocessor. One good source is computer manufacturer Web sites. Use your prior knowledge to help you understand the information. Write a short paragraph in which you describe one of the microprocessors.

NCTE 7 Conduct research and gather, evaluate, and synthesize data to communicate discoveries.

Input and Output Devices

What are the functions of input and output devices?

You use an **input device** to enter data such as text, photographs, and drawings into a computer. Examples of common input devices are shown in Figure 3.4. For example, a **graphics tablet** allows you to create sketches and drawings for display on a monitor.

Figure 3.4
Input devices are used to enter data. Which devices would be most useful to add video to a multimedia presentation?

Types of Input Devices

Input Device	Description
Keyboard 	A keyboard is used to input text and numbers and to send commands to a computer.
Mouse 	A mouse is used to click icons and buttons, highlight text, and drag and drop images, text, files, and folders. Many handheld computers use touch screens, which allow users to select items on the screen using a stylus.
Laptop 	Laptop computers use touch pads that act as the mouse.
Graphics tablet 	A graphics tablet, sometimes called a tablet PC, a digitizing tablet, or a digitizer, allows you to create sketches and drawings in digital format for display on a computer screen.
Joystick 	A joystick, used for computer games, controls movement on the screen.
Scanner 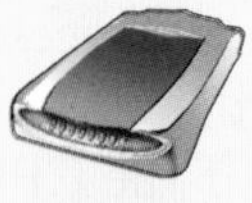	A scanner lets you convert printed images or documents into digital files.
Digital camera 	Many digital cameras and camcorders connect with computers so you can download, edit, and e-mail the photos and video you take.
Webcam 	Webcams can be used to connect with family and friends or for video conferencing over the Web.
Digital recorder 	Digital recorders are used to create speech, music, or other sounds for a multimedia project.
Synthesizer 	Synthesizers and musical keyboards allow you to use your computer to create music.

Types of Output Devices

Output Device	Description
Monitor	A monitor displays the text and graphics that you input or download into your computer. There are three types of monitors: • A plasma display creates images by passing electrical currents through a neon-xenon gas mixture sandwiched between two sealed glass plates with electrodes on the surface. • Light-emitting diode (LED) screens are small displays that light up when electricity passes through them such as those on smartphones. • Liquid crystal display (LCD) monitors use technology that displays text and images by passing electricity through a liquid crystal solution sandwiched between two magnetic sheets.
Touch screen	Touch screens are both output devices and input devices, as mentioned in Figure 3.4. Touch screens are useful in many day-to-day situations besides just smartphones, such as at an ATM or at a kiosk in an airport or at a movie theatre.
Interactive whiteboard	Interactive whiteboard technology uses projectors connected to computers to display information on a whiteboard. Users can write on the whiteboard and save the files as computer files.
Printer	A printer takes electronic information from the computer and produces a paper copy, which is also called a hard copy.
Sound system	Sound systems support multimedia application use with CD/MP3 music players and DVD players. Gaming players may enhance their experiences with surround-sound systems.

Figure 3.5
Output devices deliver processed data. **What are three types of computer monitors?**

Project Management
When you are ready to purchase any new computer component, do research about the compatibility of the component with your existing hardware. Planning ahead will save both time and money.

An **output device**, such as a printer or monitor, lets users examine the results of processed data. Examples of common output devices are identified in Figure 3.5.

 **Explain** What is the basic difference between an input device and an output device?

Storage Devices

How are computer applications and files stored?

If you shut down a computer without saving your work, you will lose your data. When you save a file, you move the information from RAM to a storage device. You usually store your applications and the files you use all the time on a hard drive. Use portable storage devices to make backup copies of your files, to move files to another computer, or to store files that are no longer needed on your hard drive.

Figure 3.6 Mobile storage devices have become increasingly popular for saving data. **What types of mobile storage devices have you used?**

Types of Storage Devices

Storage Device	What it Does	Storage Capacity
Hard drive 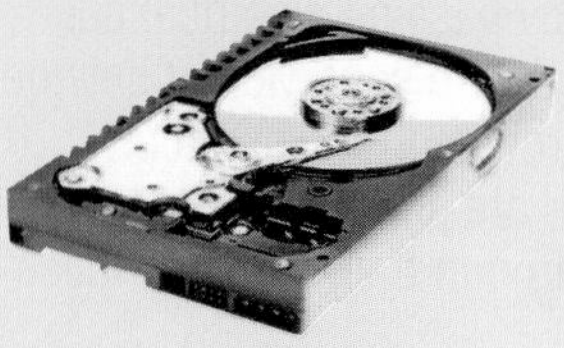	The hard drive, or hard disk, is the main storage device in your computer. This is where programs, files, and folders are permanently stored. Portable hard drives are used to back up files.	250 GB to 750 GB or more
Zip disk 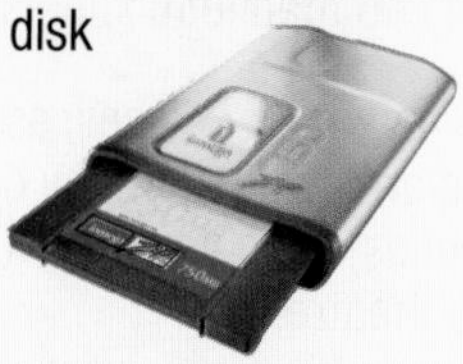	A zip disk is a portable device used to back up and store data.	100 MB to 750 MB
Optical drive (CD, DVD, BD) 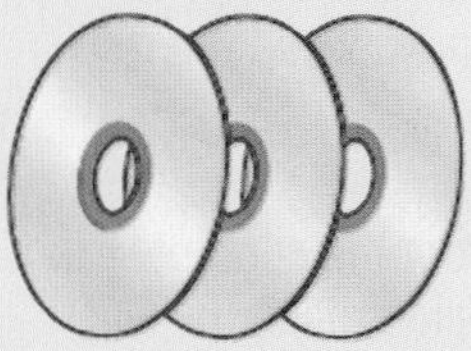	Optical drives store audio, video, and data onto discs such as CDs, DVDs, and Blue-ray discs (BDs). These discs are often categorized as read only, recordable, or rewritable. BDs were created to store large amounts of high-definition video and data.	CD = 700 MB DVD = 4.7 GB to 17 GB BD = 25 GB to 50 GB or more
Flash drive 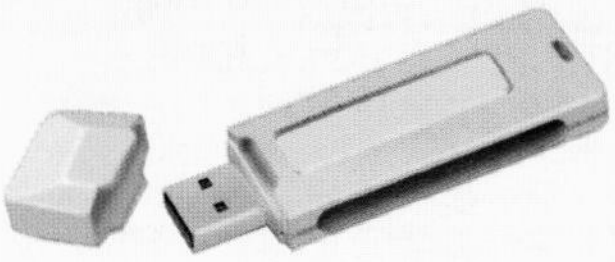	A flash drive (also called a pen USB, jump, or thumb drive) plugs directly into a computer's Universal Serial Bus (USB) port.	2 GB to 32 GB or more

Real World

Storage Devices
Removable storage devices such as DVDs and flash drives are used to back up data or transfer files between computers.

Why It's Important
How do removable storage devices help protect data?

A device's storage **capacity**, or capability, is usually measured in megabytes (MB) or gigabytes (GB). A byte is the amount of storage space required to store a single character, such as the letter "d." A kilobyte is about one thousand bytes, a megabyte is about one million bytes, and a gigabyte is about one billion bytes. The capacities of different storage devices are shown in Figure 3.6.

In the following activity, you will create a presentation about input, output, and storage devices.

YOU TRY IT

Activity 3A Identify Multimedia Hardware

1. On paper, create a grid like the one shown in Figure 3.7 on page 75.
2. Examine the hardware systems in your classroom or computer lab.
3. Enter each piece of hardware you observe into your grid.

Multimedia hardware					
Computer ID	Type of Computer	Input Devices	Output Devices	Storage Devices	Network Connection (Yes or No)
Lab01	PC	Mouse, keyboard	Printer, scanner	ZIP250	Yes

Figure 3.7
Multimedia hardware grid.

④ Include information about all the input devices, output devices, and storage devices that are part of the hardware system or are used on their own. These devices may include:

- PCs, monitors, and keyboards
- interactive whiteboards
- scanners, printers, mice, and touch screens
- cameras, camcorders, and Webcams
- graphics tablets, sound systems, and audio recording devices

⑤ Using presentation software, create a presentation that identifies what input and output devices are available in your classroom or computer lab. Explain how the input and output devices are used with other hardware and software.

⑥ Make sure your presentation includes:

- a slide about how hardware is used in your multimedia class
- a slide about input and output devices that are most important in a multimedia class

⑦ Save and close your file.

 **Reading Check** **Explain** How is a hard drive different from a removable storage device?

Academic Focus

Mathematics

Compare Prices Setting up a multimedia design business costs money. Compare two brands of a laptop computer, digital camera, and scanner. For each tool, identify the lower-priced brand. Add the three less expensive choices, making sure the decimals are aligned.

NCTM Number and Operations Compute fluently and make reasonable estimates.

Computer Software

What are the types of computer software?

Computer **software** gives instructions to the computer's hardware to make it work. Software translates a user's commands into instructions that the computer can process. Different software can help with different tasks. Software is divided into three main categories: operating system software, application software, and utility software.

Operating System Software

Every computer needs an operating system in order to work. An **operating system (OS)** controls all of the software programs on the computer. The two most common operating systems are Microsoft® Windows® (for PCs) and Mac OS® (for Apple® computers). Handheld systems, such as MP3 players and smartphones, use operating systems that were developed specifically for them, called proprietary software.

An OS moves data between RAM and other storage devices, keeps track of the computer's tasks and input devices, and sends output to the appropriate hardware. An OS also provides an interface for a user to give commands to the computer. The **graphical user interface**, or **GUI** (pronounced "goo-ee"), allows users to select words, symbols, or graphics from the desktop. As seen in Figure 3.8, GUIs are used for a variety of devices.

Figure 3.8 ●⟶
Operating systems for both laptop computers and smartphones have GUIs. **What does GUI stand for?**

Operating system

Smartphone

Application Software

Multimedia project teams use specific software to combine elements into a multimedia production. This software is called **application software** (also referred to as applications). It is used to perform different tasks on a computer.

Building multimedia projects involves both project management software and multimedia development applications. You have already learned about some of the most common project management applications. These include:

- Web browsers, such as Microsoft Internet Explorer®, Apple Safari®, Mozilla Firefox™, or Opera, for visiting Web sites.

- Word processing programs, such as Microsoft Word® or Adobe® Buzzword®, to create documents or to key text for Web sites.

- Spreadsheet software, such as Microsoft Excel® or Lotus 1-2-3®, to work with numbers and calculations and to create tables, charts, and graphs.

- Databases, such as Microsoft Access®, FileMaker Pro®, and Oracle®, to organize and retrieve large amounts of information.

- E-mail applications, such as Microsoft Outlook® and Eudora®, to exchange messages and files with other computers.

- Presentation software, such as Microsoft PowerPoint®, Apple Keynote®, and Adobe® Captivate®, to build slide shows.

Figure 3.9 lists examples of multimedia development applications with which you will need to become familiar.

Project Management It is sometimes less expensive to purchase a suite of programs than individual programs. For example, the Adobe® Creative Suite has several applications you can use in multimedia development.

Figure 3.9

Each task you do on a computer requires a specific kind of software. Which types of applications might you use to create a Web site?

Multimedia Development Software		
Type of Software	**Function**	**Examples**
Audio	Use to create and edit audio files, increase speed and volume, and filter out background noise.	Microsoft® Expression® Media, Apple® GarageBand®, Adobe® Audition®
Graphics	Use to resize, crop, and change the color of an image. Also use to create original graphics from scratch.	Microsoft® Paint, Microsoft® Expression® Design, Adobe® Fireworks®, Corel Paint Shop Pro®, Mac® iPhoto®, Adobe® Photoshop®, Serif™ DrawPlus™, Serif™ PhotoPlus™
Text editor	Use to manually key XHTML commands into a blank document.	Microsoft Notepad and WordPad, Adobe HomeSite®, HotDog Professional™, SimpleText™, BBEdit®, Amaya™
Video	Use to create, manipulate, edit, and play video.	Microsoft® Expression® Media, Adobe® Premiere®, Apple Quicktime®, Apple iMovie®, Apple® Final Cut Pro®, Serif™ MoviePlus™
Web site development	Use to create a Web site and to preview its final appearance.	Adobe® Dreamweaver®, Microsoft® Expression® Web

Utility Software

Utility applications are generally small programs designed for a specific task such as capturing screen shots, completing image management tasks, converting text and images, compressing files, or protecting data. There are four basic types of utility software:

- **Screen Capture** This software captures images of computer screen displays. This utility is useful in multimedia projects such as software tutorials. Two options for this software include Inbit FullShot® and TechSmith Corporation SnagIt®.

- **File Compression** Many multimedia files can be very large. To use less disk space and to reduce transmission time, you might want to save your files in a compressed, or smaller, format. You can do this with file compression software such as PKZip® or StuffIt®.

- **Virus Protection** It is important when working on the Internet to protect your computer and its data from outside threats such as viruses and hackers. There are many virus protection applications available from companies such as McAfee® and Symantec™.

- **Optical Character Recognition (OCR)** Use OCR software to convert scanned graphics file formats to text file formats. Two popular options for this software are OmniPage® and FineReader®.

Reading Check **Identify** What are five examples of software for developing multimedia?

Section 3.1 After You Read

Review Key Concepts

1. List common input and output devices used in a computer system.

2. Describe the different types of computer software.

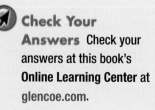 **Check Your Answers** Check your answers at this book's **Online Learning Center** at glencoe.com.

Practice Academic Skills

English Language Arts

3. **Determine** Suppose you want to start a multimedia design business. Write a list of the hardware and software you would want to buy, along with an explanation of each.

NCTE 12 Use language to accomplish individual purposes.

Mathematics

4. **Calculate** You would like to back up some files on your computer. The files you want to back up are 50.7 MB. If there are 1,000 KB in 1 MB, what is the size of the files in KB?

 **Online Student Manual • glencoe.com**

Go to your Online Student Manual and enter your password to find projects that allow you to practice and apply multimedia skills.

NCTM Measurement Understand measurable attributes of objects and the units, systems, and processes of measurement.

Follow Safety Guidelines

Potential hazards exist in any school or workplace. To keep yourself and others safe, learn to practice safety in the classroom and in the office.

Safety Regulations

Electrical components and tools in the workplace must meet certain safety requirements. Material safety data sheets (MSDS) certify that the substances used in such equipment are safe and non-toxic. Workplaces follow rules established by the Occupational Safety & Health Administration (OSHA) to prevent work-related injuries. The American Red Cross helps prepare people to handle safety emergencies at work, school, and home.

Use a hands-free headset to prevent neck injuries.

Avoid Computer Injury

To avoid computer-use problems, such as repetitive strain injury, eyestrain, or backache, make sure your workstation is ergonomically correct (that is, arranged for comfort and safety). Keep your feet flat on the floor and your wrists straight. Position the monitor about two feet away, at a height that lets you look at it without bending or twisting your neck. Take periodic breaks to stretch your body and rest your eyes. If you use the phone frequently, get a hands-free headset.

Be Safety-Conscious

You are responsible for making sure you know how to use equipment properly and for staying alert to safety hazards. Tape down loose cords, which can trip someone. Store photo, video, and audio equipment securely. Avoid horseplay, which can cause accidents and damage. Always turn off equipment before troubleshooting it. Never stick your hand into an open piece of equipment. Learn the locations of fire alarms in your school and workplace. Make sure you know the procedures to follow in case of a fire.

Keep computers safe from threats such as viruses, hackers, and spyware by using firewalls, password guidelines, data encryption, and anti-virus programs. Anti-virus software should be updated often, because new viruses are constantly released.

Skill Builder

1. **Develop a Plan** If an emergency occurred, would you know what to do? Make a presentation about your school's emergency evacuation plan or create one with the other students in your class.

2. **Research Safety** Identify common school or workplace injuries and their causes. Then, research one injury. Use resources from local, state, and federal agencies to show ways to avoid such an injury.

SECTION 3.2 Networks

Before You Read

Create an Outline Use the section's headings to create an outline. Make the headings into Level 1 main ideas. Add supporting details to create Levels 2 and 3 of the outline. Use the outline to predict what you are about to learn.

Read to Learn

Key Concepts

- **Describe** types of network configurations.
- **Explain** the functions of network hardware and software.
- **Identify** network operating systems.

Main Idea

Networks let computers share information, messages, and software. Networks utilize hardware and software in different configurations.

Content Vocabulary

◇ local area network (LAN)

◇ wide area network (WAN)

◇ server

◇ client

◇ network interface card (NIC)

◇ router

◇ network operating system (NOS)

Academic Vocabulary

You will find these words in your reading and on your tests. Use the glossary to look up their definitions, if necessary.

◆ enable

◆ convert

Graphic Organizer

As you read, list three network hardware components. Use a tree diagram like the one below to organize your notes.

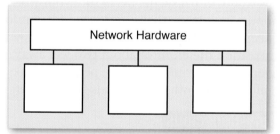

Network Hardware

 Graphic Organizer Go to this book's **Online Learning Center** at glencoe.com to print this graphic organizer.

Academic Standards

 English Language Arts

NCTE 7 Conduct research and gather, evaluate, and synthesize data to communicate discoveries.
NCTE 8 Use information resources to gather information and create and communicate knowledge.

 Mathematics

NCTM Problem Solving Apply and adapt a variety of appropriate strategies to solve problems.

NCTE National Council of Teachers of English
NSES National Science Education Standards

NCTM National Council of Teachers of Mathematics
NCSS National Council for the Social Studies

Network Configurations

What are the two main types of network configurations?

As You Read

Connect How is a computer network like a social network?

In a computer network, physical communication lines or wireless connections are used to connect computers together. Once connected to each other, computers **enable**, or allow, users to share data, communications, hardware resources, and software applications. Networks also allow users to access the Internet. Being able to store files on a network is important for two reasons:

- Multiple users can access the files. This makes it easier to work together.
- Files on networks are frequently backed up. Saving files on a network prevents important data from being lost if the system crashes.

Configuration Options

How a system of computers is arranged or set up is called its configuration. There are two main network configurations:

- **Local area network (LAN)** connects computers in a single location. A LAN may be used at home to connect just two computers or in a business to connect the whole office.
- **Wide area network (WAN)** connects computers across a wider geographical area. The largest example of a WAN is the Internet. A WAN is commonly used by large businesses to connect computers in different office locations.

The main difference between a LAN and a WAN is the area covered. A LAN can connect computers in a small geographic area such as a company, department, or complex of buildings. WANs, on the other hand, can connect computers in different countries.

Client/Server Networks

Most LANs used by businesses today are client/server networks. A **server** is a powerful central computer used by a network. A **client** is an individual computer that is part of a network. The job of the server computer is to respond to requests from the client computers. For example, a client can request information that is stored on the server. The server then finds the information and sends it to the client.

Peer-to-Peer Networks

Another networking option is a peer-to-peer (P2P) network. Like a client/server network, this type of network allows users to share files and communications. However, a P2P network does not use a server. Instead, users link their computers directly to one another using the Internet. A P2P network generally does not have the speed or security of a client/server network.

 **Reading Check** **Identify** Is the Internet a LAN or a WAN?

Network Hardware and Software

What are the hardware and software components of a network?

Network hardware includes the physical components that connect computers to one another. For a network to function properly, all the hardware components must be compatible. For example, a scanner must be compatible with each of the computers used on the network.

Modems

Many networks use a modem to allow the computers to "talk" to one another and to the server. A modem is a piece of hardware that enables a computer to send and receive signals through telephone wires or cable. A modem **converts**, or changes the form of, digital signals from a computer into analog, or voice, signals that can be transmitted over standard telephone lines.

Network Adapters

Some computers use a network adapter instead of a modem or in combination with a modem. A network adapter can be either a network interface card or a wireless adapter. A **network interface card (NIC)** is a circuit board or PC card that allows a client computer to connect to a network. The NIC provides the place to plug the network cable into the computer. It also creates and sends the signal from one network component to another. A wireless adapter allows the client computer to send and receive radio signals to and from the network. A wireless adapter is often an external device that connects through the USB port.

Routers

A special hardware device called a **router** is used to join LANs. Companies may connect two or more LANs so that employees using different networks can share e-mail and data. A router also allows computers on a LAN to access the Internet. The router helps manage network traffic by determining the fastest route for a message.

Network Software

Networks are controlled by a specific type of software called a network operating system. A **network operating system (NOS)** is an operating system with special functions for linking computers and other devices in LANs.

These operating systems are installed on a network's servers so they can communicate with each other, with the PCs on the network, and with the other shared hardware such as scanners and printers. The network operating systems have many functions such as:

- Managing network resources.
- Controlling who can access different network components.
- Keeping the network running smoothly.

Commonly used network operating systems are shown in Figure 3.10.

Network Operating Systems	
Operating System	**Description**
Microsoft® Windows Server®	Some versions offered as both PC OS and NOS.
Linux	Free NOS that runs on millions of servers around the world. Useful for Web servers that store Web pages and make them available on the Internet.
Mac OS X	Both a Mac OS and an NOS.
Novell® Open Enterprise™	Successor to Novell's Netware NOS.
Apache	Web server software that is distributed free so people and organizations can customize it to adapt to their needs.

← **Figure 3.10**
Network operating systems make sure that networks run smoothly and control who can access network components. Which network operating systems are available for free?

Operating systems and networking software work together to help users organize and retrieve files. In the following activity, you will explore how files are organized on a computer system.

YOU TRY IT

Activity 3B Explore Network Files and Folders

1 Open the default file manager for your computer's operating system. This example uses Windows Explorer. The Mac OS uses the Finder to organize files.

2 With your teacher's permission, locate and open a multimedia folder on your school's network drive. Your screen should look similar to Figure 3.11, which shows the hierarchy of the main folder for a sample multimedia project.

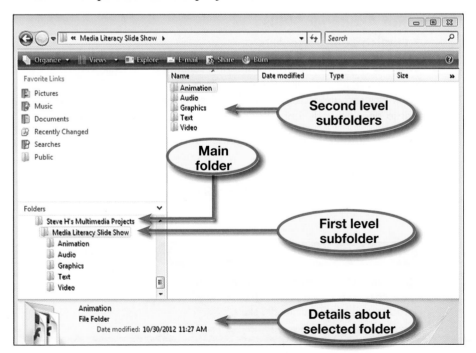

← **Figure 3.11**
This folder structure makes files easy to find.

③ Within the main folder, click a subfolder. Project files appear on the right side of the window. Depending on the size of the project, additional subfolders and files may also appear.

④ Click another subfolder. Again, further subfolders and files may appear. The hierarchy should look similar to Figure 3.12.

⑤ Study the way folders and files have been organized.Close the operating system's file manager.

Figure 3.12 ●→
Multimedia files are organized so that they can easily be found and used in projects.

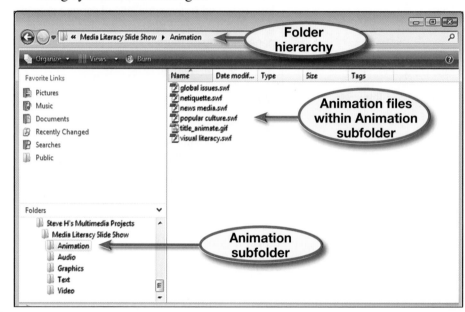

Reading Check **List** What are examples of network hardware?

Section 3.2 After You Read

Review Key Concepts

1. **Describe** the differences between a LAN and a WAN.

2. **Explain** the client/server relationship.

🚀 **Check Your Answers** Check your answers at this book's **Online Learning Center** through glencoe.com.

Practice Academic Skills

🖥 **English Language Arts**

3. **Evaluate** Suppose you are considering setting up a network for a small business. Write a paragraph that recommends either a client/server or peer-to-peer network configuration.

4. **Compare and Contrast** Create a presentation that compares features of various network operating systems. Your presentation should include the pros and cons for each option, including price and efficiency.

🚀 **Online Student Manual • glencoe.com**

Go to your Online Student Manual and enter your password to find projects that allow you to practice and apply multimedia skills.

NCTE 8 Use information resources to gather information and create and communicate knowledge.

NCTE 7 Conduct research and gather, evaluate, and synthesize data to communicate discoveries.

Chapter Summary

A computer is an electronic device that processes data. Computers range in size to meet the diverse needs of users. Computer systems consist of hardware, software, users, and data. The CPU and RAM are a computer's processing components. Input devices are used to enter data. Output devices show the results of processed data. There are many different devices for storing digital data.

LANs connect computers in a single location. WANs connect computers across a wider geographical area. Two possible network configurations are client/server and peer to peer. A network operating system allows for linking computers and other devices in LANs. Network hardware includes modems, network adapters, and routers.

Vocabulary Review

1. On a sheet of paper, use each of these vocabulary terms in a sentence.

Content Vocabulary

◇ computer (p. 69)
◇ central processing unit (CPU) (p. 71)
◇ input device (p. 72)
◇ graphics tablet (p. 72)
◇ output device (p. 73)
◇ software (p. 76)
◇ operating system (OS) (p. 76)
◇ graphical user interface (GUI) (p. 76)
◇ application software (p. 77)

◇ local area network (LAN) (p. 81)
◇ wide area network (WAN) (p. 81)
◇ server (p. 81)
◇ client (p. 81)
◇ network interface card (NIC) (p. 82)
◇ router (p. 82)
◇ network operating system (NOS) (p. 82)

Academic Vocabulary

◆ diverse (p. 70)
◆ capacity (p. 74)
◆ enable (p. 81)
◆ convert (p. 82)

Review Key Concepts

2. Explain computers and computer systems.

3. Summarize how hardware components work in a computer system.

4. Describe how computer input, output, and storage devices work.

5. Identify the categories of software, and applications for developing multimedia.

6. Describe types of network configurations.

7. Explain the functions of network hardware and software.

8. Identify network operating systems.

Critical Thinking

9. **Distinguish** List the four components of a computer system. What what might happen if one of these components were to malfunction or be missing? Which component of the system do you think is most important? Support your opinion with examples.

10. **Illustrate** List the five types of computers discussed in this chapter. Then give an example of a task that would be suited to each type of computer. Use a chart like the one below to organize your ideas.

Type of Computer	Example of Task
1.	
2.	
3.	
4.	
5.	

11. **Select** Your computer requires more memory to run a new application. Would you add RAM or ROM to your computer? Why?

12. **Classify** All-in-one printers combine several types input and output devices. Describe each of the input and output devices that you might expect to find in this type of printer.

13. **Analyze** You are in the market for a new computer and monitor. You have decided on the computer you want and now must decide which monitor to purchase. Create a list of questions to consider before the purchase.

14. **Compare and Contrast** Choose two types of computer hardware storage devices. Research to learn how the devices are similar and how they are different. Use a Venn diagram to organize your findings.

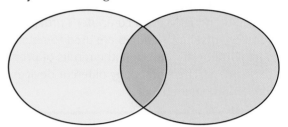

15. **Determine** Explain whether a LAN or WAN would be appropriate in each of the following situations.

   A. Your company has opened an office in another state and the employees need to access your office's computer files.

   B. The school principal wants to monitor computer activity in the school's lab.

   C. You and your brother need to access the same files from your PCs.

   D. Your biology teacher needs to e-mail the class syllabus to you.

16. **Evaluate** Based on what you know, which network operating system would you choose to support a Web design service? Support your opinion with examples.

Go Online e-RESOURCES
glencoe.com

Go to the **Online Learning Center** to find additional activities and career resources.

Practice Quizzes Test your knowledge of the material in this chapter.

Career Resources Find out more about careers, including information about résumés portfolios, and interview and workplace tips.

Academic Connections

17. English Language Arts—Research and Write a Report

Network operating systems come in several varieties. Commercial software is developed by companies and sold for a profit. Open-source software, such as Apache, is free to use. Research the development of Apache software.

A. As you research, look for the answers to the following questions:

- Who developed Apache?
- Why is Apache free to use?
- When was Apache developed and why?
- How has Apache changed since it was first developed?
- How might Apache be used in the future?

B. Write a two-page report summarizing your discoveries.

C. Proofread and spell-check your report.

> **NCTE 7** Conduct research and gather, evaluate, and synthesize data to communicate discoveries.

Standardized Test Practice

Reading Tables

Read the paragraph and table below and then answer the question.

Your neighbor, Cherise, found a new hobby—digital photography. For the last six months, she has taken photography classes. With her new skills, she decided to turn her hobby into a home-based business, which she named Cherise Designs.

For her first money-making project, Cherise has decided to make a calendar to sell. To create the calendar, she plans to take photos of scenes around your community. To save costs, she wants to print the photos on her own printer. Cherise asks your advice on what resolution to set her camera.

> **Test-Taking Tip** When answering multiple-choice questions, read the question first, then read all the answer choices before choosing your answer. Eliminate answers you know are not right.

General Resolution Guidelines	
Resolution	**Use**
72 dpi	Use a low resolution for pictures to be displayed on computer monitors, such as photos in Web sites and electronic presentations.
150 dpi–300 dpi	Use a higher resolution when printing the image on a personal printer so the picture prints more clearly.
higher than 300 dpi	Use the highest resolution for high-end printers.

18. Based on the table above, what resolution should Cherise use to save her photos?

- **A.** 72 dpi
- **B.** 150–300 dpi
- **C.** higher than 300 dpi
- **D.** 73–149 dpi

19. Create a Troubleshooting Guide

Your company, KT Enterprises, uses a local area network (LAN) to share documents and other files between departments. Your manager has asked you to create a LAN user's guide so that employees can understand how to access files.

A. Sketch an outline of KT Enterprises' LAN folders and possible files (see page 83 for an example). KT Enterprises has three main departments that work together to design, produce, and distribute multimedia presentations: Design Department, Production Department, and Distribution Department.

B. Create subfolders for each department to include in your sketch. Subfolders may include project names, delivery dates, and so on.

C. Create a troubleshooting guide for employees. In the guide:

- Explain the LAN's organization.

- Give instructions on how to access folders and files. Provide instructions on how to use hardware and software to improve productivity. Provide the instructions in the form of a step-by-step guide.

- Use illustrations as appropriate to help make your instructions more clear.

D. Edit, proofread, and spell-check your guide.

> **NETS 2b**
> Communicate information and ideas effectively to multiple audiences using a variety of media and formats.

20. Create a Presentation About LANs and WANs

The company you work for has asked you to create a presentation for your co-workers. The purpose of the presentation is to give information about local area networks (LANs) and wide area networks (WANs).

A. Use appropriate software to create your presentation. Remember that your audience is a group of professionals.

B. In your presentation, be sure to:

- Explain the difference between LANs and WANs.

- Explain what kind of network is set up at your company. Use your school as a model.

- Use illustrations such as photos, drawings, or clip art to add interest.

- Make sure the text on each slide is concise and accurate. Check your presentation for spelling or factual errors.

C. Share your presentation with the class using a computer system so that you can point to items as you talk about them. Ask classmates to recommend ways to improve your presentation.

> **NETS 3C** Evaluate and select information sources and digital tools based on the appropriateness to specific tasks.

21. Get Involved

You decide to help a local charitable organization promote an important fund-raising event by creating a flyer.

A. Work in small groups as directed by your teacher. With your group, choose a local charitable organization. If the organization does not have an upcoming event, imagine one that would work well for the organization, such as a bake sale, concert, fun run, or yard sale.

B. With your group, create a flyer to advertise the event. Include important points, such as the name of the charity, the purpose of the fund-raiser, and the date and time of the event. Also consider if the event will require a ticket purchase for participation or advance registration.

C. Scan pictures from various magazines to highlight points in the flyer. Use a table similar to the one shown to keep a record of the scanned pictures along with their description and purpose. Decide with your group which pictures you will use. Give credit to the source of the pictures in small print on your flyer.

PICTURE NUMBER	DESCRIPTION	PURPOSE
#1		
#2		
#3		

22. Create the Ideal Computer

Create a combined list of things you already do with your computer, such as writing reports for school and sending e-mail, and things you would like to be able to do with a computer, such as creating graphics, managing your schedule, and playing video games. Using the list, write questions you could use to interview a salesperson at a computer store. Phone a local computer store and interview a salesperson. By the end of the interview, you should be able to define the following requirements:

● What are my hardware needs?

● How much memory does my system need, and how does this number relate to my computer activities?

● What are my software needs?

● Which computer is the best one for my needs?

● Which input and output devices do I need?

Write a dialogue of the interview with the salesperson to share with your class.

Project 1

Research Computer History

English Language Arts Research the history of computers. Write a one- to two-page essay or create a presentation.

Plan

1. Before you begin your research, create a list of what you know about the history of computers and what you want to learn about the history of computers.

Research

2. Use search engines or books to research the history of computers. Evaluate the information to ensure accuracy. Take notes as you research. In your research, identify the key people involved in the development of computers and include their contributions.

Create

3. Based on your research, organize and summarize ideas and details. Then outline your essay. Write a thesis statement that summarizes how computers evolved Use your outline and thesis statement as the basis of the first draft of your essay. Provide two or three examples to support and illustrate your essay's points.

Review

4. Proofread and spell-check your essay.

> **NCTE 7** Conduct research and gather, evaluate, and synthesize data to communicate discoveries.

Project 2

Conduct an Operating System Analysis

English Language Arts Use the Internet to research computer operating systems. Write a one-page essay that compares and contrasts three different operating systems. Use language and vocabulary that demonstrates your knowledge of technical concepts. Use your current knowledge to enhance your understanding of technology.

Plan

1. Use information provided in Section 3.2 to write a paragraph about what you already know about the three operating systems you have chosen to research.

Research

2. Take careful notes during your research, paying close attention to the differences among the operating systems and why people choose one over another.

Create

3. Based on your research, outline your essay. Write a thesis statement for the essay. Use your outline and thesis statement as the basis for a first draft. Predict who might choose to use the different operating systems and why.

Review

4. Proofread and spell-check your essay.

> **NCTE 8** Use information resources to gather information and create and communicate knowledge.

Project 3

Analyze the Contributions of Technology

Social Studies There are not many things that you do daily that are not influenced by computers in some way. But there are many people who did not use computers when they were young. Conduct research and do an interview to find out how life was different before computers became widely used.

NCSS VIII Make judgments about how science and technology have transformed the physical world and human society.

Research

1. Research the different ways computers are used today. Your list might include electronic displays in cars, ATMs, television, smartphones, and medical equipment.

2. Talk to an individual such as a parent, grandparent, or family friend. Ask questions such as, "Do you think life was better without the influence of computers or better today with the influence?" Apply active listening skills to obtain and clarify information.

3. Use a chart like the one shown to record answers to your questions.

Interview Question	Answer
What contributions have computers made to your life?	
How was life different before computers?	
How do you think our society has been influenced by computers?	
Was life simpler without the influence of computers, or do computers make life simpler?	

Create

4. Write an essay that follows MLA style. The essay should be double-spaced and properly formatted. The essay should include:

   - A thesis statement.

   - At least four quotations from four different sources, as well as a Works Cited list.

   - A summary of your interview.

   - A paragraph or two of your conclusions.

Review and Revise

5. Share your essay with a classmate. Discuss your conclusions and how you arrived at them. Ask your classmate to read your essay and tell you whether your thesis statement is accurate.

6. Make changes to your paper based on the feedback. Proofread and spell-check your essay.

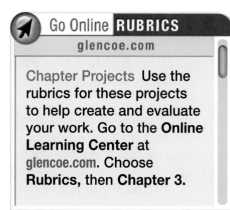

Go Online RUBRICS

glencoe.com

Chapter Projects Use the rubrics for these projects to help create and evaluate your work. Go to the **Online Learning Center** at **glencoe.com**. Choose **Rubrics**, then **Chapter 3**.

Portfolio Project

Create a Multimedia Presentation

In this unit, you learned that the term multimedia refers to using computer technology to integrate elements such as text, graphics, animation, audio, and video. In this project, you will apply your new skills to create a slide show that explains how multimedia affects your life.

Project Assignment

In this project, you will:

- Create a presentation that shows how multimedia impacts you over the course of a single day.
- Begin by creating a plan that clearly states the presentation's purpose and target audience.
- Use your plan to guide you as you develop the presentation.
- Include at least six slides in your presentation.
- Create a single slide for each multimedia item you encounter over the day. In the slide's text, describe its multimedia elements. For example, a tutorial you use in biology class might contain both audio and animation.
- Insert appropriate multimedia elements, including graphics, animation, audio, and video clips, into your slides.

Multimedia Design Skills Behind the Project

Your success in multimedia design will depend on your skills:

- Effectively use your presentation software.
- Create consistently formatted content, including bulleted lists.
- Choose an attractive design theme and color scheme.
- Create and/or choose appropriate graphics and animation.
- Use at least one audio clip and one video clip.
- Apply slide transitions.

Academic Skills Behind the Project

Remember these key academic concepts:

Writing Skills

- Use correct grammar, punctuation, and terminology to write and edit multimedia documents.
- Use language that is appropriate for the presentation's goals and audience.
- Employ effective verbal and nonverbal communication skills.

Problem-Solving Skills

- Employ planning and time-managment skills.
- Solve problems and think critically.

 **English Language Arts**

NCTE 4 Use written language to communicate effectively.

NCTE 5 Use different writing process elements to communicate effectively.

NCTE 12 Use language to accomplish individual purposes.

Mathematics

NCTM Problem Solving Apply and adapt a variety of appropriate strategies to solve problems.

STEP 1   Analyze and Plan the Project

Create a written plan that includes:

- A statement of the presentation's purpose.

- A description of the presentation's target audience.

STEP 2   Design Your Presentation

Perform all of the following tasks to design the presentation:

- Sketch out the contents of each slide and how the slide will be laid out.

- Choose an appropriate design theme and color scheme for the presentation.

- Locate or create the multimedia elements to be used in the presentation.

STEP 3   Develop Your Presentation

Follow these steps to develop your presentation:

- Use presentation software, such as Microsoft PowerPoint, to create the presentation.

- Insert each slide's text and multimedia elements.

- Apply transitions to the slides.

STEP 4   Share Your Presentation

Ask a classmate or trusted adult to review your presentation.

- Ask for feedback, constructive criticism, and suggestions for changes.

- Encourage your reviewer to ask questions.

STEP 5   Test and Evaluate Your Presentation

Follow these steps to evaluate and test your presentation:

- Use the Portfolio Project Checklist to evaluate your presentation.

- Make final changes, if necessary.

Portfolio Project Checklist

ANALYSIS AND PLANNING

- ☑ A written plan has been developed that states the presentation's purpose.
- ☑ The target audience is identified.

DESIGN AND DEVELOPMENT

- ☑ The presentation's contents match its purpose and are appropriate for its target audience.
- ☑ The design theme and color scheme are appropriate and attractive.
- ☑ The individual slides' layout and formatting are consistent and well chosen.
- ☑ Each slide presents an example of how the student interacts with multimedia in a single day.
- ☑ The text is clear and concise and uses proper spelling and grammar.
- ☑ Bulleted lists have been used when appropriate.
- ☑ The content is free of spelling and grammar errors.
- ☑ The presentation includes graphics and animation that enhance it.
- ☑ The presentation uses at least one audio clip and one video clip and the clips enhance the presentation.
- ☑ Transitions are used to move from one slide to the next.

TESTING AND EVALUATION

- ☑ The slide show demonstrates proficiency in the use of presentation software.
- ☑ All multimedia components function properly.
- ☑ Rules and restrictions regarding the use of third-party information and multimedia files have been followed.
- ☑ The presentation automatically moves from one slide to another.
- ☑ The presentation has been reviewed by a classmate or trusted adult and appropriate changes have been made.

Go Online RUBRICS

glencoe.com

Go to this book's **Online Learning Center** at glencoe.com for a rubric you can use to evaluate your final project.

UNIT 2

Multimedia Design

| Chapter 4 | The Multimedia Development Process |
| Chapter 5 | Visual Design for Multimedia |

UNIT Portfolio Project Review

Plan a Web Site

After completing this unit, you will understand the stages in the multimedia project development process. You will also learn how to apply visual design elements and the principles of design to your multimedia projects. In the Unit Portfolio Project, you will use the skills you have learned to plan the purpose, audience, and mission of a Web site. You will create the visual design concept for the site, following design principles.

 Go Online **PREVIEW**

glencoe.com

Go to the **Online Learning Center** and select your book. Click **Unit 2>Portfolio Project Preview** to learn more about planning, designing, and developing a Web site.

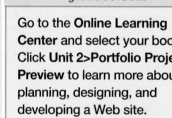

Multimedia elements enable you access e-mail, do research for your term paper, download music, view your favorite movies, and meet friends on social networking Web sites. *How much time do you spend online each day creating multimedia content?*

The Multimedia Development Process

Section 4.1
Project Analysis and Planning

Section 4.2
Project Design and Development

Section 4.3
Testing, Implementation, and Maintenance

CHAPTER OBJECTIVES

After completing this chapter, you will be able to:

❖ **Identify** the five stages of the project life cycle.

❖ **Develop** a project plan.

❖ **Determine** the scope of a multimedia project.

❖ **List** the types of navigation schemes.

❖ **Map** navigation structure.

❖ **Create** a storyboard.

❖ **Explain** the steps in the project development stage.

❖ **Describe** the testing stage of the multimedia development process.

❖ **Identify** ways to implement a project.

❖ **Discuss** proper evaluation and maintenance of a multimedia project.

Explore the Photo

It is important to organize your time to make the most of your resources. *How might you organize the tasks you need to accomplish for a school project?*

21st CENTURY SKILLS
Get Organized

The most important way to get organized is to make a plan and follow it. The steps you take will develop into good habits to help you stay organized. Planning ahead will help you achieve your goals.

Quick Write Activity Paragraph Development

Write about a time when you made a plan and followed it. What strategies did you use to develop your plan, and how did it help you stay organized?

Writing Tips

To write an effective paragraph, follow these steps:

1. Write a topic sentence that clearly expresses the main idea of the paragraph.
2. Each sentence should have one or more details that support the main idea.
3. Make sure all of your sentences are linked clearly and logically to one another.

Reading Guide

Before You Read

Prior Knowledge Look over the Key Concepts at the beginning of the section. Write down what you already know about each concept and what you want to find out by reading the section.

Read to Learn

Key Concepts

- **Identify** the five stages of the project life cycle.
- **Explain** the purpose of a project plan.
- **Determine** a multimedia project's purpose, goals, and audience.
- **Evaluate** the scope of a multimedia project.

Main Idea

There are five stages in the multimedia development process. During the first stage, analysis and planning, you should identify the multimedia production's purpose, goals, audience, mission statement, and scope.

Content Vocabulary

◇ project plan   ◇ mission statement

◇ objective   ◇ deliverable

◇ target audience   ◇ scope

Academic Vocabulary

You will find these words in your reading and on your tests. Use the glossary to look up their definitions, if necessary.

◆ comprehensive   ◆ analyze

Graphic Organizer

As you read, identify four positive qualities that every project team member should have. Use a diagram similar to the one below to help organize your information.

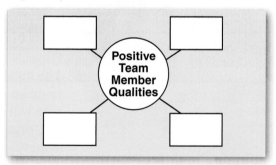

 Graphic Organizer Go to this book's **Online Learning Center** at **glencoe.com** to print this graphic organizer.

Academic Standards

 **English Language Arts**

NCTE 3 Apply strategies to interpret texts.
NCTE 12 Use language to accomplish individual purposes.
NCTE 4 Use written language to communicate effectively.

 Mathematics

NCTM Problem Solving Solve problems that arise in mathematics and in other contexts.

NCTE National Council of Teachers of English
NSES National Science Education Standards

NCTM National Council of Teachers of Mathematics
NCSS National Council for the Social Studies

Multimedia Project Life Cycle

What are the five stages of multimedia development?

Multimedia projects are often created by project teams. Project teams follow a basic sequence of tasks to create multimedia. This pattern is sometimes called the project life cycle. The five stages of the multimedia project life cycle are shown in Figure 4.1. In each stage, it is important that team members have a **comprehensive**, or thorough, understanding of their role on the project team. To function effectively as part of a team, a project team member should practice the following positive qualities and behaviors.

- **Know the role.** Each team member must understand his or her specific responsibilities and know how his or her tasks fit into the mission and goals of the overall project.

- **Remain flexible.** In some cases, team members must finish certain tasks before they can start others. However, the amount of time assigned to each stage varies based on the project, and stages may overlap. Team members must be cooperative, openminded, and flexible.

- **Communicate clearly and consistently.** Communication with team members and with clients is essential to completing the project.

- **Keep the mission and goals in mind.** Each member of the team should be clear about the project's mission and goals and know the relationship between his or her role and the final project.

As You Read

Connect In what other areas of your life is it important to remain flexible?

Real World

Be Prepared Every team member must understand his or her role, and know what tools are needed to complete the task. Being prepared helps you to accomplish goals.

Why It's Important
In what other areas of your life has being prepared helped you to complete the task at hand?

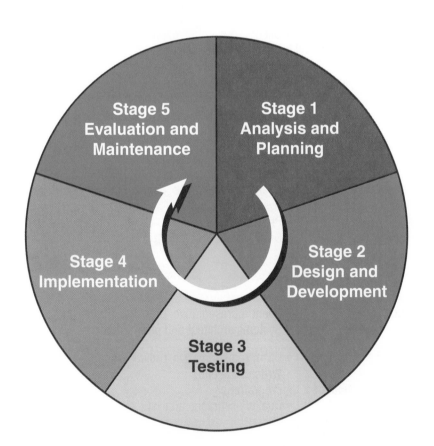

Stage 5
Evaluation and
Maintenance

Stage 1
Analysis and
Planning

Stage 4
Implementation

Stage 2
Design and
Development

Stage 3
Testing

Figure 4.1
Every stage of the multimedia development process has distinct boundaries, goals, and deadlines. Why do you think a circle is used to illustrate the development process?

The number of people on a multimedia project team varies according to the type of project being developed. For instance, the team required to develop a complex simulation or video game may be larger than the team needed for a small print publication. Some typical team members include a client, project manager, producer, user interface designer, graphic artist, audio specialist or videographer, writer, and programmer. These roles are described in detail in Chapter 10.

Different team members work during different stages of the multimedia project. For example, as shown in Figure 4.2, some team members are not involved until the testing stage, while others are involved in every stage. Every team member should understand the project's life cycle and know his or her role. It is also important for each team member to identify the tools and resources needed to complete the job.

Figure 4.2

Teams work through basic stages to develop multimedia. **What happens during the implementation stage?**

 **Reading Check** **Recall** What positive qualities and behaviors should project team members possess?

Project Life Cycle		
Life Cycle Stage	**Job Duty**	**Team Members Actively Participating**
Analysis and Planning	• Meet with client • Set up budget • Research site's audience • Develop schedule for project milestones and deliverables • Set up quality assurance process	• Client representative • Project manager • Producer
Design and Development	• Determine structure or navigation • Develop content • Develop media • Plan layout and visual appearance	• Client representative, project manager, and producer • User interface designer • Motion designer • Graphic artist • Audio specialist and videographer • Writer and editor • Systems architect • Programmer • Quality assurance analyst
Testing	• Create quality assurance test plan • Finalize multimedia's alpha version • Evaluate alpha version • Finalize multimedia's beta (final test) version • Evaluate beta version • Report bugs	• Client representative, project manager, and producer • Systems architect • Programmer • Quality assurance analyst
Implementation	• Deliver finished product • Publicize multimedia	• Client representative, project manager, and producer • Systems architect and programmer
Evaluation and Maintenance	• Complete quality assurance tests • Assess finished product • Fix problems and make improvements • Update content	• Client representative, project manager, and producer • Writer and editor • Programmer • Quality assurance analyst

Analyze and Plan
What aspects of a project does a project plan define?

Developing multimedia begins with the analysis and planning stage. During this stage, you organize your ideas and determine what you want the project to do and what it will include. Identifying the format, size, and complexity of a multimedia project will help you determine the resources and the amount of time needed to complete the project. A **project plan** defines the purpose, audience, technical needs, and design needs of a project. A multimedia project plan should:

- define the project's purpose and goals.
- identify the project's target audience.
- include the project's mission statement.

Define the Purpose and Goals

How you develop your multimedia project depends on the purpose of the project and the people who will view or use the final production. Most multimedia projects are developed for people or businesses, also called clients. A successful project plan **analyzes**, or determines the nature of, the client's reasons for doing the project. For example, imagine you are a developer meeting with the owner of a health club. The health club wants to create a new on-air radio ad. The project plan should outline the client's needs and wants and define what you need to do to meet the client's goals. Questions for the client may include:

- What are the specific goals for the ad?
- Who is the audience for the ad?
- What is the budget for the ad, and when will it need to be completed?
- Who is my point of contact for approval and how often does the contact want status updates?

As you develop the project plan, you will answer each of these questions. The answers will help you identify the specific objectives for the project. **Objectives** are the items you must complete to meet the project's goals. For example, an objective for an educational Web site for very young children, as shown in Figure 4.3, might be to include music or audio that appeals to this age group when the Web site first loads, brightly colored graphics that are picture-based, and information for parents.

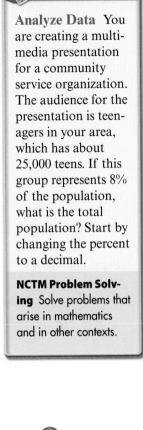
● **Figure 4.3**
The purpose and goals of a project help you identify the project's objectives. **How might the objectives differ if this Web site was targeted to teenagers?**

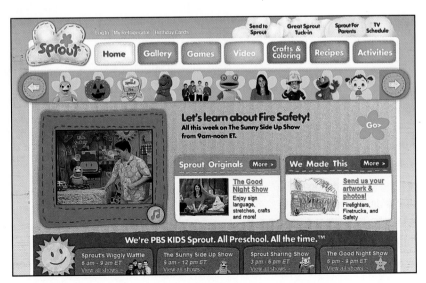

Audience The content of a multimedia presentation should reflect the needs of the audience. A presentation, for example, might include personal stories to engage interest. Examine a government Web site. Write a paragraph summarizing the audience that the site is targeting.

NCTE 3 Apply strategies and interpret texts.

Identify Target Audience

After you have identified the goals for your multimedia project, you must define the project's target audience. Your **target audience** is the group of people who will use or view the multimedia production you are creating. For example, if you are creating a multimedia presentation for an English class, your target audience will probably be the students in your class, as well as your teacher.

If you are developing a Web site about nutrition and fitness, as another example, your multimedia project might have to address the needs of a much broader audience. The site's target audience might include visitors of both sexes in a wide-ranging age group. It must appeal to visitors who know a lot about good nutrition and exercise, as well as visitors who do not know anything about nutrition and fitness. To help determine the wants and needs of your target audience, ask yourself questions similar to those listed in Figure 4.4.

Determine a Target Audience for a Multimedia Project

Question	Hint
What characteristics do the members of my target audience have in common?	• What is the target age group? • How are members of the target audience alike? • Consider their interests and skills, where they live, and other factors.
How do I want my audience to use my multimedia project?	• Consider how you want your multimedia project to appeal to your target audience. • Create targeted content and designs that are appropriate for the age group and the context of the project.
How does my target audience want to use the multimedia project?	• Consider the wants and needs of your target audience, as well as the wants and needs of your client. • Survey potential members of your target audience to find out how they use similar multimedia products.
How will my target audience access the multimedia project?	• Will most users have a high-speed Internet connection? Will users access the multimedia using a smartphone or personal digital assistant? • Consider methods for creating multimedia that your entire audience can access and use easily.
Should my project include special features?	• Consider colors or graphics that are accessible for visually impaired or color-blind users. • Include features that show sensitivity and respect for other cultures. Avoid American slang, for example.

Figure 4.4 Defining your target audience is an essential step in multimedia development. **Why is it important to identify the target audience?**

Create a Mission Statement

Once you have identified the multimedia project's purpose and target audience, you are ready to write your mission statement. A **mission statement** is a brief statement that describes the purpose and audience of your project. The mission statement helps you determine what content and components to include in your project. This statement is the foundation for your project as you move on to the design and development stages. You should refer to your mission statement frequently as you continue to design and develop your multimedia production. This will help you stay on target.

For example, a tri-fold brochure for a local theatre company provides information about the upcoming season's performances. The theatre company also wants to promote a Summer Youth program that introduces children and teens to theatre and the dramatic arts. Imagine that this print brochure has not yet been developed. It is your job to create it. To write a mission statement, ask yourself questions like those listed in Figure 4.5. Consider your audience, your goals, and assumptions you may be making about your audience. Your mission statement should address these assumptions.

Project Management It is common for projects to get off track. Review your project plan regularly to make sure that the project still meets its purpose and goals.

 **Describe** What information is essential to a project plan?

Figure 4.5
A mission statement is a reminder of the project's purpose. How might the mission statement differ if the theatre company offered a special program for season ticket holders?

Problem		Solution
What is the purpose of this brochure?		• To provide general information about the theatre company • To provide specific information about the upcoming season's performances and the Summer Youth program
What are the brochure's immediate goals?		• To supply general theatre information • To provide performance and Summer Youth information
What are the brochure's long-term goals?		• To expand awareness of the theatre company • To encourage people to order tickets for performances • To encourage participation in the Summer Youth program
Who is the target audience?		• Theatre members, theatre patrons, adults, and young adults • The audience will receive the brochure via mail or by picking it up in the theatre lobby

Mission Statement
The theatre company brochure will promote the awareness of the theatre company by providing performance and program information.

Caution Research the multimedia tools you will need ahead of time to make sure your budget is as accurate as possible.

Determine and Evaluate Project Scope

What factors define the scope of a project?

During the analysis and planning stage, the project manager works closely with the client to analyze the project's design and development in detail. The project manager and client define the **deliverables**, or the actual multimedia elements the team will submit. At this time, the project's scope is developed. The **scope** is the set of features and content the project will include. The project team must balance the desired content and features against the time, money, and other resources available. The team must determine what can realistically be accomplished.

The project manager may present a proposal or sketches so that the client can visualize the project's elements and structure. To define the scope of a project, you must set priorities and make decisions about the project's budget, content delivery format, and schedule. Omitting some content or features is often necessary to avoid exceeding the project's budget or missing its deadline.

Budget

A client or organization must determine what financial and human resources they will need for a project. A budget defines the total amount of financial resources available for multimedia development. Budgets help to define the scope of the project. For example, an organization may want to create a database that can provide personalized recommendations to customers. However, their Web site budget may limit the site to providing just basic product information. Or, a business may decide to create a one-page flyer or opt for black and white because it will be less expensive than a full-color brochure with multiple pages.

Businesses must also decide whether to use in-house employees to help with the development of the multimedia. A business must consider the cost to purchase and deploy the software or other multimedia development tools needed to develop the project, as well as the cost to deploy and run the multimedia itself. For example, a company's server and telecommunications lines may not be able to handle the amount of customer traffic that an e-commerce Web site will receive. The company must determine whether the cost of a new server and telecommunications lines are within their budget before hiring a developer to create an online store for their Web site.

Content Delivery

Whether you are developing a slide presentation of a book report for your English class or creating a radio ad for a client's business, you must determine the best way to deliver the project to your audience. A deliverable is the final format your project will take. There are two things to consider when deciding on a deliverable format:

- tools you have to create the project
- tools the target audience has to receive the project

The technical requirements of your project depend on a combination of the multimedia production's purpose and the hardware and software needed to create and use it. For example, if you are giving a book report and would like to show a video clip from a movie based on the book you have read, you would need presentation software to create and use the video clip.

There are two main categories of deliverables. Each category has its own set of technical needs and requirements to consider.

Print Media When developing print multimedia, you need to consider the tools you need to create and deliver the physical document. For example, if you are creating a flyer for a holiday food drive, you may need word processing or presentation software that allows you to create a layout that will work well on the printed page, and a scanner to upload and add a logo. Some print media can also be viewed digitally (see Figure 4.6).

Digital Media When developing digital multimedia, the hardware, operating systems, and networks the application will run on must be considered, as well as the tools needed to create the multimedia itself. Size limitations are a factor and are often determined by the hardware and software used to deliver them. As you determine the scope of the project, you will need to consider the Internet connection speeds of various devices, such as cell phones or smartphones.

Will a training application, for example, be offered on a CD that does not require an Internet connection? Devices with small screens will limit the amount of content that can be displayed at one time. For example, you are creating a Web site for movie fans. The site will have the latest releases, movie reviews, and movie times at various theaters. You want to make sure viewers can download your site and the movie times from their cell phones. To do this, you must limit the size of your Web site. Figure 4.6 shows an example of a newsletter that can be viewed digitally or printed.

The Development Process The process of creating a multimedia presentation is similar to developing and completing an academic project. Multimedia designers brainstorm, outline, research, create drafts, and revise their work just as you do when writing a report for a class. Write a paragraph explaining how developing a report is similar to determining a multimedia project's purpose and goals.

NCTE 5 Use different writing process elements to communicate effectively.

Figure 4.6
A newsletter can be published in print or in a digital format. What are some other deliverables you can think of for a print project?

Time Line and Schedule

When the project's scope and budget are clear, you can create a schedule and time line for developing your project. Project managers are responsible for determining a multimedia project's schedule. The schedule identifies the milestones for building, testing, and implementing the project as well as the order in which these tasks must take place and a final date for completion.

Project managers often determine milestone due dates by working backwards from the completion date. Milestones are the important dates you need to hit to move your project forward. Creating a detailed schedule and timeline task list makes it easier to determine how long particular stages of the project will take to complete.

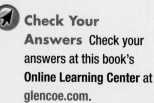

YOU TRY IT

Activity 4A Create a Multimedia Project Plan

1 At the top of a new document key: Museum Slideshow Content Plan. Navigate to your data files for this chapter. Locate and open the data file **ProjectPlan.doc**.

2 Use the information in the data file to create a project plan for a slide show promoting the museum's benefit auction. The project plan should be less than one page.

3 Proofread your project plan. Save and close your file.

Reading Check **Recall** What is a deliverable?

Section 4.1 After You Read

Review Key Concepts

1. Identify the elements you would include in a project plan.

2. Explain Why is it important to identify your target audience for a multimedia project?

Check Your Answers Check your answers at this book's **Online Learning Center** at glencoe.com.

Practice Academic Skills

English Language Arts

3. Analyze Write an essay describing why you should develop a project plan before creating a multimedia project.

4. Conclude Write a short essay in which you describe what might happen if you fail to identify your target audience for a multimedia project.

NCTE 12 Use language to accomplish individual purposes.

NCTE 4 Use written language to communicate effectively.

Online Student Manual • glencoe.com

Go to your Online Student Manual and enter your password to find projects that allow you to practice and apply multimedia skills.

Reading Guide

Before You Read

Helpful Memory Tools As you read, look for opportunities to use acronyms to help you remember information. For example, each letter in the acronym HOMES stands for one of the five Great Lakes.

Read to Learn

Key Concepts

- **Explain** the types of navigation schemes.
- **Outline** the best navigation scheme for a multimedia project.
- **Summarize** the functions of storyboards and mock-ups.
- **Describe** the steps in the development stage of a multimedia project.

Main Idea

The design stage of a multimedia project includes determining the navigation scheme and visual presentation. The development stage involves creating the project's various media elements and integrating all components.

Content Vocabulary

◇ navigation scheme

◇ storyboard

◇ mock-up

Academic Vocabulary

You will find these words in your reading and on your tests. Use the glossary to look up their definitions, if necessary.

◆ specific

◆ flexible

Graphic Organizer

As you read, identify the four main types of navigation schemes. Under each scheme, list one fact about the scheme. Use a diagram like the one below to organize your thoughts.

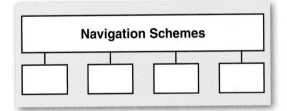

Navigation Schemes

 Graphic Organizer Go to the book's **Online Learning Center** at **glencoe.com** to print this graphic organizer.

Academic Standards

 English Language Arts

NCTE 4 Use written language to communicate effectively.

NCTE 5 Use different writing process elements to communicate effectively.

NCTE 12 Use language to accomplish individual purposes.

NCTE National Council of Teachers of English
NSES National Science Education Standards

NCTM National Council of Teachers of Mathematics
NCSS National Council for the Social Studies

As You Read

Connect How is navigating similar to giving someone directions to your house?

Design the Structure of Multimedia

Why is navigation important in a multimedia production?

Most Web sites, from large corporate sites to smaller personal sites, include certain basic elements on every page. Logos, page headers, page footers, and navigation links help visitors use a Web site. These elements also produce a consistent, user-friendly appearance. As another example, most newsletters contain a masthead (a graphic at the top of the page), body text, and headlines or titles. Some newsletters also contain a table of contents, subheads, and bylines. These standard elements help readers find and use information.

Once you know the goals and audience of a multimedia project, you can begin planning its structure and the relationships among elements. Multimedia that works well helps users navigate, or find their way through the multimedia project. The **navigation scheme** is the plan that defines how the elements of a multimedia project relate to each other. Types of navigation schemes are show in Figure 4.7

When choosing a navigation scheme, think about how users will interact with the multimedia. Will they go directly to **specific**, or particular, topics? Will they access information in a specific order? There are four main navigation schemes: linear, hierarchical, non-linear, and composite. Each scheme has particular uses and advantages.

Figure 4.7

The four types of navigation schemes. Which scheme arranges content in a hierarchical or linear structure through parts of a production, but allows a user to move in any direction through other parts?

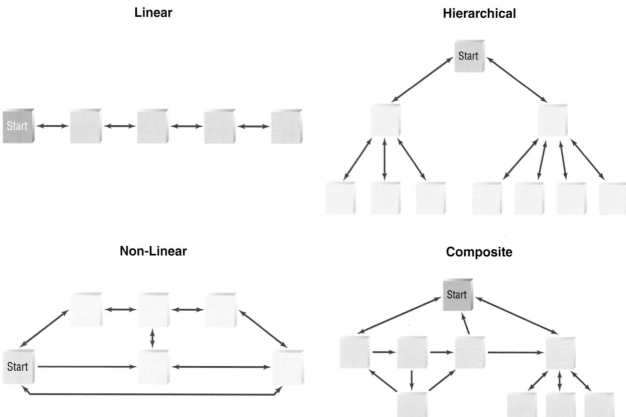

Types of Navigation Schemes

Linear

Hierarchical

Non-Linear

Composite

The structure and navigation of a successful multimedia project support the project's mission statement, meet the project's goals, and appeal to the project's target audience. Viewing your project from the audience's perspective can help you develop multimedia that the audience will enjoy using. Understanding how users are likely to move through your multimedia project will help you design navigation that lets them find information easily.

Linear Navigation Scheme

In a linear navigation scheme, every page or screen display exists at the same level. Each page in this scheme is accessed from the previous page, moving from one page to the next. A visitor navigates linear multimedia by moving sequentially through a line of pages or screen displays, one after another—the same way you read a book.

Multimedia that uses a linear navigation scheme usually has a starting point that the user accesses or sees first. The user must then move in a specific order and is limited to going forward or backward. A linear scheme is useful for stepping through a process, such as baking a loaf of bread. Most print multimedia and slide presentations use linear navigation.

Hierarchical Navigation Scheme

A hierarchical navigation scheme arranges pages, display screens, or other elements of a multimedia production in levels from top to bottom, much like the branches of a tree. In order to move from the top level to the bottom level, the user must move down one level at a time. Hierarchical navigation can contain multiple levels depending on the content. Lower levels typically contain more specific information about the topic. Figure 4.8 illustrates how content in a hierarchical structure can be organized.

Academic Focus

English Language Arts

Create an Outline
A hierarchical navigation scheme organizes information into levels, similar to an outline. The most general information is always at the top. The more detailed information appears at lower levels. Write an outline of this section. The outline should have a hierarchical structure.

NCTE 12 Use language to accomplish individual purposes.

● **Figure 4.8**
Web pages in a hierarchical navigation scheme are arranged in levels. Which page is always at the top in a hierarchical navigation scheme?

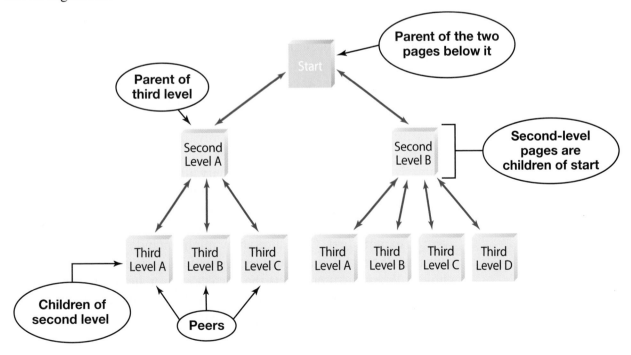

Go Online ACTIVITY
glencoe.com

Explore Navigation Schemes **Find out more about different navigation schemes for multimedia at the Online Learning Center. Go to glencoe.com. Choose Activities, then Chapter 4.**

The home page, or starting point, is at the top or highest level of the structure. The home page contains links to the pages below it, on the second level. Pages that are all on the same level are often referred to as same-level pages. The second-level pages contain links to third-level pages. You can access any of the second-level pages from the start page. However, you can only get to third-level pages from a second-level page.

A page that is connected to a page one level below it has a parent-child relationship with that page. In this relationship, the page that is on the level above is the parent, and the page that is on the level below is the child. A parent may have many children, but in a hierarchical scheme, each child may only have one parent. Two or more child pages with the same parent have a peer-to-peer relationship, which is also called a "sibling" relationship.

A hierarchical navigation scheme has specific advantages.

- Users get an overview quickly by examining the start, home, or top-level page.

- Users can then move from the top level to the pages or content that interests them.

- This ability to move around prevents users from becoming overwhelmed by information they already know or do not want.

- With this scheme, users can also track where they are in relation to the start.

Non-Linear Navigation Scheme

In a non-linear navigation scheme, users can navigate randomly through multimedia content in any order they choose. Non-linear navigation allows users to choose the direction in which they want to go. With no predetermined sequence, non-linear navigation may cause confusion, or distract the audience from the multimedia's purpose. It is important for a project that uses non-linear organization to remain focused on the goals and needs of its audience. Non-linear navigation is less common.

Instead of focusing on how users are expected to move through the presentation, non-linear content is organized based on relationships between content. Non-linear navigation is useful for multimedia projects where organizing a lot of constantly changing information is necessary. Users are encouraged to navigate to only the parts of the production that are of interest to them. Non-linear navigation can add interest and interactivity to multimedia. Interactivity allows the user to perform an action to which the multimedia will respond.

For example, a non-linear slide show might include slides that have several links to explore, allowing the user to choose which content they want to explore first. Or, a slide show might include a multiple-choice quiz near the end that encourages users to select an answer from several choices. When the user selects the correct answer, he or she can move on to the next question. If the user selects the wrong answer, he or she can either go back and try again or navigate to and review a specific part of the presentation.

Composite Navigation

With a composite navigation scheme (sometimes called a mixed structure), users can navigate freely in any direction (as in non-linear navigation) but are constrained to a hierarchical or linear structure for part of the material or application. Figure 4.9 shows an example of a composite navigation in action.

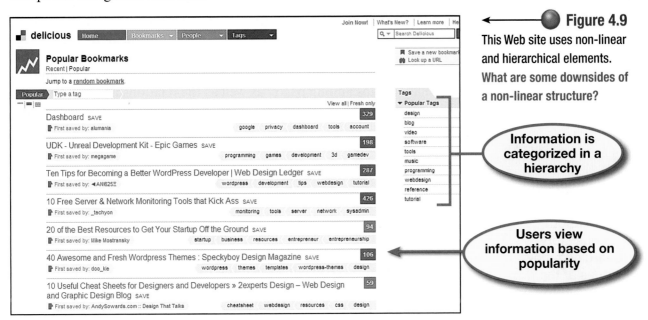

● **Figure 4.9**

This Web site uses non-linear and hierarchical elements. What are some downsides of a non-linear structure?

Information is categorized in a hierarchy

Users view information based on popularity

Many Web sites use a combination of hierarchical and linear navigation. For example, a Web site containing photographs from a vacation might let the visitor go directly to a specific photo (hierarchical) as well as see a slide show of the photos in the order in which they were posted (linear). Mixed structure can be very useful because it offers more than one way for users to access information. This structure makes multimedia **flexible**, or capable of changing to meet more than one purpose.

Once you have determined the navigation scheme for your multimedia project, you should map, or sketch, the pattern of navigation. Most multimedia projects use a navigation map, or flowchart, to visually illustrate how a user can move through the multimedia production. A navigation map is usually based on the rough outline or description of content that the project manager developed with the client during initial discussions about the project plan. A navigation map provides an overall look at the contents of your multimedia project and helps you see whether your ideas will work well before you begin creating the actual pages.

Earlier in this chapter, you created a project plan for a slide show promoting a museum's benefit auction. In the following activity, you will map the navigation structure for the slide show.

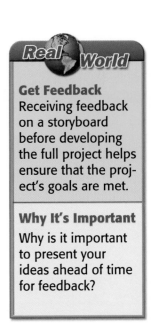

Real World

Get Feedback
Receiving feedback on a storyboard before developing the full project helps ensure that the project's goals are met.

Why It's Important
Why is it important to present your ideas ahead of time for feedback?

Reading Check

List What are the four main navigation schemes for multimedia productions?

Create a Storyboard or Mock-up

How can storyboarding help you visualize the final product?

After you have mapped the navigation for your project, you will develop a storyboard that shows the content of all pages, screen displays, or slides. A **storyboard** is a visual representation of a multimedia project. Storyboarding helps you see whether your ideas will work before you begin developing multimedia. It also helps verify that you have chosen the best navigation scheme. If your navigation scheme does not work well, you will need to make revisions to your storyboard.

Storyboarding illustrates your project's organization by showing the relationships among pages, as well as the relationships among the elements on each page. You should know what navigation scheme your project will use before you begin creating a storyboard. If you are not sure which navigation scheme you will use, you can brainstorm what you want users to see, as well as the order in which you want them to see it. You can even create more than one storyboard.

Many developers find it helpful to sketch their ideas on paper. As you become more familiar with multimedia design and development, and as your projects become more complex, you will learn which approach works better for you: sketching on paper or diagramming on a computer. It is sometimes helpful for designers to use this time to brainstorm some of the written content of the project. They may develop catch phrases or slogans, for example. It is also common to experiment with multiple storyboards, each with unique changes, such as logos or various color schemes.

Some designers use computer software to create a mock-up, or prototype, of a multimedia project. A **mock-up** is a working model of the production's screen designs and navigation elements. A mock-up is helpful because it represents how the layout will look on the published page, and even how pages will link to each other.

In the following You Try It activity, you will storyboard and create a slide show for a museum's benefit auction.

YOU TRY IT

Activity 4B Create a Storyboard

1. Open a new word processing document. At the top of the page, write or key Benefit Auction Storyboard. Underneath this, key Linear Scheme.

2. On a separate document or piece of paper, key Benefit Auction Storyboard. Underneath this, key Composite Scheme.

3. Using the information provided in Figure 4.10 on page 113, map both linear and composite navigation schemes. For each navigation scheme, be sure to include each slide's title in a box and draw lines showing the relationships among slides.

4. Consider how the multimedia elements you might include will impact your choices.

5 If necessary, create multiple variations of the storyboard. For example, if you include a video about the museum, clickable graphics with descriptions of the auction items, or a form guests can fill out to make a bid, all of these elements may impact the order in which slides are viewed.

6 Evaluate both charts to determine which structure will work better for the auction slide show. Write a paragraph that explains which choice you prefer and why.

7 Save and close your file.

Benefit Auction Slide Show Presentation	
Slide Title	**Brief Description**
The Museum Benefit Auction	Welcomes the auction attendees and serves as a jumping-off point to other pages.
About Us	Describes the purpose of the benefit auction.
Auction Schedule	Lists schedule of auction events (preview silent auction bidding, appetizers, dinner, auction, desserts, etc.)
Sponsors	Lists sponsors for the auction and explains what the proceeds support (children's art education programs at the museum).
Contact Us	Includes membership information and contact information for the museum.

Figure 4.10
Use this table to map possible navigation schemes for your presentation.

 **Reading Check** **Paraphrase** What is a storyboard?

Multimedia Development

How are elements integrated during the multimedia development stage?

Once the project plan and the storyboards have been approved by the client, you are ready to create, or develop, your multimedia production. This stage is called development. Multimedia development involves locating, creating, and editing the multimedia components. These components might include text, graphics, animation, audio, and video. The development stage also involves bringing all of these elements together into a unified system of pages or screen displays. It is important at this stage to make sure that the elements work well together.

As just mentioned, producing multimedia involves integrating, or putting together, all of the components of a project. Following the project plan, you must incorporate text, graphics, animation, audio, and video, as appropriate, into pages or screen displays. For digital media, this step includes creating hyperlinks so that users can move from one location of a multimedia production to another according to the navigation map.

Project Management It is important to have your project evaluated. Make sure you have enough time to review the feedback you receive and to make the appropriate revisions.

You might produce multimedia using XHTML, a Web design program, a presentation program, or a multimedia authoring tool, depending on the project. A multimedia authoring tool is software used to create multimedia productions that integrate text, graphics, animation, audio, and video. The most widely used multimedia authoring tool is Adobe® Director®. Figure 4.11 shows an example of an integrated multimedia Web site.

Multimedia must help meet the project's goals and overall purpose. As you plan a project, think about each type of multimedia element and how it effectively enhances the user's experience.

Figure 4.11
The development stage of a project brings all of the multimedia components into a final form. **Why is evaluation important in the multimedia development process?**

YOU TRY IT

Activity 4C Create a Slide Show

1. Open the storyboard that you created in You Try It Activity 4B. Using what you know about the relationships among elements on each slide, as well as the relationships among the slides, create a slide show.

2. Using presentation software, plan the content, design, and layout for the presentation. Use the information in Figure 4.12 on page 115 to help plan the slide show.

3. Think of a catch phrase for the benefit auction. Include this catch phrase with the name of the museum on the first slide.

4. Identify the text, colors, and graphics you plan to use, and estimate where you would place the content on the page.

⑤ Write the content for the slides. Consider the audience, assumptions, and goals of the presentation. Avoid propaganda methods for persuading viewers. Figure 4.12 shows an example slide of the presentation.

⑥ Save and close your file.

Slide Show Presentation Storyboard Tasks

Target Audience	Describe your target audience.
Slides	List the slides you will include in your slide show.
Color Scheme	Describe the color scheme you will use in your slide show.
Actions	List the actions you would like to occur when you click or hover over an object or element.
Slide Layout	• Plan your slide layout design. • List the number of graphics to be included. • Describe how you will transition from slide to slide. • Determine how much text you will include on each slide.

Figure 4.12
Storyboarding helps you keep track of the important tasks that are necessary for developing an organized presentation.

 **Reading Check**

Identify What elements might be integrated during the development stage of a multimedia project?

Section 4.2 After You Read

Review Key Concepts

1. **List** the steps of the design and development stages of a multimedia project.

2. **Identify** the uses and advantages of different navigation schemes for a multimedia production.

Check Your Answers Check your answers at this book's Online Learning Center through glencoe.com.

Practice Academic Skills

English Language Arts

3. **Evaluate** Write a paragraph describing how the navigation scheme affects the development of a project. How does navigation contribute to the effectiveness of multimedia? What happens if navigation is difficult?

4. **Compare and Contrast** Write a one-page essay in which you compare and contrast the roles and functions of navigation maps, storyboards, and mock-ups in multimedia design and development.

Online Student Manual • glencoe.com

Go to your Online Student Manual and enter your password to find projects that allow you to practice and apply multimedia skills.

NCTE 5 Use different writing process elements to communicate effectively.

NCTE 4 Use written language to communicate effectively.

Reading Guide

Before You Read

Prepare with a Partner Read the headings in this section to a partner and ask each other questions about the topics that will be discussed. Write down the questions. As you read, answer the questions you have identified.

Read to Learn

Key Concepts

- **Describe** strategies for successfully testing a multimedia project.

- **Identify** ways of implementing a project.

- **Summarize** the importance of properly evaluating and maintaining a project.

Main Idea

After the components of a multimedia project have been integrated, the product is tested to make sure it looks and works as desired. The finished product is then implemented, or delivered to the audience. Finally, the project is evaluated and updated as necessary.

Content Vocabulary

◇ alpha test
◇ accessibility
◇ implementation
◇ evaluation
◇ maintenance

Academic Vocabulary

You will find these words in your reading and on your tests. Use the glossary to look up their definitions, if necessary.

◆ accurate ◆ edit

Graphic Organizer

As you read, identify factors to consider when testing multimedia. Use a diagram like the one below to help organize your information.

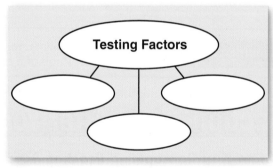

Testing Factors

 Graphic Organizer Go to this book's **Online Learning Center** at **glencoe.com** to print this graphic organizer.

Academic Standards

 English Language Arts

NCTE 4 Use written language to communicate effectively.

NCTE 5 Use different writing process elements to communicate effectively.

NCTE National Council of Teachers of English
NSES National Science Education Standards

NCTM National Council of Teachers of Mathematics
NCSS National Council for the Social Studies

Multimedia Testing

Why is it important to test your multimedia project?

As You Read

Connect Why is it important to check your work before submitting it?

After all the pieces of a multimedia project have been integrated, the finished product must be tested to ensure that it displays and functions as desired. An **alpha test** is used to check that an application runs correctly, is free of errors, and is easy for the audience to use. For an elaborate project, alpha testing may include quality assurance (QA). Quality assurance involves testing the computer code that underlies an application to ensure that it runs correctly and performs as expected.

Many programmers, writers, graphic artists, and others who contribute during the development stage test their work continuously and correct any problems they find. When all the components are brought together, more testing is needed to make sure the combined multimedia elements are **accurate**, or free from error, and work well together.

It is important to do a thorough check for a variety of potential problems, including:

- graphics or video clips that appear pixilated or have difficulty downloading or playing.
- hyperlinks that do not work, including links to Web sites that no longer exist.
- prompts that fail to appear.
- spelling or grammatical errors in the content.
- accessibility issues for people with disabilities.

Accessibility enables people with different needs to access and use multimedia resources. To make multimedia products accessible, it is important to present information in as many ways as you can. This allows people with difficulty seeing, hearing, or moving to access the project. In Chapter 5, you will learn about the federal law that developers must follow in order to make multimedia accessible. During the testing stage of a project, check that the following steps have been taken to make multimedia accessible:

- A script has been provided with audio
- Alternative text descriptions, which tools called text readers can convert to audio, have been provided for visual information
- There are controls for pausing video streaming
- Text is readable and there is enough contrast between the content and the background
- Color has not been used as the only cue that users should click an element
- Elements can be accessed using the keyboard, and not just the mouse

The testing stage of a multimedia project also includes checking that the customer's needs and wants have been met. You should also make sure that visual elements look good and are used consistently. Visual elements might include text, graphics, colors, backgrounds, and navigation buttons. The principles of visual design in multimedia are covered in more detail in Chapter 5.

You Should Know
Before alpha testing your multimedia, create a list of everything you want to check. Use your checklist as you are testing, to guarantee accuracy.

Proofreading is crucial during testing because misspelled words create a negative impression. No matter how informative the content is or how appealing the project's graphics, audio, and video components are, misspellings and other errors make the developer seem careless. It is important to **edit**, or revise and correct, your project. Clean, error-free content creates a positive impression.

The spell check function of word processors is a useful tool for proofreading, but you cannot rely on it alone. For example, if you key "hare" when you mean "hair," the spell check function will not catch the error because the wrong word is spelled correctly. Careful proofreading includes reading the text word for word and correcting any errors you find.

After revisions are made based on the alpha test, multimedia may undergo a final beta test, or beta review. During the beta review, the development team checks that the errors found during the alpha test have been fixed and that there are no new errors or concerns. The beta version may also be shown to untrained users from the target audience to make sure it is ready for general use. The usability test, sometimes called a "pilot project," confirms that the audience can utilize the user interface without difficulty. A project may not undergo beta testing if it is small, or if the schedule and budget do not allow it.

Figure 4.13 identifies several factors you should consider when testing multimedia.

Figure 4.13
You must continually test your components as you work through your project. Why is testing needed to make sure that the project works correctly?

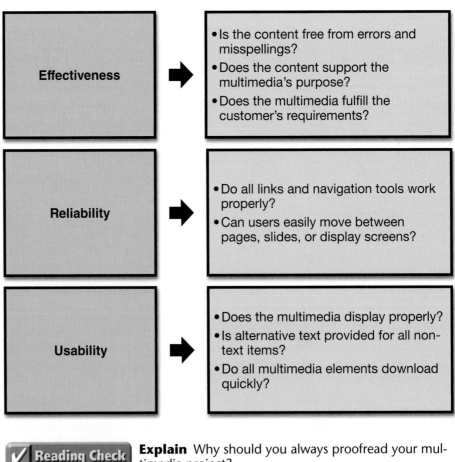

Effectiveness
- Is the content free from errors and misspellings?
- Does the content support the multimedia's purpose?
- Does the multimedia fulfill the customer's requirements?

Reliability
- Do all links and navigation tools work properly?
- Can users easily move between pages, slides, or display screens?

Usability
- Does the multimedia display properly?
- Is alternative text provided for all non-text items?
- Do all multimedia elements download quickly?

✔ Reading Check **Explain** Why should you always proofread your multimedia project?

Multimedia Implementation

How is a completed project made available to the target audience?

Once a project's testing is complete, it is ready for implementation. **Implementation**, sometimes called "roll-out," is the stage in which the finished project is delivered to the audience. You can implement your project only after resolving all the problems that turned up during testing. Implementation can take many forms, such as:

- Uploading the multimedia to a Web server for Internet use.

- Installing the multimedia on a network server, where it becomes available to authorized users. For example, you might upload a Web-based training program for employees in a company's shipping department. As another example, you might upload a multimedia sales presentation or e-commerce application to a kiosk.

- Recording the multimedia on a removable disk, and then creating and distributing copies of the disk. For example, if you develop computer-based training (CBT), you might burn the application onto CDs or DVDs for distribution.

Implementation often involves installing hardware or customizing an application so that it works with a customer's server and other equipment. It can also involve training the customer's employees. This stage includes any steps necessary to make the completed project available for the intended audience to view or use.

 **List** What are three possible methods for implementing a multimedia project?

Evaluation and Maintenance

Why should you always evaluate your completed multimedia project?

After you have completed and implemented your multimedia project, your work is not done. All the components that make up your multimedia production must be evaluated and modified accordingly. These components include text, graphics, animation, audio, video, user interface design, and programming.

Evaluation refers to the process of judging how effective your multimedia project is. When you deliver the finished product, ask for feedback from the client and audience. Expect to get both positive and negative comments during the evaluation stage. It is important not to be defensive if you receive feedback that you feel is unimportant or negative. Quite often, clients just want to state their opinions and know you are listening. Document this input and learn from it, because it can help improve your next project.

Any work that takes place after implementation occurs in the maintenance stage. **Maintenance** refers to the regular care needed to

keep your multimedia production up-to-date and working properly. Depending on the needs of the project, maintenance may include diagnosing and repairing hardware and software issues, or replacing or backing up critical data. Maintenance might also include incorporating feedback from the client and users that has been gathered during the evaluation stage (see Figure 4.14).

Most multimedia requires maintenance to remain useful. If a project contains hyperlinks, they must be checked frequently to make sure they still work. Maintenance also includes adding or updating content and deleting old information. For example, a video may require a newer version of the Flash plug-in, or the client may decide to offer users the opportunity to download a demo from the Internet instead of distributing the demo on CDs or DVDs.

Figure 4.14

During the evaluation and maintenance stage, updates and improvements are made based on user feedback. Why is a successful project never "finished?"

It is common to have a few errors in a finished project. An evaluation and maintenance plan can help eliminate these errors. In order for evaluation and maintenance to be successful, all people responsible for updating and maintaining the multimedia production must follow the same process.

Imagine you are ready to complete the final project stages for the museum's slide show. In the next activity, you will create a plan to test, implement, evaluate, and maintain the presentation.

YOU TRY IT

Activity 4D Create a Plan for the Final Stages of a Multimedia Project

1 Study Figure 4.15 on page 121, which is a checklist for the final three stages of a multimedia project. The figure lists questions to ask yourself during testing, implementing, evaluating, and maintaining a multimedia production.

2 Based on the information in Figure 4.15 on page 121, create a plan to test, implement, evaluate, and maintain the slide show you created in previous activities for a museum's benefit auction. For each of the three final stages of multimedia development, write a paragraph describing the steps you would take to address that stage. Remember to customize the information in the checklist to refer to the slide show for the museum's benefit auction

3 Proofread and spell-check your document.

4 Save and close your file.

Multimedia Project Stage Checklist

Figure 4.15
Use a checklist to help you complete the final stages of your project.

TEST

☑ Is the content free from factual, grammatical, and spelling errors?

☑ Does the content support the project's purpose and fulfill the client's needs?

☑ Does the multimedia production display properly?

☑ Do all links and navigational tools work correctly?

☑ Does every graphic, video, and page download quickly?

☑ Can users move easily between pages, slides, or display screens?

☑ Can users easily find the information they need?

☑ Have measures been taken to make the product accessible to people with disabilities?

IMPLEMENT

☑ Have all problems found during testing been fixed?

☑ Has the method of implementation been determined?

☑ Has the project been successfully rolled out to the audience?

EVALUATE AND MAINTAIN

☑ Have any errors noticed after implementation been fixed?

☑ Have feedback and updates been addressed, tracked, and documented?

☑ Are links still up-to-date?

☑ Has critical data been backed up?

☑ Have any hardware and software issues been diagnosed and addressed?

☑ Are performance statistics being monitored?

✔ Reading Check **Identify** List three tasks that take place during the maintenance stage.

Section 4.3 After You Read

Review Key Concepts

1. Identify three methods commonly used to implement a multimedia project.

2. Explain what happens in the evaluation stage of the multimedia development process.

 Check Your Answers Check your answers at this book's Online Learning Center through glencoe.com.

Practice Academic Skills

 English Language Arts

3. Analyze Write a paragraph that explains the three final stages for a multimedia project. Discuss the importance of each in the multimedia project life cycle.

4. Create Imagine you have just finished creating a personal Web page. Create a testing plan that explains the steps you will take to ensure your site will be viewed properly by Internet users.

 Online Student Manual • glencoe.com

Go to your Online Student Manual and enter your password to find projects that allow you to practice and apply multimedia skills.

NCTE 4 Use written language to communicate effectively.

NCTE 5 Use different writing process elements to communicate effectively.

Multimedia Accessibility

Multimedia products often include elements that can limit their usability for many people.

Design for Different Needs

Making multimedia content accessible to differently-abled users was not always a priority for multimedia developers. Yet such individuals make up an important segment of multimedia users. People may not be able to access multimedia for many reasons, including:

- physical disabilities or environments that make it difficult to see, hear, or understand visual or auditory elements.
- limited movement that restricts the use of input devices.
- poor language or technology skills.
- old technology and software or slow Internet connections.

Accessibility Guidelines

The World Wide Web Consortium (W3C) and Section 508 of the United States Rehabilitation Act provide guidelines for creating accessible multimedia. Some guidelines include the following.

- **Text Options** Provide text versions of graphics or audio. For example, if a photo of chili can be clicked to display a recipe, the text version might read "Recipe for making chili." Tools called text readers can convert this text to audio.

A graphic artist with limited mobility might be able to use a stylus to draw on a tablet.

- **Color** Make sure viewers can understand images without relying only on color. If foreground and background colors are too similar, it will be difficult for viewers to understand the information on the screen.
- **Input Devices** Design multimedia features that can be used with multiple input devices. For example, if a form control on a Web site can only be used with a mouse, it will limit use by people who must use voice recognition or non-pointing devices.

These technologies are likely to advance over time, making user interactions easier for those who might otherwise be excluded.

Skill Builder

1. Identify Find out what accessibility tools are available on your word processor, operating system, or authoring software. Make a chart listing at least five tools, the disabilities they address, their functions, and how to activate them.

2. Research Guidelines Use online resources to learn more about the accessibility guidelines issued by the W3C or Section 508 of the Rehabilitation Act. Create a checklist with additional guidelines for multimedia accessibility.

Chapter Summary

Creating multimedia often requires a team. Teams vary in size, but each member has specific responsibilities. He or she works with other team members to develop multimedia that meets the client's expectations.

The multimedia development life cycle includes the stages of analysis and planning, design and development, testing, implementation, and evaluation and maintenance. During analysis and planning, the multimedia developer works with the client to identify the project's purpose, goals, and audience. This informa-tion becomes the project plan. This stage also involves determining the project's scope, or the features and content the project can include given the delivery format and the time and resources available.

The design and development stage involves determining the navigation and visualizing the layout of a project, and developing and incorporating the text, audio, and visual components. The final stages of the process include testing and implementing the project, and evaluation and maintenance.

Vocabulary Review

1. On a sheet of paper, use ten of these content and vocabulary terms in a paragraph.

Content Vocabulary

◇ project plan (p. 101)
◇ objective (p. 101)
◇ target audience (p. 102)
◇ mission statement (p. 103)
◇ deliverable (p. 104)
◇ scope (p. 104)
◇ navigation scheme (p. 108)

◇ storyboard (p. 112)
◇ mock-up (p. 112)
◇ alpha test (p. 117)
◇ accessibility (p. 117)
◇ implementation (p. 119)
◇ evaluation (p. 119)
◇ maintenance (p. 119)

Academic Vocabulary

◆ comprehensive (p. 99)
◆ analyze (p. 101)
◆ specific (p. 109)
◆ flexible (p.111)
◆ accurate (p. 117)
◆ edit (p. 118)

Review Key Concepts

2. Identify the five stages of the project life cycle.

3. Explain the purpose of a project plan.

4. Determine a multimedia project's purpose, goals, and audience.

5. Explain how the scope of a multimedia project is determined.

6. List the four types of navigation schemes.

7. Discuss the usefulness of a navigation map and visualizing the layout of a project.

8. Summarize the functions of storyboards and mock-ups.

9. Describe the steps in the development stage of a multimedia project.

10. List strategies for successfully testing a multimedia project.

11. Identify ways of implementing a multimedia project.

12. Summarize the importance of evaluating and maintaining a multimedia project.

Critical Thinking

13. Identify Describe the three things that a project plan should always do. Use a graphic organizer like the one below to organize your answer. Explain why these three actions are important.

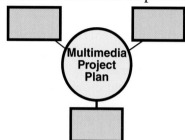

14. Analyze What factors should you consider when defining the project's purpose and goals? What factors should you consider when defining the project's scope, and why? Why is it important to consider what assumptions you are making about the audience?

15. Compare and Contrast What is the difference between a hierarchical and a linear navigation scheme? How are they similar? Use a Venn diagram to organize your thoughts.

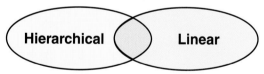

16. Illustrate the steps for designing and developing a multimedia project. Use a graphic organizer similar to the one below to help illustrate your answer. At what stages is the project manager's role important?

17. Evaluate Why do most developers use a linear navigation scheme when creating slide show presentations? Explain your answer. When would it make sense to consider a nonlinear navigation option?

18. Analyze The company you work for is behind schedule in developing a multimedia project for an important client. You are considering postponing the testing phase. List the pros and cons for this idea. Analyze how postponing testing might affect the intended outcome of the project. Develop a table or chart that illustrates and supports your thoughts.

19. Outline Create an outline of the stages of the development life cycle. In your outline, map out important milestones, including the development of the project plan, development of the navigation scheme, the creation of the storyboard, when the finished product is rolled out, and when feedback is received.

20. Evaluate In your opinion, which positiv work quality is most important to team success? Explain your opinion by providing an example.

Go Online e-RESOURCES

glencoe.com

Go to the **Online Learning Center** to find additional activities and career resources.

Practice Quizzes Test your knowledge of the material in this chapter.

Career Resources Find out more about careers, including information about résumés, portfolios, and interview and workplace tips.

Academic Connections

21. **English Language Arts–Write a Mission Statement**

NCTE 8 Use information resources to gather information and create and communicate knowledge.

A mission statement is a brief description of a multimedia project's purpose and target audience. The mission statement helps you identify essential content for your multimedia project and stay "on target" during the development process.

Use the Internet to research mission statements for non-profit organizations, such as the American Red Cross and United Way. You have been asked by an organization called Helping the Homeless to develop a postcard to help spread its mission and thank its top supporters.

A. What questions would you ask to better understand the organization's needs and the requirements of the project? Use your Internet research to determine how these questions might be answered. Use a table like the one below to organize the information.

B. Using the mission statements from your research as models, create a mission statement for the project. The statement should be one or two sentences long, clearly state the purpose of the organization, and describe the target audience.

C. Use the mission statement to brainstorm which images you might include in the postcard. When considering possible images, consider your assumptions about the audience, as well as propaganda techniques that might be used to influence the audience. Proofread and edit your project.

Question	Answer
Mission Statement	

Standardized Test Practice

Short Answer

Read the paragraph below and then answer the questions.

The applications in a software suite are designed to work together smoothly. Suites use consistent menus, icons, and other user interface features across programs so that if users are familiar with one program they can quickly learn to use the others. The price of a suite is less than the combined prices of the individual programs sold separately. It is economical for multimedia developers to buy software suites if they need multiple programs to create and manage their projects.

22. Based on the paragraph above, answer the following questions. Write your answers using complete sentences.

A. If you are familiar with one program in a software suite, explain why you should be able to learn other programs in the suite fairly quickly.

B. Why is it more economical to purchase software suites if you will need multiple programs to design and develop a multimedia project?

Test-Taking Tip When responding to a short-answer question, write as neatly as possible. Double-check your grammar, spelling, and punctuation. Neatly written answers often get higher scores.

23. Analyze Your Target Audience

NETS 4c Collect and analyze data to identify solutions and/or make informed decisions.

You have been asked to develop a Web site for a local garden club. The club wants the Web site to contain information and activities for visitors in all age groups—children, young adults, and adults. To develop the best possible Web site, you need to research existing Web sites that have been created with different age groups in mind.

A. With your teacher's approval, visit some Web sites that have been created for different age groups, such as local museums. As you examine the Web sites, analyze how they deal with the following: color (muted, bright, primary); text (size, font, color); photos (size, placement, age of people in photos); graphics (size, placement, animation); content (density, or how much on each page); and navigation (linear, hierarchical, non-linear, composite).

B. Record your data in a table similar to the one below. Analyze the data you collect. Use the data to determine how you will plan the garden club's Web site. Write a one-page essay describing how the Web site will address the needs and interests of each age group (children, young adults, and adults). Explain why a developer must assess the needs of each age group in the target audience when deciding how to present information on a Web site. What might happen if a developer did not do this? Proofread and edit your essay.

	Children	**Young Adults**	**Adults**
Color			
Text			
Photos			
Graphics			
Content			
Navigation			

24. Create a Multimedia Development Presentation

NETS 2b Communicate information and ideas effectively to multiple audiences using a variety of media and formats.

Your supervisor has decided that there is no money in the budget to hire an outside developer to handle the development of a multimedia project. She asks you to create a presentation to train in-house employees on the multimedia development process, specifically the following steps: developing the multimedia components (such as text, graphics, animation, audio, and video) and integrating the components into the final product.

A. Use presentation software to develop a multimedia tutorial to teach this information to your coworkers.

B. Be sure to consider all of the following: purpose, goals, objectives, target audience, mission statement, design, delivery format, text, graphics, animation, audio, video, and programming or production. Proofread and edit your project.

25. Get Organized

You have been asked to develop a kiosk for the after-school club Academic Boosters. The purpose of the club is to help college-bound students prepare for the challenges of taking academic courses at the college level. The club wants the kiosk to contain text, photos, video, and audio to stimulate interest among the high-school-aged audience at the school's next career day.

A. You know how to plan the project from analysis to delivery of the finished product. But how do you organize your work as you go? How will you keep track of all of the components of the project? Will you store everything on the computer? Will you create a spreadsheet to track all components of the project? Consider the components: project plan, display, text files, photographs, audio files, and video files.

B. Write a half-page plan for organizing all of the components for the Academic Boosters' kiosk project. Proofread and spell-check your document.

26. Conduct a Survey of a Target Audience

You are developing a multimedia presentation to be viewed by the students in your social studies class. Imagine the class will be viewing the project from their homes. Create a survey of the students to determine how best to deliver the content—on a CD, DVD, or online.

A. In this survey, the target audience is social studies students in your class. Construct a questionnaire to get information about home computers of the target audience. Find out about their Internet connections, presentation software programs they have on their computers, and whether they have access to a CD/DVD drives at home.

B. Ask ten students to complete the questionnaire. Use spreadsheet software such as Microsoft Excel to make a table and a bar chart plotting the data. Give the chart an appropriate title and descriptive labels. After you have completed your bar chart, exchange it with a partner. Compare and contrast the two tables. Summarize your findings. Draw a conclusion about the best delivery format for the presentation. What would your second choice be?

Content Delivery Survey Results	
Equipment	Number of People
Dial-up connection	
Broadband connection	
Wireless connection	
CD drive	
DVD drive	
Presentation software	

Projects Across the Curriculum

Project 1

Develop a Navigation Scheme

NCTE 1 Read texts to acquire new information.

English Language Arts A navigation scheme ensures that a multimedia project will be clearly understood by the viewer. You will do online research to plan a navigation scheme for a Web site that explains the project development life cycle and managing project schedules.

Research

1. Look at different types of Web sites and try to identify their navigation schemes. Think about how the navigation schemes you see might work for a Web site educating viewers about accessibility online.

Create

2. Using research and what you learned in this chapter, develop a navigation scheme for your Web site. Your scheme should include five pages.

3. Draw a storyboard of the navigation scheme. Write two paragraphs. In the first paragraph, name each page of the Web site and explain the relationships between the pages. In the second paragraph, summarize how you chose the navigation scheme. Explain why it is the right choice for the site's purpose and audience.

Review

3. Edit, proofread, and spell-check your document.

Project 2

Create a Project Mock-Up

NCTE 4 Use written language to communicate effectively.

English Language Arts A mock-up, or storyboard, is a tool that lets you see a concrete representation of your multimedia project. For this project, you will create a mock-up of a poster that will advertise an event, such as a school dance, sporting event, or art exhibit.

Plan and Research

1. Decide what your poster will advertise. Then answer the following questions: Who is the target audience? What text must appear? What font style, size, and color are appropriate? What graphics will enhance the look and message? How should elements be placed for best effect? How big will the final poster be?

2. Analyze the effectiveness of posters around your school and your community.

Create

3. Using your analysis of the posters you see, create a mock-up of your own poster by drawing it or using computer software.

Review

4. Ask two classmates to critique your mock-up. Make appropriate changes.

5. Review your work to make sure the mock-up contains the necessary elements. Proofread and spell-check the mock-up.

Project 3

Create a Multimedia Project Plan

NCTE 8 Use information resources to gather information and create and communicate knowledge.

English Language Arts The project plan helps determine a multimedia project's content and the resources required for the project. For this activity, you will develop a project plan for a multimedia presentation about generating publicity using social media tools such as blogging and podcasting.

Research

1. Conduct online research to find information on social media and how it can be used to generate publicity. Then research and find Web sites that incorporate social media. As you view the multimedia presentations, take notes about the different components you can include in your own presentation.

Create

2. Based on your research, create a project plan for the presentation. Be sure to include the following:

   - Define the project's purpose and goals.

   - Identify the project's target audience, as well as assumptions about the audience.

   - Develop the scope—all the features and content that will be included, given the project's budget.

   - Determine the deliverables, meaning how you will deliver the content to your intended audience.

   - Create a time line task list.

Item	Comments/Suggestions
Scope	
Tasks to accomplish	
Budget	
Schedule	
Deilverables	

Review

3. Share your plan with three classmates. Ask each classmate to review your plan and record their comments in a chart similar to the one shown here. Be sure to ask for positive as well as negative feedback.

Revise

4. Based on your classmates' comments, make changes to your project plan. Then write a half-page analysis describing how well you think your project would turn out based on your project plan. Draw on your knowledge of multimedia design and planning to determine what changes you might make to future plans. Include a statement describing what you learned from completing this exercise.

5. Proofread and spell-check your project plan and analysis.

Go Online **RUBRICS**
glencoe.com

Chapter Projects Use the rubrics for these projects to help create and evaluate your work. Go to the **Online Learning Center** at glencoe.com. Choose **Rubrics**, then **Chapter 4**.

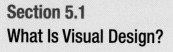

CHAPTER 5 Visual Design for Multimedia

Section 5.1
What Is Visual Design?

Section 5.2
Using Visual Design in Multimedia

CHAPTER OBJECTIVES

After completing this chapter, you will be able to:

❖ **Identify** the elements of art.

❖ **Desribe** the principles of visual design.

❖ **Analyze** visual design.

❖ **Understand** how to use visual design in multimedia.

❖ **Describe** multimedia accessibility options.

❖ **Explain** the visual design evaluation process.

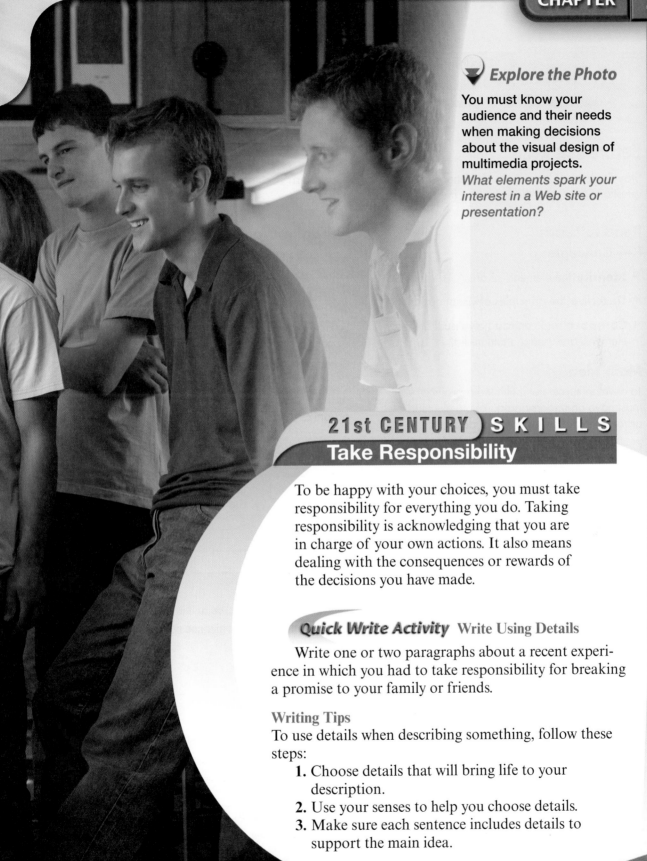

Explore the Photo

You must know your audience and their needs when making decisions about the visual design of multimedia projects. *What elements spark your interest in a Web site or presentation?*

21st CENTURY SKILLS
Take Responsibility

To be happy with your choices, you must take responsibility for everything you do. Taking responsibility is acknowledging that you are in charge of your own actions. It also means dealing with the consequences or rewards of the decisions you have made.

Quick Write Activity Write Using Details

Write one or two paragraphs about a recent experience in which you had to take responsibility for breaking a promise to your family or friends.

Writing Tips

To use details when describing something, follow these steps:

1. Choose details that will bring life to your description.
2. Use your senses to help you choose details.
3. Make sure each sentence includes details to support the main idea.

SECTION 5.1 What Is Visual Design?

Reading Guide

Before You Read

Stay Engaged One way to stay engaged when reading is to turn each of the headings into a question. Then read the section to find the answers.

Read to Learn

Key Concepts

- **Identify** the elements of art.
- **Describe** the principles of visual design.
- **Compare** and contrast how visual design elements are used in multimedia.

Main Idea

To develop successful multimedia projects, you must have an understanding of the elements of art and the principles of visual design.

Content Vocabulary

- ◇ visual design
- ◇ line
- ◇ shape
- ◇ form
- ◇ space
- ◇ focal point
- ◇ perspective
- ◇ color theory
- ◇ texture
- ◇ balance
- ◇ harmony
- ◇ emphasis
- ◇ proportion
- ◇ pattern

Academic Vocabulary

You will find these words in your reading and on your tests. Use the glossary to look up their definitions, if necessary.

- ◇ communicate
- ◇ distort

Graphic Organizer

As you read, identify the elements of art. Use a diagram similar to the one below to help you organize your information.

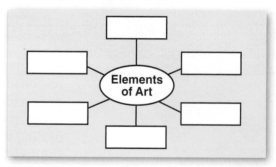

 Graphic Organizer Go to this book's **Online Learning Center** at **glencoe.com** to print this graphic organizer.

Academic Standards

 English Language Arts

NCTE 4 Use written language to communicate effectively.
NCTE 5 Use different writing process elements to communicate effectively.

NCTE 6 Apply knowledge of language structure and conventions to discuss texts.

NCTE National Council of Teachers of English
NSES National Science Education Standards

NCTM National Council of Teachers of Mathematics
NCSS National Council for the Social Studies

Elements of Visual Design

What are the elements of visual design?

A multimedia project's visual design can be just as important as its navigation and content. In Chapter 4, you were introduced to the multimedia project life cycle. This chapter focuses on the most creative part of multimedia development, using elements (such as lines, colors, and shapes) and principles (such as balance, harmony, and proportion) to build the look and feel of the multimedia projects.

Visual design is the process of planning, arranging, and integrating visual elements of art to accomplish or address a particular purpose. The elements of art are basic visual symbols or pieces that are put together to communicate ideas (see Figure 5.1). The principles of visual design are the guidelines for how to arrange or use these elements.

As You Read

Connect How does a picture help you understand new content more quickly and easily?

The Elements of Art in Visual Design

Element	Definition
Line	A line is a continuous mark made on some surface by a moving point.
Shape	A shape is a two-dimensional object or area.
Form	A form is an object with three dimensions.
Space	Space refers to the real or implied distance between, around, above, below, and within objects.
Color	Color is derived from reflected light. Color has three properties: hue, value, and intensity.
Texture	Texture refers to making things feel or look as they would feel or look in the real world.

Figure 5.1

Multimedia projects use the elements of art in different ways. Why is it important to know how to use the elements of art in multimedia projects?

Understanding how these elements work together will help you to **communicate**, or express your ideas, visually. When creating multimedia, you should incorporate the elements of art just as an artist would use them in a painting or a drawing. However, instead of using a brush or pencil, you use computer software and other multimedia tools to design and create the layout. From there, you may change colors, add text formatting, incorporate graphics, and use video and special effects. Which elements of art you choose to include will depend on the purpose, goals, and audience of your multimedia projects. The goal of effective visual design is always the same. Visual elements should:

- Add visual appeal.
- Improve clarity of multimedia projects.

Line

Line is the element of art that is a continuous mark made on some surface by a moving point, such as a pen. Lines can vary in width, direction, and length. The five main types of lines are: horizontal lines, vertical lines, diagonal or slanting lines, curved lines, and zigzag lines.

The type of lines you choose will suggest different feelings and ideas. You can use lines to guide the user's eye movement up, down, and across the page, imply motion, or suggest direction or orientation. For example, if you use curved lines to outline a banner on a Web site, the lines will suggest a relaxed, flowing movement. Curved lines create a calm, natural tone. Sharp, jagged lines are more dynamic and aggressive. Horizontal lines are used to convey tranquility and rest, while vertical lines are often associated with power or strength.

Shape, Form, and Space

When you join, or combine, the points of a line, you create a shape. A **shape** is a two-dimensional object. A two-dimensional object has height and width, but no depth. Shapes fall into two categories:

- Geometric shapes look as though they were made with a ruler or drawing tool. Examples of geometric shapes include circles, squares, triangles, and rectangles.

- Organic or free-form shapes are not regular or even. Clouds and flower petals are examples of free-form shapes.

In Figure 5.2, geometric shapes organize information for the viewer. By contrast, if you put the information in circles that are hard to see or positioned randomly on the page, the information might appear to float, communicating a lack of organization or sense of confusion.

A **form** is an object with three dimensions: height, width, and depth. Your textbook is an example of a three-dimensional form. Sculptures are three-dimensional forms. Form can also refer to the three-dimensional appearance of a two-dimensional object. For example, a computer-generated image of a cube uses light and dark areas that provide contrast to give the object depth.

Space refers to the real or implied distance between, around, above, below, and within objects. When creating multimedia projects, you should leave enough room around objects so that elements are not too close together. White space is an area without content where the eye can take a break as it scans the page. White space helps draw attention to content.

Figure 5.2

The boxes in this design organize information. What is the difference between a geometric and a free-form shape?

Shadows and Shading In order to create the appearance of form in a multimedia project, you can use light, shadow, or shading. Shadows are shaded areas. Shadows show the surfaces of the subject that reflects the least light. When an object is shaded, light and dark values are used to create contrast. For example, if you are creating a program for the school play, you might use a drop-shadow behind photos of the actors to make the pictures stand out on the page.

Depth You can create depth through the placement of objects or components. Consider the following guidelines:

- Place business names, logos, or graphics in the foreground, or in front. Pick one of these to be the **focal point**, or the element that you want to first attract the attention of the viewer.

- Place less important design elements, such as borders and textures, in the background. These elements should support the content without overpowering it.

- The middle ground, or middle distance, is the area between the foreground and the background. This area includes most of the text and other design elements for the project.

Depth of field creates depth in a special way. Depth of field is the part of an image or design that seems to be in the sharpest focus. In photography, for example, a small depth of field focuses on a single object so that it stands out as as a focal point, blurring the background. A large depth of field makes everything in the image appear as if it is in focus (see Figure 5.3).

Quick **Tip**

Troubleshoot When designing multimedia, eliminate clutter. Too much content can confuse the audience. Only include information and elements that you really need. Avoid using too many different elements.

Figure 5.3
In photography, a large depth of field eliminates a focal point and a small depth of field emphasizes a focal point. **How else can you create depth?**

Perspective Another way to create depth is through three-dimensional effects such as perspective. **Perspective** is a technique that creates an illusion of depth and volume on a two-dimensional surface. Perspective is created by overlapping, size variation, placement, and converging lines.

Color

Color is one of the most important elements of art. Of all the design elements, it is the one that most people notice first. **Color theory** is a standard set of guidelines about using color. You can apply color theory to multimedia development to help set the mood, evoke different emotions, and enhance your visual design.

Hue, Value, and Intensity Color is derived from light and has three distinct properties:

- Hue refers to the name of a color. Red, yellow, and blue are types of hues.

- Value refers to the lightness or darkness of a color. For example, the lightest value of red is pink, and its darkest value is maroon. You can make a hue lighter by adding white. You can make it darker by adding black.

- Intensity refers to the brightness or dullness of a color. A strong and bright hue, such as red, has high intensity and tends to stand out (see Figure 5.4). A dull hue has low intensity. Brighter colors are better when used sparingly.

Choose colors carefully to create a mood. A flyer or Web site for a party planning company might use a light yellow or intense greens and reds to create a bright, energetic mood. A less intense cool blue can create a calm, relaxed mood for a spa's business card.

Multimedia developers use two very different color models—one for color that will display on-screen and one for color on print deliverables.

RGB Color Model The RGB color model is designed specifically to display color on-screen. Computer monitors and televisions emit color as RGB (which stands for red, green, and blue) light. The RGB color model is called an additive color model because the three colors (red, green, blue) are added together to create a variety of colors.

Figure 5.4

In this Web site, color intensity is used to make buttons stand out. **What is the difference between the value of color and its intensity?**

CMYK Color Model The CMYK (cyan, magenta, yellow, and black) color model is generally used for print deliverables, such as this textbook or a brochure. With the CMYK model, the dyes that are used to make printing inks take in and reflect color when light shines on paper. This model is the opposite of the RGB model in that it is a subtractive color model. In a subtractive color model, the inks subtract brightness from white.

Color Schemes

A color scheme, or color palette, is the selection of colors you use throughout your multimedia project. Using color schemes make multimedia presentations effective without altering the content or elements. You can also use a color scheme to tie pages together or to distinguish between different groups of related displays. Color schemes contain a combination of contrasting and complementary colors.

- **Complementary colors** are similar in hue and intensity. They make content more consistent. Red and pink are similar hues that work together without clashing. In Figure 5.4 on page 136, green and blue are complementary colors.

- **Contrasting colors** are obviously distinct from each other. For example, in Figure 5.4 red, blue, and white are contrasting colors (white is used for text). It is important to use contrasting colors for all text in your multimedia projects. Contrasting colors make information easier to read. This is because the contrast keeps items from blending together.

As you choose a color scheme, limit the number of colors as much as possible. Think about how your audience will be using the multimedia project. Select colors that work with the project's theme and purpose. Also remember that many colors and color combinations have cultural meaning or symbolism to certain audiences. For example, when the colors red, white, and blue are used together, they are often associated with the 4th of July, and the color green is often associated with St. Patrick's Day.

Texture

Texture refers to the surface characteristic or quality that you see or feel. Common textures are rough or smooth, dull or shiny, and soft or sandy. Texture can also be a repeated pattern of lines that is used to suggest how the fur on an animal or weave of fabric might feel. Texture can be created by using different color values and color patterns. For example, light and dark colors can be used to suggest the rough surface texture of tree bark. Texture can imply movement or rhythm, or add energy to a multimedia design. Always make sure that the textures you use are not distracting and that they work well with the other elements to support the entire design of the multimedia project.

Web-Safe Colors It is important to pick Web-safe colors when deciding on color schemes for computer-based multimedia projects. A Web-safe color appears the same on a Macintosh computer as it does on computer with the Windows operating system or any other operating system.

Why It's Important Why is it important to provide reliable color within a project?

 **Reading Check** **Describe** What are the elements of art?

Principles of Visual Design

What are the principles of visual design?

Once you are familiar with the elements of art, you can begin to focus on how to put these elements together to best communicate your ideas. Multimedia developers follow a set of guidelines, known as the principles of visual design, to organize various elements to create an effective design that supports the project's purpose and goals and creates greater visual interest. Figure 5.5 shows the principles of visual design and their primary purposes.

Figure 5.5
Multimedia projects use the principles of visual design. What is the purpose of creating an area of emphasis in a multimedia project?

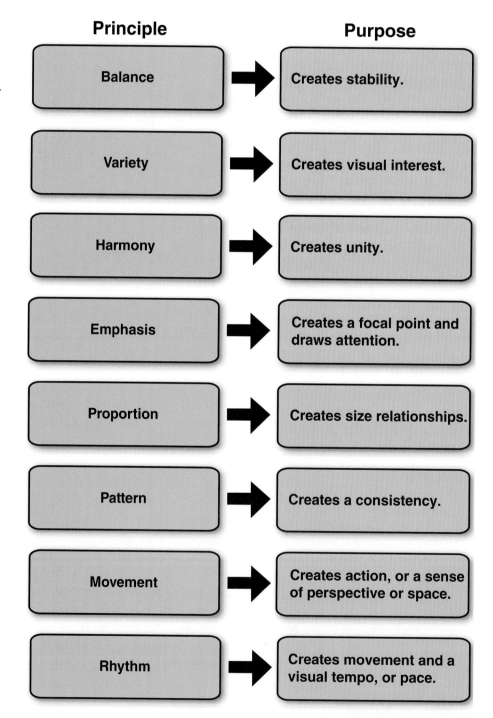

Principle	Purpose
Balance	Creates stability.
Variety	Creates visual interest.
Harmony	Creates unity.
Emphasis	Creates a focal point and draws attention.
Proportion	Creates size relationships.
Pattern	Creates a consistency.
Movement	Creates action, or a sense of perspective or space.
Rhythm	Creates movement and a visual tempo, or pace.

Go Online ACTIVITY
glencoe.com

Select Color Schemes
Investigate techniques for using color effectively by visiting this book's **Online Learning Center**. Go to glencoe.com. Choose **Activities**, then **Chapter 5.**

 Figure 5.6
The picture on the left shows informal balance. The picture below shows formal balance. **Why is symmetry important to creating an effective visual design?**

Balance

Balance is the arrangement of elements so that no one part of the work overpowers or seems heavier than any other part. Balance creates a feeling of equal weight across the project. Without balance, a design might be less visually appealing. In fact, an unbalanced presentation can even make viewers uncomfortable. This is because viewers expect and want balance, just as a skateboarder wants balance when riding. Balance can be formal or informal (see Figure 5.6).

- **Formal balance**, or symmetry, is an exact mirror reflection. Whatever appears on one side of the design is mirrored on the other. Symmetrical balance is formal, ordered, and stable.

- **Informal balance** does not have symmetry. Instead, different elements appear to have equal weight even though the two sides of the design are different in size, form, texture, or color. Objects are not perfectly mirrored on each side, but are placed in relation to each other.

A visual design that is not balanced usually has too many elements in one area and not enough in another. For example, if you are creating a poster of a slideshow presentation, you could use a darker, larger font on the left side to balance a large, dark chart that appears on the right side.

Academic Focus

Mathematics

Multiple Variables
You are planning a project that has a header, navigation bar, and content area. The header will be twice the size of the navigation bar. The content area will be three times the size of the header and navigation bar combined. If the header is 100 centimeters, how big will the content area be? Start by assigning values to the known variables.

NCTM Algebra Use mathematical models to repesent and understand quantitative relationships.

Academic Focus

English Language Arts

Symbolism In literature, a symbol represents an idea. It is important to understand the symbolism of colors when designing multimedia presentations. Colors may have a symbolic meaning to cultural groups. Conduct research on a color and its symbolism in specific cultures. Report your results in a paragraph, citing your sources.

NCTE 2 Read literature to build an understanding of the human experience.

Variety, Harmony, and Emphasis

Variety means combining art elements with slight changes to increase visual interest. Using several multimedia components such as photos, animation, and artwork in a project increases the project's variety. Without variety, viewers may find a presentation dull and uninteresting. For example, a photo may look fine on the first page of a slide show, but it may lose appeal if you used the same photo on every slide in the presentation.

In order to use variety effectively, elements in a presentation should still have something in common. **Harmony** occurs when the visual design elements have similarities. Developers use color, pattern, or common shapes to create harmony. For example, if you are creating a presentation for your business class, you might use a consistent color scheme from slide to slide in order to create harmony. When possible, use similar types of graphics and shapes to create harmony. In a consistent, harmonious presentation, elements work together to support the whole design and meet the multimedia project's purpose and goals.

Emphasis is a point of interest that the user sees first. It can be used to create a focal point or to make an element or object in a work stand out. For example, a press release should make the company logo prominent to attract attention to the company's brand. The placement of an element creates emphasis. A logo in the top-left corner of a press release creates more emphasis than one in the bottom-right corner.

Proportion

Proportion refers to the size relationships of certain elements to the whole and to each other. With proportion, you can decide how large or how small objects will be in relation to each other. For example, if you are developing a personal Web page, you might categorize information by size. If you want to draw attention to the newest blog entries, you might make this section of your Web site design larger than your photo album or comments section.

Sometimes developers use exaggerated proportion in a design. A developer might **distort**, or twist, an image to make it larger than its natural or original proportion. You might use exaggerated proportion to create a humorous effect. For example, a flyer for a senior class breakfast might show a giant stack of pancakes. While it would be impossible to eat all of the pancakes, the exaggerated size is funny.

Pattern, Movement, and Rhythm

Pattern is a two-dimensional decorative effect achieved through the repetition of colors, lines, shapes, or textures. Patterns are used to create consistency in visual design. A multimedia designer might decide to repeat the same shapes, colors, dots, or lines throughout a multimedia project to create a pattern that ties different pages to each other and creates harmony. Patterns can add visual interest to a flyer, or they can be used to echo, or carry, a theme throughout an entire presentation.

Colors and shapes create movement and emphasis

MUSEUM OF NEON ART

ABOUT MONA   BRIGHT FUTURE   GLOWING HISTORY   MEMBERSHIP   STORE   RESOURCES   MONA NEWS

Larry Albright

CURRENT
EXHIBITIONS
NEON CRUISE
CLASSES
LOCATION

DONATE TODAY

TAKE A SURVEY!

CLICK FOR DETAILS,
MUSEUM HOURS
AND ADMISSION

ALSO AT MONA:

A Cautionary Tale

PHOTOGRAPHS BY

Tom Zimmerman

Our Famous
NEON CRUISES
Continue!

CLICK FOR SCHEDULE

Figure 5.7
The principles of pattern, movement, and rhythm are demonstrated in this design. What has been done to make this design unified?

Movement combines elements to create the appearance of action to guide a viewer's eye throughout a work of art. A poster for your school's swim team might use swirling lines to illustrate water in motion.

Rhythm refers to the regular repetition of elements or objects to indicate activity or create the feeling of movement or dynamic energy. Rhythm can also be varied to create visual interest. For example, using a row of patterned dots will create a rhythm. However, a row of patterned dots that vary in size or pattern will generate more viewer interest. The visual design in Figure 5.7 illustrates how movement and emphasis have been used to increase visual appeal.

In the following You Try It activity, you will compare and contrast how the elements of art are used in the visual designs of several online news publications.

Activity 5A Compare and Contrast Visual Design Elements

YOU TRY IT

1. With your teacher's permission, locate and review several online magazines or news sites. What differences do you see between the magazines?

2. Examine how the elements of art appear in each magazine or news site. Examine the text. Pay close attention to the font size, type, and color. Then, examine the photos and graphics.

③ Use the checklist provided in Figure 5.8 to compare and contrast how the elements of art are displayed in each Web site.

Figure 5.8
Use this checklist to compare and contrast how the elements of art are used in each online news source.

Visual Design Elements Checklist

- ☑ Is the page balanced?
- ☑ What kind of balance is employed?
- ☑ What kind of color scheme is employed?
- ☑ Is there variety in how the elements are used?
- ☑ Is space used effectively?
- ☑ Is there harmony among all of the content?
- ☑ Are visual elements used to create pattern, movement, or rhythm?
- ☑ Do size relationships emphasize the level of importance among items?

④ Evaluate your findings. Which news site do you think you would visit every day?

⑤ Key your evaluation in a word processing document. Write a brief paragraph explaining your choice.

⑥ Save and close your file.

 **Reading Check** **Define** What are the principles of visual design?

Section 5.1 After You Read

Review Key Concepts

1. **List** the elements of art and principles of visual design.

2. **Describe** how you would use each visual design principle to create an effective class presentation.

Check Your Answers Check your answers at this book's **Online Learning Center** through glencoe.com.

Practice Academic Skills

English Language Arts

3. **Evaluate** Write a short essay that explains why a user might lose interest in multimedia that does not follow the principles of visual design effectively. Use examples to explain your reasoning.

4. **Analyze** You want to create a Web site to share information about your school's book club. Write a proposal that identifies how you plan to use the elements of art and visual design principles in the site's design.

Online Student Manual • glencoe.com

Go to your Online Student Manual and enter your password to find activities that allow you to practice and apply multimedia skills.

NCTE 6 Apply knowledge of language structure and conventions to discuss texts.

NCTE 5 Use different writing process elements to communicate effectively.

Reading Guide

Before You Read

What You Want to Know Write a list of what you want to learn in this section about using visual design. As you read, write down the heads in this section that provide information.

Read to Learn

Key Concepts

- **Describe** how to apply principles of visual design.
- **Explain** how the delivery format may affect the visual design of a multimedia project.
- **Describe** accessibility issues for multimedia.
- **Describe** the evaluation and peer review process.

Main Idea

Applying principles of visual design will help you create successful multimedia projects. Evaluating your design will give you the opportunity to reflect on your developing skills.

Content Vocabulary

- ◇ layout
- ◇ fundamental
- ◇ peer review

Academic Vocabulary

You will find these words in your reading and on your tests. Use the glossary to look up their definitions, if necessary.

- ◆ evident
- ◆ evaluate

Graphic Organizer

As you read this section, identify three layout guidelines for applying the principles of design. Use a web diagram like the one below to help organize the information.

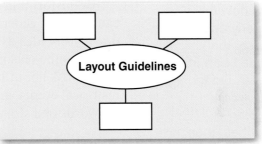

 Graphic Organizer Go to this book's **Online Learning Center** at glencoe.com to print this graphic organizer.

Academic Standards

 English Language Arts

NCTE 4 Use written language to communicate effectively.

NCTE 5 Use different writing process elements to communicate effectively.

 Mathematics

NCTM Problem Solving Solve problems that arise in mathematics and in other contexts.

NCTE National Council of Teachers of English
NSES National Science Education Standards

NCTM National Council of Teachers of Mathematics
NCSS National Council for the Social Studies

As You Read

Connect How is planning the visual design of a multimedia project like arranging furniture in a room?

Layout Guidelines of Visual Design

How do I apply visual design principles to multimedia?

Users are attracted to multimedia that is interesting and easy to use. An appealing layout will be **evident**, or obvious, if the elements of art and the principles of design work together. It is important to consider your audience at all times. If multimedia elements are inviting, attractive, and useful, users will feel comfortable. How you use the elements of art in multimedia will depend on your own personal style.

Determine Layout

Layout is the arrangement of text and graphics on each page or display screen. A good layout uses these elements to tie the entire project together. There are several methods you can use to develop your visual design. Some people use storyboards, mock-ups, or graphic organizers, such as web diagrams, to illustrate and expand upon their ideas.

In Chapter 4, we discussed creating storyboards or mock-ups. Storyboards can help you create an effective page layout for your multimedia projects. Using your story with your mission statement can help you to see what the project will look like and plan what the content will say. Others prefer to use their project plan to create an outline, or write all thoughts that come to them about the page design. Whatever option you choose, it is important to make time for this step when developing a visual design.

Brainstorming is an important part of the planning process that can help you generate layout ideas. Brainstorming involves writing down every idea as it comes to you. Then write a word or phrase that identifies the reasoning behind each idea. If you are developing a museum kiosk about Denmark, you might use keywords like geography, historical events, and culture. After you create your list, review your keywords and storyboards to decide which elements to apply.

Apply Visual Design Principles

Once you have brainstormed or outlined a page's layout, think about how you can use visual design principles and the elements of art to help communicate. You may want to use a different color or shape, or include more space or a bold pattern in your design. Or, you may want to use one or more elements of art to create a more consistent or user-friendly design. Remember not to mix too many elements on a page. Having too many elements could confuse a user. For example, when working on a museum kiosk about Denmark, you might consider the following questions:

- Should the design include a picture of the Danish flag or use its colors?

- How can you use design elements to emphasize historical events?

- What is the most user-friendly location for navigation buttons?

- What techniques should be used to create visual relationships between elements?

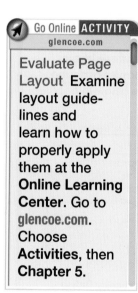

Go Online ACTIVITY
glencoe.com

Evaluate Page Layout Examine layout guidelines and learn how to properly apply them at the Online Learning Center. Go to glencoe.com. Choose Activities, then Chapter 5.

Evaluating visual design in multimedia will help you understand how to use the principles of visual design.

- Content should be easy to read.
- Text should stand out from graphics and other objects.
- Graphics should be both visually appealing and informative.
- Elements should not be distracting. Content should follow rules of proximity.

When applying the principles of visual design, you will want to follow some **fundamental**, or essential, guidelines to help make your visual design more user-friendly. The best visual designs have clear, attractive layouts that make users feel at ease and comfortable. To apply visual design principles to the page layout of multimedia, ask yourself a series of questions like those listed in Figure 5.9.

Page Layout Guidelines for the Principles of Visual Design

Principle	Questions
Balance	• Is the design divided into logical sections or areas? • Is there an equal amount of objects or elements in each area? • Are there too many elements on the page? • Is there effective use of white space to give users a visual break? • How can I create more stability in the design?
Variety	• Is there enough variation in the design? • Can I vary the types or thickness of a line, the size of a shape, or a color's hue to enhance visual interest?
Harmony	• Do lines, shapes, and colors complement each other? • Do all the elements work together to create a unified design? • How can I achieve better unity and consistency throughout the project?
Emphasis	• Is focus placed on the correct objects or content? • How can I draw more attention to the focal point? • Can I use bright colors or different textures to make a design element more interesting?
Proportion	• Do all the elements relate well to each other? • Are elements on the page sized in proportion to their importance? • How can I use size relationships to better illustrate the relationships between objects and content?
Pattern	• Is there consistency in the elements and objects used in the layout? • How can I make the design more consistent?
Movement	• Does the page layout guide the viewer's eye throughout the design? • How can I use perspective and space to improve upon the design?
Rhythm	• Is repetition used to strengthen the page's visual interest? • How can I use repetition to make users more comfortable?

PLAN AHEAD

Design Proximity refers to the closeness of items to each other on a page. Proximity is related to balance and proportion. The proximity of elements can cause users to make assumptions about how elements relate to each other. Do not create false impressions by placing items too close together.

Figure 5.9
Applying the principles of design effectively can help make multimedia more successful. **Why is it important that multimedia be visually appealing?**

In the next activity, you will develop a flyer for your school's Student Council Pancake Breakfast. Apply the principles of visual design to develop and create a flyer for the event.

YOU TRY IT

Activity 5B Apply Visual Design Principles to a Flyer

1. Decide on a theme and color scheme for the flyer. You can use your school's colors or create colors using another kind of theme.

2. Plan and write the text for the flyer.

3. Make sure to include a catch phrase, the purpose of the flyer, and the location and time of the breakfast.

4. Decide on the graphics and images you will use.

5. Plan how you will incorporate the elements of art and apply the design principles.

6. Using pen and paper, sketch the layout for your flyer. Use the checklist in Figure 5.10 to help you develop your design.

PLAN AHEAD

Design Visual design uses words and images to capture the users' attention and provide information. A successful design should support this information.

Visual Design Checklist

- ☑ Does the design add visual interest?
- ☑ Does the design only include content that I really need?
- ☑ Is the page balanced?
- ☑ Is a color scheme employed?
- ☑ Is there variety in how the elements are used?
- ☑ Is space used effectively?
- ☑ Are related items grouped together to create pattern, movement, or rhythm, if necessary?
- ☑ Do size relationships emphasize the level of importance among items?
- ☑ Do all the elements work together to create unity?
- ☑ How can I make the design more appealing?

Figure 5.10
Use the questions in this checklist to help you create a layout for your flyer.

7. Using your sketch as a guide, open word processing or presentation software and create the flyer for your school's pancake breakfast.

8. With your teacher's permission, print the flyer. Carefully proofread the flyer.

9. Save and close your file.

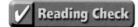 **Reading Check** **Identify** What is harmony?

Layout Guidelines for Digital Media

What should I consider when creating digital media designs?

When applying visual design principles to multimedia projects, you need to organize and present the information specifically for the deliverable. Designs that work well for books, newsletters, and other print media do not necessarily work well for digital media such as slide show presentations or the Web. Long pages of text, for example, are difficult to read on a large screen or on a video or computer monitor.

Slide Show Presentations

A slide show presentation's design must be easy to understand and large enough to be read from the back of a room. Size elements in proportion to their importance and use colors for text that contrast with the background. If you include video or images, use them sparingly. Too many visual components will clutter the a slide show layout, especially when viewed from a distance.

Some designers use a template, or premade design, to help control the consistency and layout of a slide show presentation. Templates can control layout and formatting, including color schemes and fonts, but they can also help to create the visual elements that are specific to slide show presentations, such as slide effects, transitions, and timings. An example of a Microsoft PowerPoint template for a quiz show is seen in Figure 5.11.

Designers may also wish to incorporate interactivity into digital presentations with hyperlinks, buttons, and menus. It is important to use these elements in a consistent and appealing way.

Quick Tip

You Should Know
When making a presentation, the topic headings are generally larger and a different color from the other elements and objects on the screen. Remember that without balance, the topic headings may overwhelm the other items on the slide.

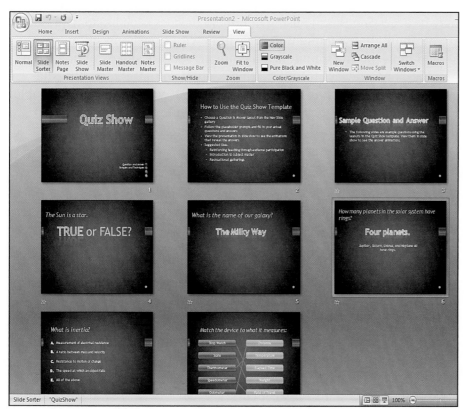

Figure 5.11
This quiz template can be modified to meet individual project needs. How can a template help you with the layout of your presentation?

CD and DVD Design

Navigation and usability are important to consider when you create the visual design for the interface and background images for a CD or DVD menu. The visual design for a CD and DVD should be easy to navigate and communicate important information clearly.

The design should use colors that display on television and computer monitors with different capabilities, but should not include colors that distract from the navigation. Sometimes, it is necessary to include a short description of how to use the content of the CD or DVD. This description is sometimes called a "readme" file or a FAQ (frequently asked questions).

Web Site Design

The visual design for a Web site must organize and present information specifically for the Web. You need to know how your visitors' monitors and various browsers will affect how your site is viewed.

The goal will be to make sure that the Web site looks the same in all browsers and on all operating systems. In order to accomplish this goal, you must test the visual design in various browsers, such as Microsoft Internet Explorer, Apple Safari, and Mozilla Firefox. If graphics or fonts look quite different between browsers, you may have compatibility issues. You should correct these issues before you finalize your Web site design. When possible, use style sheets (such as CSS) to create a consistent appearance.

When creating content for the Web, you must consider your audience's physical limitations. Although your site might have unlimited server space, visitors to the site might have slow connection speeds or may be accessing the site using handheld devices such as smartphones. If you think that you might have visitors with slow connections, you should limit the site's multimedia content, such as video, audio, and graphics, or find ways to stream this content so that the multimedia can be viewed while it is being downloaded. If you put a downloadable PDF on your Web site, you should also provide a link for visitors to download Adobe Acrobat Reader if necessary.

 **Explain** Why is it is important to consider your audience when creating digital media?

Multimedia Accessibility

Why is accessibility important to multimedia design?

Making multimedia accessible involves making sure that all types of people can access and use its content. Training and informational video and multimedia productions, for example, need to provide accessibility features so that they can be used by individuals with different needs. Some of the disabilities that can affect multimedia usability include visual impairments, hearing impairments, different learning styles, and motor skills impairments.

Section 508 is a 1998 amendment to the U.S. Rehabilitation Act. It states that federal agencies must make technologies accessible to all visitors, including those with disabilities. The amendment provides a number of accessibility standards that affect technologies, including:

- software and operating systems.
- Web sites and Web-based applications.
- telephones, cell phones, and smartphones.
- video and multimedia products and kiosks.
- computers and laptops.

Many of the Section 508 standards encourage designers to make it easier for all users to understand, scan, and respond to elements included in multimedia. To make multimedia accessible, you should try to present information for users with

- Blindness, limited sight, and color blindness
- Hearing difficulties
- Different learning styles, and mobilities that affect users' ability to use a mouse.

Consider users who have difficulty moving. Figure 5.12 outlines some techniques for making multimedia accessible.

 **Reading Check** **Describe** What is the purpose of accessibility in design?

Ways to Make Information Accessible

Accessibility Techniques

- Provide descriptions of video content and transcripts of slide show presentations.
- Provide alternative text that describes a kiosk's multimedia elements, such as audio or video, allowing people who have difficulty hearing to understand the audio.
- Provide controls to pause and continue playback in video slide show presentations.
- Limit the amount of information on a slide or Web page to make it easier to understand.
- Use colors that provide a high contrast between content and its background.

- Create elements that can be accessed using the keyboard instead of a mouse, improving usability for users with limited mobility.
- Provide a text-only version that contains the same information using only words.
- Include alternative text that summarizes an image, graph or chart's content.
- Use voice-enabled multimedia and screen readers can make multimedia content more accessible to people who have difficulty seeing.
- Use speech synthesis and voice recognition technology, allowing users to replace keyboard input with spoken words.

Figure 5.12
Follow the suggestions shown in the table to make your multimedia accessible. Why is it important to include alternative text in multimedia?

Evaluation and Peer Review

Why is it important to be able to evaluate the quality of a visual design?

Once you have created a visual design, you can **evaluate**, or study, your design. This is the time to reflect on the methods you used to combine the elements of art and how well your visual design suits your multimedia project. See Figure 5.13 for an example of a well-designed Web site.

Conducting an evaluation can help you determine if you met your purpose and goals.

Once you have created your visual design and evaluated it on your own, you can conduct a peer review to get objective feedback from your project team. A **peer review** is an informal editing process in which team members review and critique each other's work. When you get the recommendations and evaluation comments back from your peers, review the comments carefully.

In the following activity, you will conduct a peer review of your visual design work for the flyer you created in Activity 5B. Be prepared to ask questions about the feedback. You can use this constructive criticism to help you refine, or improve, your multimedia's visual design.

Figure 5.13

Evaluating your layout is an important part of the design process. What are some features that make this a good visual design?

YOU TRY IT

Activity 5C Conduct a Peer Review of a Multimedia Project

1. With your teacher's permission, form groups of four and review the visual design of each other's flyers.

2. Review each flyer separately. Examine the text. Pay close attention to the font size, type, and colors used.

3. Look at the photos and other graphics and elements used. Pay close attention to the placement and number.

4. Using the peer review checklist in Figure 5.14 on page 151, evaluate each flyer. Make sure to be positive and constructive in your feedback.

5. Ask: What elements of art are used? Have the principles of design been applied successfully?

6 Think of two additional questions you can add to the checklist. Include these questions and answer them for each flyer.

7 Using Word processing software, write a report documenting the results of your peer review for each.

8 In your evaluation, be sure to mention at least two positive things about the project.

9 Proof and spell-check your document. Save and close your file.

Figure 5.14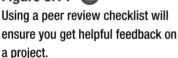

Using a peer review checklist will ensure you get helpful feedback on a project.

Multimedia Peer Review Checklist

☑ Relates logically to the multimedia's purpose. The design clearly supports the purpose of the multimedia.

☑ Visually appealing and appropriate for the target audience. Organization is logical and helpful to the viewer. The design is balanced, has variety, and uses space effectively.

☑ Effectively applies visual design principles to the elements of art. The designer has chosen the best way to combine text, figures, and other elements to create a unified design.

☑ Draws attention to the correct or most pertinent elements. Size relationships emphasize the level of importance among items. Items are grouped together to create pattern, movement, or rhythm to make a more visually appealing design.

☑ Accessible to all users without imposing any interpretation. Each element can be understood, without referring to the text. Alternative text present if needed.

✓ Reading Check **Recall** What is a peer review?

Section 5.2 After You Read

Review Key Concepts

1. **Explain** the importance of evaluating a multimedia project's visual design.

2. **Summarize** how you can use visual design principles to make your multimedia project's message clear.

 Check Your Answers Check your answers at this book's **Online Learning Center** through glencoe.com.

Practice Academic Skills

 **English Language Arts**

3. **Analyze** Select three forms of multimedia and determine what visual design principles are dominant in each. Write a paragraph that describes the considerations that may have led to the selection of those design principles.

Math

4. **Calculate** You are creating an online photo gallery for nine photos arranged in three columns and three rows. You decide to include 27 photos instead of nine, but you still want the table to have three columns. Calculate how many rows of photos would be on the page.

 Online Student Manual • glencoe.com

Go to your Online Student Manual and enter your password to find projects that allow you to practice and apply multimedia skills.

NCTE 5 Use different writing process elements to communicate effectively.

NCTM Problem Solving Solve problems that arise in mathematics and in other contexts.

Careers & Technology

Interface Designers

Think about the things you do each time you sit down to use your computer. You probably use the mouse to click icons and buttons. You might open your e-mail software to open and read e-mail. You use your Web browser to surf the Web.

Whether you notice it or not, you are using a carefully designed interface every time you use your computer. Every aspect of what you see on the screen—from the colors and shapes of the menus and toolbars right down to the position and appearance of icons—is designed to make using software as easy and intuitive as possible.

This is where the interface designer comes in. An interface designer's job is to create the look and feel of software, including color schemes, font sizes, and so on. This person also makes sure that menus and buttons work logically.

Every element you see or on your computer was created by an interface design team.

Innovative Thinking

Creative thinking skills are necessary for interface designers. Becoming familiar with current trends, multimedia tools, and technology will help you to think creatively about design. Building an understanding of specific computer applications will allow you to think critically to find innovative design solutions.

Teamwork and Communication

Of course, nobody designs an entire interface by him- or herself. Interface designers work in teams. Designers collaborate with engineers, focus groups, and others. This teamwork is necessary because it makes it more

likely that the interface will appeal to a majority of potential users.

Teams must be productive and are often held accountable for their actions and work flow. As a team member, you are responsible for your own actions and should take leadership roles when appropriate. Learning to communicate effectively while working collaboratively to achieve project goals is an important 21st century skill. It is also important to be flexible when working with others.

Skill Builder

1. **Describe Communication Challenges** What are some of the unique challenges facing interface designers? What skills would come in handy?

2. **Analyze Skills** What skills do you feel are most necessary in order to succeed in a technology career? Which skills would you like to develop?

Chapter Summary

Good visual design is important to develop multimedia that is consistent with the project's purpose and easy for the viewer to understand. Well-designed multimedia projects are created using the elements of art and principles of visual design. Use visual elements like line, color, and shape, and principles, such as balance, harmony, and proportion as tools to help build visually appealing multimedia projects.

When applying visual design principles to multimedia projects, organize and present the information specifically for the deliverable. Designs that work well for print media do not necessarily work well for digital media. Accessible multimedia projects allow people with different needs and abilities to access and use their content. It is important to make sure your multimedia projects are accessible to all users. Evaluate the visual design to ensure that it reinforces the project's purpose and goals. Evaluation and peer review allow you to determine whether the design successfully communicates, or expresses, your ideas visually.

Vocabulary Review

1. Use these words to create a crossword puzzle on graph paper. Use the definitions as clues.

Content Vocabulary

◇ visual design (p. 133)
◇ line (p. 134)
◇ shape (p. 134)
◇ form (p. 134)
◇ space (p. 134)
◇ focal point (p. 135)
◇ perspective (p. 136)
◇ color theory (p. 136)
◇ texture (p. 137)

◇ balance (p. 139)
◇ harmony (p. 140)
◇ emphasis (p. 140)
◇ proportion (p. 140)
◇ pattern (p. 140)
◇ layout (p. 144)
◇ fundamental (p. 145)
◇ peer review (p. 150)

Academic Vocabulary

◇ communicate (p. 133)
◇ distort (p. 140)
◇ evident (p. 144)
◇ evaluate (p. 150)

Review Key Concepts

2. Identify the elements of art.

3. Describe the principles of visual design.

4. Compare and Contrast how visual design elements are used in multimedia.

5. Summarize how to apply principles of visual design.

6. Describe how the delivery format may affect the visual design of a multimedia project.

7. Discuss accessibility issues for multimedia.

8. Explain the evaluation and peer review process.

Critical Thinking

9. Summarize Use a graphic organizer like the one below to explain what the elements of art are. How can they be used to help communicate ideas?

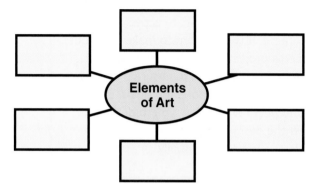

10. Explain Why is it important to use white space when creating a design? Why is variety important when creating a design?

11. Evaluate Explain how the principles of visual design can be used to solve specific art problems.

12. Discuss Your aunt is making a multimedia presentation. The presentation includes text but no graphics or other elements of art. She has asked for your input. Explain to your aunt what she might do to improve her presentation.

13. Apply You have been asked to teach visual design principles to a small group of classmates. Use your knowledge of visual design to develop a graphic to enhance your classmates' understanding. Use a chart similar to the one below to organize your thoughts.

Principles of Design	
Principle	Purpose

14. Compare and Contrast Explain the difference between the principles of balance and proportion in visual design. Use a graphic organizer like the one below to help you.

15. Analyze You are developing a new multimedia presentation. You want to make sure that your presentation is accessible to as many people as possible. What types of things should you consider when designing the layout in order to make sure that the project is accessible? What might happen if you do not create an accessible design? Write a paragraph describing how it might affect the final project.

16. Discuss Imagine you are designing a Web site about your favorite book. Identify the elements that you would include on your home page and the principles you would use to put them together. Explain your answers.

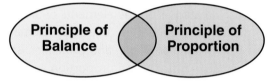

Go to the **Online Learning Center** to find additional activities and career resources.
Practice Quizzes Test your knowledge of the material in this chapter.

Career Resources Find out more about careers, including information about résumés, portfolios, and interview and workplace tips.

Academic Connections

| NCTE 4   Use written language to communicate effectively. |

17. English Language Arts–Create an Oral Presentation

Assume that you are a visual designer and a company has hired you to design the user interface for a menu that will be used on a CD. Use the Web to learn more about CD and DVD interface design. Then, prepare an oral report.

A. The company sells instructional materials such as books, videos, and interactive multimedia CDs for various musical instruments. Which elements of art would you use to enhance the CD's interface design? Consider the benefits of each visual design principle and the message each principle elicits. Use a table like the one below to help organize the results of your research.

B. Prepare an oral presentation summarizing the importance of visual design principles in the development of CD and DVD interfaces. Explain why the visual design's message is important and how an interface that is pleasing to the eye can increase the likelihood that users will read and use multimedia.

Multimedia Visual Design Principles		
Design Principles	**Purpose**	**Benefit**

Standardized Test Practice

True/False

Read the paragraphs below and then answer the question.

The two senses—sight and touch—give the sensation of texture. When you look at art, you see patterns of light and dark. These patterns call to mind memories of how the objects might feel when touched. When this happens you are experiencing *visual texture*. If you touch pictures on a printed page, they feel smooth and flat. Through your eyes,

however, you may imagine the feel of rough concrete, the cool smoothness of glass, or the soft warmth of fur.

Texture adds interest to multimedia presentations. Careful use of texture can catch the viewer's attention and create emotion and connection. Emotion and connection are effective tools in advertising.

18. Based on the paragraphs above, decide if the following statement is true or false.

When choosing art for a multimedia advertising project, it is never necessary to consider texture.

    A. T

    B. F

Test-Taking Tip On a true/false test, look for words such as always or never. These mean the statement must be true all of the time or none of the time.

19. Create a Home Page

You have decided to start a small business to review products for teens. You want to create a Web site to promote your business. Since your Web site will be the first place customers "meet" you, it must present you in the very best way.

NETS 1b Create original works as a means of personal or group expression.

A. Use multimedia software to design the layout of your Web site's home page. Your home page should correctly use the elements (line, shape, form, space, color, and texture) of art and apply the principles of visual design. Include effective use of white space, depth, perspective, and color.

B. Plan and write the content that will summarize your skills to review products for teens.

C. Share your design with classmates. Ask them to evaluate your use of the elements of art and principles of visual design. Incorporate their feedback.

20. Analyze Visual Design

You are a page designer for a magazine. Your manager has asked you to analyze the visual designs for the print and online editions.

A. With your teacher's permission, locate and review the print and online versions of a magazine. Compare and contrast how the elements of art are used in each version of the media. What visual design principles are applied in each?

B. What differences do you see between the print and digital media? How is the page layout different? How is each layout specific to the type of medium used? Use a chart like the one shown to organize your findings.

C. Write a brief summary of your findings. In your summary, explain how each deliverable targets a specific audience. Which magazine do you think you would read every day?

Elements	Print	Digital
Lines		
Shapes		
Form		
Space		
Color		
Texture		

NETS 4c Collect and analyze data to identify solutions and/or make informed decisions.

21. Take Responsibility

Did you know that there are several kinds of color schemes? For example, there are monochromatic, complementary, analogous, and accented neutral color schemes. You are responsible for researching and developing visual information to explain the different kinds of color schemes. You will use the information to teach the concepts to other classmates.

With your teacher's permission, choose one of these color schemes to research and explain to the class. Collect information and visuals that will allow you to teach this color scheme to the class.

You are responsible for the following tasks:

A. Collect information and visuals that explain and illustrate basic color theory as well as your assigned color scheme.

B. Prepare the pictures you will use as teaching aids.

C. Accept feedback from your teacher and your classmates as you prepare, plan, and create your presentation.

D. Make changes to information, visuals, and teaching based on feedback. Ask your teacher for permission to teach the class about your assigned color scheme.

CHALLENGE YOURSELF

22. Create a Visual Design

You have been asked to design a Web site to advertise a local restaurant that wants to cater to teens. The site will consist of three pages: the restaurant home page, a page of promotions directed at teens, and a menu. The restaurant owner would like you to develop a presentation to show her how you are going to plan, create, evaluate, and update the site and its visual design. Use a chart like the one below to help organize your thoughts. To develop your presentation, you will need to:

A. Research and brainstorm ideas for the Web site's visual design and for your presentation.

B. Sketch a visual design for each of the three Web pages. Use the elements of art and visual design principles to help you create the visual design. Write a brief summary of the text that will appear on each Web page. Explain what color scheme you will use and why this is important to the final product output.

C. Explain how you plan to evaluate and update the site.

D. On your own paper, create an outline for your presentation. Then, use presentation software to create your presentation. With your teacher's permission, give your presentation to your class.

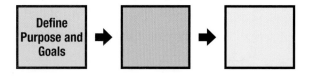

Project 1

Compare and Contrast Visual Design Principles

 Social Studies With your teacher's approval, choose a battle from the American Revolution. Locate a Web site about your battle and compare and contrast the use of balance and space in its visual design. Create a presentation based on your findings.

Plan

1. Before locating the Web site, write a paragraph that discusses balance in design and a paragraph that discusses the use of space in design.

Research

2. Locate a Web site to evaluate. Choose a site that includes graphics as well as text.

Create

3. Based on your study of the Web site, outline your presentation. Write a thesis statement that summarizes your comparison of the use of balance and space.

4. Create your presentation. Provide examples to support and illustrate your evaluation. If possible, include screen captures from the Web site to illustrate your presentation. Include the conclusions you have drawn.

Review

5. Edit your presentation. Proofread and spell-check your presentation.

> **NCSS VI A** Examine persistent issues involving the rights, roles, and status of the individual in relation to the general welfare.

Project 2

> **NCTE 4** Use written language to communicate effectively.

Evaluate Multimedia

English Language Arts Locate two different multimedia presentations. Write a one-page essay in which you evaluate their design and accessibility.

Plan

1. Create a list of questions for the evaluation. Use questions such as:

   - Are the goals of the multimedia presentation clear, and is the target audience clear? What assumptions are made about the audience?

   - Are design principles and the elements of art applied effectively?

   - Is the layout engaging and visually interesting?

   - Is content appropriate, and are the ideas communicated effectively?

Create

2. Write down your answers to these questions and to any others you ask.

3. Evaluate your findings, and outline your essay. Write a thesis statement. Use your outline and your thesis statement as the basis for a first draft of your paper.

4. Edit your final paper. Proofread and spell-check the document.

Project 3

Analyze the Importance of Design

NCTE 12 Use language to accomplish individual purposes.

English Language Arts Different people respond in different ways to advertising. In this project, you will design a multimedia advertisement and survey people in your target audience to get their reactions to the ad. Then you will analyze your results, revise your design based on the results, and draw a conclusion.

Research

1. Conduct research about the art of advertising. Find information on the Internet or in magazines or books that will help you understand what it takes to make an advertisement appealing to a specific target audience. Consider such things as:

Adapting Visual Design to Your Audience		
Color	**Font**	**Graphics**
• What color should the background be, and what color should the text be? • Is creating an ad in black and white an option? • What color scheme should you use?	• Which fonts are the most readable? • How large should the font be to be readable?	• Should you use photographs or clip art? • How should you balance the graphics on the page? • Should you use animation or any special effects?

Create

2. Based on your research, create a design for an advertisement for a product of your choice. Use a product that will appeal to your age group. Use presentation or multimedia software to create your advertisement.

Review

3. Share your ad with the class. Ask for their reactions to your design. Do they like it? Do they dislike it? Are they undecided? Why do they feel the way they do? Record your survey findings.

Revise

4. Based on your survey results, make changes to your design. Then, write a half-page analysis describing how age and other factors may affect perception of design. What conclusions can you draw? Why is it important to analyze your audience before you start to design and develop multimedia?

5. Proofread and spell-check the document.

Go Online RUBRICS
glencoe.com

Chapter Projects Use the rubrics for these projects to help create and evaluate your work. Go to the **Online Learning Center** at **glencoe.com**. Choose **Rubrics**, then **Chapter 5**.

UNIT 2

Portfolio Project

Plan a Web Site

In this unit, you learned how to create a content plan that specifies items such as project goals, the target audience, a mission statement, and project requirements. You also learned how to develop a project that applies the elements and principles of visual design. This portfolio project gives you the opportunity to strengthen these new skills by planning a Web site for a school club or organization, such as the multimedia club or the athletic department.

Project Assignment

In this project, you will:

- Develop a content plan that includes your school Web site's purpose, goals, target audience, mission statement, and requirements.
- Create a storyboard showing the pages and the layout of the text and multimedia elements of the home page.
- Apply the elements and principles of visual design.
- Write a testing plan that explains how you would test the site.
- Write an implementation plan that explains how you would implement the site.

Multimedia Skills Behind the Project

Your success in multimedia design will depend on your skills:

- Choose an appropriate navigation scheme.
- Determine how to divide the site into individual pages.
- Design a home page that is well composed, making it easy for visitors to locate what they need.
- Apply the elements of visual design.
- Apply the principles of visual design, including balance, proportion, rhythm, and unity.
- Demonstrate planning and time-management skills such as project management and storyboarding.

Academic Skills Behind the Project

Remember these key academic concepts:

Writing Skills

- Use correct grammar, punctuation, and terminology to write and edit multimedia documents.
- Employ effective verbal and nonverbal communication skills.
- Adapt language for audience, purpose, situation, and intent.

Problem-Solving Skills

- Determine the needs of the site's visitors and how these needs can best be met.
- Solve problems and think critically.

 **English Language Arts**

NCTE 4 Use written language to communicate effectively.

NCTE 5 Use different writing process elements to communicate effectively.

NCTE 12 Use language to accomplish individual purposes.

 **Mathematics**

NCTM Problem Solving Apply and adapt a variety of appropriate strategies to solve problems.

STEP 1   Analyze and Plan the Project

Follow these steps to develop the content and project plans.

- Develop a list of project goals.

- State the target audience, write a mission statement, list the project requirements, and state the project's scope.

STEP 2   Design Your Project

Apply the elements and principles of visual design as you follow these steps:

- Choose an appropriate navigation scheme.

- Create a storyboard that shows the basic layout and contents of each page and indicates how pages will be linked to one another.

- Create a detailed sketch showing the layout and contents of the home page.

- Specify the text, audio, and visual content that will be contained on the home page.

- Choose a color scheme using Web-safe colors.

STEP 3   Share Your Presentation

Ask a classmate or a trusted adult to review your content and project plans and your Web site design.

- Ask for feedback, constructive criticism, and suggestions for changes.

- Encourage your reviewer to ask questions.

STEP 4   Plan the Implementation of Your Project

Use what you have learned about project implementation to write a paragraph explaining how you might implement your Web site.

STEP 5   Evaluate and Test Your Project

Apply what you have learned about project testing to perform these tasks:

- Write a paragraph describing how you would test this Web site.

- Use the Portfolio Project Checklist to evaluate your work.

- Make final changes, if necessary.

Portfolio Project Checklist

ANALYSIS AND PLANNING

☑ A content plan that includes a mission statement and the site's purpose, goals, and target audience, has been written.

☑ A project plan that defines the project's scope has been written.

DESIGN AND DEVELOPMENT

☑ An appropriate navigation scheme has been chosen.

☑ A storyboard has been created that shows the basic layout and contents of each page and indicates how pages will be linked to one another.

☑ The storyboard shows the layout and contents, including all multimedia elements, of the home page.

☑ The elements and principles of visual design have been followed.

☑ An appropriate color scheme has been chosen.

IMPLEMENTATION

☑ The implementation plan explains how the Web site will be made available to the target audience, for example by uploading it to a Web server.

TESTING AND EVALUATION

☑ The testing plan explains that the Web site will be checked to make certain that all components, including multimedia elements, are error-free.

☑ The testing plan explains that visual elements will be checked for consistency in look and placement and that all content will be proofread and checked for spelling and grammar errors.

☑ The project has been reviewed by a classmate or trusted adult and appropriate changes have been made.

Go Online RUBRICS

glencoe.com

Go to this book's **Online Learning Center** at glencoe.com for a rubric you can use to evaluate your final project.

UNIT 3

Multimedia Components

- Chapter **6** Text
- Chapter **7** Graphics and Animation
- Chapter **8** Audio
- Chapter **9** Video

UNIT Portfolio Project Preview

Design an Online Newsletter

In this unit, you will understand how to use multimedia components such as text, graphics, animation, audio, and video. You will use these components to enhance a variety of multimedia projects. In the Unit Portfolio Project, you will develop an online newsletter for a local organization.

 Go Online PREVIEW

glencoe.com

Go to the **Online Learning Center** and select your book. Click **Unit 3>Portfolio Project Preview** to learn more about planning, designing, and developing a multimedia project.

Explore the Photo

It is important to use all multimedia components, such as text and graphics, to enhance your project's goals.

How might you use text and graphics to create a logo for a community service organization at your school?

Section 6.1
Text in Multimedia

Section 6.2
Work with Text

CHAPTER OBJECTIVES

After completing this chapter, you will be able to:

❖ **Recognize** the role text plays in multimedia.

❖ **Describe** the kinds of software applications used for working with text.

❖ **Distinguish** among the major file formats for storing text.

❖ **Identify** the characteristics of text you can control through formatting.

❖ **Explain** how software is used to edit and manage fonts.

❖ **Apply** recommended guidelines for working with text in screen displays.

Explore the Photo

Text used in multimedia can help you get the most from the other multimedia elements. *How can text be used to enhance a home video?*

21st CENTURY SKILLS
Prioritize

Every day, numerous tasks compete for your attention. Addressing them in order of importance can help you use your time and energy wisely.

Quick Write Activity Cause and Effect

Write about a time when prioritizing led to the successful outcome of a situation.

Writing Tips

To write an effective cause-and-effect paragraph, follow these steps:

1. Focus on how the cause, being able to prioritize resources, created a positive effect.
2. Write a clear thesis statement. Make sure your paragraph takes a clear position.
3. Include an introduction and conclusion. Use appropriate transitional words between the cause and effect, such as therefore and because.

SECTION 6.1 Text in Multimedia

Reading Guide

Before You Read

Use Notes Whenever you come across a term or concept in the section that is unfamiliar or unclear, write it down on a notepad. After you are done reading, look up the answers to your questions.

Read to Learn
Key Concepts

- **Identify** the functions of text in different multimedia productions.
- **Name** types of computer applications for working with text.
- **Distinguish** among the common formats for text files.

Main Idea

Text is an important component of most multimedia productions. It is typically combined with other media. Text can be saved in different formats for different purposes.

Content Vocabulary

◇ banner ad
◇ text message
◇ open source
◇ text editor
◇ file format

Academic Vocabulary

You will find these words in your reading and on your tests. Use the glossary to look up their definitions, if necessary.

◆ role
◆ incorporate

Graphic Organizer

As you read the section, note the role of text in multimedia projects. Use a table like the one shown to note examples of multimedia in which text may appear.

Project	Role of Text

 Graphic Organizer Go to this book's **Online Learning Center** at glencoe.com to print this graphic organizer.

Academic Standards

 English Language Arts

NCTE 5 Use different writing process elements to communicate effectively.
NCTE 6 Apply knowledge of language structure and conventions to discuss texts.

NCTE 12 Use language to accomplish individual purposes.

NCTE National Council of Teachers of English
NSES National Science Education Standards

NCTM National Council of Teachers of Mathematics
NCSS National Council for the Social Studies

Use Text in Multimedia

How is text used in different multimedia projects?

Text consists of letters, numbers, and other symbols. In multimedia, the **role**, or job, of text may be to inform, persuade, or entertain. Most multimedia includes text. Text almost never appears on its own in multimedia projects. It is used with other multimedia elements. The role of text in a multimedia project should always be consistent with the goals, purpose, and audience of the project. Whenever you use text in a project, whether it is a letter, an advertisement, or a brochure, you must plan what you want to say before you write it. It is always important to revise your written work.

Web Pages and Online Advertisements

Every Web site contains text. It is often used to explain the site's purpose or to promote the site in some way. Some text may be hypertext. Hypertext links to another location on the site or on the Web when it is clicked. A hypertext link, also called a hyperlink or simply a link, usually stands out because it is a different color than the rest of the text on the Web page.

One role of text on a Web site is to advertise a product or service, as shown in Figure 6.1. A **banner ad** is a type of advertisement used on the Web that, when clicked, takes the user to the sponsor's home page. A banner ad promotes a product or service. Banner ads may contain animation, audio, or video. When users click a banner ad, they are led to the advertiser's Web site.

Other online ads are similar to banner ads. A rollover ad changes from a banner to a larger ad when users move their mouse over it. A pop-up ad appears in a new browser window.

As You Read

Connect In the last 24 hours, what multimedia projects with text have you seen?

Visibility Color can play an important role in the design of a banner ad. Using a bold color for text may attract viewers to your ad.

Why It's Important

If no one notices a banner ad, how effective do you think it will be?

Figure 6.1
Almost every Web site uses text to inform, persuade, or entertain. **How is text used on this Web page?**

E-mail and Text Message Marketing

Marketing is the process of advertising, selling, and distributing a product or service. E-marketing combines text and graphics to encourage repeat business and to get new customers. The most common e-marketing is done via e-mail. A **text message** is a brief electronic message between mobile devices. Businesses can send customers ads and news as text messages. Short Message Service (SMS) is the technology that makes text messaging possible. Text messages sent using Multimedia Messaging Service (MMS) may include multimedia files, such as graphics, audio, and video.

Mobile Applications and Games

Software applications developed for handheld devices such as mobile phones often use text. These applications, also called apps, can be purchased or downloaded for free (see Figure 6.2). Mobile apps include study tools, media players, and games. Text for games and apps may be used for rules and instructions, chat features, character descriptions, background story, feedback, and other information.

Figure 6.2
Mobile apps allow users to study, work, and play games on mobile phones. **How is text used in mobile apps?**

CBT, Presentations, and Kiosks

Most computer-based training (CBT), including Web-based training (WBT), relies on text to deliver lessons, exercises, tests, and user feedback. Some CBT programs come with printed workbooks for trainees to use when they do not have access to computers.

Multimedia presentations often include text on a projection screen or interactive whiteboard. Typically, a presentation consists of a series of slides, and some slides present a list of the main points the speaker would like to make. Some presentations include text handouts, which are copies of the slides that may include the presenter's notes.

A kiosk is a stand-alone display without a presenter. The text used in a kiosk presentation is usually integrated with other media, such as graphics, audio, and video. Museums use kiosks to provide information. Airports, hotels, stores, and other businesses may use kiosks to complete registration, check in guests, or to complete sales transactions..

 **Reading Check** **Name** What are eight types of multimedia projects that may use text?

Project Management
If your multimedia project requires a specific format, decide which applications you need to create it. Also consider what software users might need in order to view it.

Software for Working with Text

What kinds of software and file formats are used for working with text in multimedia projects?

When working with text in multimedia, it is important to understand the software used to create and edit text. You should also be familiar with the various file formats for storing text.

You might use the following types of programs to develop text for a multimedia project: word processing, text editing, Web design, desktop publishing, presentation, multimedia authoring, graphics editing, video editing, and optical character recognition (OCR).

Word Processing and Text Editing

Word processing applications, such as Microsoft Word, can be used to create letters, reports, and other documents. **Open source** programs are ones that can be freely copied and modified. Adobe® Buzzword®, shown in Figure 6.3, and Google Docs™ are open-source word processors that operate within a Web browser, letting you create, edit, and share documents such as letterhead, letters, memos, reports, flyers, brochures, advertisements, newsletters, certificates, postcards, and business cards.

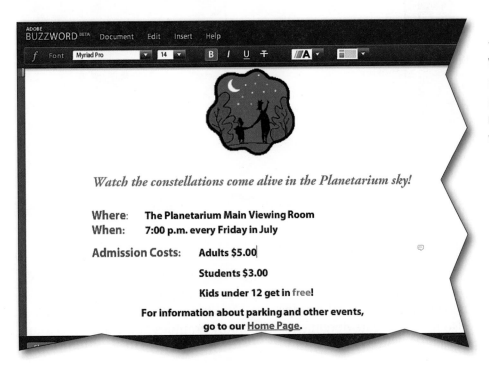

Figure 6.3
Word processing documents might combine text with graphics. What types of documents have you created using word processing software?

A **text editor** is a program for modifying plain text files. Text editors come standard with both the Windows® and Mac® operating systems. Text editors do not allow users to make complex formatting changes, but text files can be viewed using different word processing software. Microsoft Windows has two text editors: Notepad and WordPad. The Mac OS® offers a text editor called TextEdit. Text editors are sometimes used to create content for the Web. Web developers might save the file with the .html extension and then view the files in a Web browser or in Web design software.

Web Design

Web design programs such as Adobe® Dreamweaver® and Microsoft Expression® Web have features for creating, editing, and formatting text and hyperlinks for Web site pages (see Figure 6.4). This software allows developers to create a consistent appearance for text across very large Web sites.

You can copy text from a word processing document and paste it into a Web design program. Word processing software also allows you to save documents in the .html format and then open the new XHTML file in a Web design program.

Figure 6.4
Web design software allows you to create, edit, and format text and hyperlinks. How can you use word processing software and Web design software together?

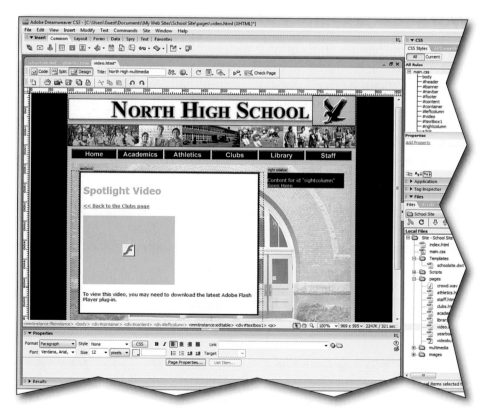

Desktop Publishing

Desktop publishing (DTP) programs are more powerful than word processing programs for working with very large documents, such as books, magazines, and newspapers. Desktop publishing programs are also used to create documents with many graphics and complex layouts.

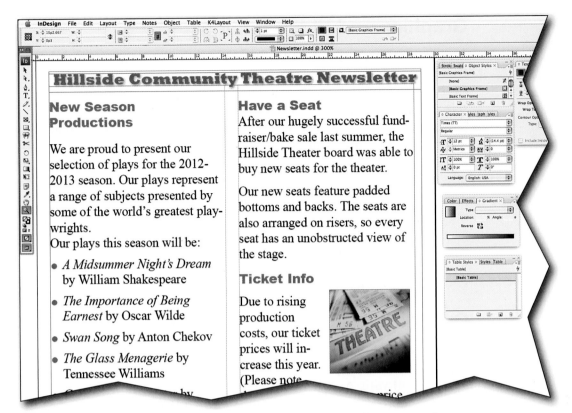

Desktop publishing programs are used to prepare documents for printing. In addition, desktop publishing programs are used to publish manuals, catalogs, and other content in an online format.

Popular desktop publishing programs include:

- **Microsoft Office Publisher** This inexpensive and easy-to-use program is suitable for flyers, brochures, postcards, letterhead, ads, and business cards.

- **Adobe InDesign®** Professional designers use InDesign to create print and online products such as posters, newsletters, magazines, and books (see Figure 6.5). InDesign allows publications to be delivered with video, sound, animation, and interactivity.

Text plays an important role in most pieces produced with desktop publishing software. Whether such publications are printed or appear online, they may also **incorporate**, or include, other media elements.

Presentation and Multimedia Authoring

Presentation and multimedia authoring programs can be used to assemble various media elements into a finished product. The product might be a presentation, demonstration, tutorial, computer-based training, game, or kiosk content. Text can be developed in these programs or imported from another program. Typically, text is combined with animation, special effects, video, graphics, and sound. Microsoft Office PowerPoint® and Apple Keynote® are examples of presentation software. Multimedia authoring programs include Adobe Director® and Adobe Authorware®.

Figure 6.5
Adobe InDesign is a popular desktop publishing program. What types of documents are commonly created using desktop publishing programs?

Go Online **ACTIVITY**
glencoe.com

Evaluate Writing Styles Learn more about writing for multimedia presentations at the **Online Learning Center**. Go to **glencoe.com**. Choose **Activities**, then **Chapter 6.**

Graphics and Video Editing

Graphics editing programs, such as Adobe Photoshop®, Adobe Illustrator®, and Microsoft Paint, have features for creating titles, captions, labels, and other text. These programs generally offer a selection of fonts and formatting options. You can control the color, placement, and other characteristics of text added to images in a graphics editing program.

Video editing programs have features for adding titles, credits, and other text to videos. Like graphics editors, video editing programs generally offer a variety of fonts and formatting options. When selecting a font to use with a video, keep in mind how the font will appear when displayed on a large screen or on a video or computer monitor. Common video editing programs include Adobe Premier Pro®, Adobe After Effects®, Avid® Xpress Pro, and Apple Final Cut Pro®. Windows Movie Maker is basic video editing software included in Windows.

Optical Character Recognition

If you want to place text from a printed document into a digital presentation, one option is to retype the text with word processing or other software. Another method is to scan the text and digitize it. Scanners store pages as graphics. Optical character recognition (OCR) software converts the text to digital format. Most OCR programs have options for saving the resulting text into a format that can be brought into a multimedia production. Even the best OCR software makes errors, though. It is important to proofread converted text.

 **Identify** What are two popular desktop publishing programs?

Text File Formats

Which file formats can be used by most word processing programs?

A text file is a file created with software that is used mainly for composing text, such as a word processing program. A **file format**, also called file type, refers to the way a document is saved. The file format determines which programs can open it. It is also important to consider what software other team members or viewers might be using to access or view your multimedia project. Text-based documents generally have one of the file formats listed in Figure 6.6.

- Documents are often saved with the .doc file extension. If you need to convert such a file to a format that can be read by any word processing application, convert the file to a TXT (plain text) or RTF (rich text) format. Remember that during the conversion, text formatting may be lost.

- PDF is the most common format for text documents downloaded from the Web. Saving a document as a PDF file maintains its formatting. Users must have Acrobat Reader, which can be downloaded for free, in order to read PDF files.

Accessibility PDF files can be created specially for use by people with disabilities. PDFs can include codes that allow screen readers to translate text into artificial speech or electronic Braille.

Text File Formats	
File format	**Description**
DOC (.doc)	Stands for Document. The default file format for many word processing programs, including Microsoft Word. Files with the .doc extension can contain text, graphics, tables, and hyperlinks.
PDF (.pdf)	Stands for Portable Document Format. A snapshot of a final document, which can contain text, graphics, and hyperlinks. A PDF cannot be edited as typical text files can.
TXT (.txt)	Stands for TeXT. All word processors and many other programs can save and open TXT files. Also called "plain text" because it contains few formatting options. Files with the .txt file extension are often used to create Web content. The file extension is changed to a .html extension so that the file can be viewed in a Web browser.
RTF (.rtf)	Stands for Rich Text Format. Many programs can save documents as RTF files, which keep text attributes such as underlining, bold, and font specifications when opened in other programs.
XHTML (.xhtml, .xht, .xml, .html, .htm)	Stands for EXtensible HyperText Markup Language. Uses embedded codes called tags to create hypertext links and specify text formats in Web pages.

Figure 6.6
Text files are created by text editors and word processing programs. Which file format contains little or no text formatting and can be opened by many programs?

It is important to know how to convert files for your multimedia projects. You may need to convert files in order to meet the needs of your audience. For example, imagine that you work for a local planetarium. You have created a flyer to print and post to promote an upcoming event. You also would like to post the flyer as a Web page. In the following activity, you will edit a flyer and save two versions of the file, one as a word processing document and the other as a Web page.

Activity 6A Edit a Flyer and Save It as Multiple File Types

1. Locate and open the data file folder for Chapter 6. Open the **Flyer.doc** data file.

2. You need to update the prices for adults and students. Key the new price for adults as **$5.00**. Key the new price for students as **$3.00**.

3. Proofread the file. When you are ready to save the file, click **File>Save As**. Click the **Save as type** drop-down arrow. Choose **Rich Text Format (*.rtf)**. With your teacher's assistance, select the location where you will save the file. Click **Save**.

YOU TRY IT

DATA FILE

④ The file extension on the title bar should be .rtf. Click **File>Save As**. Click the **Save as type** drop-down arrow.

⑤ Choose **Web Page (*.htm, *.html)**. Save the file in the same location as the **Flyer.rtf** file.

⑥ Close the file.

⑦ Browse to the folder where you saved the files. There should be two versions of the **Flyer** file. Open the version named **Flyer.htm**. The file should open in your default Web browser, as shown in Figure 6.7.

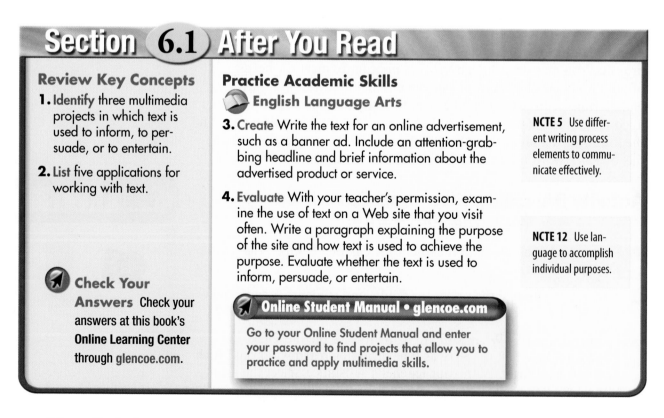

Figure 6.7
The edited Flyer.htm file as it appears in a Web browser.

✔ **Reading Check** **Recall** What does PDF stand for?

Section 6.1 After You Read

Review Key Concepts

1. Identify three multimedia projects in which text is used to inform, to persuade, or to entertain.

2. List five applications for working with text.

🎯 **Check Your Answers** Check your answers at this book's **Online Learning Center** through glencoe.com.

Practice Academic Skills

🌐 **English Language Arts**

3. **Create** Write the text for an online advertisement, such as a banner ad. Include an attention-grabbing headline and brief information about the advertised product or service.

4. **Evaluate** With your teacher's permission, examine the use of text on a Web site that you visit often. Write a paragraph explaining the purpose of the site and how text is used to achieve the purpose. Evaluate whether the text is used to inform, persuade, or entertain.

🎯 **Online Student Manual • glencoe.com**

Go to your Online Student Manual and enter your password to find projects that allow you to practice and apply multimedia skills.

NCTE 5 Use different writing process elements to communicate effectively.

NCTE 12 Use language to accomplish individual purposes.

SECTION (6.2) Work with Text

Reading Guide

Before You Read

Pace Yourself To keep yourself focused, read for ten minutes. Take a short break. Then read for another ten minutes.

Read to Learn

Key Concepts

- **Select** appropriate fonts and text formatting for multimedia projects.
- **Identify** ways to control fonts for use in multimedia productions.
- **Demonstrate** recommended practices for using text in multimedia.

Main Idea

The way text is formatted contributes to its readability and impact in multimedia. Understanding the technology behind fonts helps you select and manage them effectively.

Content Vocabulary

◇ typography   ◇ point

◇ typeface   ◇ alignment

◇ font   ◇ tracking

◇ serif   ◇ kerning

◇ sans serif

Academic Vocabulary

You will find these words in your reading and on your tests. Use the glossary to look up their definitions, if necessary.

◆ common   ◆ guideline

Graphic Organizer

As you read, look for the four text alignment options. Use a main idea chart like the one shown to help organize your information.

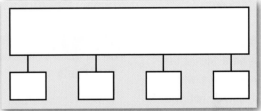

 Graphic Organizer Go to this book's **Online Learning Center** at glencoe.com to print this graphic organizer.

Academic Standards

📖 English Language Arts

NCTE 4 Use written language to communicate effectively.
NCTE 9 Develop an understanding of diversity in language use across cultures.
NCTE 12 Use language to accomplish individual purposes.

Mathematics

NCTM Measurement Understand measurable attributes of objects and the units, systems, and processes of measurement.

NCTE National Council of Teachers of English
NSES National Science Education Standards

NCTM National Council of Teachers of Mathematics
NCSS National Council for the Social Studies

As You Read

Connect What text formatting do you recognize in the pages of this book?

Typography and Fonts

How does text formatting contribute to the text's impact in a multimedia project?

Typography is the style, arrangement, and appearance of text. Typography plays a role in how text communicates the message of a multimedia production.

Until a few decades ago, typography generally involved hard type. Hard type refers to text characters that were cast in metal or carved in wood. These characters were combined to make impressions on paper or to make printing plates. Today, desktop publishing programs make it much easier to edit a document and add formatting to text.

A **typeface**, also called a **font**, is a design for an alphabet, including letters, numbers, punctuation marks, and symbols, that share a consistent style. Arial, Times New Roman, and Helvetica are three of the most common typefaces.

Fonts are classified in two categories. **Serif** fonts have additional lines or curves on the ends of most letters. Serif fonts are generally thought to be easier to read and are often used for printed text, such as in newspapers and books. **Sans serif** fonts are clean. They do not have additional lines. Sans serif fonts are often considered easier to read online. For this reason, they are commonly used in online multimedia projects. The titles and headings in this book use sans serif fonts. The body text is a serif font. Some common serif and sans serif fonts are shown in Figure 6.8.

Figure 6.8

Serif fonts have lines at the ends of most letters, while sans serif fonts do not. Which types of fonts are generally used in print?

Basic Font Types	
Serif Fonts	Sans Serif Fonts
Times New Roman	Arial
Courier New	Futura
Garamond	Verdana

Font Technologies

Software companies have developed several different font technologies, or standards, over the past decades. Newer technologies provide more design options and other features. The most popular font technologies are **TrueType** and **OpenType**.

TrueType, the dominant font technology for PCs, was developed by Apple. Windows and Mac OS both come with some TrueType fonts, which are scalable. A scalable font can be resized. Scalable fonts provide high-quality text for both screen display and printing.

OpenType is a font technology developed jointly by Adobe and Microsoft. (See Figure 6.9 on page 177.) It extends TrueType technology by allowing larger character sets and more typographic control. Like TrueType fonts, OpenType fonts can be resized and used on either Windows or Macintosh computers.

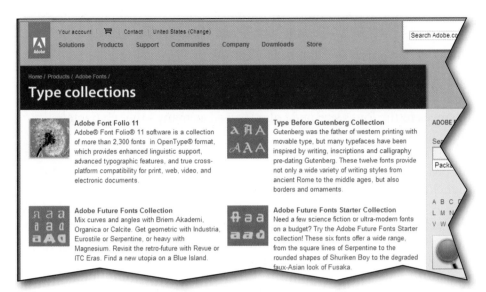

Figure 6.9
Many fonts can be downloaded from the Internet, giving you more options for your multimedia project. **What are OpenType fonts?**

Edit and Manage Fonts

Computers have different fonts on their hard drives. The Windows and Mac OS come with some **common** (shared) fonts. Each also has fonts the other does not. In fact, fonts may vary among different versions of the same operating system. Further, many PC users install additional fonts that other users do not necessarily have.

When you open a file that uses a font your PC does not have, the computer generally substitutes a font with a similar appearance. The substitution is often not noticeable, but font substitutions can cause problems. For example, on a Web page, font substitution might make the labels on buttons unreadable. Font substitution can also move elements in a multimedia presentation out of their proper positions. To avoid these problems, use a font manager and make sure that you use fonts that work across platforms, as shown in Figure 6.10.

A font manager organizes all the fonts on a system. Font managers, such as Extensis® Suitcase Fusion, are essential in multimedia development because projects may require numerous fonts. A font editing program, or font editor, provides tools for making changes to fonts. Two popular font editors are FontLab Fontographer™ and High-Logic FontCreator™.

Figure 6.10
It is important to use fonts that, when substituted, will not alter the page or screen layout in multimedia. **Why can font substitution cause problems?**

Mac OS and Windows Font Substitutions	
Mac OS System Font	Windows System Font
Courier	Courier New
Helvetica	Arial
Times	Times New Roman

 **Reading Check** **Explain** What is the difference between a font editor and a font manager?

Format Text for Readability

In what ways can text be formatted for use in multimedia projects?

When you work with text for a multimedia project, you can make many kinds of formatting changes. You can select the fonts and make changes to the font's size and color, as well as many other characteristics, such as alignment and kerning.

It important to consider readability when making formatting changes to text. When text is readable, the most important information is highlighted, and readers will want to continue reading the details.. Readable text is formatted with the purpose, audience, and goals for the multimedia project in mind. Be careful to avoid making formatting changes that make text difficult to read. Readability will be affected by size, style, color, special effects, alignment, and text wrapping.

Modify Size, Style, and Color

Type size is often measured in points. The larger the point size, the bigger the text. A font's **point** size is based on the height of the characters, and a single point is one seventy-second of an inch. Size is also sometimes measured in picas instead of points. A pica is about one-sixth of an inch.

Text of the same font size might seem wider in one font than another. For example, each of the three typefaces in Figure 6.11 is illustrated in 28-point size type. As you can see, the Arial font is slightly wider than the Optima and Garamond fonts at the same point size.

A typical Web page, presentation slide, or other multimedia display uses fonts at several point sizes. Point size shows the relative importance of different text items.

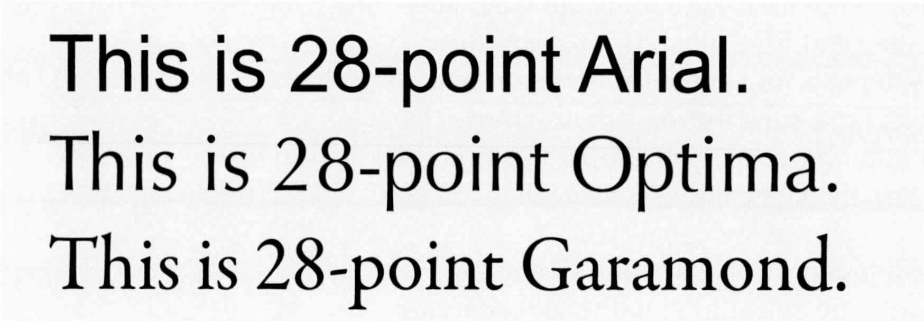

This is 28-point Arial.
This is 28-point Optima.
This is 28-point Garamond.

Figure 6.11
Different fonts will have different appearances even in the same point size. What point size should a heading be?

- The title or main heading is usually the largest text, between 18 and 72 points.
- The next level of heading is generally two sizes smaller than the main heading.
- Body text is at least two sizes smaller than headings, typically 10 or 12 points.

Headings should be highly readable. Body text should be smaller, but not so small that it cannot be easily read. Figure 6.12 on page 179 illustrates the way font size is commonly used to make different kinds of information more readable. In this document, you would expect all the body text to be a consistent font and size.

It is common to use a smaller font size for text elements that are less important than the body text, such as footers and footnotes. When

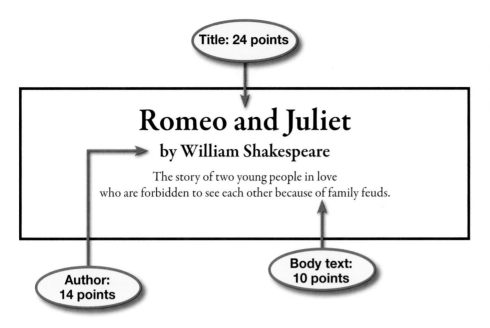

Figure 6.12
The size of the text indicates what is important. **What is the most important element on this page?**

selecting type sizes for a multimedia project, think about how the text content will convey meaning.

You can apply basic font styles such as bold, italic, and underlining to text. These styles are used to emphasize individual words or phrases.

- Bold type is darker and thicker than the surrounding type.

- The characters in italic type tilt to the right, as in book titles.

- Underlines may be solid or broken. Underlining is often used to show a hyperlink, so it should be used carefully.

You can apply color to text for emphasis, impact, or visual appeal. Color can also be used to distinguish headings from body text. Use color sparingly to increase its impact.

Special Formatting and Effects

Desktop publishing software allows you to create special formats. It is important to use these formats in a manner that keeps text readable.

- Outline gives characters a hollow look: Romeo and Juliet.

- Drop shadow, or just shadow, is a soft outline, generally below and to the side of characters: Romeo and Juliet.

- Superscript is a smaller number or symbol appearing slightly above other characters, as in Einstein's formula: $e = mc^2$.

- Subscript is a smaller number or symbol appearing slightly below other characters, as in the chemical formula for water: H_2O.

Perspective can make text appear to be shaped, such as three-dimensional, rounded, or curved. Depending on the software you are using, you might be able to use special effects and perspective to add interest and draw attention to text (see Figure 6.13 on page 180).

Special effects can create a sense of dramatic impact on your multimedia projects. Too many special effects can be distracting, though.

Academic Focus

 Mathematics

Determine Height
The title slide for a multimedia presentation has two lines of text. The first line uses a 44-point font and the second a 32-point font. The distance between the two lines is 104 points. What is the total number of inches this title takes up? Remember that there are 72 points in an inch.

NCTM Measurement
Understand measurable attributes of objects and the units, systems, and processes of measurement.

Quick Tip

You Should Know Use special formatting sparingly in a multimedia presentation. It is best used to make a special point. If you use it repeatedly, it will make your text distracting and hard for your viewer to follow.

Figure 6.13
There are many special effects that can be applied to change the way text looks. What is the difference between embossed and engraved?

In general, it is a good idea to limit these special effects to the portions of a project that you want viewers to read immediately. Focus on using these effects on headings and short pieces of attention-getting text.

- **Embossing** gives the three-dimensional effect that characters are being pressed into paper.
- **Engraving** makes characters appear to be carved into paper.
- **Watermark** is an imprinted word or words intended to be only faintly visible behind the text on a page.
- **Animation** Makes text move, stream across a screen, or rotate. Some text animation is done with graphics programs, which is discussed in Chapter 7.

Align, Space, and Wrap Text

Most programs allows you to align, or line up, text in several ways. **Alignment** is the position of text on a page. Figure 6.14 shows four alignment options. Left-aligned is the default setting for all word processing and desktop publishing programs.

Left-aligned is the most common type of alignment. The other three options are less frequently used because they are distracting and

Figure 6.14

Text can be left-aligned, centered, right-aligned, or justified. Which alignment is most common?

Left-aligned text is positioned flush with the left edge of the page. Text is usually left-aligned automatically when you enter it on a page.	Centered text is positioned in the middle of the page.	Right-aligned text is positioned flush with the page's right edge.	Justified text is positioned so that all lines have the same left and right margins.

make text harder to read. Centered text is generally used for headers or text such as quotes that need to be set apart from the rest of the text.

You can choose how much space appears between lines and paragraphs and between individual characters. Leading is the space between lines. **Tracking** is the amount of space between characters. **Kerning** is the space between a specific pair of characters. For example, in most fonts, the shapes of the letters A and V make them appear farther apart than they actually are. You can kern this pair of letters (that is, remove a portion of the space between them) for a smoother look. See Figure 6.15 for examples of tracking and kerning.

Most multimedia applications illustrate text with graphics, such as drawings, photos, or design elements. Text wrap is the flow of text around graphics in a multimedia production. Notice the way text flows around some of the graphics in this book.

In the next activity, you will use a desktop publishing program to practice text formatting and font effects in a restaurant menu.

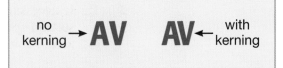

Loose Tracking

SUSPECT VANISHES
West-Side Police Lose James in Corn Field

Tight Tracking

SUSPECT VANISHES
West-Side Police Lose James in Corn Field

Figure 6.15

Tracking allows letters in a sentence to be closer or further apart. **What is kerning?**

Activity 6B Format Text in a Desktop Publishing Program

YOU TRY IT

1. Open a desktop publishing program, such as Adobe InDesign.

2. Create a new document. Make sure the document has a landscape orientation, which means that it is wider than it is tall.

3. Locate and open the data file folder for Chapter 6. Open the **Restaurant.doc** data file. Copy the text from the data file into your desktop publishing program. Position the text in two columns.

4. Use a right-aligned tab with leaders to position the prices on the right side of each column.

5. Change the menu section names (such as "Appetizers") to a font with thick, heavy serifs (such as Rockwell Extra Bold) at 16 points.

6. Change each menu item and its price to a bold, sans serif font (such as Arial) at 10 points.

7. Change each menu item description to a serif font (such as Times New Roman), italicized, at 10 points.

8. Change the spacing after the menu section heads to 9 points.

9. Apply a dark color and a special effect (such as shadow, outline, emboss, engrave, or perspective) to the menu section heads.

⑩ If necessary, adjust the alignment of the text so that each menu section appears completely within one column and does not break across columns.

⑪ Key a name for the restaurant and center it vertically and horizontally within the right column.

⑫ Try using a fanciful or playful font, in a size, color, and style appropriate for a restaurant's logo.

⑬ Try applying a color with a gradient to the background of the menu. Watch to make sure that the background color isn't too dark so that you can not read the menu items.

⑭ Save the document as **Your Name Restaurant Menu** and close your desktop publishing software. Figure 6.16 shows an example of how the menu might look.

Amici's

Appetizers and Soups

CHICKEN LETTUCE WRAPS 7.95
Our signature appetizer—often copied, never equaled

ANTIPASTO 8.95
Delectable meat, cheese, and vegetable plate

TOMATO SALAD 5.95
Fresh Roma tomatoes, garlic, and basil marinated to perfection

DAILY SOUP SPECIAL 4.95
Fresh, homemade soup made daily

Sandwiches

MEATLOVER'S SUB 7.95
Delicious deli meats and cheese on a fresh-baked roll

VEGGIE LOVER'S SUB 7.95
Fresh vegetables and Italian dressing on a fresh-baked roll

LIGHT LUNCH COMBO 5.95
A half sandwich and a bowl of fresh soup

Pizzas

MARGHERITA 8.95
Delicious pizza with the freshest ingredients

GARLIC AND OLIVES 7.95
Garlic lover's special! Comes with a free breath mint

Pastas

PENNE PESTO 7.95
Delicious whole-wheat penne pasta and homemade pesto

LINGUINE ALFREDO 8.95
Al dente linguine with a delicious cream sauce

LASAGNE WITH MEAT SAUCE 8.95
Meat lover's special with fresh tomato sauce and homemade pasta

MARINARA SPECIAL 7.95
Linguine, fettuccini, or penne pasta with a delicious marinara sauce

SEAFOOD LOVER'S SPECIAL 10.95
Delicious linguine with clam sauce or shrimp

Desserts

TIRAMISU 6.95
Simply delectable

ICE CREAM 6.95
Try vanilla, chocolate, strawberry, or all three

CHOCOLATE CHEESECAKE 7.95
You'll love our homemade chocolate cheesecake

FRUIT AND CHEESE PLATE 5.95
Seasonal fruit and light cheese—perfect for sharing

Figure 6.16
Using different fonts and font characteristics can make a document visually appealing, even without graphics.

Create Lists

Formatting text in lists organizes information so that it is easier to read. Items in lists can be ordered or unordered. An ordered list uses numbers or letters to present information in steps or in sequential order. An unordered list uses bullets or symbols to present information that does not need to be in a specific order. A bullet is a small graphical symbol, such as a dot or a diamond. See Figure 6.17 for examples of numbered and bulleted lists.

Figure 6.17
Lists can be ordered using numbers or unordered using bullets. **When would it make sense to use an ordered list?**

Numerical list of instructions:	Bulleted list of types of fonts:
1. Turn on computer.	• Courier New
2. Enter user name and password.	• Garamond
3. Open My Documents folder on desktop.	• Times New Roman
4. Click on Multimedia folder.	• Verdana

 **Reading Check** **Describe** What are the four ways to align text?

Text Formatting Guidelines
What are guidelines for formatting text in multimedia projects?

There are some important guidelines you should follow when using text in multimedia. A **guideline** is a rule or principle that provides advice for appropriate behavior. Text in a multimedia production should be readable, formatted consistently, and attractive. A presentation is more likely to be successful when the text is attractive, informative, and used consistently.

Readability

Readability is the foundation of all text formatting. Follow these guidelines in order to create readable text in your multimedia projects.

- **Provide good contrast.** Contrast is the obvious distinction between two elements, such as text and a background. Some colors show up poorly against certain backgrounds. For example, there is not enough difference between pink and red for pink text to stand out against a red background. Avoid patterned backgrounds that make text difficult to read. Figure 6.18 shows you how patterns and contrast can negatively impact the presentation of text.

- **Use increased point size to emphasize information.** Make sure the text for a presentation that will be viewed by a large group of people, such as a slide show, is visible from the back of the room. Follow the guidelines given earlier in this chapter for making headings consistent and readable.

- **Use an appropriate amount of text on-screen to avoid scrolling.** Some multimedia applications (especially Web sites) may require a certain amount of vertical scrolling for the content to make sense.

- **Use serif and sans serif fonts appropriately.** As a general rule, sans serif fonts are more readable in online publications, so consider consistently using sans serif fonts for headings and other attention-getting text. Avoid fanciful fonts.

Figure 6.18

Contrast is the distinction between two elements. Which of these pictures use contrast the best?

PLAN AHEAD

Project Management
Make sure to plan ahead of time the fonts you will use for each component of your multimedia project. This way, you will develop a project that is consistent in design.

Academic Focus

English Language Arts

Active Voice
Multimedia presentations should contain active sentences. An example of a passive sentence is, "The ball was thrown by the boy." To make the sentence active, rearrange the words: "The boy threw the ball." Rewrite the following sentence so that it is more active: "This site was created by the Language Club."

NCTE 12 Use language to accomplish individual purposes.

Consistency

Typeface selection and text formatting should reflect the kind of multimedia project you are developing, as well as its purpose. How text works with other elements, such as audio, video, and graphics, should also be considered and applied consistently.

- **Use bold, italic, and underlining sparingly, for emphasis.** Hyperlinks are typically underlined. You may choose to consistently bold key terms or phone numbers.
- **Use style options consistently.** Typeface, size, white space, and color should be used consistently throughout your multimedia project.
- **Style important text consistently.** Place titles and hyperlinks consistently to make navigation easier.
- **Avoid using all uppercase letters, even for headlines and titles.** Text that combines uppercase and lowercase letters is easier to read. It is also more attractive.
- **Test your presentation at different screen resolutions and on both a Mac and a PC.** Different monitors are set at different resolutions, so they display fonts differently. Also, font substitution issues across platforms can cause text formatting to be inconsistent.

Style Sheets and Templates

Templates and styles (also called style sheets) ensure consistent formatting in a document. For example, you might create a style called "Heading" that uses Arial at 24 points with bold formatting. You can then easily apply the style to every heading in a project.

A template is a collection of style and formatting specifications that can be reused for multiple documents or parts of documents. For example, a slide show might contain two types of slides: title and information.

You can use existing templates that come with your word processing or desktop publishing software, or you can create your own templates. You can also edit existing templates. When you apply the appropriate template to a slide or document, text and other elements are automatically formatted as desired.

In the following activity, you will evaluate the menu you created in Actvity 6B to make sure that it follows text readability guidelines.

YOU TRY IT

Activity 6C Assess the Readability of Text in a Multimedia Project

1. With your teacher's permission, open your saved Restaurant Menu project.

2. Read the readability checklist in Figure 6.19 on page 185.

3. Review your project and make any necessary changes to improve readability. Save your revised project.

④ In a word processing document, write a paragraph that explains what you like best about your Restaurant Menu project. What would you like to work on in future projects? Why?

⑤ When you are done with your evaluation, save and close your file.

● Figure 6.19
Use this checklist to make sure the text in your multimedia project is as readable as possible.

Text Readability Checklist

- ☑ Are appropriate fonts used for all text elements?
- ☑ Are fanciful or playful fonts and all uppercase letters used sparingly, if at all?
- ☑ Do the fonts appear correctly on both Windows and Mac OS, and at various resolutions?
- ☑ Does the organization (bullets, numbering, alignment) of text help present ideas clearly?
- ☑ Is the use of fonts and text formatting consistent throughout the presentation, creating an organized appearance?
- ☑ Is the text readable against the background?
- ☑ Are titles and hyperlinks placed consistently, and do they work?
- ☑ Is the text visible from the back of the room (if the text will be projected)?
- ☑ Has text been used on-screen in a way that avoids or minimizes scrolling?
- ☑ Is the text current, correct, free of spelling mistakes, and free of grammatical errors?
- ☑ Is it clear that the situation, purpose, and audience were considered when planning, writing, and revising the project?

 Reading Check **Explain** How does the contrast between text and a background affect readability?

Section 6.2 After You Read

Review Key Concepts

1. Describe how font size is measured.

2. Recommend three important rules to follow to improve layout and readability of your multimedia project.

 Check Your Answers Check your answers at this book's **Online Learning Center** through glencoe.com.

Practice Academic Skills

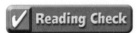 **English Language Arts**

3. Create Create a flyer or poster that celebrates an upcoming holiday or event. Choose colors for the text that best represent the holiday. Write a paragraph explaining your choices.

4. Recommend A friend of yours would like to advertise her new dog-walking business. With your teacher's permission, write an e-mail to your friend recommending different multimedia products she could create, such as letterhead, business cards, flyers, a Web site, or brochures. Suggest techniques for making text in these projects consistent, readable, and attractive.

NCTE 9 Develop an understanding of diversity in language use across cultures.

NCTE 4 Use written language to communicate effectively.

 **Online Student Manual • glencoe.com**

Go to your Online Student Manual and enter your password to find projects that allow you to practice and apply multimedia skills.

Ethics & Technology

Fair and Responsible Use of Technology

Widespread access to computers and the Internet raises issues of responsibility. These technologies make it possible to create, duplicate, and distribute material unethically, or even illegally. As a student, you have a social responsibility to use these resources ethically. This includes exhibiting ethical conduct such as respecting privacy online and providing proper credit for ideas. You must also comply with all laws.

Software and Digital Media

When you purchase software, you are a licensed user. It is considered fair use, in most cases, to re-install the software on the same PC. It is illegal to make more copies than the license allows or to provide copies to others. Using, copying, or sharing computer programs without permission is software piracy. Shareware programs are often available on the Internet for free download, to be purchased after a trial period on an honor system.

When you purchase a music CD, you cannot lawfully copy the music and share it on the Internet.

The Internet

News and media sites often allow the public to leave anonymous comments. Social networking sites allow a network of people to exchange information. It is possible to say unflattering or untrue things about others on a network. You should always follow proper netiquette and fair use guidelines. File-sharing software makes it easy to trade digital copies of music or full-length movies, but this activity violates the law. You do not have the right to make copies of music or movies, and you do not have the right to post copies on a Web site without permission from the copyright holder.

Skill Builder

1. **Research Laws** Examine the First Amendment, Federal Communications Commission regulations, the Freedom of Information Act, liability laws, and other regulations for compliance issues. Report on how these laws impact your decision making about the use of technology.

2. **Evaluate Policies** Write a report that examines the liabilities, copyright laws, fair use guidelines, and duplication of materials associated with multimedia productions. Correctly cite all sources.

Chapter Summary

Most multimedia projects include text, which may be used to inform, persuade, or entertain. In developing multimedia projects, you might create, edit, or add text, or transfer text from one program to another. There are several types of software applications used for developing text including word processing programs, Web design programs, desktop publishing programs, presentation programs, and authoring programs. It is important to consider how text will be used and viewed when deciding what file format to use to save your text.

Virtually all programs that let you work with text offer options for controlling how the text looks. The look of the text can be altered by modifying the font, size, basic styles, and color, as well as other characteristics such as alignment and spacing. When creating and editing text, you should always strive for easy readability. Special formatting and effects should be used sparingly, and for emphasis. Style sheets and templates can be used to help maintain consistency throughout your multimedia project.

Vocabulary Review

1. Write six sentences. Include in each sentence two or more of these content and vocabulary terms. Each sentence should clearly show how the two terms are related.

Content Vocabulary

◇ banner ad (p. 167)
◇ text message (p. 168)
◇ open source (p. 169)
◇ text editor (p. 170)
◇ file format (p. 172)
◇ typography (p. 176)
◇ typeface (p. 176)

◇ font (p. 176)
◇ serif (p. 176)
◇ sans serif (p. 176)
◇ point (p. 178)
◇ alignment (p. 180)
◇ tracking (p. 181)
◇ kerning (p. 181)

Academic Vocabulary

◇ role (p. 167)
◇ incorporate (p. 171)
◇ common (p. 177)
◇ guideline (p. 183)

Review Key Concepts

2. Identify the functions of text in different multimedia productions.

3. Name types of computer applications for working with text.

4. Distinguish among common formats for text files.

5. Select appropriate fonts and text formatting for multimedia projects.

6. Identify ways to control fonts for use in multimedia productions.

7. Demonstrate recommended practices for using text in multimedia.

Critical Thinking

8. Identify Text is used in different types of multimedia projects. Depending on the type of project, the text must be written to fit the situation, purpose, and audience. Use a chart like the one below to identify eight types of multimedia projects that use text in different ways.

Multimedia Projects	
1.	5.
2.	6.
3.	7.
4.	8.

9. Explain Discuss how you would plan, write, and revise text for use in an online multimedia project. What choices would you make regarding fonts, alignment, and special formatting? Why?

10. Evaluate Compare and contrast print and digital communications products that demonstrate appropriate and inappropriate design and layout of text. What are some of the design and layout problems evident in the project with an inappropriate use of text? Use a table like the one below to share your analysis.

	Appropriate Use of Design and Layout	Inappropriate Use of Design and Layout
Project 1		
Project 2		

11. Make Recommendations With your teacher's permission, use the Internet to locate a site that allows you to download different fonts. Import your favorite font. Write a paragraph describing why you think the font would be effective in a text document or multimedia presentation.

12. Design Create a business proposal for a student store at your high school. Remember to consider your target audience for the proposal. Add visual elements such as tables, graphs, and maps. Your proposal should be presented in a text document, such as a brochure or report. Apply typography guidelines, including design and layout principles, as well as a variety of formats. Include at least one special effect, such as embossing, watermarking, or engraving. Be sure to include the appropriate use of alignment, headers, and fonts.

13. Give Examples Conduct research to find examples of the use of left-aligned text, right-aligned text, centered text, and justified text. Provide two examples for when you might use each alignment option. Use a graphic organizer to help organize your answers. Which alignment is the most common? Which is the most effective? Why?

Alignment	Example 1	Example 2
Left-aligned		
Right-aligned		
Centered		
Justified		

Go Online **e-RESOURCES**

glencoe.com

Go to the **Online Learning Center** to find additional activities and career resources.

Practice Quizzes Test your knowledge of the material in this chapter.

Career Resources Find out more about careers, including information about résumés, portfolios, and interview and workplace tips.

Academic Connections

NCTE 8 Use information resources to gather information and create and communicate knowledge.

14. Language Arts–Compare and Contrast Software

With your teacher's permission, research and download an open source word processing software application. You may choose OpenOffice.org Writer, AbiSource's AbiWord, KOffice Project's KWord, Adobe Buzzword, or Google Docs. Familiarize yourself with the software you choose.

A. Compare and contrast the software to the commercial word processing software installed on your computer. Consider ease-of-use and the following criteria as you analyze the software.

- What are the software's strengths?
- What are the software's weaknesses?
- How is the software similar?
- How is the software different?

B. Use a table to help organize your thoughts.

Software	Strengths	Weaknesses	Similarities	Differences

C. Write a one-page recommendation for the software that you felt performed the best. Edit, proofread, and spell-check your recommendation.

Standardized Test Practice

Multiple Choice

Read the paragraph below and then answer the question.

In the 1990s, most computer monitors were standardized to display only 256 set colors. To Web designers, this posed challenges when designing Web sites and onscreen multimedia. Certain colors and combinations were not displayed as intended on the monitor or in the Internet browser. It was also possible to "use up" the colors available for display, leaving text and graphics looking drab or distorted. Despite the advances in display technology, most multimedia and Web designers design with a color palette of 216 colors.

15. Based on the paragraph above, answer the following question.

What happened to Web designers who "used up" the available monitor colors in the 1990s?

A. They could not finish their Web page.

B. They were given new color palettes.

C. They were left with text and graphics that looked drab or distorted.

D. They never "used up" all of the colors.

> **Test-Taking Tip** Referring back to a specific term to review a difficult concept can help you to choose the correct answer. Go back to the reading sections that mention Web designers to determine whether each statement is correct or false.

16. Compare Software

You have just been hired to work as a sales representative for a software distributor. The company sells many different kinds of software, and you must be able to tell customers about the software and answer questions. You decide to develop a table to enter information about each type of software.

NETS 3c Evaluate and select information sources and digital tools based on the appropriateness to specific tasks.

A. To begin, you decide to focus on desktop publishing programs. You will need to know:

- the name of the software.
- a brief description.
- customer uses for the software.

NETS 6b Select and use applications effectively and productively.

B. Create a table to help you organize your information. List at least six desktop publishing programs.

Software/Program	Description	Uses

17. Guidelines for Using Text

Your company has asked you to create guidelines for creating, formatting, and laying out text in all of the company's multimedia projects. Consider typography guidelines, such as font type, size, color, and alignment of text.

NETS 2a Interact, collaborate, and publish with peers, experts, or others employing a variety of digital environments and media.

A. Research guidelines for best use of text in print, computer presentations, and Web pages. Use the information provided in your textbook. With your teacher's approval, do online research for more ideas.

B. Plan and analyze the information you collect and use it to design a printable page of important guidelines that must be followed for all of the company's projects. The print page can be a newsletter, flyer, or brochure.

C. Write the guidelines. The guidelines should contain acceptable fonts, font sizes, colors, and alignment, as well as other design, layout, and formatting options for text.

D Include a statement in the guidelines that explains why consistency and readability are important to a clear presentation of text.

E. Proofread and spell-check your presentation before printing and presenting it to your class. Answer questions and revise the project based on your classmates' feedback.

18. Prioritize

You have been hired to develop a Web site for a nonprofit organization that raises money to help send students to college. The message the organization wants to share is that everyone who wants a higher education should be able to get it. The organization wants the Web site to attract attention without being flashy. The main goal of the Web site is to provide information that explains the purpose of the organization.

A. The home page of the site will contain two headings, an unordered list explaining the organization's goals, and ordered list that provides instructions for registering to become a member of the organization.

B. Plan the text you will create for the Web site. Determine how you will prioritize the planning of these text components. Rank each item in order of importance. Include the estimated amount of time each component will take to complete.

C. Write a short explanation of your plan. Edit and proofread your explanation.

19. Create a Style Sheet

You have been asked to create a sample design for your school yearbook. You want the sample to look professional. You realize that you must keep the look of the text consistent throughout the booklet and so you must develop a style sheet.

Create an 8-page style sheet that displays your ideas for the main club pages, student photos, and faculty pages. Use your knowledge of typography guidelines, along with your creativity, to develop styles for each of the following:

- Body text
- Heading 1
- Heading 2
- Text that requires emphasis
- Unordered lists and ordered lists
- Captions

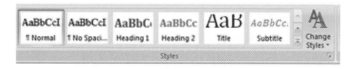

- Alignment
- Special formatting

With your teacher's permission, print your style sheet and share it with the rest of your class. Make sure there are no errors in the style sheet. Incorporate feedback from classmates before saving the stylesheet.

Project 1

Analyze Text Use

NCTE 4 Use written language to communicate effectively.

English Language Arts With your teacher's approval, locate five Web sites to compare and contrast their use of text. Create a presentation to share your findings with the class.

Plan

1. Plan questions you will use to analyze the Web sites, such as: What is the role of text? Are font, text style, size, and color used consistently? Are appropriate fonts used? Are fanciful or playful fonts used sparingly? Does the text formatting make it easy to read, emphasizing key information?

Research

2. Locate five Web sites. Take notes as you evaluate the Web sites.

Create

3. Develop an outline before you create the presentation. Provide examples, such as screen captures, to support and illustrate the presentation. Include conclusions you have drawn about the appropriate use of text. Apply typography guidelines.

Review

4. Edit, proofread, and spell-check the presentation.

Project 2

Evaluate Animated Text

NCTE 12 Use language to accomplish individual purposes.

English Language Arts Many multimedia projects use animated text to draw attention. For this project, you will survey people on the use of animated text and write an essay on your findings.

Plan

1. With your teacher's permission, locate two or three Web sites that use animated text as part of their design.

Research

2. Choose five people from different age groups to survey. Record their answers to questions such as: Do you like the animated text? Does the animated text draw your attention? Why or why not?

Create

3. Evaluate your findings by answering these questions: Do people tend to like animated text? Do opinions vary by age group? What conclusions can you draw?

4. Outline your essay and write a thesis statement.

5. Use your outline and your thesis statement to write a first draft of your essay.

Review

6. Edit, proofread, and spell-check the essay.

Project 3

Design a Poster or Newsletter

NCTE 5 Use different writing process elements to communicate effectively.

 English Language Arts A promotional poster or newsletter can inform your target audience about a project and help generate business for your company.

Plan

1. Using pen and paper, draw a storyboard for your poster or newsletter. See the chart below to help decide which format you will use. Consider the following: Which format would better serve your target audience—a poster or newsletter? What is the message you want to deliver to the target audience? What graphics

ADVANTAGES AND DISADVANTAGES OF POSTERS AND NEWSLETTERS		
Type of Handout	**Advantages**	**Disadvantages**
Poster	• One page • Quick to create • Can post on bulletin boards or use as handouts	• Cannot include as much information as a newsletter • Limited space for graphics
Newsletter	• Two or more pages • Provides various kinds of information on each panel • Can use as handouts	• May take more time to create than a poster • May be difficult to post on bulletin boards because it is difficult to read quickly

will you need?

Create

2. Use a word processing or desktop publishing application to create your poster or newsletter. Use the typography guidelines checklist in Figure 6.19 on page 185.

Evaluate

3. Evaluate the following:

   • Does the overall appearance of the document generate interest?

   • Is the document readable?

   • Are the text, graphics, and background well integrated?

   • Does the text of the document support the document's purpose?

   • Is the content clear?

   • Does the layout of the document guide the reader to important information?

4. Write a one-page essay explaining your evaluation. Edit, proofread, and spell-check your essay.

Go Online **RUBRICS**

glencoe.com

Chapter Projects Use the rubrics for these projects to help create and evaluate your work. Go to the **Online Learning Center** at **glencoe.com**. Choose **Rubrics**, then **Chapter 6**.

Graphics and Animation

Section 7.1
Graphics in Multimedia

Section 7.2
Animation in Multimedia

CHAPTER OBJECTIVES

After completing this chapter, you will be able to:

❖ **Recognize** the role of graphics and animation in various multimedia productions.

❖ **Differentiate** between the functions of the two types of graphics.

❖ **Distinguish** among the major standard image formats.

❖ **Analyze** the conditions that affect the quality and appearance of graphics.

❖ **List** types of tools for editing computer graphics.

❖ **List** examples of the two types of animation.

❖ **Explain** different methods for creating animation.

Explore the Photo

Good judgment comes from experience. Every day you make judgments in social situations. Think about how your judgments will affect yourself and others before you make decisions. *What experiences have you had that illustrate good judgment?*

21st CENTURY SKILLS
Use Good Judgment

When you find yourself in a situation that requires your judgment, investigate all aspects before making a decision to determine the difference between fact and opinion. Good judgment is the most important quality of a strong leader because the decisions a leader makes must be good ones.

Quick Write Activity — Personal Narrative

In a personal narrative, the writer describes thoughts and feelings about an event or experience in his or her own life. Write a personal narrative about how you resolved a problem using good judgment.

Writing Tips
To write a personal narrative, follow these steps:
1. Test your ideas by talking them through or by freewriting.
2. Ask yourself questions to fill out details of the narrative.
3. Construct a time line or other graphic organizer for your narrative.

SECTION 7.1 Graphics in Multimedia

Reading Guide

Before You Read

Adjust Reading Speed Slow down the rate at which you read to match the difficulty of the text. Reread each paragraph if needed.

Read to Learn

Key Concepts

- **Explain** the role of graphics in multimedia projects.
- **Distinguish** between types of graphics.
- **Describe** aspects of graphics files, including quality, format, and function.
- **Identify** tools and techniques for editing digital images.

Main Idea

Graphics help contribute to the meaning and impact of multimedia. Programs make creating and editing graphics easy even for a novice.

Content Vocabulary

◈ raster graphic
◈ pixel
◈ vector graphic
◈ native file format
◈ standard image format
◈ resolution
◈ file compression
◈ color mode

Academic Vocabulary

You will find these words in your reading and on your tests. Use the glossary to look up their definitions, if necessary.

◈ attribute
◈ distinct

Graphic Organizer

As you read, note the similarities and differences between raster graphics and vector graphics. Use a Venn diagram like the one shown to help you organize your information.

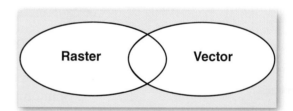

 Graphic Organizer Go to this book's **Online Learning Center** at **glencoe.com** to print this graphic organizer.

Academic Standards

 English Language Arts

NCTE 7 Conduct research and gather, evaluate, and synthesize data to communicate discoveries.

NCTE 12 Use language to accomplish individual purposes.

Mathematics

NCTM Algebra Understand patterns, relations, and functions.

NCTM Measurement Apply appropriate techniques, tools, and formulas to determine measurements.

NCTE National Council of Teachers of English
NSES National Science Education Standards

NCTM National Council of Teachers of Mathematics
NCSS National Council for the Social Studies

Using Graphics in Multimedia

What role do graphics serve in multimedia?

A graphic is an image used to illustrate, inform, or entertain. Graphics are basic components of communication because they convey information quickly in a way that can be understood by many people. Graphic images include photographs, logos, diagrams, drawings, tables, charts, maps, and paintings. You encounter multimedia productions that contain graphics every day. Examples of various types of graphics are shown in Figure 7.1.

Graphics are often used to advertise a product, clarify information, promote a name brand, convey an idea or illustrate a concept, demonstrate a process or procedure, add visual interest or entertain viewers, or grab the viewer's attention. Graphics may have multiple roles at the same time. For example, a Web site might use a single image to promote the corporate brand and add visual interest.

Find Graphics on the Internet

Many graphics files can be downloaded online. Online sources of graphics include stock image sites and Clip Art providers. Corbis and iStock are examples of popular stock image providers.

Stock photos are often royalty-free images. A royalty-free image is a graphic that can be used in an unlimited number of projects for a one-time fee. Other types of images may require additional fees depending on how the user plans to use the image. For example, some owners give permission to use an image as long as it is not modified. Many Clip Art sources, such as Microsoft Office Online, offer images for free. Always be sure to follow the published terms and conditions for using any graphics you download from the Internet. Unless you are given specific permission to use someone else's images, downloading and using graphics violates copyright laws.

As You Read

Connect What kinds of graphics do you see every day?

Go Online ACTIVITY
glencoe.com

Locate Graphics Online Learn how to find images, such as photos and drawings, for your multimedia presentations at the **Online Learning Center.** Go to **glencoe.com.** Choose Activities, then Chapter 7.

Figure 7.1
Graphics add visual interest to multimedia. What other purposes do graphics serve in multimedia projects?

Use Graphics Appropriately

While graphics can add appeal and value to your multimedia project, they can also distract from your project's goal if not used appropriately. By planning your project thoroughly, you can ensure that any graphics used will support the goals of your project. Remember that too many graphics can clutter your project and distract viewers from its purpose. Use the Graphics Evaluation Checklist in Figure 7.2 to help you analyze the use of graphics in your multimedia project.

Figure 7.2 ●——→

A multimedia project that uses graphics should follow these guidelines. **Why is the file size of a graphic important?**

Graphics Evaluation Checklist

- ☑ Do the graphics support the project's goals?
- ☑ Do the graphics distract viewers?
- ☑ Are the graphics an appropriate file size for the type of multimedia project?
- ☑ Have necessary permissions been obtained and cited?
- ☑ Have I included alternative text to describe my graphics?
- ☑ Do the colors in the graphics contrast with the background?
- ☑ Do I have too many graphics?
- ☑ Are they distracting for viewers?

During the design and development stage of production, you should identify the role of any graphics that you may want or need to include. If you are developing a Web site, the size of the file will affect the download times for the Web site. This will be important in deciding what type of image you will create and the file format you will save it in.

In addition to how you can use graphics to support your project's goals, you must also keep in mind the accessibility guidelines discussed in Chapter 5. This will ensure that as many people as possible are able to view your project and understand your project's purpose. When using graphics, this can mean using alternative text to describe your graphics to assist people with visual impairments and choosing colors in your graphics that will contrast well with your background colors.

 **Reading Check** **Recall** List three ways graphics can be used in multimedia projects.

Types of Graphics

What are the two types of graphics?

There are two types of computer-generated images: raster graphics and vector graphics. The type of graphic is determined by how it is created. Each type of graphic has advantages and disadvantages.

Raster Graphics

A **raster graphic**, also called a bitmapped graphic or a bitmap, is an image made up of tiny dots, or pixels. A **pixel** (short for picture element) is a single point in a graphic image. Each pixel is assigned a color, like the areas of a paint-by-numbers picture. Many raster graphics are continuous-tone images, which means that they have an unlimited number of colors or shades of gray that create a continuous appearance.

Photographs are the most common examples of continuous-tone images. Other raster graphics may be photo-realistic images that are created by artists.

Enlarging a bitmap enlarges individual pixels, so the pixels are more obvious and the image loses crispness, as seen in Figure 7.3. When using raster graphics, remember these tips:

- Raster graphics lose clarity if their size is reduced drastically.
- Raster graphics are generally a good choice when the image will not be resized and a more complex image is required.
- Raster graphics are generally larger files than vector graphics, which is an important consideration for download times.

Raster graphics editing programs, sometimes called photo editors or paint programs, allow you to create bitmaps. Examples of these programs include Adobe® Photoshop®, Adobe Fireworks®, Corel® Paint Shop Pro®, Microsoft Expression®, Microsoft Picture Manager, and Microsoft Paint. You can zoom in and edit individual pixels or make sweeping changes to larger areas. These programs typically let you create montages or compositions that contain multiple photos and draw new illustrations. Some programs will allow you to create 3-D images and animations. Be sure to research any software before purchasing it to ensure it can do what you need it to.

Vector Graphics

A **vector graphic** is an image drawn in lines, curves, and shapes. These "paths," which can be filled with color, are defined by mathematical formulas. Vector graphics can be easily resized without losing quality or clarity so they are good for designs like logos that will be reproduced in many sizes (see Figure 7.4). Another advantage of vector graphics is that the files are generally much smaller than those for similar bitmaps. Vector graphics are not appropriate for photographs and other images with millions of colors.

Vector graphics editing programs, sometimes called draw programs, allow users to create vector graphics. With this type of software, users can draw lines and curves, and fill shapes with color. You might use a vector graphics editor to create an artistic or technical illustration, logo, chart, or diagram. Some popular draw programs include Adobe Illustrator®, CorelDRAW®, and Microsoft Office Visio®.

Figure 7.3
Adobe Photoshop can be used to create raster graphics. **What are some advantages to using raster graphics?**

Quick **Tip**

Jargon A montage is a grouping of multiple pictures to create one larger image. It is similar to a collage.

Figure 7.4
Vector graphics are created using draw programs. **What types of graphics are better as vector graphics than raster graphics?**

Graphic File Formats

What is the best graphic file format for print products?

The default format in which a file is saved is the **native file format**. This format is specific to the software used to create the file. A graphic being transferred to another application should be converted to a **standard image format**, which is a format that is supported by most graphics applications. Figure 7.5 shows the most common image formats, along with their filename extensions and advantages and disadvantages. A file's extension identifies the file's format. For example, the extension for a tagged image file format (TIFF) file is ".tif". Standard image formats are readable by various programs.

The best file format for graphics in a multimedia project depends largely on how the graphics will be used. The two most commonly used standard image formats for use on the Web are GIF (graphic interchange format) and JPEG (joint photographic experts group) format. The TIFF format is a popular choice for print products.

One of the biggest factors in choosing a file format is generally the **resolution**, or the number of pixels per inch (ppi). In general, the higher the resolution, the crisper the image. However, higher resolutions also mean larger file sizes, which can slow down download times. Graphics that are to be used only on the Web are generally fine with a file resolution of 72 ppi. Graphics that need to look clear when printed need a higher ppi. You may also hear the term "dpi" referred to. This stands for dots per inch and refers to the resolution of printed publications.

Figure 7.5
Different software applications save files in different formats. What file formats have you encountered?

 **Reading Check** **Explain** What is the difference between a native file format and a standard image format?

Standard Image Formats

File Format	Advantages	Disadvantages
BMP (.bmp)	• Supports millions of colors • Good for creating computer icons or wallpaper	• Very large files, download slowly • Generally not used for Web pages
GIF (.gif)	• Small file size; downloads quickly • Good for line drawings and simple graphics	• Only supports up to 256 colors • Limited colors make it inappropriate for saving photos
JPEG (.jpg or .jpeg)	• Supports millions of colors • Color support makes it good for saving photos • Compatible with most graphics editing software	• Files are often large to accommodate higher quality, which means slower downloads
PICT (.pict, .pct, or .pic)	• Can be used for both raster and vector images • Compatible with Mac OS® graphics software	
PNG (.png)	• Supports more colors than GIF files, and still downloads quickly • Good for non-professional graphics and images that will be edited multiple times	• Earlier Web browser versions do not support PNG format
TIFF (.tiff or .tif)	• Supports millions of colors • Good for saving photos and creating line art • Good for importing images into documents • Compatible with most graphics editing software	• Files are often large to accommodate higher quality, which means slower downloads • Generally used for print

File Compression

Why is file compression important?

Multimedia files, especially graphics files, are often very large. E-mailing, uploading, or downloading a large file can take a long time. **File compression** is a way of saving a file in a compressed, or smaller, format. The file then requires less disk space and the transmission time is reduced. When referring to graphics, compression reduces an image's file size by removing some color information. However, while compression makes files smaller, it can also reduce an image's quality.

Most images on the Web are compressed JPEG or GIF files. Image editing software contains file compression tools. Both the Mac OS and Microsoft Windows have built-in file compression utility programs, allowing you to share photos and other graphics quickly and easily in compressed formats.

Lossy and Lossless Compression

There are two types of compression schemes used for graphics—lossy and lossless.

- Lossy compression reduces file size significantly but loses some data—and image quality—in the process. Keep in mind that decompressing the file will not restore the lost data and the image will have a reduced image quality.

- Lossless compression means that the graphic does not lose data (detail) when it is compressed. However, this means that you also do not greatly reduce file size or the download time.

Depending on the needs of your multimedia project, you must weigh the advantages and disadvantages of lossy and lossless compression (see Figure 7.6).

Lossy vs. Lossless Compression		
Type of Compression	**Sample File Formats**	**Use When...**
Lossy	• JPEG	• A smaller file is required • Image quality is not as important
Lossless	• GIF, TIFF	• A larger file is acceptable • Image quality is very important

Figure 7.6
The compression of graphics files can be lossy or lossless. Which type of compression is more appropriate for a graphic that must be published in print with great clarity?

To help manage file size and transmission times, many graphics editing programs display the approximate download times. You can use this estimate to help you choose the compression option that gives the best balance between image quality and file size.

Figure 7.7
The original JPEG alongside several GIF options. When is it better to use a lossless compression scheme?

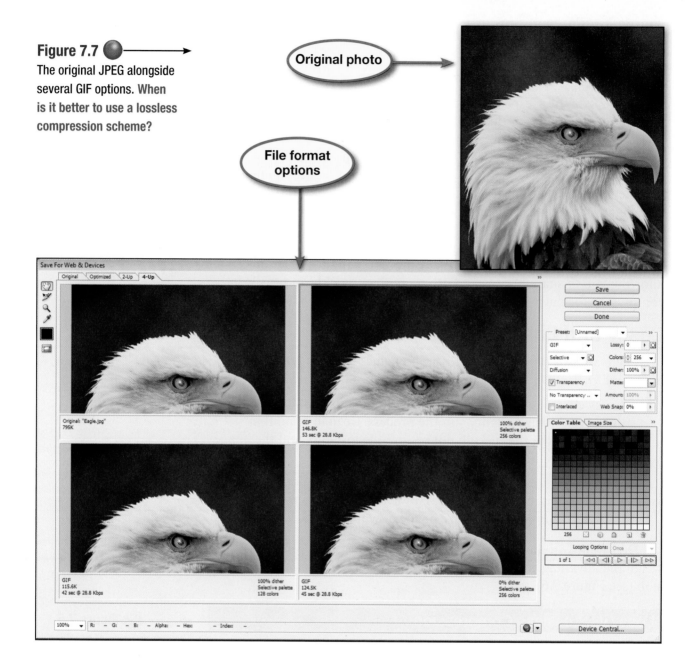

Original photo

File format options

PLAN AHEAD

Publishing Multimedia projects can be very large and take a long time to download. Research options for decreasing transmission time when including large files in a project.

Converting Graphic Formats

Many image editing software applications allow you to open a graphic in one format, and save it in another format. For example, Adobe Photoshop will open a JPEG file and then allow you to resave the image as a GIF file. This can be useful when you need the image for use in a program or browser that will only accept certain file formats. Be aware, however, that when a file is converted from one format to another, the converted image may not look exactly like the original. In the example shown in Figure 7.7, when the JPEG file is converted to a GIF file, the resulting image does not have as many colors and looks distinctly different from the original JPEG image.

Reading Check **Define** What are lossy and lossless compression schemes?

Edit Graphics

How can you change the way an image looks in a graphics editing program?

Graphics editing programs let you create images or change the way they look to best suit a particular multimedia production (see Figure 7.8). These programs have features for adjusting the size, color, texture, and many other attributes of images. (Such features may differ between raster graphics editors and vector graphics editors.) An **attribute** is a descriptive property or characteristic of an object or image.

● **Figure 7.8**
The original graphic (far left) has been edited to show three different ways it can be changed. What are some of the ways you can change graphics?

Crop, Resize, and Rotate

Cropping is eliminating unwanted parts of an image from the top, sides, or bottom. You can make a picture more effective by cropping it so that attention is focused on the desired subject.

Graphics editing software also lets you resize an image. Resizing is changing the height and width of an image to be larger or smaller. Resizing a bitmap changes its resolution (pixels per inch). If you double the size of a bitmap, for example, you cut its resolution in half. Therefore, enlarging a bitmap (or shrinking it drastically) reduces its clarity. Vector graphics, on the other hand, do not lose clarity as you resize them.

Changing one dimension of an image without changing the other dimension equally will distort, or stretch, the image. To avoid this, maintain the image's aspect ratio. Aspect ratio is the proportion of width to height. For example, an image with an aspect ratio of 2:1 is twice as wide as it is tall. Most graphics editing programs will let you maintain the aspect ratio automatically.

If you transfer photos from a digital camera or scanner onto a computer, you might notice that some photos appear angled to the left or right or even upside-down. In a graphics editing program, you can flip an image to be right-side-up. Or you can turn an image in a circle around a central point to a desired angle. Changing the angle at which an image is displayed is called rotating.

Academic Focus

Mathematics

Aspect Ratio A 2:1 aspect ratio means that an image is twice as wide as it is tall. Assume that a graphic is 2 inches wide and 0.5 inches high. If it is enlarged so that it is 2 inches tall, what width is needed to maintain its aspect ratio? Begin by determining the aspect ratio.

NCTM Measurement Apply appropriate techniques, tools, and formulas to determine measurements.

Adjust Contrast, Brightness, and Color

Figure 7.9

Adjusting the brightness and contrast of a photo can make a dark background lighter **How do brightness and contrast differ from one another?**

Contrast refers to the difference between the lighter and darker areas of an image. The brightness of an image is the degree to which it appears light or dark overall. Contrast and brightness are often adjusted together (see Figure 7.9). For example, you might increase the brightness of a photo to lighten a dark sky. Then the contrast might be adjusted to make a dark object, such as fishermen, appear more distinct from the dark background of the sky. **Distinct** means distinguishable to the eye as being separate.

You can control the color in an image by adjusting the balance, hue, and saturation. For example, you might need to balance the color in a photo that appears greenish because it was taken under fluorescent lights. In this case, you would reduce the green in the image and add some magenta. You can also alter all the pixels of one specific hue, or color, in an image or adjust the saturation, or intensity, of the pixels.

Dithering When developing multimedia applications, you might need to reduce the color depth of an image. In a bitmapped image, color depth refers to the number of bits of data used to represent the color of an individual pixel. It also describes the number of distinct colors an image can contain. The higher the color depth, the more lifelike the image will look. For example, black and white images have a color depth of 1 bit, or 2 colors. Every pixel can be either black or white (on or off).

- Graphics with 8-bit color depth, producing 256 colors, are referred to as indexed color images.
- A 24-bit image has a color depth of about 16.7 million colors; called a true color image, it closely mimics colors in the real world.
- A 32-bit graphic can include over 4.2 billion distinct colors.

Remember that converted files may not look like the original images. You might have to convert a 24-bit TIFF to an 8-bit GIF that will load faster on a Web page. The resulting image might show bands of color instead of smooth transitions between shades. To minimize this effect you can apply the technique of dithering, which simulates the lost colors from the available palette and intersperses pixels of those colors.

Color Mode Selection **Color mode** refers to the model used to create color. You will recall from Chapter 5 how important color selection is in multimedia development. The RGB color model combines red (R), green (G), and blue (B) light to make a broad range of colors. Traditionally, the RGB color model is used for screen displays (such as those for televisions and computers). In the CMYK color model, colors result from mixing partial amounts of cyan (C), magenta (M), yellow (Y), and black (K). Cyan is light blue and magenta is a shade of red. CMYK is the color model used for the printing process. When you work with digital graphics, you can specify the color mode (RGB or CYMK) that suits your purposes. You might also work in grayscale mode, which shows an image in shades of gray between black (weakest light intensity) and white (strongest light intensity).

Layers and Masks

In editing a digital graphic, a layer is used to separate elements and effects. Layers are transparencies stacked on top of each other in front of a background. A standard layer contains a picture or piece of text that can be superimposed on, or laid over, another. An adjustment layer applies an effect such as saturation, brightness, or contrast to the layers below it.

A mask can be linked to a layer. Masking means to isolate an area of an image so that part of the image can be adjusted separately from the rest. The area defined by the mask hides that part of the layer from the picture. (See Figure 7.10.) Layers and masks are helpful in merging multiple images to create montages and collages. To reduce file size, multiple layers can be "flattened" into a single layer. This should only be done when you are done editing the image and should be saved as a new file so you can return to the original image layers later, if needed.

Figure 7.10
A mask effect can hide or emphasize a specific part of an image. **Why do graphic artists use layers and masks?**

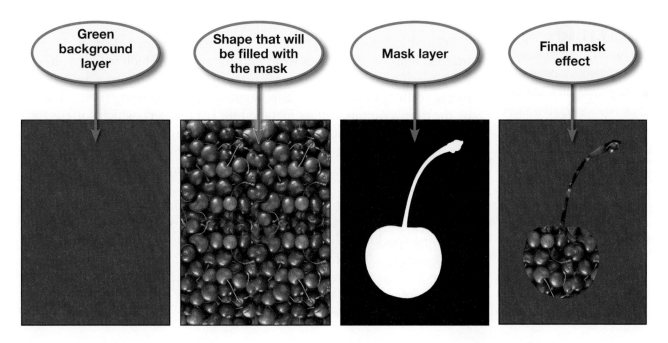

Green background layer

Shape that will be filled with the mask

Mask layer

Final mask effect

Filters

Figure 7.11
You can choose from many types of filters, including underpainting, craquelure, and paint dabs. How can you use filters to appeal to your audience?

Graphics editing programs use filters to apply special effects to images. The concept comes from photography, in which you can alter the look of a picture by placing a filter over the camera lens. In digital image editing, thousands of effects can be achieved using filters. Two of the more common filters include blur (or feather), which softens the focus of an image, and sharpen, which makes an image clearer. You can use other filters to make a picture look like a piece of art created with charcoal, pen, colored pencil, pastel, watercolor, or paint dabs (see Figure 7.11).

You can also use filters to add texture (such as mosaic tiles and cracked paint), distortion (such as ripple), or noise (for adding or removing speckles). Filters can be used alone or in combination with each other. Be careful not too apply to many filters. Your image could end up looking distorted. Remember, also, not to make permanent changes to your only copy of an image. Always save a copy of the file before making changes.

Graphics Editing Tools

Tools in graphics editing software applications let you accomplish specific tasks, such as the following:

- Transform, or change the physical characteristics of an image
- Draw, or create vector lines, curves, and shapes in an image
- Focus, or adjust how sharp or blurry an image appears

Many programs also have tools to create drastic special effecs. You can create 3-D effects, adjusting foreground, middle distance, and background. These effects can be used to meet specific needs, attract your audience, and keep them engaged in your project or presentation.

Figure 7.12 identifies the main types of tasks that can be done within most programs. Each task might be accomplished using a variety of individual tools, depending on the software and the task. For example, to paint an image, or apply color to it, you might use a pencil, brush, paint bucket, pattern stamp, or gradient. Note that the tools to accomplish these tasks will vary from program to program and may differ between raster and vector graphics editors. Complex image editing software can contain thousands of tools that will transform your projects, while free programs perform simpler tasks.

Graphics Editing Tasks

Task	Description
Navigate	Maneuver to another area of an image more easily than using scroll bars, usually with a Hand tool
Select	Specify elements or areas of an image you will modify using other tools or commands
Transform	Alter one or more of the physical characteristics of an image, such as scaling, resizing, rotating, flipping, or moving
View/choose/ adjust color	View color values, change color saturation, or pick a color at a defined spot on an image
Paint	Apply color as if by painting to make soft strokes, fills, gradual tones, hard-edged lines, patterns, and gradients
Draw	Create vector paths such as lines, curves, and shapes, which can be filled with color
Focus	Change how clearly defined an image is, by adjusting color contrast or by blending
Erase	Remove a portion of an image
Type	Add and format text

Figure 7.12

Each task in a graphics editing program can adjust images in specific ways. **How does paint differ from draw?**

Design Always make a copy of files before making permanent changes to them. This includes cropping and more complex edits.

Activity 7A Edit a Digital Photo

① Open a raster graphics editing software application, such as Adobe Photoshop.

② Open the student data file **Eagle.jpg**.

③ Choose the selection tool. Select the area around the eagle's eye.

④ Examine the filter effects available in your photo editing software. Select the lens flare filter or a similar filter. Click the center of the eagle's eye to apply the filter. Adjust the brightness of the filter to **100%**.

⑤ The lens flare effect should look like rings, circles, or starbursts of brightness on a photo (see Figure 7.13).

Figure 7.13
The lens flare filter gives the eagle a starry-eyed look.

Eye lens flare filter applied

Figure 7.14
The background behind the eagle is selected.

⑥ Use a selection tool, such as the Magic Wand in Photoshop, to select the back-ground around the eagle (see Figure 7.14).

⑦ Set the background color to **black**. Set the foreground color to **blue**. Apply a cloud or similar filter to the background.

Background selected

8 Deselect the background. Confirm that the background is now blue with a cloudy effect (see Figure 7.15).

9 Save the file as **Your Name Eagle.jpg**.

10 If your program includes the option to save the photo for the Web, select this option. Review and compare the choices for saving the photo. Select the option that you feel is the best.

11 Close your photo editing software.

Background color changed

Figure 7.15
The green background is replaced by a blue and black background with a cloud filter effect.

 **Reading Check** **Explain** What does it mean to crop, resize, and rotate a graphic?

Section 7.1 After You Read

Review Key Concepts

1. **Explain** how raster graphics and vector graphics are different.

2. **Identify** five tasks that you can do to manipulate digital images.

 Check Your Answers Check your answers at this book's Online Learning Center through glencoe.com.

Practice Academic Skills

English Language Arts

3. **Conclude** There is a saying that a picture is worth a thousand words. Find a photo or illustration, and write at least one paragraph detailing what the image shows. Based on this exercise, do you agree with the meaning of the saying? Why or why not?

NCTE 12 Use language to accomplish individual purposes.

Math Concept

4. **Apply** Suppose an image has an aspect ratio of 3:2. Its width is how many times its height? Explain your reasoning.

NCTM Algebra Understand patterns, relations, and functions.

 **Online Student Manual • glencoe.com**

Go to your Online Student Manual and enter your password to find activities that allow you to practice and apply multimedia skills.

SECTION 7.2 Animation in Multimedia

Reading Guide

Before You Read

Survey Look at the figures and read their captions. Then write one or two sentences predicting what the section will be about.

Read to Learn

Key Concepts

- **Examine** the role of animation in multimedia.
- **Compare and Contrast** the two types of animation.
- **Summarize** the techniques for creating and editing computer animation.

Main Idea

Animation can deliver a big impact in a multimedia production. Understanding how animation is formatted and created helps you integrate it effectively into multimedia.

Content Vocabulary

- ◇ wireframe model
- ◇ computer-generated imagery (CGI)
- ◇ virtual reality
- ◇ frame-by-frame animation
- ◇ tweening
- ◇ rollover

Academic Vocabulary

You will find these words in your reading and on your tests. Use the glossary to look up their definitions, if necessary.

- ◆ via
- ◆ automatic

Graphic Organizer

As you read, note the different file formats available for saving animation files. Use a graphic organizer like the one shown to help you organize your information.

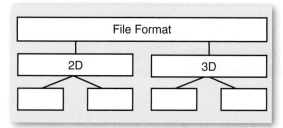

File Format — 2D / 3D

 Graphic Organizer Go to this book's **Online Learning Center** at **glencoe.com** to print this graphic organizer.

Academic Standards

 English Language Arts

NCTE 3 Apply strategies to interpret texts.
NCTE 7 Conduct research and gather, evaluate, and synthesize data to communicate discoveries.

 Mathematics

NCTE Geometry Analyze characteristics and properties of two- and three-dimensional geometric shapes and develop mathematical arguments about geometric relationships.
NCTM Number and Operations Compute fluently and make reasonable estimates.

NCTE National Council of Teachers of English
NSES National Science Education Standards

NCTM National Council of Teachers of Mathematics
NCSS National Council for the Social Studies

Use Animation in Multimedia

What role does animation perform in multimedia?

As You Read

Connect What examples of multimedia animation do you see every day?

Animation is the art of using graphics to create the illusion of motion. Attention-grabbing by nature, animation can be a particularly effective component of a multimedia presentation (see Figure 7.16).

This animation fades in and out of view.

Figure 7.16
Animation can be used to enhance a multimedia production such as a Web site. What roles might animation play on a Web site?

Traditional animation, drawn by hand, was used for most cartoons and animated movies until the beginning of the 21st century. Computer-generated animation is now popularly used in cartoons, movies, video games, mobile applications, Web sites, online and television advertisements, electronic greeting cards, slide show presentations, and computer-based training.

Animation might play various roles in multimedia, including telling a story, entertaining, advertising, illustrating a concept, demonstrating a process or procedure, adding visual interest, and grabbing the viewer's attention. For example, a video game might use animation to simulate complex interactions. A presentation might use animation to transition from one slide to another. A Web site might use animation to present navigation elements or to illustrate a process.

Find Animation on the Internet

Animation files can be downloaded from online sources in various formats, such as GIF, SWF, and MOV. (File formats for animation will be discussed later in this section.) Sources of animation include Clip Art providers and stock image sites. Keep in mind that you may need to obtain permission to use animation files in a multimedia project. Be sure to follow the terms and conditions of the source.

Use Animation Appropriately

As with text and graphics, it is important to plan the animation for your multimedia project to be sure that it helps reach the aims of your project and that it is accessible by all viewers. Animation, like graphics, can be easily overdone if you are not careful. Be sure that any animation you use has a purpose and is not distracting.

Too much animation can make it difficult for viewers to read text or locate needed information in your multimedia project. Use the checklist in Figure 7.17 to help evaluate the animation in your multimedia project.

Figure 7.17
Use this checklist when planning the animation for your multimedia project. **Why should you identify the purpose of any animation you want to use?**

Animation Evaluation Checklist

☑ Does the animation support the project's goals?

☑ Does the animation draw the viewer's attention to important content?

☑ Do the animation files take too long to download?

☑ Have necessary permissions been obtained and cited?

☑ Have I included alternative text to describe my animation?

☑ Do I have too much animation? Is my project cluttered?

☑ Does the animation distract the viewer (for example, does it flash on and off)?

☑ Do viewers have the option to skip the animation?

✔ Reading Check **Identify** Name three roles of animation in multimedia.

Types of Animation

What are the two types of animation?

Computer animation creates the optical illusion of motion in a sequence of digital images. Animation files are played back **via**, or by way of, different formats.

Computer animation is commonly described as one of two types: two-dimensional (2D) or three-dimensional (3D). Two-dimensional animation has width and height. Three-dimensional animation has width, height, and depth.

Two-Dimensional Animation

Also called vector or path animation, two-dimensional animation has the "flat" look of paper. Two-dimensional animtion has the following characterisics:

- It has width and height.
- It can be developed using raster or vector graphics.
- It defines movement by formulas.
- It is used commonly on the Web because it loads quickly.

This traditional type of animation involves photographing a series of images drawn or painted by hand on transparent cellulose acetate sheets. Banner ads, e-cards, and Web sites often use 2D animation because it loads quickly and is easy to use. Figures in 2D animation are developed using raster or vector graphics. Movement in 2D animation is defined by formulas. Two-dimensional animation can be made to look three dimensional (with shadows, for example).

Three-Dimensional Animation

Three-dimensional animation (shown in Figure 7.18) seems to bring inanimate objects to life. It has the following characteristics:

- It has width, height, and depth.
- It is sometimes called computer-generated imagery (CGI).
- It is developed by modeling, animating, and rendering.
- It is used in video games, animated movies, special effects

The basic steps in 3D animation are modeling, animating, and rendering. In modeling, polygons (plane figures with straight edges) are used to build the surface of a three-dimensional object. This mathematical representation, called a **wireframe model**, lets you visualize the entire 3D structure of the object. The object is then placed within a scene, and its motion is specified. Finally, the model is rendered as an image.

Three-dimensional animation is used in video games, animated movies, and special effects in live-action films. These 3D special effects applied to computer graphics are also called **computer-generated imagery (CGI)**. Science, medicine, and the military use 3D animation to create virtual simulations that would be too difficult or dangerous to create in reality. **Virtual reality** lets you interact with an artificial environment by moving around in it and manipulating simulated objects.

Figure 7.18
In three-dimensional animation, images have width, height, and depth. **What is CGI?**

Software for Developing Animation

Two-dimensional and three-dimensional animation are created with different types of software. Adobe Flash® is a popular tool for creating 2D animation, especially for Web sites. An animation created in Flash is sometimes called a movie. There are also various programs available for developing animated GIFs. An animated GIF is a relatively small and simple 2D animation that often appears on the Web. Multimedia authoring and presentation programs such as Adobe Director® and Microsoft Office PowerPoint offer relatively simple features for adding movement to text and graphics.

Popular programs for developing 3D animation include: Autodesk® Maya®, Audodesk 3ds Max®, NewTek Lightwave 3D®, and Maxon Cinema 4D. These applications allow you to rotate or bounce an object, zoom in or out of a scene, and fade text or graphics in and out.

Animation File Formats

As with graphics, you must decide what file format you will use to save your animation. Animation must be saved in a file format that allows it to be played on the Internet or another delivery device, such as a DVD. The best format for animation depends largely on whether it is 2D or 3D animation.

2D File Formats Two of the most common standard formats for 2D animation files are animated GIF and SWF.

- Animated GIF is a file format for small, simple animations. An animated GIF consists of a series of GIF graphics displayed in succession, creating the appearance of movement.

- SWF (pronounced swiff) is a playable movie file. The native file for animation produced with Adobe Flash is an FLA. FLA files must be saved in SWF format in order to view them without the original software. This is necessary, for example, when you load the files onto the Internet. Software for running SWF files, called Adobe Flash Player, is built into most browsers or is available as a plug-in.

3D File Formats Three-dimensional animation programs generate a variety of file formats. To be played back, these native files must be converted to a standard animation or standard video format.

- Standard animation files are generally SWF files.

- Standard video files include AVI (Audio Video Interleave), FLV (Flash Video), or MOV (QuickTime Movie).

 **Reading Check** **Identify** Which type of animation is developed with width, height, and depth?

Edit Animation

What are the two main techniques for editing animation?

In animation, multiple images are used to achieve the illusion of motion. Typically, a storyboard is developed as a guide before production begins. The storyboard might be sketched on paper or prepared electronically.

Recall from earlier in the section that the images used to create 2D animation can be raster or vector graphics. The images used to create 3D animation are rendered using mathematical models. Both 2D and 3D animation can be accomplished using the same techniques: frame-by-frame and tweening.

Frame-by-Frame and Tweening

Frame-by-frame animation uses the same principle as live video. What appears to be continuous motion is actually a series of many frames. Each frame shows the same graphic with a tiny change in position to simulate motion (see Figure 7.19). The quality of frame-by-frame animation depends on the frame rate, or how quickly the frames are changed. The more frames displayed per second, the smoother the action seems. In video games, for example, the standard frame rate is 32 frames per second (fps).

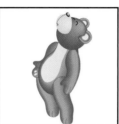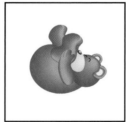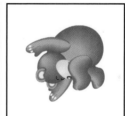

The animation technique of tweening creates frames in a special way. **Tweening** is the process of generating transitional frames between two keyframes. Keyframes are intermediate frames that blend so that one appears to change into the next. Tweening is short for in-betweening. Tweens, or the frames in-between, are generated mathematically to give the appearance that the first keyframe transforms smoothly to the second. Creating the in-between frames is **automatic**, or programmed to occur. You do not create frames yourself, as in frame-by-frame animation.

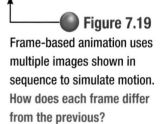

Figure 7.19
Frame-based animation uses multiple images shown in sequence to simulate motion. **How does each frame differ from the previous?**

Rollovers

The use of rollovers in multimedia applications are so widespread that these little animations deserve special attention. A **rollover** consists of two or three images that switch when the cursor rolls over a navigation button or other on-screen element. The rolled-over item might light up, display shadowing as if it has been pressed, or otherwise seem to change. When the cursor moves away, the item reverts to its original appearance.

Rollovers are important for navigating many types of multimedia productions, including Web pages, computer-based training, kiosks, and video games. A rollover's animation is controlled by a set of instructions within a Web design program such as Adobe Dreamweaver®; a 2D animation program such as Adobe Flash; or a graphics editing program such as Adobe Fireworks, Adobe Photoshop, or Adobe Illustrator. Rollovers can also be created using programming code, such as JavaScript® (in a small application called an applet).

In the following You Try It activity, you will create an animation program to create 2D animation.

YOU TRY IT

Activity 7B Create a 2D Animation

DATA FILE

① Open a 2D animation program, such as Adobe Flash.

② Create a new document.

③ Import the student data file **Kitten.jpg** to the stage (see Figure 7.20).

Figure 7.20
You can create animation by adding effects to a single image.

④ Convert the image to a symbol, name it **Kitten**, and specify its behavior as that of a graphic. Change the size of your document to match the size of the contents.

⑤ Insert a keyframe at frame **35**.

⑥ Change the brightness of the picture to **100%**. The picture disappears (see Figure 7.21 on page 217).

⑦ Insert a keyframe at frame **70**.

⑧ Change the brightness of the picture to **0%**. The picture reappears.

⑨ Create a motion tween between frames **1** and **35**.

⑩ Create a motion tween between frames **35** and **70**.

⑪ Play your animation. The picture should disappear and reappear.

⑫ Select **File>Export Movie**. Name the file **Your Name Kitten.swf**. Click **OK**.

⑫ Save and close your file.

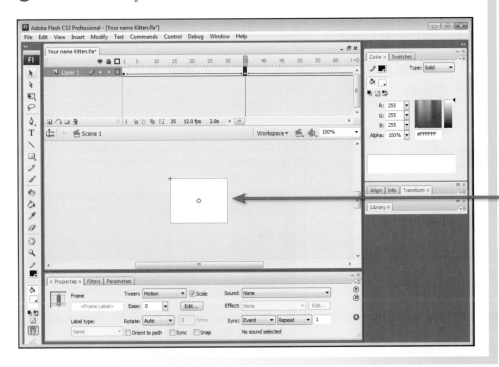

● Figure 7.21
Changing the brightness of the picture to 100% makes the kitten disappear.

Brightness at 100%

 **Reading Check**   **Explain** How does the technique of tweening create the illusion of motion?

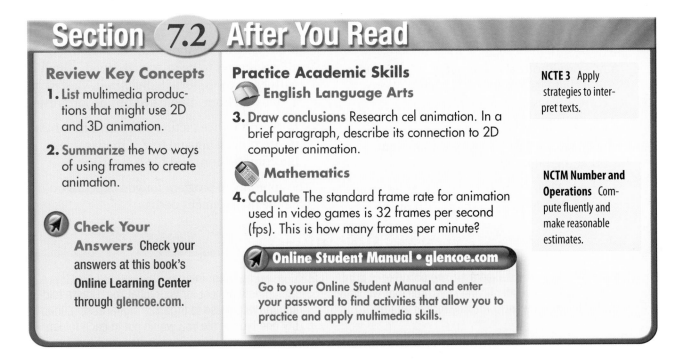

Section 7.2 After You Read

Review Key Concepts

1. List multimedia productions that might use 2D and 3D animation.

2. Summarize the two ways of using frames to create animation.

Check Your Answers Check your answers at this book's **Online Learning Center** through glencoe.com.

Practice Academic Skills

English Language Arts

3. Draw conclusions Research cel animation. In a brief paragraph, describe its connection to 2D computer animation.

Mathematics

4. Calculate The standard frame rate for animation used in video games is 32 frames per second (fps). This is how many frames per minute?

Online Student Manual • glencoe.com

Go to your Online Student Manual and enter your password to find activities that allow you to practice and apply multimedia skills.

NCTE 3 Apply strategies to interpret texts.

NCTM Number and Operations Compute fluently and make reasonable estimates.

Real World Technology

Manage Multimedia Elements

File management refers to organizing graphics, animation, audio, video, and other multimedia elements on a computer. You can organize the files yourself, or you can use file management software to help you. Graphics are the most common digital asset, so most file management software includes specific image management tools.

File Management Tasks

Depending on your goals and purposes, you might need to organize multimedia elements, also called assets, in directories or folders. One reason you might want to organize elements is so that you can assign keywords to the files. Files that include keywords can be searched and sorted so that they are easier to find and use.

File Management Software

Several programs allow you to manage images and other multimedia elements. Most software makes it possible to group, sort, and organize files both online and offline. Following are a few examples:

- Adobe Bridge available with most of Adobe's professional creative applications, lets you group, browse, and search digital assets.

- ACDSee Photo Manager offers a home version that lets you locate and view photos, correct flaws, and share favorites.

- Extensis allows you to find, sort, preview, organize, archive, track, and share fonts and other digital assets.

- Google Picasa is free software that lets you create Web albums to share with others.

File management software allows you to manage all the digital assets used in your multimedia projects.

- iPhoto, made by Apple Inc. for Mac OS X, allows images to be imported, titled, edited with basic tools, sorted, organized, viewed on a Mac or iPhone, published online, or printed.

- Microsoft Office Picture Manager offers basic photo processing and image management, file compression, and file conversion.

The appropriate program for you depends on your file management needs.

Skill Builder

1. Identify Keywords Find a picture online or in print. List at least five identifying keywords that would be helpful if you were searching for the image.

2. Construct a Plan Imagine that you are creating a multimedia project for your local zoo. Create folders you might use to organize digital assets. Identify one type of file you would put in each folder.

Chapter Summary

Graphics are images. Graphics can be logos, charts, drawings, paintings, or photographs. Types of graphics include raster and vector. Animation is the art of using graphics to create the illusion of motion. Animation can be created in two or three dimensions.

Graphics and animation can have a big impact on the effectiveness of multimedia. Productions that often contain graphics or animation include Web sites, online ads, mobile applications, presentations, and CBT. The role of graphics or animation might be to advertise, inform, illustrate a concept, demonstrate a process, tell a story, or add visual interest.

Understanding how graphics and animation are created and edited helps you prepare them effectively for use in multimedia. Graphics editing programs let you crop, resize, and rotate images; adjust contrast, brightness, and color; and layer, mask, and filter images. Both 2D and 3D animation can be accomplished through frame-by-frame and tweening techniques.

Vocabulary Review

1. Use at least seven of these content and academic vocabulary terms in a short essay about the use of graphics and animation in multimedia.

Content Vocabulary

◇ raster graphic (p. 198)
◇ pixel (p. 198)
◇ vector graphic (p. 199)
◇ native file format (p. 200)
◇ standard image format (p. 200)
◇ resolution (p. 200)
◇ file compression (p. 201)
◇ color mode (p. 205)
◇ wireframe model (p. 213)
◇ computer-generated imagery (CGI) (p. 213)
◇ virtual reality (p. 213)
◇ frame-by-frame animation (p. 215)
◇ tweening (p. 215)
◇ rollover (p. 215)

Academic Vocabulary

◇ attribute (p. 203)
◇ distinct (p. 204)
◇ via (p. 212)
◇ automatic (p. 215)

Review Key Concepts

2. Explain the role of graphics and animation in multimedia projects.

3. Compare and Contrast the two types of graphics.

4. Describe aspects of graphics files, including quality, format, and function.

5. Identify tools and techniques for editing digital images.

6. Examine the role of animation in multimedia.

7. Compare and Contrast the two types of animation.

8. Summarize the techniques for creating and editing computer animation.

Critical Thinking

9. Examine Find five important events in the evolution of computer graphics. Use information from your text and, with your teacher's approval, research the history of computer graphics online. Use a graphic like the one shown to help you create a time line showing the dates and events you identified.

10. Evaluate Which color mode (RGB, CMYK, or grayscale) would you use to create projects for the following products? Explain your answers.

   A. television
   B. magazine
   C. black and white photo
   D. textbook
   E. computer monitor

11. Describe How do pixels per inch (ppi) determine the resolution of a bitmap?

12. Summarize Think about each type of multimedia production you have seen over the past few days. List the types of multimedia that caught your attention. How were graphics and animation used in each? What functions did they perform?

13. Compare and Contrast Use a Venn diagram to organize information about 2D and 3D animation. Where the circles do not overlap, list characteristics specific to 2D or 3D animation. Where the circles overlap, list characteristics that 2D and 3D animation have in common.

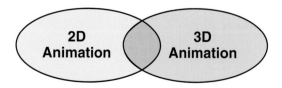

14. Analyze Graphics have different roles in multimedia productions. Record the roles in a table similar to the one below. Enter the roles in the first column. In the second column, identify the graphic(s) you think would work best for each role. One example is provided.

Graphic Use in Multimedia	
Purpose	**Type of Graphic**
Deliver information	Table, chart, diagram

15. Outline Create an outline including six different methods for modifying graphics. Include two facts about each method. The first method has been outlined for you.

Methods Used to Modify Graphics
I. Crop
   A. Eliminates unwanted parts of an image
   B. Focuses attention on the desired subject

Go Online **e-RESOURCES**
glencoe.com

Go to the **Online Learning Center** to find additional activities and career resources.

Practice Quizzes Test your knowledge of the material in this chapter.

Career Resources Find out more about careers, including information about résumés, portfolios, and interview and workplace tips.

Academic Connections

16. **English Language Arts–Analyze Information** NCTE 3 Apply strategies to interpret texts.

With your teacher's permission, use the Web to locate four different types of Web sites (e.g., commercial, informational, educational). Analyze the sites according to the following criteria: How does the site use graphics and animation to meet the purpose of the site? Are graphics and animation overused on the site? What, if any, graphics or animation should not have been used?

A. Use a table similar to the one shown to organize your information.

B. Write a one-page analysis that compares and contrasts the Web sites and their use of graphics. Which Web site had the most effective use of graphics and animation? What considerations may have led to the selection of those graphics and animation? Explain what changes, if any, you would make to the Web sites.

	Type and Purpose of Web Site	Effective Uses of Animation	Graphics to Keep	Graphics to Delete
Web Site 1				
Web Site 2				
Web Site 3				
Web Site 4				

Standardized Test Practice

Multiple Choice

Read the paragraph below and then answer the question.

Graphics are essential to most Web sites, contributing not only to their visual appeal but also to their content. Videos can also make Web sites more informative and entertaining, and special effects such as animation can add to their appeal. When selecting graphics, video, and animation, Web designers should keep the following in mind: file size and download time, memory requirements, monitor size and resolution, and browser type.

Test-Taking Tip In a multiple choice test, read the question before you read the paragraph and answer choices. Try to answer the question before you read the answer choices. This way, the answer choices will not throw you off.

17. According to the paragraph, which of the following statements is true?

   A. Videos are used for entertainment but not for information purposes on Web sites.

   B. Graphics are nonessential to most Web sites, contributing only to their visual appeal and not to their content.

   C. Web designers should keep monitor size and resolution in mind when developing content for Web pages.

   D. It is not necessary for Web designers to consider file size and download time when developing a Web site.

18. Evaluate Animation

NETS 5b Exhibit a positive attitude toward using technology that supports collaboration, learning, and productivity.

You work for a company that wants to update the animation on its Web site. Your boss asks you to lead a team to evaluate animation used in other corporate Web sites and make specific recommendations about how the company should use animation on its Web site.

A. Working in a small group, locate five corporate Web sites that include animation. Use a table similar to the one below to evaluate the sites.

Animation Evaluation			
Site	Animation Enhances Site	Animation Distracts	Text Readable
1			
2			
3			
4			
5			

B. After you have evaluated the Web sites, use presentation software to create a presentation that highlights the top 10 best uses of animation. In your presentation, include at least one reason to support each best use choice. Illustrate your presentation with specific examples from the Web sites. Be sure to properly cite any sources you use.

C. Proofread and spell-check your presentation.

19. Develop a Photo Collage

A client has asked you to create a custom photo collage for an ad. Select a local business for your client. For example, you could select a local dance studio, realtor, or pet groomer. After you have selected a business, create a collage to sell the business' product(s) or service(s).

A. Use four to six photos acquired from at least two different sources. Once all the images have been selected, create a mock-up of the collage. Find or create additional graphics and text to enhance the ad.

B. Use an image-editing program to create the collage. Use feathering, masking, and color enhancement to soften and blend the edges of the photos into a collage.

C. Include a title and a byline with your name. Be sure to properly cite any sources you use.

NETS 1a Apply existing knowledge to generate new ideas, products, or processes.

20. Use Good Judgment

Imagine that you are the leader of a team creating a virtual tour for a local recreation center. As the team leader, part of your role is giving feedback to other team members and resolving issues. The team has brainstormed some ideas for the virtual tour. You have created a rough mock-up of what you envision for the navigation and design. However, the virtual tour's structure and design do not seem to work well together. You need to resolve these problems while keeping the team motivated.

A. Draft your thoughts on a separate piece of paper, examining the issues from all angles.

B. Include information about what the issues are and ask your team to use the Internet to research other Web sites that offer effective virtual tours. Summarize what you want your team to look for and ask them to rate the sites' tours for their navigation, usability, effectiveness of visual design, and so on. Ask the team to look for sites that offer tours of: museums, exhibits, art galleries, designer homes, and sports facilities.

C. Revise your thoughts and rework them into a memo for your next team meeting. Be sure to proofread and spell-check your memo. Ask your teacher where and how to save the file.

21. Develop a Proposal

Your friend's business is reporting slow sales. He advertises online and in the local newspaper, but sales are still slow. You ask to see his ad and notice that it does not include graphics. Your friend asks if you will develop a proposal for a series of ads with graphics in them. Include the following in your proposal:

A. The type of business your friend has.

B. The purpose and audience of the business, including any assumptions you might have about the audience.

C. The graphics recommendations for the Web site.

D. An explanation of why you would recommend those types of graphics.

E. A description of the kind of logo you might design for the business.

Use a graphic organizer similar to the one shown to help you organize the information. Then, use the information in the graphic organizer to write your proposal. Proofread and spell-check your proposal.

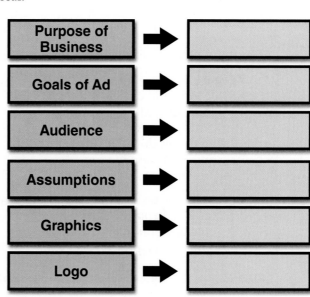

Project 1

NCTE 8 Use information resources to gather information and create and communicate knowledge.

Research Careers in Graphic Design

 English Language Arts Use newspapers, books, or the Internet to locate information about and view work done by graphic artists. Research and identify job opportunities, job duties, and job skills that relate to a career in graphic design.

Research

1. Answer the following: What type of education and experience do graphic artists need? What types of companies hire graphic artists? What is the salary range for graphic artists? What are the roles and responsibilities of a graphic artist? What is the job outlook for graphic artists? What technical and artistic skills are are needed to pursue a career in graphic design?

Create

2. Use the information you gather to create a presentation or a print publication. Include answers to the questions above. Then, identify your career goals and explain whether you hope to have a career in graphic design. Explain your reasoning. Proofread and spell-check your document.

Project 2

NCTE 7 Conduct research and gather, evaluate, and synthesize data to communicate discoveries.

Develop a Multimedia Tutorial

English Language Arts Working in a small group, develop a tutorial about how to use graphics to enhance a multimedia production.

Plan

1. Determine the different tasks of the project. Use a chart similar to the one shown. Decide who will be responsible for the tasks shown in the chart.

Research

2. Locate graphics on the Web, on CDs, and in books to use in your presentation.

Create

3. Modify and create graphics as needed. Make sure you can legally use the images you copy, download, or scan for use in your presentation.

4. Write the text for your tutorial. Explain how each type of graphic is used to enhance the project. Cite your sources. Proofread and spell-check your tutorial.

Team Tasks for Tutorial Project	
Task	Name(s)
Research Web sites	
Locate graphics	
Draw sample images	
Integrate graphics into the presentation	
Crop, adjust graphics' brightness, contrast, hue, and saturation	
Create and edit text	

Project 3

Integrate Graphics and Animation

NCTE 3 Apply strategies to interpret texts.

NCTE 8 Use information resources to gather information and create and communicate knowledge.

English Language Arts Some graphics take a short time to create, while others, such as animation, may take longer.

Plan

1. Select a topic for a multimedia project. Then, use a table similar to the one below to track all the images you plan to include in the project and their description and type (graphics, photos, animations). Determine whether you already have all of the graphics or photos you need. List the applications you will need to create new images or animation. List applications you will use to modify existing graphics or photos. If you will be using graphics from an outside source, remember to cite the source in your table.

Multimedia Graphics and Animation Plan			
Graphic Description	**Graphic Type**	**Application to Be Used or Source Retrieved From**	**Time Needed to Create**

Create

2. Create at least two different types of graphics or animation for your project. If using digital photography to create new photos, use equipment and techniques appropriately. Be sure to incorporate photo composition techniques such as lighting, perspective, candid versus posed, the rule of thirds, and level of horizon.

3. Use at least two different graphics or animation from an outside source. Modify the graphics to meet your needs, using appropriate software and following standard visual design principles. Be sure to consider image size, resolution, and orientation. Also consider whether photos will need to be retouched and whether the color mode is appropriate. Apply layers, if needed, to make edits.

Review

4. Share the graphics you have created and the graphics you modified with at least two other classmates. Ask for their feedback based on your plan for placement in the production, size, resolution, orientation, retouching, and coloring.

Revise

5. Based on feedback from your classmates, revise the graphics. Modify the time needed to create graphics in your table if necessary.

6. Proofread and spell-check your table.

Go Online RUBRICS
glencoe.com

Chapter Projects Use the rubrics for these projects to help create and evaluate your work. Go to the **Online Learning Center** at glencoe.com. Choose **Rubrics**, then **Chapter 7**.

CHAPTER 8 Audio

Section 8.1
Audio in Multimedia

Section 8.2
Work with Audio

CHAPTER OBJECTIVES

After completing this chapter, you will be able to:

❖ **Identify** the different types of audio used in multimedia projects and computing.

❖ **Explain** the various reasons audio might be used in multimedia projects.

❖ **Describe** how presentations containing audio can be made accessible to people who have difficulty hearing.

❖ **List** ethical principles for using audio found on the Internet.

❖ **Describe** the technological aspects of audio, including sound quality, file size, and file format.

❖ **Explain** the ways sound can be modified using audio editing software.

❖ **List** examples of popular audio editing programs.

❖ **Identify** audio devices often used in developing multimedia projects.

Explore the Photo

Working with audio requires good decision-making skills. You must decide how audio will contribute to the project without being distracting.
What guidelines do you follow when making decisions?

21st CENTURY SKILLS
Make Informed Decisions

When making an informed decision, you should gather and evaluate the most current and relevant information on the topic. Having access to as much up-to-date information as possible allows you to think through the pros and cons of the situation.

Quick Write Activity Coherent Paragraphs

Write about a time when you made a decision without having all the facts. What was the result? On what was your decision based? What would you do differently if you had to make the decision again?

Writing Tips

To write coherent paragraphs, follow these steps:

1. Use transition words and phrases.
2. Use repeated words, parallel structures, or synonyms to link sentences and paragraphs.
3. Use pronouns to avoid unnecessary repetition.

SECTION (8.1) Audio in Multimedia

Reading Guide

Before You Read

Predict Browse the section's headings, bold terms, and figure captions to predict what you will learn.

Read to Learn

Key Concepts

- **Identify** forms of audio used in multimedia.
- **Explain** the role of audio in multimedia.
- **Identify** principles for using audio ethically.
- **Compare and Contrast** common audio file formats.
- **Describe** audio file size and sound quality issues.

Main Idea

Audio plays many roles in multimedia. Effective audio use in multimedia requires an understanding of audio file formats, sound quality, and file sizes.

Content Vocabulary

◇ sound effect ◇ sample size
◇ voice-over   ◇ channel
◇ analog   ◇ codec
◇ sampling   ◇ bandwidth
◇ sampling rate

Academic Vocabulary

You will find these words in your reading and on your tests. Use the glossary to look up their definitions, if necessary.

◇ principle
◇ proprietary

Graphic Organizer

As you read the section, identify two ways to capture sound waves. Use a tree diagram like the one below to map out your ideas.

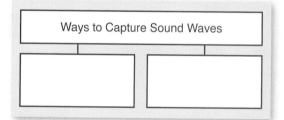

Ways to Capture Sound Waves

 Graphic Organizer Go to this book's **Online Learning Center** at glencoe.com to print this graphic organizer.

Academic Standards

 English Language Arts

NCTE 8 Use information resources to gather information and create and communicate knowledge.
NCTE 12 Conduct research, gather, evaluate, and synthesize data to communicate discoveries.

NCTE National Council of Teachers of English
NSES National Science Education Standards

Mathematics

NCTM Problem Solving Build new mathematical knowledge through problem solving.
NCTM Problem Solving Monitor and reflect on the process of mathematical problem solving.

NCTM National Council of Teachers of Mathematics
NCSS National Council for the Social Studies

Audio in Multimedia

How does my audience and purpose affect my audio choices?

The next time you play a video game, turn off the sound on the television or computer monitor. How does your experience change? Does the game seem less realistic? Is it less enjoyable? If so, the game's developers have made effective use of audio. Audio is live or recorded sound. Using audio in multimedia projects can help capture and hold your audience's interest and provide information using all the senses.

Audio may be incorporated into a range of multimedia projects, from Web pages and video games to mobile applications and kiosks. Some forms of audio used in multimedia projects include:

- **Music** You probably hear music every day, on the radio, television, or a personal audio player (see Figure 8.1). Music refers to sounds produced by voices or instruments. In multimedia projects, music might set the mood for a Web site, complete the action in a video, or add interest to a presentation.

- **Sound Effects** A sound effect is an artificially created or enhanced sound used to achieve an effect (without speech or music). The sound might imitate another sound, such as applause or thunder. Echoes might be used to suggest the locations of sounds in space. Sound effects can add a sense of realism to the action of a video game or training simulation. Other media that commonly use sound effects include movies, plays, television shows, radio programs, and music.

- **Voice-over** Voice-over uses the human voice to narrate all or part of a presentation. A voice-over might tell a story, provide directions, or give feedback to the user of a video game or computer-based training (CBT) simulation. Human voices can help add to the authenticity of characters in video games and animations. Other multimedia, such as electronic dictionaries and online encyclopedias, also offer spoken narrative.

- **Alerts and Prompts** Computers provide beeps and other sounds to warn you of problems such as a low battery, a hardware glitch while booting up, or a disconnected printer. Operating systems and software applications often use audio to let you know when a process, such as downloading a file, is complete. Audio signals also alert users to on-screen messages that require action, such as inserting a CD or clicking a button.

As You Read

Connect What types of audio do you listen to on a regular basis?

Go Online **ACTIVITY**
glencoe.com

Web Accessibility Find out more about the W3C's Web Accessibility Initiative at the **Online Learning Center**. Go to **glencoe.com**. Choose **Activities**, then **Chapter 8**.

Figure 8.1
Mobile audio players let you listen to songs, podcasts, and other audio files whenever and wherever you want. **What other types of audio are used in multimedia?**

Locating Audio Files Online

You can use search engines to locate audio files for your multimedia projects. For example, the Music Robot WAV search engine lets you search for specific sounds and MIDI files. Many stock sound sites and Clip Art providers also offer sound effects and short audio files.

Stock sounds are often royalty-free, but you may need to obtain permission or pay a fee to use other audio files in a multimedia project. Always be sure to follow the terms and conditions for using any audio you download or purchase from the Internet.

Online music stores such as Apple's iTunes Store, Amazon MP3, Rhapsody, Zune Marketplace, and Walmart MP3 Music Downloads offer a legal way to download, play, and share audio files online (see Figure 8.2). These files may include music files as well as other types of audio files.

Certain ethical principles apply to downloading or purchasing music, as well as how you can use the music. A **principle** is a rule or code of conduct. Peer-to-peer file-sharing applications make it easy to trade digital copies of music. This practice, however, could violate the license, or agreement, entered into when you purchased the music. Licenses are sometimes called licensing agreements. You do not have the right to make copies of audio files for others or to post copies of files on a Web site without permission from the copyright holder.

Most music cannot legally be used without paying a fee to the publishing company. If you are unsure, contact the source of the music. Always be sure to provide credit for any type of media you use that you did not create yourself.

Figure 8.2

Online music stores offer movies, television shows, music videos, and other media for download. **Why is a licensing agreement important?**

The Role of Audio in Multimedia

Sounds and music can perform a variety of functions in multimedia projects. They should always be used to enhance your project. By planning your project thoroughly, you can ensure that any audio used will support your project's purpose and goals. Remember that too many sounds can distract viewers from the multimedia project's purpose. Use the Audio Evaluation Checklist in Figure 8.3 to help you analyze the use of audio in your multimedia project.

Audio should have a specific role and should not be used unless you have specific reasons for including the sound. Be sure to identify the role of any sounds that you want to include in your multimedia project. Does the audio add interest, convey meaning, or direct attention to an important element or event? The role of audio can vary based on the type of multimedia project you are building.

Figure 8.3
Use this checklist when you plan your multimedia projects. **Why should you identify the role of any sounds you want to include in multimedia?**

Audio Evaluation Checklist

☑ Does the audio support the project's goals?
☑ Does the audio distract viewers?
☑ Are the audio files in the most appropriate file format?
☑ Is the level of sound quality appropriate for the file format and deliverable?
☑ Are the audio files an appropriate file size for the type of multimedia project?
☑ Have necessary permissions been obtained and cited?
☑ Have I included alternative text, or a transcript to describe my sounds and audio?
☑ Do I have too many sounds in the multimedia project?

- An online promotion might include such projects as a Web page, an online ad, or e-mail or text message marketing. These might use audio to add interest or set a mood.
- A mobile multimedia project might be video or music applications, communication applications like e-mail, or data tracking programs like GPS systems. The role of audio in these projects might be to convey meaning, direct attention, give feedback, prompt action, or provide directions.
- An entertainment multimedia project might be a video, video game, cartoon, or movie. These projects might use audio to add a sense of realism, complement action, prompt action, set a mood, or tell a story.
- A multimedia project used for informational purposes might include CBT, presentations, or a kiosk. In these instances, audio can appeal to people who learn best by listening, clarify information, direct attention, help improve understanding, and provide directions.

Think about the types of sound that are most appropriate for your project. Also consider the software you will need to create and modify the sounds you want to use. This will help you to identify the audio file formats and files sizes that are best for the type of multimedia project you are developing. Files sizes can affect download times and sound quality, and be a key factor in deciding on the type of sound you will use or create and the file format you will save it in. Be sure that the file is not so large that users will have trouble downloading it.

Real World

Ethical Use of Audio Multimedia developers must conduct themselves ethically when using copyrighted audio and other media in projects for clients.

Why It's Important
Why is it important to consider ethics when working with clients?

Accessibility Issues

When using audio, you must also think about accessibility issues. For someone with difficulty hearing, it can be a challenge to understand and benefit from a multimedia presentation that contains audio. Think about the accessibility guidelines discussed in Chapter 5 and what you would need to do to ensure that as many people as possible are able to access and understand your project. When using sound, alternate text must be provided to describe the audio for people with hearing impairments. This can be provided as a transcript that includes the audio's content word for word, with descriptions of sounds (such as laughter). When the transcript is timed to appear with the visual presentation, it is called captioning.

Figure 8.4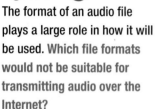
The format of an audio file plays a large role in how it will be used. **Which file formats would not be suitable for transmitting audio over the Internet?**

 **Explain** How can audio in a multimedia project be made accessible to someone who has difficulty hearing?

Audio File Formats

Format (Extension)	Features	Function
AIFF (.aif, .aifc, .aiff)	• Developed specifically for Macintosh® computers • Uncompressed, so it is much larger than MP3	One of the main file formats used by professional audio (and video) programs
AU, SND (.au, .snd)	• Can be played on Windows or Macintosh computers that have appropriate software and hardware • Do not compress audio nearly as much as MP3	Early formats for exchanging sound files on the Internet that are no longer widely used
MIDI (.mid)	• Refers to a method and format for recording music from synthesizers and electronic instruments • Contains data describing the pitch, length, and volume of musical notes played on an electronic instrument • Can rarely compete with high-quality digital audio on PCs	• Early format for cell phone ringtones • Occasionally used for simple sounds on the Internet (due to its small file size)
MPEG Audio-Player 3 (.mp3)	• Developed by the Moving Picture Experts Group • Can compress an audio file to about one-twelfth the space it takes up on a CD, with no significant loss in sound quality	Standard audio file format for storing and exchanging music
Wave® (.wav)	• Created by Microsoft® and IBM® for Windows sound files • Does not compress audio as much as MP3 and other formats • Mainly used for short audio clips	Standard format for sound effects and other very short sounds (such as system alerts)
Windows Media® Audio (.wma)	• Proprietary format used by Windows Media® Player • Uses lossy compression • Can be played back using a range of consumer devices	• Used for music files • Not as popular as MP3 music files
MPEG Audio-Player 4 Part 14 (.mp4, .m4a)	• Developed by the Moving Picture Experts Group • Allows streaming over the Internet • Can store subtitles	File format used for streaming audio and video

Using Audio Technology

Why is it important to consider file size when using audio in multimedia projects?

When you use audio in a multimedia production, you must think about its technical aspects. Technical considerations include file format, sound quality, and file size.

Audio File Formats

There are many different formats for audio files, each with specific strengths and weaknesses. An audio file's format determines which devices can interpret, open, and properly play the file's content; how much space it occupies on a disk; and how long it takes to travel over the Internet. Figure 8.4 on page 232 shows the most common audio file formats, along with their filename extensions and functions. Standard formats can be supported by various programs. If a format can be used only with a specific program, the file format is called **proprietary**.

The best format for audio files depends largely on how they will be used in the multimedia. MP3 is the standard audio file format for storing and exchanging music and WAV is the best format for sound effects and systems alerts. Always test multimedia projects containing audio files to make sure that the audio plays properly, the sound quality is high and the file size is not too large.

Sound Quality

Sound is a series of waves that vibrates your eardrums or other objects (see Figure 8.5). How well a multimedia application delivers sound depends partly on the user's equipment (which the developer cannot control) and partly on how the sound was recorded and edited (which the developer can control). There are two ways to record, or capture, sound waves:

- **Analog** audio recording captures continuous waves of sound (a stream of data) on the surface of magnetic tape or the groove of a record. The quality of an analog recording deteriorates over time.

- Digital audio recording captures individual units of data to reproduce sounds more accurately than analog recordings. In general, digital recordings delivered on CDs, DVDs, networks, and the Web have replaced analog recordings because they are more durable and accurate than cassette tapes and records.

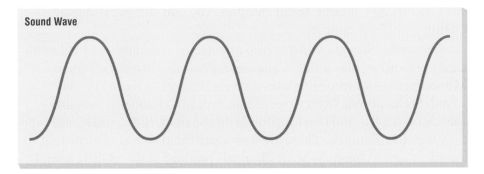

Sound Wave

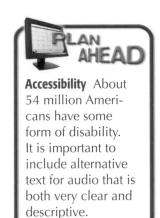

Figure 8.5

This image represents a sound wave. To use audio in a multimedia project, sound waves must be recorded. What equipment do you need to record sound?

Plan Ahead

Accessibility About 54 million Americans have some form of disability. It is important to include alternative text for audio that is both very clear and descriptive.

Sampling Digital audio recording devices capture sound by **sampling**, or recording fragments of, a sound wave. Sampling and sampling rates determine the quality of a sound recording. Sampling turns the waves of an audio file into points on a grid that can be measured and recorded. (See Figure 8.6.)

The **sampling rate** is the number of times per second a recording device samples sound waves. It is expressed in kilohertz (kHz). The higher the sampling rate, the better the audio file's sound quality. However, higher sampling rates mean larger file sizes, which can take longer to download. Multimedia sampling rates generally vary, but commercial CDs and other computer audio are sampled at 44.1 kilohertz (kHz), or 44,100 samples recorded per second. To the human ear, this is a near-perfect recording. The other two sampling rates typically used for multimedia productions are 22.05 kHz and 11.025 kHz.

Figure 8.6 🔵 ➡

Sampling transforms sound waves into points on a grid. Does a higher or lower sampling rate create better sound quality?

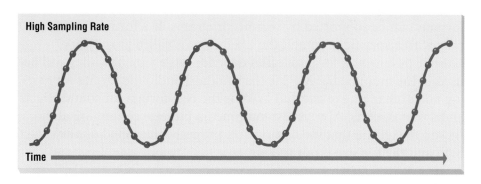

High Sampling Rate

Time

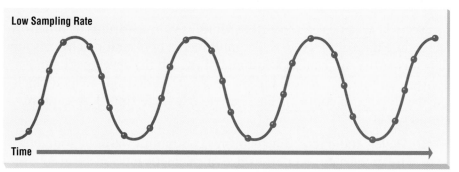

Low Sampling Rate

Time

Another factor in digital sound quality is sample size, also called audio resolution. **Sample size** is the number of bits of data in each sample, typically 8 or 16 bits. In general, the higher the resolution, the clearer the audio. While 8-bit has long been the most universal sample size, most sound cards are now made with 16-bit sample size. The standard audio CD contains 16-bit samples. You can still get good sound quality with 8-bit samples.

Channels Sound quality is also affected by the number of channels used to record or play a file. A **channel** represents a stream of audio. Monaural (mono) recording uses a single channel to record or play sound. Stereophonic (stereo) recording uses two channels—one for sounds on the left and one for sounds on the right. Surround sound typically uses five channels. There are newer surround sound systems that use six or seven channels. More channels produce more realistic sound.

File Size

Audio files are often very large. The size of an audio file depends on the following data:

- Number of channels
- Sample size
- Sampling rate
- Length

If you know this information, you can calculate the size of an audio file. For example, suppose a song on a CD (recorded in 16-bit, 44 kHz stereo) is four minutes long. Use the following formula:

> 2 (stereo channels) x 16 (bits) x 44,000 (samples per second) x 240 (seconds of music)
> = 337,920,000 bits

The file is over 40 megabytes. This relatively large file size translates to a level of sound quality appropriate for delivery on a home audio system. Sending a file that size over the Internet, however, could take a very long time. Even loading and playing it on a laptop for a presentation would be cumbersome.

Compression File compression reduces the size of audio files for transmission over the Internet or slow network connections. As with images, audio compression is a way of saving an audio file in a smaller format that requires less disk space and transmission time. Audio editing software typically contains file compression tools that allow you to save your audio files as lossy or lossless.

- In lossy compression, some less important data is discarded. For most multimedia productions, this slight loss in audio quality is an acceptable trade-off for a smaller file size.
- Lossless compression maintains sound quality but generates larger files than lossy compression.

When deciding which compression format to use, you must consider both the quality and file size. Ask yourself: Which is more important for the type of multimedia project I am creating? You might need to consult with your client or employer. Practice will help you find the right balance for different types of projects.

Streaming Streaming audio (or video) also reduces the user's wait time. Streaming audio is a process that breaks the transmission into pieces. Those pieces are continuously received and played back by a media player as they are downloaded from a source device. Each downloaded piece plays as the rest of the file is still arriving. The result is a continuous stream of content, without the long download time.

Streaming audio is increasingly popular for listening to large files that must be downloaded from the Web. Streamed audio might include a live radio broadcast, or it might be a file that you download or receive with e-mail.

Academic Focus

Mathematics

Audio Compression A compression scheme used for audio has a 6:1 compression ratio. An uncompressed audio file has a size of 540MB. What would be its size after compression? Start by dividing 540 by 6. If you wanted the file size to be less than 70MB, what compression ratio would you need?

NCTM Problem Solving Monitor and reflect on the process of mathematical problem solving.

Figure 8.7
Users must have a media player to hear streaming audio. What is streaming audio?

To hear streamed audio, you need the appropriate media player, such as QuickTime (see Figure 8.7). To create or transmit a streaming audio file, you must select a codec. A **codec** (**co**mpression/**dec**ompression scheme) is the means of compressing and decompressing data. The choice of codec, which determines audio quality and consistency, is based on the type of audio and available bandwidth. **Bandwidth** is the amount of data that can be transmitted to the receiver in a given amount of time.

 **Reading Check** **Define** What are sampling, sampling rate, and sample size?

Section 8.1 After You Read

Review Key Concepts

1. **Identify** three audio file formats used for exchanging music. Which is the most popular?

2. **Summarize** the relationship between an audio file's sound quality and its file size.

 Check Your Answers Check your answers at this book's **Online Learning Center** through **glencoe.com**.

Practice Academic Skills

Mathematics

3. **Calculate** A song on a CD recorded in 16-bit, 44 kHz stereo is three minutes long and contains 253,440,000 bits. Assuming there are 8 bits in a byte, and 1,000,000 bytes in a megabyte, calculate the approximate size of the file.

English Language Arts

4. **Analyze** Locate a brief video that includes speech and sound effects (such as a dog barking, or waves crashing on the beach). As you play the video, write a properly punctuated transcript of all spoken words. Include descriptions of sounds. Make a list summarizing your accessibility options, listing the pros and cons of each.

Online Student Manual • glencoe.com

Go to your Online Student Manual and enter your password to find projects that allow you to practice and apply multimedia skills.

NCTM Problem Solving Build new mathematical knowledge through problem solving.

NCTE 12 Conduct research, gather, evaluate, and synthesize data to communicate discoveries.

SECTION (8.2) Work with Audio

Before You Read

Vocabulary To gain a better understanding of vocabulary, divide a piece of paper into three columns with the following heads: *Term, What is it?,* and *What else is it like?* Write down each new word you come across and answer the two questions about it as you read the section.

Read to Learn
Key Concepts

- **Describe** methods for recording, editing, and analyzing audio.

- **List** common tools for creating and editing audio for multimedia.

- **Explain** how audio in multimedia can be accessed by people with impaired hearing.

- **Describe** the hardware needed to work with audio in multimedia.

Main Idea

Audio editing software is used to create and modify sound for multimedia. Effective audio should support a multimedia project's content.

Content Vocabulary

◇ speech synthesis

◇ voice recognition

◇ audio card

Academic Vocabulary

You will find these words in your reading and on your tests. Use the glossary to look up their definitions, if necessary.

◆ professional   ◆ adequate

Graphic Organizer

As you read this section, identify four audio devices used in building a multimedia production. Use a Web diagram like the one below to organize your information.

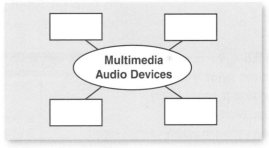

 Graphic Organizer Go to this book's **Online Learning Center** at glencoe.com to print this graphic organizer.

Academic Standards

 English Language Arts

NCTE 6 Apply knowledge of language structure and conventions to discuss texts.
NCTE 7 Conduct research and gather, evaluate, and synthesize data to communicte discoveries.
NCTE 8 Use information resources to gather information and create and communicate knowledge.

 Mathematics

NCTM Number and Operations Compute fluently and make reasonable estimates.

NCTE National Council of Teachers of English
NSES National Science Education Standards

NCTM National Council of Teachers of Mathematics
NCSS National Council for the Social Studies

As You Read

Connect How could you use audio in your next class presentation?

Go Online ACTIVITY
glencoe.com

Audio Editing Software Learn more about the features of various audio editing applications at the Online Learning Center. Go to glencoe.com. Choose Activities, then Chapter 8.

Editing Audio

What equipment and software do you need in order to record and edit sound?

Devices for recording and playing back sound have existed since at least 1877, when Thomas Edison recited "Mary Had a Little Lamb" into a cone and recorded it on a sheet of tinfoil wrapped around a cylinder. When Edison invented the phonograph, he probably could not have imagined today's technology. We can now record sound and make it available within moments to listeners throughout the world via the Internet, radio, and television.

Audio editing software lets you create audio files or change the way files sound to best suit the purpose of a particular multimedia project (see Figure 8.8). These programs have tools for recording, editing, or applying effects to sounds; importing, exporting, or converting audio from one format to another; combining or mixing two audio files; or analyzing certain aspects of audio, such as rhythm and pitch.

Record, Edit, and Apply Effects

You can use audio editing hardware and software to record, edit, or apply effects to sounds for a multimedia project. You may want to record a voice-over narration for simulations or a Web site, or adjust the volume of an existing audio file in a CBT program or video game. Or, you may want add a sound effect, such as applause, that fades in or out, or plays automatically when users successfully complete a segment of a tutorial. Sound effects, such as birds chirping or the roar of a waterfall, can also help set a mood.

Figure 8.8

Audio editing software provides the tools to create quality audio files. **What are some of the ways you can modify audio files?**

Features of Audio Editing Software	
Feature	**Description**
Import, export, convert	Importing, exporting, or converting an audio file involves saving it in a different format that is usable by a particular program or device.
Record	Through a computer's line input, audio editing software might let you record sound from a microphone, mixer, cassette, vinyl record, radio, or a live performance on electronic instruments.
Edit	You can edit sound in many ways, such as make it louder or softer, mute it, shorten or lengthen it, clear it of background noise, or loop (repeat) it.
Mix	Different audio tracks, such as vocal and instrumental, can be blended electronically to produce a combined recording.
Apply effects	Numerous special effects can be applied to audio, including fade, reverse, echo, reverberate (resound), and distort.
Analyze	Audio analysis refers to pulling out and interpreting certain aspects of audio signals, such as rhythm and pitch.

Recorded and edited sound effects can be useful to achieve a desired effect in a multimedia project. You can offer feedback, for example, such as "Sorry" or "Try again" to show the user that they have made a mistake in a slide show quiz. Other sound effects are useful in games and simulations to simulate common and ambient sounds that contribute to the environment set up by the software.

Remember, before you decide how you want to incorporate audio, you should consider whether it reflects and supports the content of the multimedia project.

Convert, Combine, and Analyze

Many audio editing programs allow you to convert audio from one format to another. This can be helpful when you need the audio file for use in a program that will only accept certain file formats. You may also convert a file format to create a smaller file. An old AU file that you want to include in your multimedia project, for example, can be converted to the smaller, compressed MP3 format.

Audio editing software also lets you combine or mix two audio files to create sound for your multimedia project. For example, you might want to make a new recording from an old source and mix it with a sound effect that you have created on an electronic keyboard, or combine sections from two or more music tracks.

Some audio editing software includes audio analysis capabilities that are designed to let you pull out, analyze, and interpret various characteristics of audio signals, such as rhythm and pitch.

 **Reading Check** **Name** Identify the audio editing technique for blending different tracks to produce a combined recording.

Audio Editing Software

What software is needed to create audio for a multimedia project?

Audio files are created with different types of software. Most new computers come with some software and hardware for editing audio. You can also purchase audio editing software with powerful features. There are also various programs for creating written music using input from electronic instruments or from your computer's keyboard.

Audio editing programs range in price and features. You can use applications such as GoldWave, Sound Forge, and Audacity to create and edit high-quality audio files. Microsoft Windows contains an application called Sound Recorder that lets you create and save audio files. While Sound Recorder allows you to make some changes, it does not provide the sophisticated features of commercial and professional audio applications. Some popular programs for creating and editing audio include:

- **Adobe Audition**, formerly Cool Edit Pro, offers professional tools for recording and editing audio. A **professional** is someone who engages in an activity as an occupation. Professional audio tools are used by people who have a career in audio editing. Audition is available for Windows PCs.

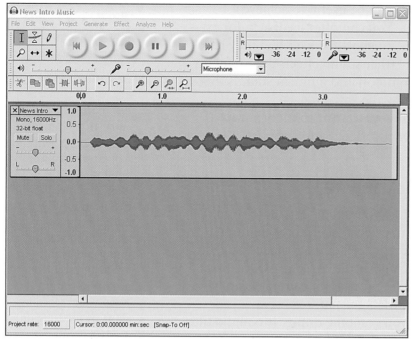

- **Adobe Soundbooth**, included in Adobe's Creative Suite, is a basic audio editor for home and semi-professional users. It operates on Windows and Mac OS.

- **Audacity** is a popular open-source, cross-platform audio editing software that can be downloaded free from the Internet (see Figure 8.9). Windows, Mac OS, and Linux versions are available.

- **Cakewalk SONAR V-Studio** is used by professional editors in the music studio. It integrates hardware and software, providing advanced audio recording and editing capabilities.

Figure 8.9

Audio editing software allows you to select parts of an audio file to record, compress, or convert file formats. What are some advantages of audio editing software?

- **GoldWave by GoldWave Inc.** is a popular and relatively inexpensive program that offers advanced audio editing tools for achieving professional results. GoldWave works on Windows OS.

- **Logic Pro by Apple Inc.** lets you record, professionally mix, and edit audio on a Macintosh computer.

- **Sony Sound Forge** is a full-featured audio editing suite utilized by music professionals and semi-professionals. Sound Forge operates on Windows PCs.

- **Sound Recorder**, a simple audio recording application, comes with Windows. Starting with Vista, basic features for editing and adding effects to audio were removed from Sound Recorder.

MIDI Software

Some conventional audio editing programs also have features for recording, storing, replaying, and editing MIDI files. These programs include Cakewalk SONAR for Windows (and Mac OS with a certain utility) and Apple's Logic Pro for Macintosh computers.

Software for Composers

Creating new music is actually one of the least common uses for sound in multimedia projects. However, if you have composition software, you can create sheet music and musical scores for many voices or instruments. Or you can create and record music with your computer keyboard or with a MIDI instrument. MakeMusic, Inc., offers a range of composition programs. Songworks, by Ars Nova Software, lets you compose, notate, and print music. Both MakeMusic's products and Songworks are available for Windows and Mac OS.

Activity 8A Edit Audio Clips

❶ Open an audio editing software program such as Microsoft Windows Movie Maker or Audacity.

❷ Create a new project and name it *Your Name* **News Music**.

❸ Locate and open the data file folder for Chapter 8. Import the student data file **News Intro Music** that is compatible with your program (or music you recorded using audio equipment and transferred to the computer). This clip is about 3 seconds.

❹ Import the version of the student data file **News Story Music** that is compatible with your program (see Figure 8.10).

❺ Listen to the two clips play solo. Then, listen to the clips play together. The second clip is about 16 seconds, but notice that the music stops several seconds before the clip ends.

❻ Trim the excess time off the News Story Music clip so that it stops just after the music ends (see Figure 8.11).

❼ Play the sequence again to confirm that the second clip ends at the appropriate place.

❽ Save the file and close your audio or video editing software.

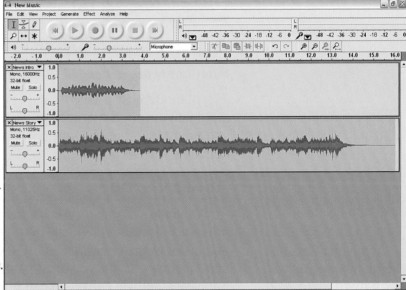

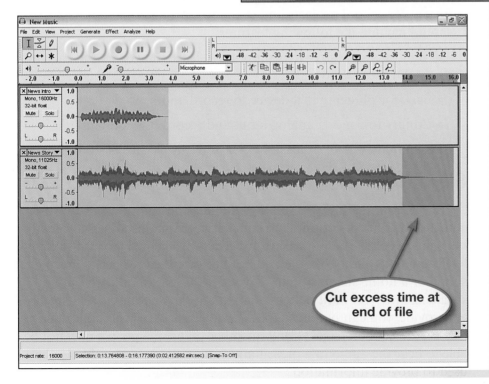

Cut excess time at end of file

● **Figure 8.10**
The audio editing software allows you to "see" both of the clips you have imported at the same time.

● **Figure 8.11**
The software allows you to hear and see how you are editing the audio clip.

Accessibility Software

Remember to think about how the audio you are using might limit people with special needs. Technologies such as speech synthesis and voice recognition make some multimedia elements more accessible to people with impaired hearing, speech, or mobility. **Speech synthesis** software uses a computer to articulate human speech. This software allows people with speech disorders to talk to others through a computer. **Voice recognition** uses human speech as an input device for a computer. Voice recognition programs accept spoken words in place of keyboard strokes. Some video games use speech instead of text to direct play. As computing power increases, these technologies are likely to improve.

 **Reading Check** **List** Identify three popular audio editing programs.

Audio Hardware

What hardware is needed to use audio in a multimedia project?

All modern PCs have the capability of playing system sounds. The input and output devices, or physical components that create, process, and produce audio for multimedia productions, however, may or may not come with a computer.

Audio Cards

An **audio card**, also called a sound card, is a circuit board that processes sound and sends it to a computer's speakers. The card plugs into a slot in the computer's CPU. All Macintosh computers and most new Windows PCs have built-in audio cards. If your computer does not have a built-in card, you can purchase an inexpensive one that is sufficient for school projects and even most professional applications. It should include the following features:

- Built-in synthesizer that supports at least 100 voices and can turn MIDI into audio
- Jack for plugging in a device to record audio
- Ability to convert analog input and record it in a digital file
- Sampling rate of at least 44 kHz and sample size of 16 bits

Speakers

Speakers will allow you to play and hear the audio you create and edit. All Macintosh computers and most new Windows PCs come with built-in speakers. These speakers are generally **adequate**, or sufficient, for listening to audio, but they do not produce the crisp, clear, deep sound of a home stereo system. If your PC has a sound card but no speakers, or if you want better sound quality than your current speakers provide, you can purchase speakers to connect to your computer (see Figure 8.12 on page 243). Remember that some people may not be able to hear the audio in a presentation, so visual cues should also be used to provide information.

Academic Focus

Mathematics

Compare Prices
Audio software and hardware cost money. Compare two brands of the following audio editing tools: audio editing software, audio card, speakers, and microphone. For each tool, subtract the lower price from the higher price. Be sure to make the decimals properly aligned. Assess which brands are the least expensive.

NCTM Number and Operations Compute fluently and make reasonable estimates.

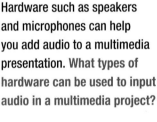 **Figure 8.12**

Hardware such as speakers and microphones can help you add audio to a multimedia presentation. What types of hardware can be used to input audio in a multimedia project?

Microphones

You will need a microphone to record audio and save it in a file. If your computer did not come with a microphone, you can usually purchase one very inexpensively. Plug the microphone into a jack in the audio card to record voice input, such as narration for a multimedia presentation. Alternative input methods, such as special keyboards and bite sticks, allow developers (and users) with special needs to enter data without a microphone.

MIDI Hardware

MIDI input devices include synthesizers, portable keyboards, and other instruments. Working with MIDI instruments requires additional hardware or software and devices for connecting the instruments to PCs. You can also buy MIDI cards, which have jacks for MIDI instruments and features for saving the MIDI input.

CD/DVD Burners

Most new PCs have drives for recording on rewritable CDs and DVDs, a process referred to as "burning." These devices are too slow, however, to be practical for commercial purposes. Multimedia producers can purchase peripheral CD and DVD burners that are many times faster than a standard CD-RW drive in a home PC. These devices connect to the CPU but operate separately.

PLAN AHEAD

Accessibility When developing multimedia projects that include audio, ask yourself if you would understand the purpose and meaning of the project if you were unable to hear it. If not, create alternative content that will make it accessible to people who have difficulty hearing. Synchronize the transcript with the presentation.

Audio Safety Considerations

You should handle audio equipment only if you understand how it operates. Always read the user manuals. There are some general safety precautions to follow when working with audio equipment:

- Avoid contact with electrical connectors and cables.

- Tape down and flag all audio cable that crosses areas where people walk or work.

- Do not repair broken audio equipment yourself unless you are trained or qualified to do so. Report any damaged equipment to your supervisor and others who use the equipment.

- Return audio equipment to its appropriate storage area when you are done using it. Store audio equipment in containers designed for this type of equipment.

YOU TRY IT

Activity 8B Add Sound Effects

① Open your audio editing software.

② Open the *Your Name* **News Music** media file you created in You Try It Activity 8A.

③ Navigate to and import the version of the student data file **Ocean Waves** that is compatible with your software (or a sound effect you recorded using audio equipment and transferred to the computer). This clip is about 36 seconds.

④ Shorten the Ocean Waves (or sound effect) clip to the length of the News Intro Music clip (see Figure 8.13). The two audio clips will now play at the same time.

Figure 8.13

The News Intro Music and the Ocean Waves sound clips are now about the same length.

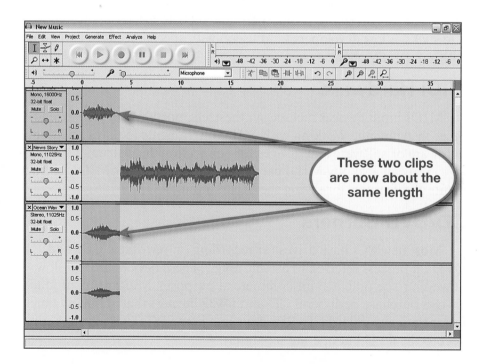

5. Adjust the start time of the News Story clip so that it starts just after the News Intro Music and Ocean Waves clips stop (see Figure 8.14).

6. Play the sequence to confirm that the first music clip plays with the sound effect, followed by the second music clip.

7. Save the finished audio clip file and close your audio editing software.

8. Play the audio clip for a classmate. Ask the classmate to evaluate your work, using the Audio Evaluation Checklist on page 231.

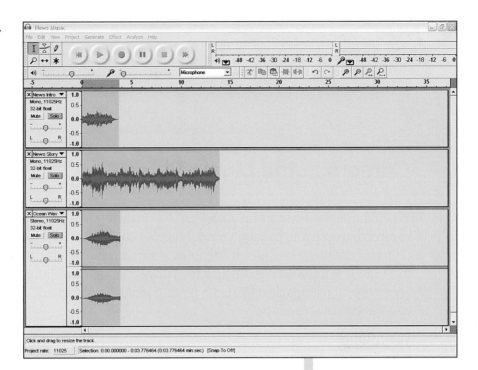

Figure 8.14
The second music clip now plays after the other two audio clips.

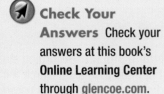 **List** Name four pieces of audio hardware.

Section 8.2 After You Read

Review Key Concepts

1. **Compare and Contrast** audio editing software tools used to create quality audio files.

2. **Identify** how the quality of sound produced by a computer's built-in speakers differs from the speakers of a home stereo system.

Check Your Answers Check your answers at this book's **Online Learning Center** through **glencoe.com**.

Practice Academic Skills
English Language Arts

3. **Summarize** Research speech synthesis or voice recognition technology. Write a paragraph describing how the hardware and software used in this technology improves accessibility for all users.

4. **Illustrate** Research the history of devices for recording and playing sound, starting with Edison's phonograph in 1877 and concluding with the digital era. Create a time line showing the dates of the main advances in audio technology.

NCTE 7 Conduct research and gather, evaluate, and synthesize data to communicate discoveries.

NCTE 8 Use information resources to gather information and create and communicate knowledge.

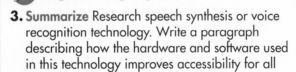
Online Student Manual • glencoe.com

Go to your Online Student Manual and enter your password to find projects that allow you to practice and apply multimedia skills.

Careers & Technology

Careers in the Music Studio

When music was recorded on analog tape, a single mistake often meant re-recording an entire passage. Overdubbing analog tracks (recording one on top of another) was difficult, requiring enormous skill. Today, however, most music is recorded digitally to a hard drive. The captured information is analyzed and manipulated by studio professionals using high-end computers and specialized software.

Producer

The producer works with every aspect of a music project and is often seen "at the helm" of a recording studio's mixing console. He or she is chiefly responsible for the sound of the finished piece. Many music experts feel that digital audio has a "cold" sound, compared to the "warmth" of analog media like magnetic tape and vinyl. Talented producers can use digital effects to create the richest sound possible.

Engineer

Working alongside producers are engineers, or engineering technicians. They understand the nuts and bolts of audio hardware and software. They are responsible for the microphones, speakers, and recording equipment, as well as the tools used to edit the recording. While producers are the team members that direct the artistic aspect of the recording, engineers handle the technical side. They help producers use the right multimedia tools to create the sounds they desire.

Digital technology has opened career opportunities for music specialists.

Sound Editor

After music has been recorded, the sound editor works with the producer and the musicians to piece together dozens of separate audio files. These files, called "takes," represent different instruments or vocals. Editors use sophisticated software to mix audio and create the illusion of a single, complete recording.

Skill Builder

1. **Analyze Music** Listen to one of your favorite musical recordings. Try to imagine what the different takes for instruments and vocals might have been when the song was recorded in the studio. List these possible takes.

2. **Research Recording Studios** Recording studios typically consist of three rooms. Research the design of recording studios and write a paragraph identifying and explaining the purpose of each of the three rooms.

Chapter Summary

Audio is live or recorded sound. Using audio effectively can help you enhance your multimedia project. Audio can include music, sound effects, voice-overs, or alerts and prompts. Audio is often used to convey meaning, set a mood, prompt action, add interest or direct attention to an important event, add a sense of realism, facilitate understanding or provide directions, clarify visual information, complement action, or tell a story. Audio may have multiple roles at the same time, but it should always support the goals of your multimedia project. Audio should not distract your viewers. You can use the Internet to locate audio files. Be sure you have permission to use audio.

Audio comes in a variety of formats. Sound quality depends on sampling rates, the number of channels used to record or play a file, and the file size. Understanding how audio files are created and edited helps you prepare them effectively. Audio editing software lets you record, edit, or apply effects to sounds; import, export, or convert audio from one format to another; combine or mix two audio files; or analyze certain aspects of audio, such as rhythm and pitch.

Vocabulary Review

1. Write six sentences. Include in each sentence two or more of these content and vocabulary terms. Each sentence should clearly show how the two terms are related.

Content Vocabulary

◇ sound effect (p. 229)
◇ voice-over (p. 229)
◇ analog (p. 233)
◇ sampling (p. 234)
◇ sampling rate (p. 234)
◇ sample size (p. 234)

◇ channel (p. 234)
◇ codec (p. 236)
◇ bandwidth (p. 236)
◇ speech synthesis (p. 242)
◇ voice recognition (p. 242)
◇ audio card (p. 242)

Academic Vocabulary

◇ principle (p. 230)
◇ proprietary (p. 233)
◇ professional (p. 239)
◇ adequate (p. 242)

Review Key Concepts

2. **Identify** forms of audio used in multimedia.

3. **Explain** the role of audio in multimedia.

4. **Identify** principles for using audio ethically.

5. **Compare and Contrast** common audio file formats.

6. **Describe** audio file size and sound quality issues.

7. **Describe** methods for recording, editing, and analyzing audio.

8. **List** common tools for creating and editing audio for multimedia.

9. **Explain** how audio in multimedia can be accessed by people with impaired hearing.

10. **Describe** the hardware needed to work with audio in multimedia.

Critical Thinking

11. Synthesize With your teacher's permission, visit various online music stores such as the Apple iTunes Store, Amazon MP3, or Rhapsody. View each site's licensing agreements for downloads and CD purchases. In general, how would you obtain permission to use an audio file in a multimedia project? How would you legally use an audio file from the online music stores you visited?

12. Demonstrate The producer and engineer disagree about the audio file format used for an online promotion. Use a chart like the one below to explain how you would determine the best format for the ad. Then, explain how to download, edit, and convert audio files.

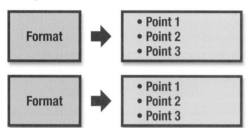

13. Cause and Effect Audio adds an important element to multimedia presentations. How might the audio in a music video or TV advertisement affect your behavior? For example, would you be more likely to purchase a CD or some other product advertised? Why?

14. Analyze What are six common audio file formats used in digital and interactive media? Explain the function of each file format. Use a graphic organizer like the one shown to help you organize your information.

File Format	Function
a.	
b.	
c.	
d.	

15. Compare and Contrast Your sister has to record some sound effects for a film she is making for class. She is not very familiar with audio editing software and asks for your help. Explain the difference between analog and digital audio recordings and how sampling and sampling rates affect sound quality. Which type of recording is most popular today and why?

16. Decide A friend is developing content for a multimedia project. She asks for your advice about the types of audio editing software and hardware needed to record and edit a voice-over for her presentation. Identify what she will need to create and play her voice-over.

17. Predict Improvements in audio technology have led to advancements in video games, Web sites, and movies. Predict some other fields or industries that will benefit from improved audio technology. Explain how the technology might improve and how it might impact each field. Use a table similar to the one below to organize your ideas.

Field	Technology	Impact

Academic Connections

NCTE 7 Conduct research and gather, evaluate, and synthesize data to communicate discoveries.

18. **English Language Arts—Summarize Technical Issues**

Write a one-page report in which you describe the technical issues with digital audio. After you have written your report, create an audio file that summarizes the parameters that affect the quality and file size of audio recording. Use a table similar to the one below to help you organize your information. Be sure to discuss the following factors:

A. sampling rate

B. bits per sample

C. number of channels

D. sample size

E. length

Technical Issue	Description

After you have read your report aloud and recorded it, re-record it until you are satisfied with the quality of the recording.

With your teacher's permission, work with a partner to demonstrate how factors such as sampling rate and bits per sample affect the quality and size of audio files. Make analog and digital recordings and compare the quality; adjust the sampling rate and the sample size of various audio files; and use lossy and lossless compression to compare the quality of compressed files.

Standardized Test Practice

True/False

Read the paragraph below and then answer the question.

Many word processing and presentation programs allow you to add sound files. Multimedia software projects can make use of sounds to draw the user's attention to something. Presentations make use of sounds to introduce bulleted text and announce transitions between screens. Multimedia programs also use sound to provide reinforcement such as hearing a "click" sound when the user accesses a navigation button on a Web site or tutorial. Sounds can help enhance our experience of many different kinds of documents and multimedia presentations.

19. Based on the paragraph above, decide if the following statement is true or false.

Adding sound to a multimedia presentation always enhances the user's experience.

    A. True

    B. False

Test-Taking Tip Usually, most of the statements are true on a true/false test. You have a 50 percent chance of getting the correct answer, even if you are guessing. If you leave the question blank, you have no chance of getting it right.

20. Analyze Audio Effectiveness

You are planning an update to an in-house training tutorial. Your supervisor has asked you to research how you might incorporate sound to enhance the effectiveness of the tutorial.

A. With your teacher's permission, use the Internet or other resources, such as CDs or DVDs available in your school or local library, to find three multimedia projects that use audio.

B. As you view the projects, analyze the effectiveness of the audio. Use a table to document the data about each project's audio.

C. Compare the use of audio in the three projects. In your table, list what is similar about the use of audio in the projects and what is different. Does the sound enhance the project or is it distracting? Is the sound quality good? Does it take too long to play or download the audio? Would you use the audio in your own multimedia project?

D. Select one use of audio that worked well in each project. For each use, be sure to explain why the audio was effective. For example, if the sound captured your attention, explain why—for example, the sound alerted me to the animation it was synchronized to, and so on. Proofread and spell-check your analysis.

NETS 3d Process data and report results.
NETS 4c Collect and analyze data to identify solutions and/or make informed decisions.

21. Create an Audiovisual Report

Your company is considering using streaming audio to reach its audience. You have been asked to create an audiovisual report about the demand for streaming audio on the Internet.

A. Conduct online research to learn more about the demand for streaming audio on the Internet. Based on your research, determine whether the company should integrate streaming audio into its operations. Do you feel confident that the company would benefit from streaming technology? Why or why not? Could the technology be improved? If so, how?

B. Use the Internet and other sources to find information, audio clips, and graphic files to support your argument. Make a list of the files you will include in your report, their file formats, and where they came from. If you need permission, draft a letter to the source or organization asking for permission to use the files.

C. Proofread and spell-check your report.

NETS 5a Advocate and practice safe, legal, and responsible use of information and technology.

22. Make Informed Decisions

As you use the Internet to gather audio, video, graphics, text, and other resources for your multimedia presentations, you will have to make decisions about the legal and ethical use of the resources you find. Knowing what is permissible, both legally and ethically, will help you make informed decisions.

Form groups of five following your teacher's instructions. As a group, conduct research to learn more about the ethical use of audio. Each person in the group will be responsible for researching one of the topics below. Decide who will be responsible for each topic. Group members should focus on safety, security, ownership, and privacy issues during their research. Make sure each group member collects enough information to write at least four paragraphs summarizing their research. All paragraphs should be compiled into one report. Be sure to use appropriate transitions when compiling the report. Proofread and spell-check your report.

A. Bill of Rights and Responsibilities for Electronic Learners

B. First Amendment of the Constitution of the United States

C. Federal Communications Commission regulations

D. the Freedom of Information Act

E. liability laws

23. Integrate Audio into a Multimedia Presentation

Assume you are a sound engineer and a company has hired you to integrate audio into a multimedia presentation. The final presentation will be distributed on a CD-ROM. Use presentation software to create a multimedia presentation on a topic approved by your teacher.

A. Determine what text, graphics, and animation you will use and how they might be enhanced by adding audio. Use a graphic organizer similar to the one below to help organize your presentation. Integrate the audio into the text, graphics, or animation in your presentation.

B. Prepare an oral report that describes how you used audio to enhance the presentation (for example, to draw viewers' attention to important text and graphics included in the production). Explain why the audio supports the presentation's purpose and how it makes the presentation easier to understand.

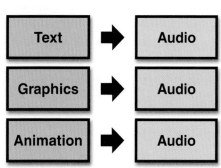

Project 1

Make an Audio Advertisement

NCTE 5 Use different writing process elements to communicate effectively.

English Language Arts A company has hired you to create a 15-second advertisement for its product. The ad will run on the radio, so you will not use any graphics or text.

Plan

1. Choose a product such as a sports drink, crunchy snack, or an automobile.

2. Develop a script that includes voice-over narration and sound effects. You may also want to include music.

Create

3. Make your own sound files using a computer and a microphone or a digital audio recorder. Be sure to follow proper safety procedures while using digital audio equipment. Transfer any audio files from the equipment to your computer.

Review

4. Listen carefully to your finished advertisement. Use sound editing software to manipulate or convert your files. With your teacher's permission, present your final advertisement to your class.

Project 2

Plan a Web Page with Audio

NCTE 7 Conduct research and gather, evaluate, and synthesize data to communicate discoveries.

English Language Arts The local arts center would like to add audio to its Web site. The program director has asked you to research the technological issues involved, as well as the hardware and software needed to integrate the audio.

Research

1. Determine what audio will be used on the site. Conduct research to find the appropriate hardware and software needed to incorporate the audio into the site. Use a table like the one shown to organize your findings. Also take notes on any technological issues that the program director should know.

Multimedia Components	Tools Needed

Create

2. Write a brief essay to outline the technological issues for the program director. Include your recommendations for hardware and software equipment.

Review

3. Proofread and spell-check your work.

Project 3

Incorporate Sound into a Multimedia Project

NCTE 12 Use language to accomplish individual purposes.

English Language Arts A multimedia presentation can be both powerful and entertaining. For this project, you will need to decide what type of multimedia project to create. The project should have a theme that incorporates visual elements, text, and audio.

Plan

1. Decide what types of sound, music, or narration you will use in your multimedia project. Create a list of the types of sound, music, and narration that you will be using in your project.

Research

2. Research how you will make or acquire these elements.

Create

3. Create a table like the one below. List all of the elements and the source of each. Decide what equipment, such as a microphone and editing programs, will be needed to create or modify the elements. If you use elements from an outside source, cite the source and examine and comply with copyright laws.

Element (sound, music, narration)	Source	Equipment Needed

4. Create a prototype, or a sample, of your project. This does not have to include the full script of all of the sound elements. With your teacher's permission, download the sound and music files from the Internet or other sources. Use appropriate equipment to create narration. Modify and edit the audio files as needed and prepare them to fit with your multimedia format. Insert the files into your sample.

Review

5. Present your prototype to the class. Ask for feedback on your use of sound, music, and narration in your project.

Revise

6. Make changes to your prototype and table based on the feedback. Create a CD of your prototype.

7. Proofread and spell-check your table.

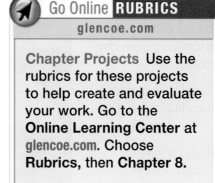

Go Online **RUBRICS**

glencoe.com

Chapter Projects Use the rubrics for these projects to help create and evaluate your work. Go to the **Online Learning Center** at glencoe.com. Choose **Rubrics,** then **Chapter 8.**

CHAPTER 9 Video

Section 9.1
Video in Multimedia

Section 9.2
Work with Video

CHAPTER OBJECTIVES

After completing this chapter, you will be able to:

- ❖ **Classify** the different kinds of video used in multimedia.
- ❖ **Explain** how presentations containing video can be made accessible to people with visual impairments.
- ❖ **Outline** the basic steps in recording video.
- ❖ **Interpret** the purpose of video in various multimedia productions.
- ❖ **Apply** knowledge of video technology to incorporating video into multimedia.
- ❖ **Identify** equipment for working with video in multimedia projects.

 Explore the Photo

To be productive, you need to use all the tools and resources around you effectively.
How can understanding how to use multimedia development tools improve your productivity?

21st CENTURY SKILLS
Be Productive

Productivity refers to using resources, such as time, people, and money, to bring about a desired result. If the time you invest in a project creates a good final product, you have been productive.

Quick Write Activity Descriptive Essay

Write an essay about a time when you were especially productive. How did your approach to the project contribute to your productivity?

Writing Tips
To write a descriptive essay, follow these steps:
1. Decide what mood you want to create in the essay.
2. Write a strong topic sentence for each paragraph.
3. Present details in a logical order.
4. Select precise transition words.

SECTION 9.1 Video in Multimedia

Reading Guide

Before You Read

Use Two-Column Notes Divide a piece of paper into two columns. In the left column, write down main ideas you find as you read. In the right column, list supporting details. This exercise will help you understand what you have read.

Read to Learn

Key Concepts

- **Identify** some common sources of video on the Internet.
- **Describe** the common types of video employed in multimedia.
- **Explain** how video quality and file size relate to one another.
- **List** frequently used formats for video files.

Main Idea

Video plays many roles in multimedia. Using video effectively in multimedia requires an understanding of its technology, including video quality, file size, and file format.

Content Vocabulary

◇ clip
◇ vlog
◇ Webcasting
◇ real time
◇ canvas
◇ streaming video
◇ buffer

Academic Vocabulary

You will find these words in your reading and on your tests. Use the glossary to look up their definitions, if necessary.

◇ auditory   ◇ crucial

Graphic Organizer

As you read, look for five types of multimedia projects, and note a possible role of video for that project.

Type of Project	Role of Video

 Graphic Organizer Go to this book's **Online Learning Center** at glencoe.com to print this graphic organizer.

Academic Standards

 English Language Arts

NCTE 5 Use different writing process elements to communicate effectively.
NCTE 7 Conduct research and gather, evaluate, and synthesize data to communicate discoveries.

NCTE National Council of Teachers of English
NSES National Science Education Standards

 Mathematics

NCTM Number and Operations Compute fluently and make reasonable estimates.
NCTM Problem Solving Build new mathematical knowledge through problem solving.

NCTM National Council of Teachers of Mathematics
NCSS National Council for the Social Studies

Use Video in Multimedia

What are some purposes of video in multimedia projects?

Video refers to live-action movies shot with a camera. Video takes graphics to the next level by creating the illusion of movement. As with other multimedia elements, you have the option of using someone else's video (with proper permission) or creating your own.

Find Video on the Internet

As with audio, ethical principles apply to downloading, copying, and sharing copyrighted video. For example, distributing digital copies of a movie without permission from the copyright holder is illegal. The Fair Use Doctrine lets you copy portions of copyright-protected work for certain nonprofit purposes, including research and backup. If you are unsure about whether you can use a video, contact the owner to ask for permission. Provide a credit and cite your source for any video you did not create yourself.

Following are a few sources of video available on the Internet:

- **Online music stores**, such as Apple's iTunes Store and Zune Marketplace, may offer music videos, movies, television shows, and video podcasts for download.

- **YouTube**, a video-sharing Web site, lets users upload and view videos they have produced on a broad array of topics.

- **Search engines**, such as Yahoo! Video, Google Videos, and Bing Video, are sources for finding free, commerical, and user-created videos (see Figure 9.1).

- **Hulu** offers video on demand (television shows and movies), with commercials, from certain networks and studios.

As You Read

Connect What are some examples of video you see regularly on the Internet?

● **Figure 9.1**
You can play or download video from Web sites such as Yahoo! Video. **What does the Fair Use Doctrine say about copying videos?**

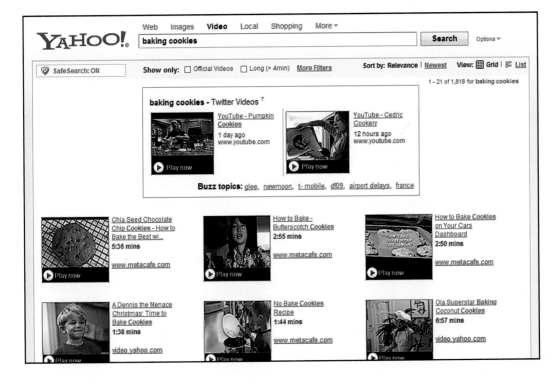

Academic Focus

English Language Arts

Use Video Ethically When you use video, follow ethical guidelines, just as you would when using text or graphics. Research guidelines for using video clips and write a paragraph explaining how to cite video sources.

NCTE 7 Conduct research and gather, evaluate, and synthesize data to communicate discoveries.

Record Your Own Video

Most video you will find on the Internet is protected by copyright. If you want to include original video in a multimedia project, a team member must record it. The basic steps in recording a video are as follows:

1. Write a script.

2. Create a storyboard to plan the content and sequence of the scenes you want to capture.

3. Use a video camera to create video clips. Use video techniques (such as panning and zooming) and lighting effectively.

4. Digitize video, if necessary.

5. Save the files on a computer.

6. Use video editing software to edit video and audio into a single project.

Use Video Appropriately

You will plan what video to include in your project during the Design and Development stage of the project life cycle. As with the other elements of your multimedia project, you must decide how to best use video to help meet your overall goals. Any video you use should ultimately help you get and retain more viewers. Use a checklist, such as the one shown in Figure 9.2, to help you appropriately evaluate any video you plan to use in your multimedia project.

People with visual impairments may miss some information in a multimedia project that features video. To make the video accessible to such an audience, **auditory** (verbal) descriptions must be provided for visual information. This information might include descriptions of people and objects, facial expressions, body language, action and movement, scenery, scene changes, and graphics. Auditory descriptions are integrated into the audio track of the video, typically where natural pauses fall. Video clips also frequently feature subtitles, transcripts, or scripts so that hearing-impaired viewers can understand dialogue.

Figure 9.2

Multimedia that uses video should follow these guidelines. **Why are auditory descriptions of visual information important?**

Video Evaluation Checklist

☑ Does the video support the project's goals and purpose?

☑ Does the video distract viewers? Does it draw the viewer's attention?

☑ Is the video an appropriate format for the multimedia project?

☑ Does the video take too long to download?

☑ Have necessary permissions been obtained and cited?

☑ Have I included auditory descriptions for the video's visual information?

☑ Can the user stop and start the video?

 **Reading Check** **Explain** What are some ways to find video on the Internet?

Types of Video in Multimedia

How does video function in multimedia?

Go Online **ACTIVITY**
glencoe.com

Evaluate Multimedia Web Sites **Find out** more about evaluating multimedia Web sites, including those using video, by visiting the **Online Learning Center** at **glencoe.com.** Choose **Activities,** then **Chapter 9.**

Video may be incorporated into a variety of multimedia productions, from Web pages to computer games to CBT. The role of the video will often help determine the type of video. The most common types of video in multimedia include clips, simulations, and broadcasts.

Clips

A video **clip** is a segment of a longer video recording, or any relatively short video (see Figure 9.3). Advances in technology have made it easy to post digital video clips online. These clips may present news, sports, music videos, television shows, movie trailers, or original productions. For example, the Web site for a news program might include video segments from an earlier television broadcast. Personal blogs (Web logs or online journals) and video-sharing sites have led to an influx of video clips on the Internet. A blog that mainly publishes video clips is called a **vlog**, short for video blog.

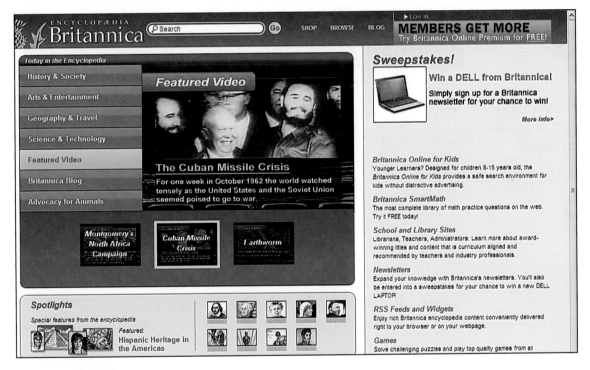

Simulations

Scientists and engineers use video simulations to explore scenarios that would be impractical or impossible to produce in real life. For example, a video simulation might test the safety of a building design during an earthquake or illustrate the probable impact of a hurricane or other event. Video simulations might teach surgeons how to perform operations, train police officers on how to behave in dangerous situations, or prepare other professionals for specialized situations. Game producers use simulations for flying, car racing, and other action games.

Figure 9.3

An online encyclopedia might include video clips illustrating various topics. **How can video add meaning to reference material?**

Broadcasts

A broadcast is the transmission of multimedia elements, such as audio and video, on radio, television, or the Web. **Webcasting** is broadcasting audio and video using the Internet. When a signal is transmitted live, without edits or delays, it is said to be delivered in **real time**. Both real-time and delayed broadcasts on the Internet use streaming media (data, audio, and video). Webcasts include videoconferences, distance-learning classes, sporting events, television shows, and movies. Broadcasts always occur at specified times so that users can "tune in."

The Role of Video

The average user can more easily view and create video. Video is commonly employed for business, entertainment, education, and other purposes. It might be used to advertise, create a setting, tell a story, or perform any number of other functions (see Figure 9.4). For example, you might use clips, simulations, or broadcasts for educational multimedia, but simulations would probably not work on a cell phone.

 **Reading Check** **Recall** What is a vlog?

Figure 9.4
Video can perform many functions in multimedia. Why should you identify the role of video you want to incorporate in a multimedia project?

Role of Video in Multimedia		
Type of Multimedia	**Examples**	**Role of Video**
Online promotion	Web page, online ad, e-mail or text message marketing	• Attract attention • Advertise • Provide information or instructions
Mobile	Types of applications: communication, data tracking, productivity, entertainment	• Achieve an effect without music or speech • Convey realism and action • Create a setting • Set a mood • Tell a story
Entertainment	Video, video game, movie	• Add visual interest • Provide information or instructions
Information	News site, simulation, videoconference, recordkeeping, presentation, kiosk	• Add visual interest • Convey realism and action • Demonstrate a process or procedure • Provide information or instructions
Education	CBT, distance learning, online encyclopedia	• Appeal to visual learners • Demonstrate a process or procedure • Provide information or instructions

Video Technology

What technical factors should you consider when using video in multimedia projects?

Understanding video technology is **crucial**, or extremely important. The video's quality and delivery method affect the file format and size, which in turn affects the development of the multimedia project. For example, a real-time broadcast, such as the teleconference shown in Figure 9.5, has specific technical needs that might be different from the needs of a Web site that broadcasts short video clips.

Video Quality

Video can enhance a multimedia project, but it can also detract from it if the video is of poor quality. The quality is determined by the following factors:

- resolution.
- capturing.
- canvas size.
- color depth.

Resolution Video quality depends largely on the resolution of individual frames and on frame rate. Recall from Chapter 7 that a frame is a single still image in a video or animation. Video frames consist of pixels. Frame rate is the speed at which frames are displayed, measured in frames per second (fps). The higher the frame rate, the sharper and smoother the action in the video appears. The standard frame rate for digital video is 32 fps, which the human eye perceives as continuous movement. Movies shown in theaters, which traditionally use analog video, run at 24 fps. Videos with greater resolution and higher frame rates contain more data and have a larger file size.

Figure 9.5
Video technology needs for real-time broadcasts can be different than for other productions. Why is it important to know the delivery method for video?

Project Management
When you convert video from analog to digital format, you set parameters for quality and file size. It is important to determine the necessary quality level before performing this task. Once a video file has been captured, the quality cannot be increased without starting the whole process over.

High-definition television (HDTV) is a system for broadcasting digital television with greater resolution (clarity) than traditional systems. HDTV digitizes and compresses images before transmission, displaying them on wider screens with twice the resolution.

Interlaced vs. Progressive Scanning	
Video Display Technique	**Features**
Interlaced scanning	• Refreshes alternate (odd and even) lines, with a slight delay in between • Produces a fluttering effect • Used in traditional television systems
Progressive scanning	• Refreshes lines in sequential order, from top to bottom • Produces a more even, detailed image • Used for most computer monitors and high-definition televisions

Another factor affecting resolution is how a video image is "drawn" by refreshing a screen's horizontal scan lines (rows). The chart shown in Figure 9.6 compares the two video display techniques—interlaced and progressive scanning.

Capturing For most purposes, video is recorded digitally (as bits of information). However, analog videotape can be converted to digital format through a process called capturing. Capturing lets you set parameters for the quality and file size of the converted video. Capturing is similar to sampling for audio clips.

Canvas Size The **canvas** is the area where a video is displayed. The size of the canvas is specified by the video developer. Software for playing video generally allows you to enlarge the viewing window, and therefore the video itself. Enlarging a clip beyond its intended size will stretch the pixels, resulting in a blocky appearance. (Video played on a PC with insufficient RAM can look the same way.)

A resolution of 320 × 240 pixels is common for videos that will be streamed to mobile devices. Higher resolutions are used when streaming video to a Web site or saving video on a CD. DVD video commonly displays at one of the following resolutions:

- 720 x 576 pixels
- 704 x 576 pixels
- 352 x 576 pixels

Color Depth You learned about the color depth of an image in Chapter 7. The color depth of video is the number of distinct colors that can be represented by a monitor or display in combination with a video card. A video card is a computer component that transfers graphical data to the monitor. A 24-bit video card, for example, has a color depth of about 16.7 million colors. The higher the color depth, the more lifelike the video will look.

Color depth is important for a realistic appearance. However, as with all the factors that affect video quality, it is important to consider the audience and delivery method of a video multimedia project. Sometimes, you have to compromise the quality of the video in order to make it accessible to a wider audience.

Streaming Video

As you read in Chapter 8, streaming technology is ideal for viewing multimedia over the Internet. RealNetworks first made use of streaming video in 1995. As broadband, or high-speed, Internet access became standard, Web publishers used streaming video more and more. **Streaming video**, which often includes audio, is a way of transferring data so that the client's browser starts to display the video before the entire file has been transmitted (see Figure 9.7).

Streaming gives the viewer a sense of a faster download time, since users do not have to wait for the entire file to download before watching the video. Streaming video might be used to play real-time video broadcasts or previously recorded clips. A certain amount of streamed data is buffered by the client's computer before playback begins. To **buffer** is to temporarily hold data in the computer's memory before it is played back. Buffering helps the video play smoothly if the transfer of data from the server fluctuates.

Figure 9.7
Streaming allows video on the Internet to start playing before the entire file has been delivered to the user's computer. What technique means to hold a certain amount of streamed data in memory before playback begins?

Buffering allows video to begin playing while it is still downloading.

Non-Streamed Video Sometimes, video must be downloaded over a network and played back from local storage media (such as a hard drive) rather than streamed. Video is also used for multimedia platforms other than the Web, such as computer-based training, slide show presentations, kiosks, and games. Such video must be stored on a hard drive, CD, or DVD to be viewed. Because it can be downloaded or played using other hardware, this video does not need to be streamed.

Quick Tip

Troubleshooting Web sites such as KeepVid and YouTube Downloader let you capture videos in FLV format. Then you need to convert the downloaded files to a more usable format or download a special player to view them.

Video File Formats

A video file's format determines the programs that can open and play it, how much space it occupies on a disk, and how fast it travels over an Internet connection. Most video capture files are stored in AVI format (for Windows) or MOV format (for Mac OS). These files can be imported into video editing software for manipulation.

Most video formats use lossy compression to eliminate unnecessary data. Less data means faster transmission, but it also means less realistic video. The Moving Picture Experts Group (MPEG) and other authorities in the multimedia industry are striving to develop formats that offer both realism and compact video. Figure 9.8 describes the features of the five most frequently used formats for video files.

You will likely develop a preference for one type of video file format based on your use and preference. While AVI is not as popular as it was in the 1990s, it is still used by novice videographers. WMV, FLV, and MOV are all common formats for streaming video on the Web. MOV is especially suited for editing video. MPEG is particularly suited to computer networks because it uses greater compression to accommodate network-based multimedia. You might experiment with more than one format before you find one you are comfortable with and that best suits your purposes.

Figure 9.8 The most prominent video file formats have been developed by Apple, Microsoft, Adobe, and the Motion Picture Experts Group. **Which file format is rarely used for streaming video on the Internet?**

Video File Formats

Format	Features
AVI	• Stands for Audio Video Interleave • Compresses audio and video • Supports streaming video but is seldom used for it • Can be viewed using Windows Media Player
FLV	• Stands for Flash Video • Supports uncompressed audio • Good for streaming video • Can be viewed on most operating systems using Adobe Flash Player
MOV	• Stands for Movie • Compresses audio and video • Good for streaming video • Can be viewed on Windows and Mac OS using QuickTime Player
MPEG Video	• Produced as a complete set of video format standards in 1988 • Compresses audio and video • Can be used for streaming video • Can be viewed using Windows Media Player or RealNetworks RealPlayer (Windows), or QuickTime (Mac OS) • Continues to evolve
WMV	• Stands for Windows Media Video • Developed for streaming video on the Internet • Compresses audio and video • Closely related to the WMA format for audio • Can be viewed using Windows Media Player or a QuickTime component on Mac OS

File Size

Video files can become large very quickly. As with audio, it is a good idea to identify your audience and delivery method before preparing video for a multimedia project. Always consider broadcasting video content to the widest audience you can. This may mean providing video files in multiple forms. For example, you might stream video, provide a higher-quality version on a DVD, and allow video to be downloaded to play using a separate media player. If you know that you can only provide video in one format, make sure that the file quality and file size are appropriate.

Ask some basic questions:

- Will you be streaming your video across the Internet? If so, sacrifice a little quality to make the file smaller, especially for users with slower Internet connections. A small file size will also download more quickly.

- Will the file be incorporated into a self-running CD or DVD demonstration? If so, file size is not as important (as CDs can hold 640 MB of data. A 4.7-GB DVD can hold an hour of standard video. A 1.46-GB DVD holds 18 minutes of video).

 **Reading Check** **Describe** What is the role of buffering in streaming video?

Section 9.1 After You Read

Review Key Concepts

1. **Compare and Contrast** video clips, video broadcasts, and video simulations.

2. **List** five video file formats, and identify a video player that can be used to view each file format.

 Check Your Answers Check your answers at this book's **Online Learning Center** through **glencoe.com**.

Practice Academic Skills

English Language Arts

3. **Create** Think about something you know how to do well, such as playing a sport, making a craft, cooking a recipe, or repairing something. Create a script for a video that would teach others how to do this activity. Include on-screen narration, as well as auditory descriptions of the scenes you would show.

NCTE 5 Use different writing process elements to communicate effectively.

Mathematics

4. **Calculate** Digital video has a standard frame rate of 32 frames per second (fps). What would be the equivalent number of frames per minute?

NCTM Number and Operations Compute fluently and make reasonable estimates.

 **Online Student Manual • glencoe.com**

Go to your Online Student Manual and enter your password to find activities that allow you to practice and apply multimedia skills.

Reading Guide

Before You Read

Study with a Buddy Study with a partner. Quiz each other on what you already know about a topic and write down any questions you have.

Read to Learn

Key Concepts

- **Discuss** devices for recording and digitizing video.

- **Compare** the features of popular video players.

- **Give** examples of video editing programs and the types of changes that can be made to video.

Main Idea

In order to use video in your multimedia project, you must have the proper hardware and software, and know how to use it correctly.

Content Vocabulary

◇ camcorder
◇ Webcam
◇ video capture card

◇ video tuner card
◇ footage
◇ batch processing

Academic Vocabulary

You will find these words in your reading and on your tests. Use the glossary to look up their definitions, if necessary.

◇ device

◇ secure

Graphic Organizer

As you read, look for three types of cameras used to record video for multimedia projects. Use a tree diagram like the one shown to help you organize your information.

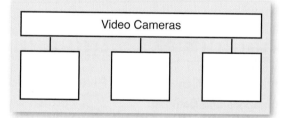

Video Cameras

 Graphic Organizer Go to this book's **Online Learning Center** at **glencoe.com** to print this graphic organizer.

Academic Standards

 English Language Arts

NCTE 6 Apply knowledge of language structure and conventions to discuss texts.
NCTE 7 Conduct research and gather, evaluate, and synthesize data to communicate discoveries.

NCTE 8 Use information resources to gather information and create and communicate knowledge.

NCTE National Council of Teachers of English
NSES National Science Education Standards

NCTM National Council of Teachers of Mathematics
NCSS National Council for the Social Studies

Video Hardware

What devices are used to record digital video for multimedia projects?

In order to work with video, you must have the proper equipment. The devices for recording and digitizing video include cameras, production equipment, capture cards, and tuner cards. A **device** is a piece of equipment, or hardware.

Cameras

Video might be captured using any of three different types of cameras. A professional video camera or camcorder can be used for capturing recorded clips. A Webcam can be used for continuous broadcasting.

Professional Video Cameras Video cameras used for professional recording may be portable (carried on the shoulder) or stationed in a studio. Professional cameras record video electronically, with higher quality and control than consumer models.

Camcorders A **camcorder** is a mobile, or portable, electronic device that combines a video camera and a video recorder. The recording medium in camcorders has been shifting from magnetic tape to digital storage. Multimedia projects can include video recorded with an analog or digital camcorder. If an analog camcorder is used, the videotape must be digitized for use in the project. Higher-end cell phones often offer a camcorder feature, although the quality of the recorded video varies.

Webcams A **Webcam** is a low-end digital camera that continuously broadcasts real-time video. Its uses include home security, traffic monitoring, and observing day-to-day activities from a source location (see Figure 9.9).

As You Read

Connect What types of video hardware have you used?

Figure 9.9
A Webcam can be used to broadcast real-time video continuously from a source location. What can you learn by watching a live feed from a particular place, such as a city square, a tourist attraction, or a natural landscape?

Go Online **ACTIVITY**
glencoe.com

Examine Video Technologies
Take a look at the various features of video, such as frame rate and color depth, that determine its quality at the Online Learning Center. Go to glencoe.com. Choose Activities, then Chapter 9.

Other common uses for Webcams include videoconferencing and communicating with friends and relatives. You can set up a Webcam to stream live images to a Web site. For example, a Webcam might "feed" video from a particular vantage point in a city, at a famous landmark, or on a college campus.

Production Equipment

Depending on how complex your video production is, you might find yourself using more than just a camera. Other production equipment might include tapes (if not recording to disc), camera lenses, lens filters, tripods, lights, microphones, power sources, batteries, and a green screen (a filming background that will be replaced by another background in post-production).

Capture Cards

You might need to transfer non-digital video into a PC for use in multimedia projects. A **video capture card** converts analog video, such as a tape from a VCR or analog camcorder, to digital format. The video capture card saves the resulting file on a PC's hard drive. You can then use software to edit the file and incorporate the video into a multimedia production.

Tuner Cards

A **video tuner card** lets a computer receive cable, aerial, or satellite television signals. Like a TV, the tuner card isolates a single channel from the many channels in a television signal. Sometimes called a TV tuner card, it commonly uses a technique called video overlay to display a television show on a computer monitor. Because most video tuner cards also function as video capture cards, they also let you record television shows and save them on a computer's hard drive.

Hardware Safety Considerations

You should handle video equipment only if you understand how it operates. Follow these tips:

- Do not repair broken video equipment yourself unless you are trained or qualified to do so. Send a damaged camera to a certified provider to be fixed.

- Report any damaged equipment to your supervisor or others who also use it.

- Protect the camera lens with a cap or hood. Keep a clear filter on the lens at all times to help protect it from damage caused by rocks and water spots.

- If you are shooting among the elements, such as on a hike, seal your camera in a plastic bag when it is not in use.

- To keep your devices **secure** (free from risk or loss), protect them with cases and bags. For travel, pack equipment in custom-made hard cases with locks and wheels. Within the cases, arrange cushioning foam perfectly around the equipment.

In the following activity, you will use video editing software to first create or import and then arrange several video clips.

Activity 9A Create a Video

YOU TRY IT

1 Record original video using a video device, such as a camcorder, or download several video clips from the Internet. Read and follow any rules about how to use the clips legally, and give cite the source.

2 Open a video editing program, such as Windows Movie Maker.

3 Import video from your video device. Select several segments of the video, creating clips. Alternately, import video clips from your hard drive. You can also capture or import images and audio files.

4 Arrange the video clips on the storyboard, timeline, or other similar workspace, in the order you desire (see Figure 9.10).

● **Figure 9.10**
Video clips can be reordered in a video editing program to create a different sequence.

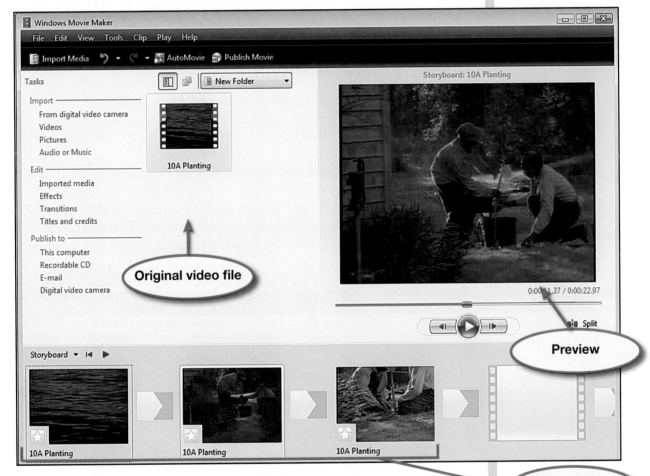

5 Preview the sequence of clips. The clips should play one after the other. You can also preview individual clips or rearrange their order.

6 When you are satisfied with the order of the clips, save the file as *Your Name* Movie and close your video editing software.

 **Recall** Identify scenarios for when you would use professional video cameras, camcorders, and Webcams.

Video Software

How is software used to edit video for use in multimedia projects?

There are two basic types of video software: programs for viewing video and programs for editing video. The features of these two applications often overlap.

Video Playing Software

Numerous applications are available for viewing video. The most popular programs for playing back video include Adobe Flash Player, Apple QuickTime Player, Microsoft Windows Media Player, and RealNetworks RealPlayer. These are all available at no charge through your browser or the Internet. Many other free and inexpensive players are also available. For example, VLC Media Player from VideoLAN is open-source software that the public can freely copy, modify, and share. All of these programs support streaming media. See Figure 9.11 for some of the other features of each of these video players.

Video Editing Software

Figure 9.11
Free video players, some offering paid versions with enhanced features, are available on the Internet. For which video player is the source code freely available to users?

You can use specialized software to edit digital video that has been uploaded from a video camera or legally downloaded from the Internet, or analog video that has been digitized. The raw scenes from a video camera, prior to editing, are called **footage**.

Video editing programs are available with basic to advanced features. Some of the more popular editing programs include Adobe Premier Pro, Apple's Final Cut Pro, Apple's iMovie, Avid Media Composer, and Microsoft Windows Movie Maker. There are free programs available for download on the Internet.

Video Playing Software	
Video Player	**Features**
Flash Player	• Available for Windows, Mac OS, Linux, and other operating systems (including mobile) • Built into some browsers and available as a plug-in for Internet Explorer, Firefox, and Safari • Originally developed to display vector animation
QuickTime Player	• Comes with Mac OS and is available for Windows • Available as a paid version with additional playback options and editing capabilities
Windows Media Player	• Comes with Windows and Windows Mobile • Has features for finding video and managing a media library
RealPlayer	• Available for Windows, Mac OS, Linux, and other operating systems • Has features for finding video and managing a media library • Available as a paid version with more powerful features
VLC Media Player	• Available for Windows, Mac OS, Linux, and other operating systems • Open-source • Offers filters for special effects

Free programs generally do not have as many features as commercial programs. When choosing which application to purchase or use, be sure to choose one compatible with your operating system and that has the features you need. Many applications offer free trials (see Figure 9.12).

- **Adobe Premier Pro** provides powerful video editing capabilities. Available for Windows and Mac OS, Premier Pro is used for television shows and feature films, among other applications.

- **Apple Final Cut Pro**, available for Mac OS only, is an industry standard for video editing. Final Cut Pro has been popular among independent moviemakers, but its user base has grown to include mainstream television and film editors.

- **Apple iMovie** is a basic video editor that comes with Mac OS. It can be used to organize and browse home movies, as well as add titles, transitions, audio, and effects to video footage.

- **Avid Media Composer** has been a high-end video editing program for film and television since the early 1990s. It can be used on both Windows and Mac OS.

- **Microsoft Windows Movie Maker** is a simple video editing program available in older versions of Windows. Its features are similar to those of iMovie. It can be downloaded for use on more recent versions of the Window operating system.

Many video editing programs offer a technique for making the editing process more manageable. **Batch processing** allows you to apply a particular action on multiple image files at once. For example, you can change the size or frame rate or modify the color and contrast, to multiple image files automatically.

Academic Focus

English Language Arts

Descriptive Writing Video demonstrations reinforce concepts and teach new skills. For example, a multimedia presentation on cooking might use video to show certain techniques. Write a paragraph describing how you might use video to explain how to prepare a recipe.

NCTE 6 Apply knowledge of language structure and conventions to discuss texts.

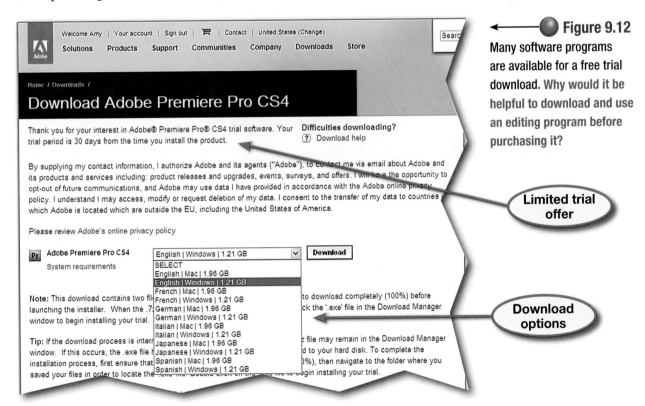

Figure 9.12
Many software programs are available for a free trial download. Why would it be helpful to download and use an editing program before purchasing it?

Quick Tip

Caution If you are using a Webcam to deliver live video to a Web site or to communicate with friends and relatives, keep in mind that software exists for turning Webcams on and off remotely. Use a lens cap to protect your privacy as well as the camera lens.

The following are some of the modifications you can make to your video footage, depending on the type of software you are using:

- Change the size or frame rate
- Extract portions to create clips or reorder the sequence of action
- Add narration, audio, text, special effects, and transitions
- Integrate still photographs
- Modify color and contrast
- Edit and synch audio clips
- Convert from one format to another
- Use encoding to create a DVD, podcast, or video for the Web or mobile devices

In the following activity, you will use video editing software to modify the video you created in You Try It Activity 9A.

YOU TRY IT

Activity 9B Edit a Video

1. Open video editing software, such as Windows Movie Maker.

2. Open the video file *Your Name* **Movie**, which you created for Activity 9A.

3. Trim each clip so that it starts later and ends earlier, removing footage that is unnecessary.

4. Apply transitions between clips so they flow more smoothly (see Figure 9.13). Preview transitions before choosing which ones to apply. Common transitions include fade (in which a scene slowly darkens and disappears) and dissolve (in which one scene fades as the next is superimposed on it).

Figure 9.13
Transitions can be added between clips to add visual interest to a video.

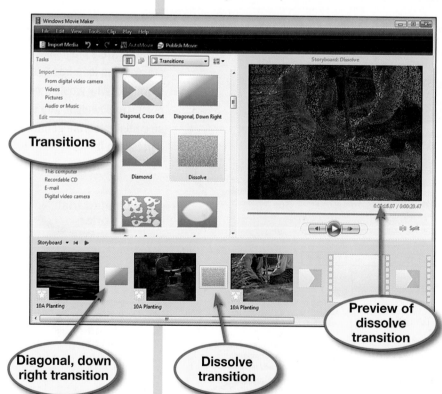

Transitions

Diagonal, down right transition

Dissolve transition

Preview of dissolve transition

5. Apply special effects to the movie. Examples include blur, sepia (for an old-time look), film grain (for texture), grayscale (shades of gray), rotate, slow down, and speed up.

6. Add background music, sound effects, or narration. Edit the audio and video to play together (see Figure 9.14). You can adjust the audio using volume, fade, and mute.

7 Add titles and credits to the movie, applying animation, font, and color choices to the text as desired.

8 Preview the movie to make sure it plays as intended, with transitions, special effects, audio, titles, and credits. When you are satisfied, save the file.

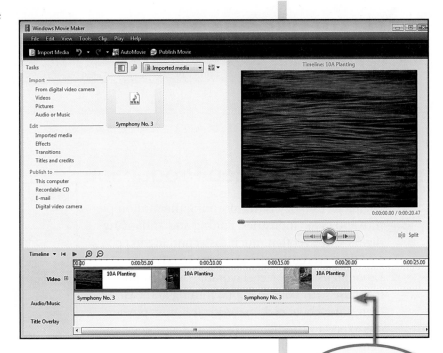

Figure 9.14

Audio added to a movie must be timed to play correctly with the video.

Audio trimmed to same length as video clips

 **Reading Check** **Define** What is footage?

Section 9.2 After You Read

Review Key Concepts

1. **Explain** how a video tuner card works. Why is it needed?

2. **Summarize** the modifications you can make to video footage using video editing software.

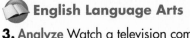 **Check Your Answers** Check your answers at this book's **Online Learning Center** through glencoe.com.

Practice Academic Skills

English Language Arts

3. **Analyze** Watch a television commercial. Evaluate how the original video recording might have been edited or enhanced. Have different clips been cut together? Have special effects been applied? Write an essay analyzing the possible modifications.

4. **Conclude** Research the "prosumer" category of camcorders and write a paragraph to answer the following questions: What does prosumer mean? How do the features and prices of prosumer camcorders compare with those of consumer and professional camcorders?

NCTE 7 Conduct research and gather, evaluate, and synthesize data to communicate discoveries.

NCTE 8 Use information resources to gather information and create and communicate knowledge.

Online Student Manual • glencoe.com

Go to your Online Student Manual and enter your password to find activities that allow you to practice and apply multimedia skills.

Careers & Technology

Careers in Video Production

Digital technology is transforming the motion picture and video industries. Editing and enhancing digital video is often much easier and less expensive than working with film. The U.S. Bureau of Labor Statistics projects favorable opportunities for those with skills in digital filming and CGI (computer-generated imagery). Training, previous experience, skill, creativity, and a professional demeanor can help you get a job in digital video.

As digital video becomes more affordable, job prospects are increasing for those skilled in digital filming.

The Industry

Most feature films and television shows in the United States are produced by the motion picture industry. However, the popularity of digital video recorders and editing software—as well as the Web, DVDs, and cable TV—has led to a rise in independent videographers. These professionals make films for specific audiences or purposes, on topics such as history, fitness, self-help, home and garden, crafts and hobbies, outdoor recreation, and travel. They also create commercials, music videos, event videos, fundraiser promotions, political spots, video for use in computer games, and similar productions.

Occupations

Jobs in filmmaking are often grouped by its three phases: preproduction (planning), production (making), and postproduction (editing and finishing).

Preproduction tasks include budgeting, storyboard and script development and revision, location scouting and planning, scheduling and running casting calls and call-backs, and set and costume design and construction. Production crews include cinematographers (sometimes called directors of photography), who design shots to match the director's artistic vision; camera operators, who do the shooting; gaffers, who set up lights; sound engineers, who oversee audio; recordists, who set up sound equipment; and boom operators, who handle microphones. Postproduction roles include film and video editors, who choose and edit the best shots (often digitally); dubbing editors, who mix sounds and visuals; film librarians, who catalog footage; and sound effects editors, who add sound effects and background music (often electronically) to shape the film into its final form.

Skill Builder

1. **Research Careers** Do online research on the topic of preproduction to find out the occupations of people who participate in this phase of filmmaking. Name five roles, and include a brief description of each role.

2. **Examine an Industry** Research and analyze how the popularity of digital video has affected the film industry. Write a paragraph that summarizes your conclusions.

Chapter Summary

Video enhances some of the most common applications of multimedia, such as simulations, clips, and broadcasts. There are a number of sources for video on the Internet, such as online music stores and YouTube. Most video found on the Internet is protected by copyright laws. You must consider a video's quality and file size. A video's quality depends on its resolution and frame rate. Streaming video allows you to view a multimedia file without having to store it to your computer's hard drive. Its format allows the Web browser to display the video segment while data is still being transferred.

Equipment needed for working with video includes cameras, production equipment, capture cards, and tuner cards. There are different types of cameras to choose from to meet different needs. Video software can be broken down into programs for viewing video and programs for editing video, but their features may overlap. Programs for playing back video include Flash Player, QuickTime Player, Windows Media Player, and RealPlayer. Popular video editing programs include Adobe Premier Pro, Apple Final Cut Pro, Apple iMovie, Avid Media Composer, and Microsoft Windows Movie Maker.

Vocabulary Review

1. List an example of ten of these content and academic vocabulary terms in everyday life.

Content Vocabulary

◇ clip (p. 259)
◇ vlog (p. 259)
◇ Webcasting (p. 260)
◇ real time (p. 260)
◇ canvas (p. 262)
◇ streaming video (p. 263)
◇ buffer (p. 263)

◇ camcorder (p. 267)
◇ Webcam (p. 267)
◇ video capture card (p. 268)
◇ video tuner card (p. 268)
◇ footage (p. 270)
◇ batch processing (p. 271)

Academic Vocabulary

◇ auditory (p. 258)
◇ crucial (p. 261)
◇ device (p. 267)
◇ secure (p. 268)

Review Key Concepts

2. Identify some common sources of video on the Internet.

3. Describe the common types of video employed in multimedia projects.

4. Explain how video quality and file size relate to one another.

5. List frequently used formats for video files.

6. Discuss devices for recording and digitizing video.

7. Compare the features of popular video players.

8. Give examples of video editing programs and the types of changes that can be made to video.

Critical Thinking

9. **Illustrate** Create a presentation to demonstrate how to capture video files in digital formats to be used in various delivery systems such as podcasting, downloadable media, and streaming. Use a chart like the one below to show the steps in the process.

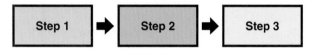

10. **Summarize** A new student has joined your multimedia class. She has a limited background in multimedia production. Your teacher has asked you to summarize the different types of video to help the new student.

11. **Evaluate** Find a multimedia Web site that includes video. Evaluate the site for its accessibility compliance. Write a brief essay explaining your findings.

12. **Make Decisions** You have been asked to prepare a multimedia presentation for a club you belong to. Prepare a list of hardware, software, and other components that are necessary for an effective presentation.

13. **Predict** Audio and video software, along with other multimedia software, are constantly being improved upon. Research emerging multimedia software. What impact do you think this new technology might have on society? Use a chart to organize your information.

Software	Description	Impact on Society

14. **Examine** With your teacher's approval, access an existing Web page. Describe the steps you would follow to develop and incorporate the video, audio, text, graphics, and motion graphics into a similar Web page. Create a presentation that demonstrates the tasks that would need to be performed.

15. **Research** Use a K-W-L chart like the one below to determine what you know, want to know, and learned about these topics: the First Amendment, Federal Communications Commission regulations, the Freedom of Information Act, and liability laws that are relevant to developing multimedia productions. Conduct research to fill in the blank spaces in the chart.

Know	Want to Know	Learned

16. **Analyze** Choose one piece of video hardware that you might use in a multimedia presentation, such as a specific camera or a microphone. Describe the proper safety procedures for using that piece of equipment. Write a summary to share the information you learn.

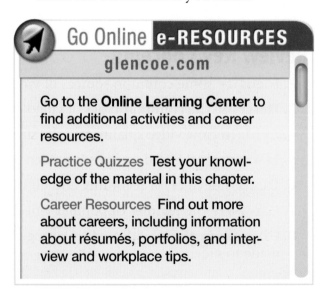

Go Online **e-RESOURCES**
glencoe.com

Go to the **Online Learning Center** to find additional activities and career resources.

Practice Quizzes Test your knowledge of the material in this chapter.

Career Resources Find out more about careers, including information about résumés, portfolios, and interview and workplace tips.

Academic Connections

17. English Language Arts–Transfer Files

With your teacher's permission, use the Internet to research different ways to transfer information and resources between software programs and systems. Use a graphic organizer similar to the one shown below to record information on how to transfer text, data, sound, video, and still images.

When you have completed your research, use the information in your graphic organizer to write a step-by-step guide explaining the methods you researched. Your step-by-step guide should:

A. Explain terms the reader may not know.

B. Provide the steps in chronological order.

C. Use appropriate transition words.

D. Use precise verbs to make the explanation clear.

Information to Transfer	How to Transfer	Software to Use
Text		
Data		
Sound		
Video		
Still Images		

At your teacher's direction, demonstrate the different methods you have researched to transfer information from equipment to computer, including a brief explanation of the software you are using.

NCTE 7 Conduct research and gather, evaluate, and synthesize data to communicate discoveries.

Standardized Test Practice

Essay

Read the paragraph below and then answer the question.

Imagine that you have been asked to create a multimedia Web page for your school. The Web page will include information about school events, clubs, sports, classes, faculty and staff, and students.

Test-Taking Tip Before answering an essay question, think about what you want to say. Write down a few notes to help you organize your thoughts. Number your thoughts in the order you will write about them.

The Web page should be as interesting and entertaining as possible, so you should include still photographs, video clips, and audio wherever possible. Your school has a digital camera and computer available for your use and has asked that you supply a list of resources that you believe you will need to accomplish this task.

18. Based on the paragraph above, write an essay that describes the digital tools or resources you would select for this task. Justify your selection based on the efficiency and effectiveness of the tools and resources.

19. Create a Presentation on Ethics

NETS 2d Students contribute to project teams to produce original works or solve problems.

At your company, you are part of a group assigned to train coworkers on the appropriate and ethical use of digital tools and resources. Working in a small group, create a multimedia presentation, which will incorporate text, charts, tables, clip art, drawing tools, and audio and video capabilities. Include special effects, title sequences, and creative scene transitions in your presentation.

A. Cover the following information: copyright and patent laws for multimedia such as video, text, sound, pictures, and intellectual property; fair use laws; First Amendment and Federal Communications Commission regulations; liability laws; licensing agreements pertaining to audio and video files; duplication of materials associated with productions and performances; ethics pertaining to scanned and downloaded clip art images, photographs, documents, video, recorded sounds and music, and trademarks.

B. Be sure to exhibit ethical conduct as you work with other group members. Also, properly cite sources for any ideas, graphics, text, audio, and video you use in your presentation. Edit your multimedia presentation before presenting it.

20. Discuss and Demonstrate Equipment

You are in charge of demonstrating for your employer several different types of equipment that can be used for developing multimedia presentations. (For this project, use equipment available at your school.)

A. Work with your partner to complete this activity. (Follow your teacher's instructions for forming into pairs.) Determine who will discuss and demonstrate the different pieces of equipment. Use a table similar to the one shown to help you organize your information.

Multimedia Development Equipment	Discussion	Demonstration
Video capture cards		
Color scanners		
Still and digital cameras		
Photocell		
Laser discs and players		
Video overlay boards		
Bar code readers		
Overhead projection systems		

B. With your teacher's permission, give your presentation to the class.

NETS 2b Students communicate information and ideas effectively to multiple audiences using a variety of media and formats.

21. Be Productive

A local service club has invited you to come to a meeting and describe and demonstrate the fundamental elements of importance to multimedia design and development. Explain how a team's approach to the project can help contribute to productivity.

A. You decide to focus on the following points:

- Drawing techniques
- Audio
- Video
- Animation
- Typography
- Digital imaging
- E-commerce
- Intellectual property
- Copyright law

B. Create and edit your demonstration. Include an outline of the methods you would use to be productive.

22. Analyze Project Costs

Your friend has a Web site to promote his business. He wants to add video to create more interest and expand his customer base. He asks you, "What equipment do I need to add video to my company's Web site?"

A. Conduct research to develop a list of the hardware and software you would use to create video for a multimedia Web site. Do not include a new PC or monitor on your list, but do include the cost of video cards or other equipment.

B. Compare your results. Specify which products you would choose, and explain why.

C. Find the total cost of your selections. Use a chart like the one shown to help organize your information.

PROJECT ANALYSIS		
Product	Reason for Using	Cost

NETS 3c Evaluate and select information sources and digital tools based on the appropriateness to specific tasks.

Project 1

Create a Video

NCTE 5 Use different writing process elements to communicate effectively.

English Language Arts Imagine that you have been asked by a local computer store to create a short audio/video sales production. The video will demonstrate how to create a video using the store's video products.

Plan

1. Name the store and choose the products you will promote. Write a script and plan what visuals you want to capture on video. Use a graphic organizer like the one shown to help keep your ideas organized.

VIDEO FOR DEMONSTRATION			
Video Clips	Shooting Location	Narration	Actors Needed

Create

2. Use a video camera to create the video clips. Demonstrate proper use of safety procedures while using the digital video equipment. Convert the video to a digital format. Use video editing software to edit your video and audio into a single presentation.

Review

3. Proofread and spell-check your presentation.

Project 2

Create a Video Demonstration

NCTE 12 Use language to accomplish individual purposes.

English Language Arts As a consultant, you have been asked to create a video that teaches a skill.

Plan

1. Choose a skill that you will teach. The skill can be a sport or other physical activity such as cooking, cleaning, or golfing. Create a video that teaches a specific skill or task that relates to that subject. For example, if you want to teach a golf skill, you might focus on putting. The final video should be 3 minutes long.

Create

2. Include the following in your video project: a storyboard of the project, an overview of what is being taught, narration and demonstration of the skill within the video, a list of equipment needed for the project, a list of locations where the video will be shot, and a timeline of events. Use your storyboard to guide your video shoot.

Review

3. Edit your video and use appropriate software to compress the video. Proofread and spell-check your final demonstration.

Project 3

Include Video in a Multimedia Presentation

NCTE 8 Use information resources to gather information and create and communicate knowledge.

English Language Arts Many CDs and Web sites use video clips or full-length videos to demonstrate a product or to provide an opportunity to teach a concept. For this activity, you will need to determine a theme for a multimedia project that includes video. The project can be a Web page or a presentation.

Plan

1. Determine the theme for your project and decide what video elements to include in your project. As with graphics and sound, creating a video or locating a video clip can take time, but it can add impact to your project and help make your project more effective.

Research

2. List the types of video you plan to include and the ways in which you will use video in the project. Research how you will make or acquire these pieces. Use the Internet or other sources available to you. Remember to obtain permissions and cite sources.

Create

3. To keep track of the video in your project, create a table like the one shown below. If you will be using pre-recorded video, list your sources (Web sites, for example). If you are planning to create your own video, list the equipment you will need. If there is narration, develop a script of what is to be said and note who will be the voice talent.

VIDEO TO INCLUDE		
Video Element	**Source or Voice Talent**	**Equipment Needed**

4. To help you use video in the most effective way, create a script that explains the sequence of action, dialogue/narration, and length of each video segment. Also consider developing a storyboard to help you work out transitions and sequencing.

5. Obtain or shoot your video. Use video editing software to edit your video and save it in the proper format for your multimedia presentation or Web site.

6. Place the video in your multimedia project.

Review

7. Carefully review your video and multimedia project.

8. Proofread and spell-check your project.

Go Online **RUBRICS**

glencoe.com

Chapter Projects Use the rubrics for these projects to help create and evaluate your work. Go to the **Online Learning Center** at **glencoe.com**. Choose **Rubrics**, then **Chapter 9.**

UNIT

3 Portfolio Project

Design an Online Newsletter

In this unit, you learned how to create and modify a variety of multimedia components, including text, graphics, animation, and audio and video clips. The unit discussed the various skills, software, and hardware required to develop and implement these multimedia elements. This portfolio project will let you use your new skills to create an online newsletter for a group in your community, like a neighborhood watch group, recycling center, or a local dog park.

Project Assignment

In this project, you will:

- Create an online newsletter for a local organization.
- Make up a name for the newsletter and create an original logo.
- Create an ad for a local business that supports the community. The ad should contain a link to the business's Web site.
- Include at least one animation and links to one audio and one video clip.

Multimedia Design Skills Behind the Project

Your success in multimedia design will depend on your skills:

- Apply the principles and elements of visual design.
- Choose appropriate typefaces, font sizes, and font styles.
- Create graphics and animation.
- Properly implement links to audio and video clips.
- Demonstrate planning and time-management skills such as project management and storyboarding.

Academic Skills Behind the Project

Remember these key academic concepts:

Research Skills

- Use Internet resources for research purposes.

Writing Skills

- Use correct grammar, punctuation, and terminology to write and edit multimedia documents.
- Employ effective verbal and nonverbal communication skills.
- Adapt language for audience, purpose, situation, and intent.

Problem-Solving Skills

- Determine the needs of the newsletter's visitors and how these needs can best be met.

 **English Language Arts**

NCTE 4 Use written language to communicate effectively.

NCTE 5 Use different writing process elements to communicate effectively.

NCTE 12 Use language to accomplish individual purposes.

 **Mathematics**

NCTM Problem Solving 2 Apply and adapt a variety of appropriate strategies to solve problems.

STEP 1   Analyze and Plan Your Project

Follow these steps to plan your newsletter:

- Develop a list of project goals.

- Describe the target audience, write a mission statement, and state the project's scope.

- Conduct research and use the information you find when writing the newsletter content.

STEP 2   Design Your Project

Follow these steps to design your project:

- Create a storyboard.

- Develop a template, choose a color scheme for the template, and choose attractive and readable typefaces and font sizes for the headings and main text.

STEP 3   Develop Your Project

Follow these steps to develop your project:

- Use software to create a logo and animation.

- Use the storyboard to create the newsletter, placing the text, logo, graphics, and the animation in their proper locations.

- Insert links to audio and video clips.

- Create an ad for a local business that contains a link to the business's Web site.

STEP 4   Share Your Project

Ask a classmate to review your newsletter.

- Ask for feedback, constructive criticism, and suggestions.

- Encourage your reviewer to ask questions.

STEP 5   Test and Implement Your Project

Apply what you have learned about project testing to perform these tasks:

- Write a paragraph describing how you would test this newsletter.

- Use what you have learned about project implementation to write a paragraph explaining how you might distribute the newsletter in an online communication.

- Use the Portfolio Project Checklist to evaluate your work.

Portfolio Project Checklist

ANALYSIS AND PLANNING

☑ A content plan that includes a mission statement that specifies the site's purpose, goals, and target audience has been written.

☑ A project plan that defines the project's scope has been written.

DESIGN AND DEVELOPMENT

☑ A storyboard has been created that shows the basic layout and contents of the newsletter.

☑ The elements and principles of visual design have been followed.

☑ An appropriate color scheme has been chosen.

☑ All text is complete and clearly and concisely written.

☑ All multimedia elements enhance the newsletter.

☑ The newsletter's banner includes its name and an original logo.

☑ The ad includes a link to the business's Web site.

☑ The newsletter contains an animation and links to an audio clip and a video clip.

TESTING AND IMPLEMENTATION

☑ The testing plan explains that all components will be checked for accuracy, functionality, and consistency.

☑ The implementation plan explains how the newsletter will be made available to the target audience, for example by being disseminated as an e-mail attachment or as a link to a Web site.

☑ The project has been reviewed by a classmate or trusted adult and appropriate changes have been made.

Go Online RUBRICS

glencoe.com

Go to this book's **Online Learning Center** at glencoe.com for a rubric you can use to evaluate your final project.

UNIT

4 The Multimedia Project Team

Chapter 10 Multimedia Project Team Roles
Chapter 11 Career Planning

UNIT Portfolio Project Preview

Create a Digital Portfolio

In this unit, you will develop an understanding of multimedia project team roles, as well as the skills needed to manage a project. You will also develop the necessary skills to plan your multimedia career. In the Unit Portfolio Project, you will put together all the components needed to showcase your employability skills, including your résumé.

 Go Online PREVIEW
glencoe.com

Go to the **Online Learning Center** and select your book. Click **Unit 4>Portfolio Project Preview** to learn more about teamwork, project management, and career skills.

Explore the Photo

You should have strong technical skills and teamwork skills in order to manage projects.
How can you use your technical skills and project management skills to promote a small business?

Multimedia Project Team Roles

CHAPTER OBJECTIVES

After completing this chapter, you will be able to:

❖ **Interpret** the meaning of teamwork.

❖ **Practice** teamwork skills and qualities.

❖ **Generalize** the relationship between client and developer of a multimedia project.

❖ **Classify** developer roles into front end and back end.

❖ **Describe** the responsibilities of developer roles on a multimedia project team.

❖ **Plan** a Web site by defining the site's goals, target audience, mission, and scope.

❖ **Evaluate** considerations in designing and developing a Web site.

❖ **Outline** the final stages of a Web site's production.

Explore the Photo

Creating a multimedia project, such as an online student newspaper or a digital yearbook, requires teamwork.
How is performing a role in a multimedia project similar to participating on a sports team or in a school club?

21st CENTURY SKILLS
Teamwork

An effective team member is responsible to the team, helps other team members, and contributes to sound decision making.

Quick Write Activity Explanation

Consider a team, such as an athletic team or the staff of the school yearbook. Each team member must complete specific tasks in order to accomplish the final goal. Write an essay explaining the role of each member of the team you chose to consider.

Writing Tips
To write an essay that explains the team roles clearly, follow these steps:
1. Describe the purpose of the team. Describe how each team member plays a role to accomplish this purpose.
2. Arrange the details in an organized, logical way.
3. Make the explanation clear and easy for the audience to understand.

SECTION (10.1) Client Roles

Before You Read

Take a Nap The more well-rested you are before you study, the more likely you will be to remember what you have learned.

Read to Learn

Key Concepts

- **Explain** how teamwork leads to the successful completion of a project.
- **Evaluate** the skills and qualities of effective team members.
- **Recognize** the client's role in a multimedia project.

Main Idea

The success of a project depends on how effectively team members achieve their personal objectives, contributing to the team's overall objectives. The client who initiates a multimedia project participates in different ways throughout the production process.

Content Vocabulary

◇ project team

◇ teamwork

◇ client

◇ proposal

Academic Vocabulary

You will find these words in your reading and on your tests. Use the glossary to look up their definitions, if necessary.

◆ team

◆ exemplary

Graphic Organizer

As you read, list the five stages in project development with an example of the client's role in each stage. Use a table like the one below to organize your thoughts.

Stage	Example of Client's Role

 Graphic Organizer Go to this book's **Online Learning Center** at glencoe.com to print this graphic organizer.

Academic Standards

 English Language Arts

NCTE 5 Use different writing process elements to communicate effectively.
NCTE 7 Conduct research and gather, evaluate, and synthesize data to communicate discoveries.

NCTE 12 Use language to accomplish individual purposes.

NCTE National Council of Teachers of English
NSES National Science Education Standards

NCTM National Council of Teachers of Mathematics
NCSS National Council for the Social Studies

Project Teams and Teamwork

What does it mean to be part of a team?

Creating a complex multimedia production requires the effort of a team. A **team** is a group of people organized to work together in an activity. A team created for a particular purpose and time period is called a **project team**. Typically, team members have different roles. This chapter introduces the possible roles of participants on a multimedia project team.

The specific makeup of the team depends on many factors, such as the type of project, complexity, budget, and schedule. For an elaborate project, such as a video game, team roles may be very specific. For a simpler project, such as a basic Web site, team members often fulfill more than one role. However, every team has at least two members: a client and a developer.

Teamwork Skills and Qualities

When the members of a team engage in **teamwork**, they work together to achieve certain goals. In order for the team to be productive and efficient, each team member must practice teamwork skills, as described in Figure 10.1. For example, it is important to listen to other team members and to communicate your ideas clearly. **Exemplary**, or model, team members commit themselves to the team, settle disagreements, are organized, and can solve problems on their own. Employers value these skills in employees.

As You Read

Connect Which teamwork skills and qualities do you already possess, and which do you need to develop?

Figure 10.1

Skills and qualities that make a person an effective team member also lead to getting a job and being a successful employee. **Why is active listening an important skill to develop?**

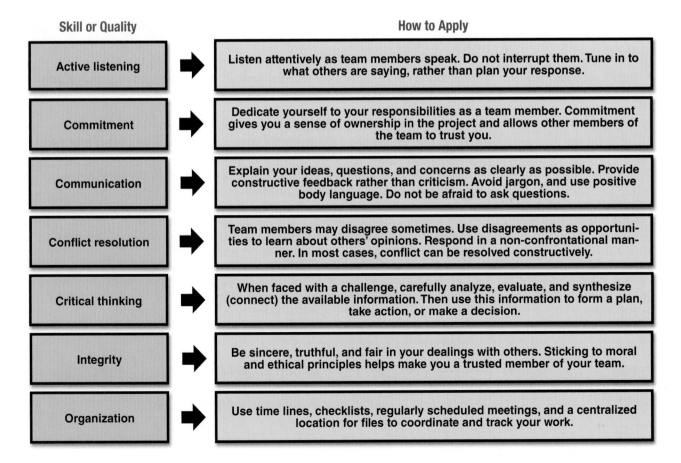

Skill or Quality		How to Apply
Active listening	→	Listen attentively as team members speak. Do not interrupt them. Tune in to what others are saying, rather than plan your response.
Commitment	→	Dedicate yourself to your responsibilities as a team member. Commitment gives you a sense of ownership in the project and allows other members of the team to trust you.
Communication	→	Explain your ideas, questions, and concerns as clearly as possible. Provide constructive feedback rather than criticism. Avoid jargon, and use positive body language. Do not be afraid to ask questions.
Conflict resolution	→	Team members may disagree sometimes. Use disagreements as opportunities to learn about others' opinions. Respond in a non-confrontational manner. In most cases, conflict can be resolved constructively.
Critical thinking	→	When faced with a challenge, carefully analyze, evaluate, and synthesize (connect) the available information. Then use this information to form a plan, take action, or make a decision.
Integrity	→	Be sincere, truthful, and fair in your dealings with others. Sticking to moral and ethical principles helps make you a trusted member of your team.
Organization	→	Use time lines, checklists, regularly scheduled meetings, and a centralized location for files to coordinate and track your work.

Troubleshooting The client should provide comments to the developer through a single person. If more than one person provides comments, and the comments do not agree, the developer will not know what action to take.

Project Development Teams

Each member of a project development team is responsible for specific tasks. Some team members will be involved in all five stages of the development process while others will be involved in only one. For a project to be successful, each team member should be aware of his or her own responsibilities, as well as the roles of the other team members. You will learn more about developer roles in Section 10.2.

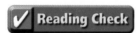 **List** What are seven teamwork skills or qualities?

The Client

What is the client's role in a multimedia project?

The **client** is the group or person who pays for and publishes a multimedia production. For a school project, you can think of your teacher as the client. The client gathers information about the project's goals, budget, and time line. Then the client asks several developers to create a **proposal**, or formal outline of the work. The client selects a developer and begins the development process.

The client is involved throughout a multimedia project. However, the extent of the client's involvement varies from stage to stage. The client expresses a vision for the project that allows the development team to meet the client's expectations. Figure 10.2 describes the client's additional responsibilities in a multimedia project.

Figure 10.2

The client participates in all stages of a multimedia project. In which stage does the client assess the audience's experience with the finished product?

Client's Role in a Multimedia Project

Stage	What the Client Does
Stage 1: Analyze, Plan	• Sets the project goals and the expected benefits, as well as deadlines and budgets • Communicates the project's goals, time line, and budget to potential developers and obtains proposals • Selects a developer and adjusts the proposal as necessary • Works with the developer to identify the target audience and determine the project's mission statement • Establishes the project content, if any, that will be provided by the client • Delivers any other information the developer requires
Stage 2: Design, Develop	• Evaluates and approves design-related items from the developer • Evaluates and approves major media components from the developer, including text, artwork and graphics, animation, audio, and video
Stage 3: Test	• Reviews the product during the testing stage, just prior to implementation • Reports bugs (errors) in content and functionality
Stage 4: Implement	• Responds to questions from the project manager as the developer rolls out the finished product
Stage 5: Evaluate, Maintain	• Assesses the audience's results with the finished product, sharing feedback with the developer • Participates in updates to fix problems and make improvements • Updates content as necessary

There are two kinds of client-developer relationships. In one, the client hires a company or individual to complete a project. In the other, the client works with a team within the client's own organization.

- **Client-Developer Relationship 1: Client hires another company.** For example, the client, the Gadget Corporation's Customer Service Department, hires the Show Me Agency to create a Web site, after approving the agency's proposal and deciding that the agency can work within the budget and meet the schedule.

- **Client-Developer Relationship 2: Client works with a department within the same company.** In this instance, the client, the Gadget Corporation's Customer Service Department, uses internal employees (such as the Internet Marketing Department) to create a Web site.

In either case, at least one representative of the client participates on the project team. This representative communicates information between the project team and the client's management.

The client's input is crucial during each stage of the project. Consistent communication among all team members is essential to the project's success. It is always important for the developer to establish and maintain a good relationship with the client, for the current project as well as future projects.

 **Categorize** What are the two main forms of client-developer relationships?

Academic Focus

English Language Arts

Communication Skills Effective verbal and nonverbal communication skills are important 21st century skills. Imagine that you have a disagreement with a teammate about how to complete a project. Write a dialogue that demonstrates effective verbal communication skills. Use descriptions to demonstrate nonverbal skills.

NCTE 5 Use different writing process elements to communicate effectively.

Section 10.1 After You Read

Review Key Concepts

1. **Identify** two positive skills or qualities that the members of a project team should possess.

2. **Describe** the client's role during the design and development stage of a multimedia project.

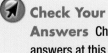 **Check Your Answers** Check your answers at this book's **Online Learning Center** through glencoe.com.

Practice Academic Skills

English Language Arts

3. **Hypothesize** Write a paragraph explaining how skills used to work with peers on school projects might translate to effectiveness on an on-the-job project team.

4. **Interpret** In Stage 1 of a multimedia project, the client requests proposals from several potential developers. Use Internet resources to research the business document called a "request for proposal" (RFP). Write a brief report to explain what a request for proposal is and how it relates to the client's role in a multimedia project.

 **Online Student Manual • glencoe.com**

Go to your Online Student Manual and enter your password to find projects that allow you to practice and apply multimedia skills.

NCTE 12 Use language to accomplish individual purposes.

NCTE 7 Conduct research and gather, evaluate, and synthesize data to communicate discoveries.

Reading Guide

Before You Read

Understanding Write down any questions you have while reading. Many of them will be answered as you continue. If not, you will have a list ready for your teacher when you are finished reading.

Read to Learn
Key Concepts

- **Summarize** the developer's general role in a multimedia project.
- **Differentiate** between the front end and back end of a multimedia production.
- **Describe** the responsibilities of developer roles on a multimedia project team.

Main Idea

The developer on a multimedia project team performs front-end and back-end roles. In these roles, the developer contributes to the project's management, user experience, media components, computer systems, functionality, and quality assurance.

Content Vocabulary

◇ developer   ◇ usability test

◇ front end   ◇ bug

◇ back end   ◇ debug

◇ prototype

Academic Vocabulary

You will find these words in your reading and on your tests. Use the glossary to look up their definitions, if necessary.

◆ goal

◆ vision

Graphic Organizer

As you read, compare and contrast the front-end and back-end roles on the developer's project team. Use a Venn diagram similar to the one below to organize your thoughts.

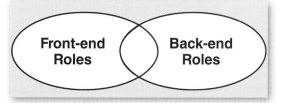

Front-end Roles   Back-end Roles

 Graphic Organizer Go to this book's **Online Learning Center** at **glencoe.com** to print this graphic organizer.

Academic Standards

 English Language Arts

NCTE 5 Use different writing process elements to communicate effectively.
NCTE 7 Conduct research and gather, evaluate, and synthesize data to communicate discoveries.
NCTE 12 Use language to accomplish individual purposes.

NCTE National Council of Teachers of English
NSES National Science Education Standards

 Mathematics

NCTM Number and Operations Understand numbers, ways of representing numbers, relationships among numbers, and number systems.

NCTM National Council of Teachers of Mathematics
NCSS National Council for the Social Studies

The Developer: Front-End Roles

Which roles on a project team contribute to the user interface?

The **developer** is the organization or department hired by the client to create a multimedia production. During the analysis and planning stage, the developer assesses the work to be done. Tasks are often categorized as front-end tasks or back-end tasks. The **front end** of a project is the visible part, with which the user interacts. The **back end** is the part that processes data and makes the production work. The roles on a multimedia project team can likewise be grouped according to whether they contribute to the product's front end or back end.

Project Management and User Experience

The project manager and the producer oversee a project's organization and creative direction from start to finish. These people may have frequent contact with the client. On a small project team, the producer and the project manager may be the same person. The interface designer is responsible for helping to plan how users will experience and respond to the multimedia production.

Project Manager The **goal**, or objective, of the project manager is to keep the project on track. The project manager works with the client to develop the goals, target audience, and mission statement for the project. This person sets up a budget for the project and develops a schedule of milestones and deliverables. The project manager also selects the members of the team and assigns specific tasks. Project managers speak for the team in meetings with the client representative, report on the team's progress, and share feedback from the client with the rest of the team.

Producer Also known as the creative director or art director, the producer helps to develop the **vision**, or concept, for the product. The producer plans and coordinates the development of the project's various media elements. The producer also creates storyboards that show the general flow of animation and video (if applicable). He or she directs the integration of different media into a unified whole. The producer usually directs others but may work hands-on, especially to integrate media using multimedia authoring software.

User Interface Designer The user interface designer is responsible for making the product work as well as possible for the user. During the design stage, the user interface designer helps construct the production's architecture, or structure; develops a unified look for the production; and storyboards the multimedia elements and navigation. The user interface designer may use diagrams called wireframes to demonstrate how users will interact with the production.

In the development stage, the user interface designer works with the project's graphic artist and programmer to create a **prototype**, which is a model of the product's screen designs and navigation elements. The prototype may be used in a **usability test**, in which untrained individuals assess how easy the product is to use. Based on the results, the user interface designer may refine the interface design.

As You Read

Connect Why is it important to consider how users will experience a multimedia production?

Project Management
The project manager may wear more than one hat depending on the size and needs of the team. For example, the project manager might write content or help evaluate the user interface.

Academic Focus

 Mathematics

Budgets People use budgets to track expenses and income. If a small e-commerce business wants to save 10% of its monthly income of $1,000, how much will it save over 12 months? Start by converting 10% to a decimal.

NCTM Number and Operations Understand numbers, ways of representing numbers, relationships among numbers, and number systems.

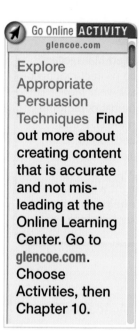
Media

Depending on the nature of the final product, a team may include creators of such media as animation, graphics, audio, video, and text. These team members produce materials during development but may also participate in the design stage.

Motion Designer Motion design refers to graphic design that uses animation or video to create the illusion of movement. Uses of motion graphics include Web animation, opening sequences for movies, commercials, music videos, and corporate presentations and logos. Motion graphics are developed by motion designers, who are also called interactive designers or multimedia developers.

Graphic Artist The graphic artist, or graphic designer, creates original graphics for a multimedia production. This artwork may include interface layouts, navigation buttons, charts, drawings, and animation. Much of this work may be done with development software. The graphic artist works closely with the user interface designer, photographers, and any others contributing to the project's visual content.

Audio Specialist and Videographer A team developing a production that uses high-quality audio and video generally includes an audio specialist and a video specialist, or videographer. These professionals may record sounds and video, edit recordings, integrate existing files, and convert files to different formats.

Writer and Editor Generally, a multimedia project includes both content writing and technical writing. On a small project team, one person may do most, or all, of the writing.

- **Content writers** prepare the content that will appear in a production. The writer researches and creates text that is reviewed by editors and subject matter experts. During maintenance, the writer may update the text or correct errors.
- **Technical writers** create documentation that supports the production. In the analysis stage, the technical writer may prepare reports about the project's needs, or benefits and costs. User documents, such as manuals, are written in the development stage and may be revised during maintenance.
- **Editors** make modifications to the language, organization, grammar, and spelling of text generated by content and technical writers. They pay attention to details, flow, readability, and tone.

 **Identify** What are three front-end roles on a multimedia project team?

The Developer: Back-End Roles

What are the back-end roles on a multimedia project team?

As you have learned, the back end of a multimedia production is the part that involves critical tasks that are not obvious to the user. The responsibilities of typical back-end roles on a multimedia project team are described below.

Computer Systems and Functionality

Certain roles focus on how the product is developed and delivered.

Systems Architect The systems architect is responsible for the overall technical design of the product, including the hardware and operating systems on which it will run, how components will work together, and programming languages and other tools that will be used to develop the product. A systems architect contributes mostly to the design stage of a project but may also be involved in other stages.

Programmer Programmers write the code for more complex multimedia projects. This work takes place during development. In the testing and maintenance stages, he or she may update the code to fix problems or make small improvements. A product that can be developed using existing software may not require programming.

Quality Assurance Analyst

The code for a multimedia production is checked for mistakes by a quality assurance (QA) analyst, a specialist on the project team who tests the product for **bugs**, or errors. During a project's design stage, the QA analyst may write a test plan that details the tools and procedures to be used during the testing stage. The QA analyst uses the product as a user would, analyzing the performance and looking for any problems. The programmer then **debugs** the code, or corrects any errors reported by the QA analyst. Testing may also be required during maintenance.

 **Reading Check** **Recall** For what three items is the systems architect responsible?

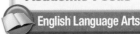

Academic Focus

English Language Arts

Quality Assurance Checking facts, spelling, and punctuation helps ensure that a literary composition is free from errors. Create a quality assurance checklist for a multimedia presentation you are developing. Exchange the list with a classmate and make changes based on the feedback.

NCTE 12 Use language to accomplish individual purposes.

 Section **10.2** After You Read

Review Key Concepts

1. **Describe** the role of the producer on a multimedia project team.

2. **Distinguish** between the front end and back end of a multimedia project.

 Check Your Answers Check your answers at this book's **Online Learning Center** through glencoe.com.

Practice Academic Skills

English Language Arts

3. **Critique** Think about an item you would like to purchase. Visit three Web sites that are likely to sell the item. Navigate to the item, noting how easy or difficult it is to find on each site. Write a paragraph evaluating your experience with the navigation of the three sites.

4. **Apply** Choose a developer role described in the text that appeals to you. List details about the role. Then write a paragraph stating how your interests or skills make you suited to that role.

 Online Student Manual • glencoe.com

Go to your Online Student Manual and enter your password to find projects that allow you to practice and apply multimedia skills.

NCTE 7 Conduct research and gather, evaluate, and synthesize data to communicate discoveries.

NCTE 5 Use different writing process elements to communicate effectively.

SECTION (10.3) Case Study: Web Site Project

Reading Guide

Before You Read

Prior Knowledge Look over the Key Concepts at the beginning of the section. Write down what you already know about each concept and what you want to find out by reading the section.

Read to Learn

Key Concepts

- **Analyze** the factors that go into planning a Web site.
- **Apply** multimedia design principles to Web sites.
- **Explain** how to develop multimedia for the Web.
- **Identify** areas of a Web site to test before publishing the site.

Main Idea

This section's case study applies the project stages introduced earlier to the creation of a Web site for a fictitious company.

Content Vocabulary

◇ demographic

◇ comp

◇ tag

◇ Web site authoring software

◇ source code

Academic Vocabulary

You will find these words in your reading and on your tests. Use the glossary to look up their definitions, if necessary.

◆ potential

◆ suit

Graphic Organizer

As you read, identify the five project stages and give examples of tasks that are completed in each stage. Use a table like the one below to organize your information.

Stage	Examples of Tasks

 Graphic Organizer Go to this book's **Online Learning Center** at **glencoe.com** to print this graphic organizer.

Academic Standards

 English Language Arts

NCTE 12 Use language to accomplish individual purposes.

 Mathematics

NCTM Algebra Use mathematical models to represent and understand quantitative relationships.
NCTM Reasoning and Proof Select and use various types of reasoning and methods of proof.

NCTE National Council of Teachers of English
NSES National Science Education Standards

NCTM National Council of Teachers of Mathematics
NCSS National Council for the Social Studies

Stage 1: Analysis and Planning

Which aspects of a Web site must be defined before design and development can begin?

This section will guide you through the process of creating a Web site for Extreme Sports Rentals, a fictitious business that rents equipment for sports that are considered risky. The work will be broken down into the project stages outlined in Chapter 4. Keep in mind that the decisions and tools used to develop a Web site can be adapted to other multimedia projects.

Project Goals and Mission

A Web site's goals must be clear from the start. A commercial (business) Web site has the general goals of establishing the company's image; attracting customers; promoting and selling products or services (called e-commerce); and providing background, employment, and contact information.

As developer of the Web site for Extreme Sports Rentals, you first need to define the site's specific goals, which may include the following:

- Draw customers to stores, located in major cities across the United States

- Let customers reserve equipment online

- Stimulate interest in mountain biking, inline skating, skateboarding, and snowboarding

- Advocate proper safety when engaging in extreme sports

Next you should define the Web site's target audience, which is the company's existing and **potential**, or possible, customers. For Extreme Sports Rentals, the target audience consists of males and females in their teens, twenties, and thirties who are active on the weekends. This kind of statistical data about a population is often called **demographics**. The Web site should be designed to communicate specifically with the target demographic.

Finally, you need to write a mission statement that summarizes the project's goals and audience. The site might have the following mission statement: "The mission of the Web site for Extreme Sports Rentals is to increase knowledge of extreme sports and the company's equipment rentals by adventure-seeking young people." You will refer to the mission statement throughout the design and development stage, to keep the project on track. Some organizations post their mission statement on their Web site, as seen in Figure 10.3.

As You Read

Connect What strategies do you use to plan school projects?

Figure 10.3
An organization, as well as its Web site, may have a mission statement. What role does a Web site's mission statement play during the production process?

Project Resources

The scope of a Web site refers to the features and content that can be included, given the project's resources. To define the scope of a project, start by listing all desired elements. Then weigh those desires against the project's resources, as seen in Figure 10.4.

Figure 10.4
The resources of a multimedia project include money, time, people, and development tools. What is the relationship between a project's resources and its scope?

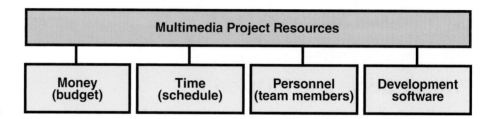

For example, the budget for the Extreme Sports Rentals site might allow for implementing a store locator but not a reservation system. Perhaps the time line requires that the site be live prior to a particular event, but videos illustrating extreme sports will not be recorded and edited by then. Leaving out some components may be necessary in order to meet the deadline and to maintain the budget.

Requirements and Content Delivery

As you have learned, a multimedia project has both content requirements and technical requirements. Both types of requirements reflect the production's goals and target audience. The Web site for Extreme Sports Rentals, for example, might require the following four types of content:

- **Text:** the company's history; store addresses, phone numbers, and hours; product details and rental packages; a reservation form; profiles of sponsored athletes; and safety tips
- **Graphics:** product photos, images of extreme sports, and maps for finding stores
- **Audio:** energetic background music for the site
- **Video:** short films of people engaging in extreme sports

A project's technical requirements are further determined by the hardware and software available to deliver and utilize the production. For instance, suppose Extreme Sports Rentals is given 200 MB of server space to store its Web site. The site's content must be limited accordingly. The Internet speeds of mobile devices on which the site might be downloaded may also restrict its size. As another technical consideration, links to any required plug-ins should be provided. For instance, the site might be viewable only using Adobe Flash Player. Or it might include PDFs (of product lists at various stores, for example), requiring Adobe Acrobat Reader.

 **Identify** What are four general goals of a commercial Web site?

Academic Focus

Mathematics

Bar Charts Most project management software can be used to create Gantt charts, which are bar charts illustrating schedules. Based on the relationships between tasks, the software automatically calculates new dates when actual dates are entered that differ from the scheduled ones.

NCTM Algebra Use mathematical models to represent and understand quantitative relationships.

Stage 2: Design and Development

Which production tasks are done during design and development?

Understanding a Web site's goals and audience helps you identify not only what content to include but how to present it. The same is true for all multimedia projects, but Web sites have special design concerns.

Design Considerations

There are several factors to consider when designing a Web site. Three key factors are the target audience, the difference between Web design and print design, and the effect of different browsers.

Target Audience A Web site's appearance and organization must appeal to the appropriate audience. For Extreme Sports Rentals, an effective design might be visually stimulating, with clever but intuitive navigation. Such an approach would reflect the adventurous spirit of the company's likely customers.

Browsers The appearance of fonts, graphics, and page layouts may differ when a site is viewed using different browsers. Therefore, the pages of a site need to be tested in all popular browsers to make sure they display properly (see Figure 10.5). If there are differences in how a page displays, the designer must analyze and adjust the design.

Quick **Tip**

Shortcut Some Web design programs, including Adobe Dreamweaver, offer features for previewing Web pages in various browsers.

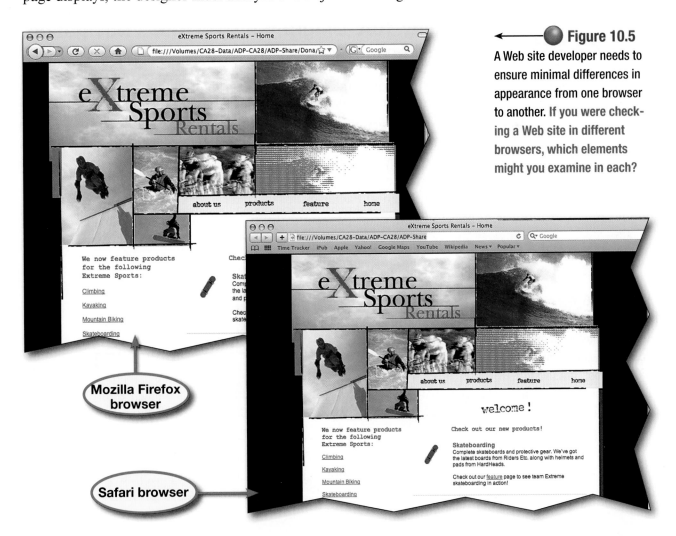

Figure 10.5
A Web site developer needs to ensure minimal differences in appearance from one browser to another. **If you were checking a Web site in different browsers, which elements might you examine in each?**

Mozilla Firefox browser

Safari browser

Web vs. Print Designs that work well for printed pieces may not work well for Web sites. Long pages of text and small type are difficult to read on a computer screen. The main text on any Web page should be easy to read and not require a lot of scrolling. With Web publishing, content can be easily revised and linked. Your Web site might use hyperlinks to connect to additional information about extreme sports.

Interface Design

A Web site's interface is where users interact directly with the site. The interface's design, therefore, is a very important tool in meeting the site's objectives with the target audience.

Navigation Scheme Chapter 4 describes four arrangements for the pages of a Web site: hierarchical, linear, non-linear, and composite. Suppose you want the Web site for Extreme Sports Rentals to benefit from the following advantages of the hierarchical form of navigation:

- The home page gives an overview of the site.
- Visitors can go directly to pages that interest them.

In the following activity, you will diagram the site's navigation. Remember that the diagram of a Web site's structure is sometimes called the site architecture.

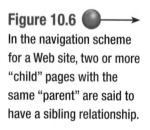

Activity 10A Diagram a Web Site's Navigation

1 Open your word processing, flow chart, or presentation software.

2 Use text boxes and lines—or a diagram tool that automatically formats an organization chart—to represent the following arrangement of pages at the Extreme Sports Rentals Web site:

- The Home page is the parent of the three pages About Us, Products, and Features.
- The Products page is the parent of the two pages Product List and Rental Packages.

3 Compare your diagram with Figure 10.6.

4 Save and close your file.

Figure 10.6
In the navigation scheme for a Web site, two or more "child" pages with the same "parent" are said to have a sibling relationship.

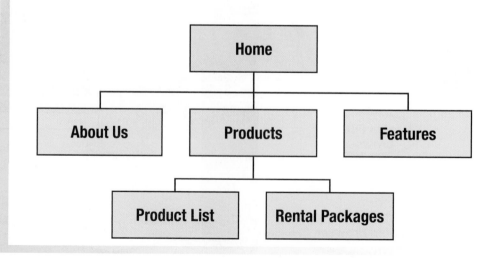

Storyboard A storyboard can be used to plan sequences in your Web site. It might include frames, sometimes called wireframes, showing the content and navigation on each page. In the next activity, you will create a wireframe for a Web site's home page.

Activity 10B Storyboard a Web Site's Home Page

YOU TRY IT

1. Open your word processing, flow chart, or presentation software.

2. Use your software's text boxes or diagram tools to represent the following elements on the Home page of the Extreme Sports Rentals Web site:

   - Navigation menu and direct links to the Product List and Rental Packages pages

   - Company logo and several photos showing extreme sports

   - Welcome text, text about two featured products, and text highlighting the product list and rental packages

   These items should appear as placeholders, which are boxes that substitute for the actual items.

3. Compare your diagram against Figure 10.7. Your diagram should contain the same elements but not necessarily in the same places.

4. Save and close your file.

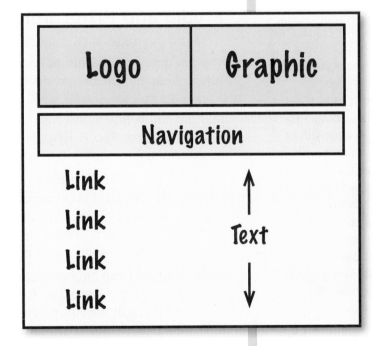

Figure 10.7
A wireframe is a diagram of content and navigation for a Web page.

Design Comps The graphic artist typically creates **comps** (short for comprehensive artwork or composite design) of key pages to illustrate the site's proposed visual design. Recall that in Chapter 5, you learned about the visual design principles of proportion, balance, variety, emphasis, harmony, pattern, movement, rhythm, symmetry, unity, and repetition.

Figure 10.8
Follow these important guidelines when designing a Web site. **What is a design theme?**

Web Design Checklist

☑ Select a design theme (unifying idea) to tie together the various elements.

☑ Tailor the design to the computer screen's landscape orientation.

☑ Make the navigation accessible, intuitive, consistent, and useful.

☑ Include short blocks of text, spread over multiple pages. White space helps balance the content and avoid clutter.

☑ Choose fonts that are easy to read.

☑ Provide enough contrast between the text and the background.

☑ Be sure the background is appropriate for the content and is not too busy.

☑ Use graphics to add interest and information, without distracting from the site's focus.

☑ Obtain permission for any text or graphics taken from another source.

☑ Cite sources of information used on the site.

☑ Make sure the design elements are used consistently.

The design comps, based on the content identified in the storyboard or wireframes, may be sketched on paper or generated using software such as Adobe Fireworks. The Extreme Sports Rentals site might have an informal look and a youthful feel, to appeal to its target audience. Follow the guidelines in Figure 10.8 to design a Web site.

Media and Programming

After analyzing, planning, and designing a multimedia production, you can develop the content and then combine all the pieces into a functioning multimedia production.

Media Development Various media, including text, graphics, animation, audio, and video, may be developed for a multimedia project. For the Extreme Sports Rentals Web site, the media developed should be determined by the content requirements.

- Text should be written to **suit**, or be appropriate for, the audience. It should avoid jargon and slang. For instance, the Extreme Sports Rentals Web site might define terms that would be unfamiliar to potential customers who are new to extreme sports. An informal tone would appeal to the young audience.

- Graphics and animation are created or acquired during the development stage. For Extreme Sports Rentals, you might photograph the equipment that can be rented. You might research stock photos showing extreme sports, and reproduce them with permission.

- Audio and video may be recorded or acquired. For Extreme Sports Rentals, you might find free music clips or copyrighted songs (used with permission). You might shoot footage of extreme sports or find video clips on the Internet (again, used with permission).

In the following activity, you will plan the "About Us" page of the Extreme Sports Rentals Web site.

Go Online **ACTIVITY**
glencoe.com

Accessible Web Sites Learn about how to make your Web sites accessible to visitors with disabilities at the **Online Learning Center.** Go to glencoe.com. Choose **Activities**, then **Chapter 10.**

Activity 10C Plan a Web Site's About Us Page

YOU TRY IT

❶ In a new word processing document or at the top of a sheet of paper, key or write the title **Planned Content for About Us Page**.

❷ Brainstorm ideas for the goals, mission, audience, and products that the company might sell. List the text and graphics you would like to include.

❸ Write keywords next to your ideas. Decide which of these keywords you would like to use in headings for the About Us page.

❹ Organize your ideas so that the most important topics are at the top of your page. Topics that are less important should be at the bottom of the page.

❺ Create a new document called **Final About Us Page**. Finalize your headings and wording. Use your notes if you have questions.

❻ The content should include a brief paragraph (no more than 200 words) written to the target audience addressing the site's goals and mission.

❼ Proofread, spell-check, save, and close the final document.

Web Programming Web sites are typically created in XHTML. This programming language contains **tags**, or codes that instruct a browser how to display a Web page. If you do not know XHTML, you can use **Web site authoring software** to create a Web page. Many Web design programs use WYSIWYG (pronounced whiz-ee-whig), short for "what you see is what you get." This system displays a page as it would appear in a browser. It also generates XHTML. Microsoft Expression Web and Adobe Dreamweaver are popular WYSIWYG programs. Web programming may use a text editor, also called an XHTML editor. The programming instructions for a Web site are called the **source code**. Knowing some XHTML is useful to troubleshoot source code.

 **Reading Check** **Paraphrase** What is WYSIWYG?

Final Stages

What are the last steps in a Web site project?

After the components have been integrated, a multimedia production such as a Web site is checked for errors and delivered to the audience.

Stage 3: Testing

Before publishing a Web site, it is important to check it for errors. Ideally, this final check should be performed by QA analysts who have not worked on the project. Their fresh perspective makes them more likely to notice mistakes. The QA analyst will test the site in various browsers and versions, ensure that sections work together, check every link, verify the design's consistency, and proofread the text.

Stage 4: Implementation

After testing and debugging, or fixing any errors, a multimedia production is ready to be released. You might implement a Web site, such as the one for Extreme Sports Rentals, by migrating the files to the final hosting environment, performing another round of testing, and moving the files to the live URL. For Extreme Sports Rentals, implementation would also require training store employees to receive reservations made through the Web site.

Stage 5: Evaluation and Maintenance

After using a new Web site for a while, the client may want changes or new features. For example, Extreme Sports Rentals might want to add a blog. The client may need to update information regularly on the site, such as available rental packages or prices. The client might make these updates through a content management system created by the developer, or the developer might implement them. In addition, hyperlinks to pages outside the site should be rechecked periodically.

YOU TRY IT

Activity 10D Evaluate a Web Site

1. In your Web browser, browse to your data files. In the **Extreme Sports Rentals** folder, open the **index.html** file.

2. Refer to the checklist provided in Figure 10.9 to evaluate the appearance and appropriateness of the various elements of the Extreme Sports Rentals Web site. The home page of the site is shown in Figure 10.10.

3. Click the navigation links, read the text, and review the graphics and other multimedia elements of the site. Assess whether the site satisfies each guideline for good Web design.

4. Key your observations in a word processing document. Include a summary of your evaluation.

5. Save and close your file. Close your Web browser.

DATA FILE

Figure 10.9
This checklist can help you assess the elements of any Web page.

Web Site Evaluation Checklist

- ☑ The page orientation is landscape, to match the computer screen.
- ☑ White space is used to balance the content and avoid clutter.
- ☑ Navigation buttons are placed to make navigation intuitive.
- ☑ Text is valuable and error-free, with a tone that appeals to the target audience.
- ☑ Text is easy to read and does not require a lot of scrolling.
- ☑ The background is appropriate for the content and is not too busy.
- ☑ Graphics are interesting and are not distracting.
- ☑ Permission has been obtained for source material.
- ☑ Sources are cited.

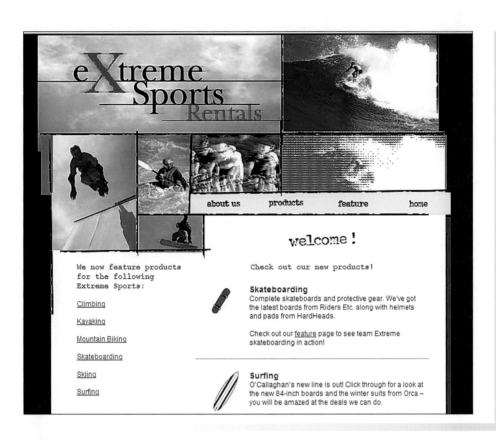

→ ● **Figure 10.10**
This is the home page of the Extreme Sports Rentals Web site.

 Reading Check **Explain** What is the advantage of having people who did not work on a multimedia project test it?

Section 10.3 After You Read

Review Key Concepts

1. Identify four types of content included on a multimedia Web site.

2. Conclude why hyperlinks on a Web site need to be checked during testing and maintenance.

⤢ **Check Your Answers** Check your answers at this book's **Online Learning Center** through glencoe.com.

Practice Academic Skills

📖 **English Language Arts**

3. Apply Imagine you have recently started a business to make some extra money after school. You want to create a simple Web site to advertise it. Write a paragraph describing the business, the site's goals, and the target audience.

🖩 **Mathematics**

4. Infer Using deductive reasoning, make your best guess at the meanings of the following XHTML tags. (As an example, the tag <br> defines a single line break.) Tags: **a.** <del>, **b.** <ins>, **c.** <img>.

NCTE 12 Use language to accomplish individual purposes.

NCTM Reasoning and Proof Select and use various types of reasoning and methods of proof.

⤢ **Online Student Manual • glencoe.com**

Go to your Online Student Manual and enter your password to find projects that allow you to practice and apply multimedia skills.

Real World Technology

Communication Choices and Decisions

Communicating is the act of conveying thoughts, opinions, or facts. Social communication refers to exchanges you might have with friends or family members. Professional communication refers to information relayed within a business. When you find yourself in a position to share knowledge with others, you must make a number of decisions regarding the content and delivery of your message.

Content

Communication consists mainly of words, although it may have nonverbal aspects. When choosing your words, consider the following:

- Audience
- Occasion
- Purpose

Depending on the audience, your language might be informal, professional, or technical. It might target a specific group or appeal to a diverse cross-section of people. For example, information about climate change would be expressed simply for the public, but a higher-level discussion could be presented to environmental experts. Depending on the occasion, your word choice might be chatty (as in a casual conversation) or polished (as in a business meeting). In all cases, your words should have integrity and never be used to mislead.

Always consider your audience, occasion, and purpose when communicating.

Delivery

The requirements of a particular assignment might determine the way you deliver a message. For example, the narration for a slide show is spoken; a research paper is written. In other circumstances, you might be able to choose how your message is delivered. For example, you might make a phone call or send an e-mail, record a radio announcement or place an ad in a newspaper. If you are giving a speech in person, be aware of the effects of nonverbal communication such as gestures, eye contact, and posture. If your words are part of a dialogue, be sure to listen actively and attentively to others.

Skill Builder

1. **Research Communication Aids** Do research about how graphics, such as tables and charts, can be used to support oral and written communication.

2. **Write a Report** The goal of public relations (PR) is to promote a good relationship between a company and the community, customers, and employees. Research and summarize how PR firms help companies connect with one of these audiences.

Chapter Summary

Good teamwork is essential in creating a multimedia production. The makeup of a project team depends on many factors, including the type of project, complexity, budget, and schedule. Effective team members possess skills such as active listening, commitment, communication, conflict resolution, and critical thinking. The client participates in various ways during all stages of the project.

The client hires a developer to create a multimedia production. Tasks for a project are typically categorized as relating to the front end, which the user sees, or the back end, which makes the production work behind the scenes.

A Web site project is typically developed in five stages: 1 Analyze and Plan, 2 Design and Develop, 3 Test, 4 Implement, and 5 Evaluate and Maintain.

Vocabulary Review

1. On a sheet of paper, use each of these vocabulary terms in a sentence.

Content Vocabulary

- project team (p. 289)
- teamwork (p. 289)
- client (p. 290)
- proposal (p. 290)
- developer (p. 293)
- front end (p. 293)
- back end (p. 293)
- prototype (p. 293)
- usability test (p. 293)
- bug (p. 295)
- debug (p. 295)
- demographic (p. 297)
- comp (p. 301)
- tag (p. 303)
- Web site authoring software (p. 303)
- source code (p. 303)

Academic Vocabulary

- team (p. 289)
- exemplary (p. 289)
- goal (p. 293)
- vision (p. 293)
- potential (p. 297)
- suit (p. 302)

Review Key Concepts

2. Explain how teamwork leads to the successful completion of a project.

3. Evaluate the skills and qualities of effective team members.

4. Identify the client's role in a multimedia project.

5. Summarize the developer's general role in a multimedia project.

6. Differentiate between the front end and back end of a multimedia production.

7. Describe the responsibilities of developer roles on a multimedia project team.

8. Analyze the factors that go into planning a Web site.

9. Apply multimedia design principles to Web sites.

10. Explain how to develop multimedia for the Web.

11. Identify areas of a Web site to test before publishing the site.

Critical Thinking

12. Distinguish Follow your teacher's instructions to form small groups and research the different multimedia project team roles. Your group should choose one or more roles so that all roles are covered. Determine the experience, education, salary range, and responsibilities of each job. Use a table like the one shown to organize your information.

Experience	Education	Salary Range	Responsibilities

13. Explain Which job on a multimedia project team would you most like to have? Why? Use the Internet or other resources to complete research about the job that is of interest to you. Create a graphic organizer that shows how your skills, personality traits, and interests relate to the job you chose.

14. List A small business has asked you to create a multimedia production to advertise merchandise. Prepare a list of hardware, software, and other components that will be needed for an effective presentation.

15. Predict Multimedia software is constantly being updated. Research new multimedia software and how it might change the way multimedia projects are currently developed. Use a chart like the one shown to organize your information.

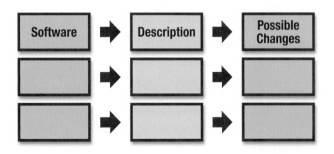

16. Analyze Suppose you are the project manager for a multimedia development agency. A small pet-sitting business wants you to create a multimedia production to advertise the business. Analyze the request and think of possible multimedia advertising solutions. Prepare a list of suggestions to share with the client.

17. Critique Suppose you are developing a Web site to promote a museum. Consider how you might use text, graphics, animation, audio, and video on your Web site. Write a brief outline of the elements you would include and why you feel these elements are suitable for this purpose.

18. Evaluate Choose three existing Web sites to evaluate based on the following factors: design and accessibility compliance. Use a table such as this to organize your evaluation of the three sites.

	Site 1	Site 2	Site 3
Evaluate/ critique design			
Evaluate accessibility compliance			

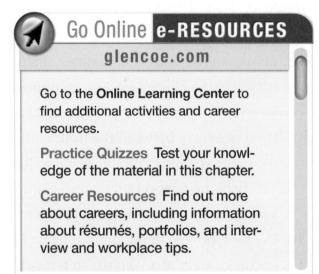

Go Online e-RESOURCES

glencoe.com

Go to the **Online Learning Center** to find additional activities and career resources.

Practice Quizzes Test your knowledge of the material in this chapter.

Career Resources Find out more about careers, including information about résumés, portfolios, and interview and workplace tips.

Academic Connections

19. Language Arts–Demonstrate Teamwork

In this chapter, you learned several skills and qualities that are necessary to good teamwork. Think of a goal that would require teamwork to accomplish. Then write a short story, using your characters to illustrate good teamwork skills and how those skills contribute to the outcome of the story. To complete your project, follow these steps:

A. Determine what event you want to write about. This might be a group project for school, a party, or a sporting event. Keep in mind that a team can be two or more people. Write a list of the teamwork skills you think would be necessary to complete the goal. Use a chart like the one shown to help organize your thoughts.

B. Write an outline for your story. Include digital photos to illustrate your story. Be sure to obtain permissions and provide proper citations for photos, if necessary. Proofread your story for spelling and grammar errors.

C. Submit your story to your teacher.

Skill/Quality	Usefulness to Goal

NCTE 5 Use different writing process elements to communicate effectively.

Standardized Test Practice

Multiple Choice

Read the paragraph below and then answer the question.

Creating large multimedia projects, such as interactive DVDs, video games, or Web-based training programs, requires the concerted effort of many people over a significant amount of time, usually several months. There is a process for developing a large-scale application and many different roles for the people involved. Each role has certain requirements, responsibilities, and rewards.

Smaller multimedia projects, such as slide shows or small Web sites, require the same project phases as larger projects. Some less complex projects may be completed by a small team or just one person.

20. Based on the paragraph, which statement is correct?

A. Small multimedia projects do not require as many phases as larger projects.

B. Large-scale multimedia applications are often developed by just one person.

C. Large-scale and small-scale multimedia projects go through the same stages of development.

D. Development of large-scale multimedia projects seldom takes more than a few weeks.

> **Test-Taking Tip** In a multiple choice test, the answers should be specific and precise. Read the question first, then read all the answer choices before you choose. Eliminate answers that you know are incorrect.

21. Produce a Presentation

Follow your teacher's instructions to form groups. Your group has been asked to develop a slide show to inform new employees about the ethical use of digital tools and resources in the workplace.

A. Choose appropriate tools to create the presentation.

B. Conduct research on your topic. Use a table like the one shown to organize the information you will include in your presentation. Determine which digital tools and resources you will discuss, as well as the ethical rules for each. Digital tools used in the workplace might include such resources as e-mail, development software, and network security. You should find additional resources used in business through your research.

C. Develop a storyboard for the presentation to share with your employer.

D. Build your presentation. Include graphics, sound, and video, as appropriate. Be mindful of potential copyright issues.

E. Review your presentation for correct spelling and grammar.

NETS 3b Locate, organize, analyze, evaluate, synthesize, and ethically use information from a variety of sources and media.

Digital Resource	Ethical Rules

22. Analyze a Multimedia Presentation

You have been asked to develop a Web site to help promote your business. The business might be a florist, a pet-sitting service, or a multimedia development agency. As part of the planning stage, your boss has asked you to analyze other business Web sites and create a list of elements you would include or not include in your Web site. You need to:

NETS 4b Plan and manage activities to develop a solution or complete a project.

A. Choose and evaluate three business Web sites.

B. Create a table or spreadsheet like the one shown below to list the elements you noted on each Web site.

C. Note whether you feel this element should be included on your company's Web site, along with the reason for your decision. For example, you might note that each Web site includes a privacy policy. This should be included on your site to protect the company.

NETS 4c Collect and analyze data to identify solutions and/or make informed decisions.

Element	Web Site URL	Include?	Reason

23. Teamwork

Each member of a multimedia project team must possess teamwork skills and qualities such as active listening, commitment, communication, conflict resolution, critical thinking, integrity, and organization. Follow your teacher's instructions to form groups of four. Create a table like the one below that lists each skill or quality and the project role or roles that would especially require it. Can you think of any other skills to add to the list?

Teamwork Skill/Quality	Project Role
Active listening	
Commitment	
Communication	
Conflict resolution	
Critical thinking	
Integrity	
Organization	

CHALLENGE YOURSELF

24. Learn New Software

As a Web designer and developer, you will need to keep current on the design applications that are available to help you do your job. With your teacher's permission, go online and locate a new application (or an application that is new to you) for developing Web design graphics, animation, or content. Compare the application to a similar application with which you are familiar. Use a Venn diagram like the one shown to compare the two applications. Use questions such as these for your comparison:

A. Who developed the application?

B. What is the cost of the application?

C. What are the application's strengths?

D. What are the application's weaknesses?

E. How are the applications similar?

F. How are the applications different?

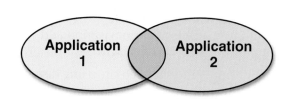

Projects Across the Curriculum

Project 1

Analyze and Plan a Web Site

NCTE 5 Use different writing process elements to communicate effectively.

English Language Arts Follow your teacher's instructions to form teams. Your team has been asked to create a Web site to promote a nonprofit organization in your community. (The organization can be real or fictional.) In this project, you will complete Stage 1, analysis and planning, of the development process.

Plan

1. Conduct research into the intended audience for the Web site, as well as the technology you will need.

2. Identify the types of elements you will include on your Web site.

Create

3. Write a mission statement for your organization's site.

4. Use a table or spreadsheet to determine the schedule, or time line, for your project. Include each stage of development with a realistic time estimate.

5. Use a word processing program to develop the content for your Web site. Include notes for graphics, audio, or video you would like to include.

Review

6. Perform a check for correct spelling and grammar.

7. Share your proposed content with your client (your teacher) and incorporate any necessary changes, based on the feedback.

Project 2

Design and Develop a Web Site

NCTE 12 Use language to accomplish individual purposes.

English Language Arts With your team, you will now complete Stage 2, design and development, of the Web site you planned in Project 1.

Plan

1. Decide which type of navigation scheme will best serve your Web site.

Create

2. Diagram the Web site's navigation.

3. Using the elements you identified in Step 2 of the previous project, develop a storyboard for your site's home page.

4. Develop or find any needed media for your site, including text, graphics, audio, and video. Keep in mind permissions for using elements from another source and plan where and how you will cite your sources on the site.

Review and Revise

5. Review your navigation and storyboard for correctness before submitting them to your client (teacher) for review.

6. Build the Web site using development software, incorporating any feedback.

Project 3

Test, Implement, and Evaluate a Web Site

NCTE 8 Use information resources to gather information and create and communicate knowledge.

English Language Arts Continue to work with your team from Projects 1 and 2. You are now ready to complete Stages 3 and 4 in the process of developing your Web site. Putting together a finished project involves many tasks within each stage. As you move through these two stages, notice how the project develops.

Research

1. Collect and review all feedback from the analysis and planning stage, and from the design and development stage.

Plan

2. Make a list of the tasks that need to be completed in the testing stage and the implementation stage of the project. Assign each task or role to a team member. Use a table similar to the one shown to record your assignments.

Create

3. Once assignments are made to team members, have each team member write out the steps for his or her role in testing and implementing the Web site.

4. Create a detailed time line, and list the elements to be included. Be sure this time line works with the overall time line you developed in Project 1. Make suggested revisions to the time line until the project is completed. Keep in mind that any revisions to the time line would need to be approved by your client.

PROJECT DEVELOPMENT					
Stage 3		Stage 4		Stage 5	
Role	Member	Role	Member	Role	Member

5. Test your Web site in various browsers and versions to ensure consistency. Be sure to verify that all links and navigation buttons work; that all text is correct; and that graphics, audio, and video work and are incorporated properly. Note any changes that need to be made, and have the appropriate team members make the corrections.

6. Follow your teacher's directions to implement your Web site by moving the files to the final hosting environment.

Review and Revise

7. Perform a final round of testing on your Web site. Make changes to the Web site based on this testing.

8. Share your Web site with your class for additional feedback. Continue to revise your Web site, if appropriate.

Go Online RUBRICS
glencoe.com

Chapter Projects Use the rubrics for these projects to help create and evaluate your work. Go to the **Online Learning Center** at glencoe.com. Choose **Rubrics**, then **Chapter 10**.

Section 11.1
Plan Your Multimedia Career

Section 11.2
Develop Your Multimedia Career

CHAPTER OBJECTIVES

After completing this chapter, you will be able to:

❖ **Define** career pathway.

❖ **Identify** multimedia career clusters, their pathways, and sample careers.

❖ **Explain** how extended learning opportunities provide insights into careers.

❖ **Describe** how conducting a self-assessment is useful when choosing a career.

❖ **List** aspects of possible career choices that should be researched during career exploration.

❖ **Examine** the roles of training, education, portfolios, and résumés in preparing for a multimedia career.

❖ **Evaluate** the importance of transferable employability skills and qualities.

❖ **Summarize** ways that one can advance in a career.

Explore the Photo

In multimedia teams, each person has a unique leadership role. *What can you do in school and on your own to develop leadership skills for your future career?*

21st CENTURY SKILLS
Identify Leadership Qualities

Leadership is not about a position or a title, but rather the positive qualities one shares to bring out the best in others. A leader communicates well, respects different points of view, and acts with the team's common interest in mind. What are other leadership qualities?

Quick Write Activity Personal Narrative

Think of someone whom you consider to be a good leader. Write a persuasive essay describing what makes this person a good leader. Your essay should convince others to agree with your opinion.

Writing Tips
To write a persuasive essay, follow these steps:
1. State your position clearly.
2. Make sure each sentence in the essay includes details to support the main idea.
3. Use facts to back up your position.

SECTION ⑪.1   Plan Your Multimedia Career

Reading Guide

Before You Read

Stay Engaged One way to maintain your interest while you read is to turn each heading into a question. Then, read the section to find the answer.

Read to Learn
Key Concepts

- **Identify** multimedia career clusters, their pathways, and sample careers.
- **Explain** how extended learning opportunities provide insights into careers.
- **Describe** how conducting a self-assessment is useful when choosing a career.
- **List** aspects of possible career choices that should be researched during career exploration.

Main Idea

Having a successful career in multimedia requires deliberate planning. The first steps include becoming familiar with multimedia careers and choosing an appropriate one.

Content Vocabulary
- career pathway
- career outlook

Academic Vocabulary

You will find these words in your reading and on your tests. Use the glossary to look up their definitions, if necessary.

- tailor
- require

Graphic Organizer

As you read, identify four types of extended learning opportunities that can provide insights into your career exploration. Use a web diagram like the one below to organize your thoughts.

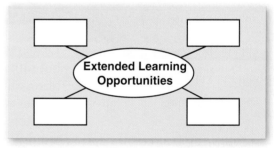

Extended Learning Opportunities

 Graphic Organizer Go to this book's **Online Learning Center** at **glencoe.com** to print this graphic organizer.

Academic Standards

 English Language Arts

NCTE 8 Use information resources to gather information and create and communicate knowledge.
NCTE 12 Use language to accomplish individual purposes.

NCTE National Council of Teachers of English
NSES National Science Education Standards

 Mathematics

NCTM Data Analysis and Probability Select and use appropriate statistical methods to analyze data.
NCTM Number and Operations Compute fluently and make reasonable estimates.

NCTM National Council of Teachers of Mathematics
NCSS National Council for the Social Studies

Explore Multimedia Careers

What are some careers in the field of multimedia?

A career is a person's chosen occupation or profession, or a sequence of jobs held in one field with increasing responsibility and authority. The U.S. Department of Education has organized similar careers into broad groups called career clusters (see Figure 1.10 in Chapter 1). The goals of presenting careers in this way are to help students like you do the following while still in school:

- Focus on a possible **career pathway**, or area of concentration within a career cluster.

- **Tailor**, or adapt, what you learn and experience to gain knowledge and skills for your chosen career.

- Plan any further education or special training the career may **require**, or demand as necessary or essential.

Multimedia Careers

Two of the career clusters defined by the U.S. Department of Education relate to multimedia:

- **Arts, Audio/Video (A/V) Technology, and Communications** involves designing, producing, exhibiting, performing, writing, and publishing multimedia content including visual and performing arts and design, journalism, and entertainment services

- **Information Technology** involves the design, development, support, and management of hardware, software multimedia, and systems integration services

The table in Figure 11.1 shows the different career pathways associated with these clusters, as well as some sample careers.

As You Read

Connect Which multimedia careers interest you?

Go Online **ACTIVITY**
glencoe.com

Career Outlook
Learn more about the future demand for multimedia careers at the **Online Learning Center**. Go to **glencoe.com**. Choose **Activities**, then **Chapter 11**.

Multimedia Career Clusters, Pathways, and Sample Careers		
Career Cluster	**Career Pathways**	**Sample Careers**
Arts, A/V Technology, and Communications	• Visual Arts • Performing Arts • Audio/Video Technology • Journalism and Broadcasting • Telecommunications Technologies • Printing Technology	• Graphic artist • Actor • Videographer • Reporter • Cable installer • Press supervisor
Information Technology	• Information Support and Services • Programming and Software Development • Network Systems • Interactive Media	• Technical writer • Programmer • Network administrator • Web designer

Figure 11.1
Broadly defined career clusters break down into career pathways that cover individual careers. Which pathway would you focus on if you wanted to be a technical writer?

Tools and Education Needs

Figure 11.2

Multimedia project team members in front-end roles come from a variety of backgrounds. For which role is a degree in English, journalism, or technical communication helpful?

As you read in Chapter 10, many multimedia careers are defined by whether the work is done on the front end or back end of a project. Figure 11.2 lists many of the roles available to front-end developers, along with suggested tools and the educational background needed for those roles. This can be useful in deciding which multimedia careers you are interested in. For example, if the role of graphic artist interests you, then you can see from the chart that you might want to start learning to use different graphics or video editing software now, as well as compiling a portfolio. In addition, when applying to colleges, you might also consider art school or technical schools.

Tools and Backgrounds for Front-End Developer Roles

Role	Possible Tools	Possible Background
Project Manager	• Project management software • Spreadsheet software • Flow chart software • Database software • Word processing software	• Degree in business or management • Basic knowledge of all project team roles • Familiarity with multimedia development tools • Ability to focus on the big picture, with excellent communication skills
Producer	• Web design and multimedia authoring software • Flow chart software	• Bachelor's degree and on-the-job experience creating media • Some knowledge of media development tools • Expertise in Web design or multimedia authoring • Ability to focus on the big picture, with excellent communication skills
User Interface Designer	• Flow chart software • Programming software • Laboratory equipment (such as video and audio recorders)	• Bachelor's degree in computer science or graphic arts • Study of human factors engineering (interaction between human beings and computers) • Understanding of XHTML and tools for adding interactivity • Good communication skills
Motion Designer	• 2D and 3D animation, multimedia authoring, and video editing software	• Bachelor's degree in computer science or degree from a technical school • Experience in graphic design, animation, or filmmaking • Software proficiency
Graphic Artist	• Raster and vector graphics software • 2D and 3D animation, multimedia authoring, and video editing software	• Degree from college or art school, or degree or certificate from a technical school • Compiled portfolio • Software proficiency
Audio Specialist and Videographer	• Digital and analog devices • Audio and video software	• Degree in audio engineering, music, or video production • Strong understanding of audio or video recording and editing techniques • Software and hardware proficiency
Writer and Editor	• Word processing, desktop publishing, and Web design software • Help-authoring software	• Bachelor's or master's degree in English, journalism, or technical communication • Excellent written communication and research skills • Ability to obtain and restate technical information • Knowledge of XHTML • Software proficiency

There are also many careers available for back-end developers, such as systems architect, programmer, and quality assurance analyst. As with the front-end roles (See Figure 11.3), there is a wide array of possible backgrounds and tools used by each role.

Figure 11.3
Both front-end and back-end roles are required for a successful multimedia project. Which type of role might this man be fulfilling?

- Systems architects often use flow chart or word processing software. Their possible backgrounds include a bachelor's or master's degree, eight to ten years of experience in information technology and programming, and a thorough understanding of hardware, operating systems, networks, and the Internet.

- Programmers generally use programming languages such as ASP. NET, C++, CSS, or XHTML. They also use scripting languages such as ActionScript® for Adobe® Flash® and Lingo for Adobe Director®. Programmers often have a bachelor's degree in computer science or a related field, and a technical understanding of the Internet and operating systems is also useful.

- Quality assurance analysts often use infrared waves, radio waves, or microwaves in addition to performance and functionality testing and word processing software, and bug-tracking systems. A college degree in computer science or another technical or scientific subject is often required for this career. Prior experience as a programmer or network engineer is often helpful.

Extended Learning Opportunities

As discussed in Chapter 1, you can learn about multimedia careers through the following types of extended learning opportunities:

- **Curricular** such as classes in computer science, desktop publishing, digital graphics, animation, multimedia, video technology, and Web design.

- **Career-based** such as interning for a graphic design firm, assisting a photographer, or writing for an online magazine

- **Extracurricular** such as participating on the school yearbook or in an after-school club that helps the community develop multimedia projects.

- **Service** such as volunteering to produce newsletters or presentations for a nursing home, the humane society, or another community organization.

Recall Identify two career pathways within the Arts, Audio/Video Technology, and Communications cluster.

Academic Focus

Mathematics

Calculate Average Salaries Total job earnings include both salary and benefits, such as paid vacations and health insurance. When considering a job, evaluate the total compensation package. Imagine you have two offers. The first job pays $40,500 a year, plus benefits worth $95 per month. The second offers $38,200 a year, plus $115 per month in benefits. Which job has a higher value?

NCTM Data Analysis and Probability Select and use appropriate statistical methods to analyze data.

Pick a Career

Which multimedia career is right for you?

Conducting a self-assessment can help you define your skills, aptitudes, interests, personality, and values. This information, in turn, can help you target a career for further research. Use self-assessment checklists similar to the ones shown in Figure 11.4 to see which of the multimedia career clusters might suit you. Remember that you do not need to answer yes to every item in the lists in order to have an interest or aptitude for those careers.

Self-assessments can also help you plan your career path and set goals for your future. In fact, you can use assessments to help you determine the training, skills, and leadership requirements for various career opportunities. Self-assessments can be taken periodically to assess your progress toward meeting your career goals. The Career Skills Handbook at the end of this book can also assist you in planning your career goals and assessing your progress.

Figure 11.4
Completing a self-assessment can help you choose a career that reflects your skills, interests, and personal qualities. Which career cluster would be appropriate if you enjoy performing?

Multimedia Career Self-Assessments

Self-Assessment 1 (Note all statements that are true for you.)	Self-Assessment 2 (Note all statements that are true for you.)
☑ I am talented in writing, art, photography, or fashion.	☑ I know how to set up computer hardware.
☑ I am interested in the technical aspects of producing films, TV shows, or plays.	☑ I learn new computer software easily.
☑ I would like to inform through broadcasting.	☑ I understand how computer networks operate.
☑ I am skilled at capturing events on video.	☑ I would like to develop interactive media.
☑ I am good at operating or repairing telecommunications equipment.	☑ I am able to explain technical information in easy-to-understand language.
☑ I like to communicate through print and online publications.	☑ I like working with computers.
☑ I want to create computer graphics or animation.	☑ I find technology fascinating.
☑ I appreciate artistic expression.	☑ My mind is logical, organized, and detail-oriented.
☑ I like to work with technology.	☑ I am good at math.
Results: If you checked two or more statements, you are probably suited to the Arts, A/V Technology, and Communications cluster.	**Results:** If you checked two or more statements, you are probably suited to the Information Technology cluster.

YOU TRY IT · Activity 11A Research a Multimedia Career

➊ Identify the career pathway that best reflects your responses to the self-assessments in Figure 11.4. (See Figure 11.1 on page 317 for more information about the pathways associated with the multimedia career clusters.) Also consider any extended learning opportunities you have had.

➋ Research your chosen career pathway to find associated careers.

③ Select a career that appeals to you.

④ With your teacher's permission, go to an online career resource such as the Bureau of Labor and Statistics. The BLS has occupational outlook information that is geared to high school students (see Figure 11.5).

⑤ Search the site for the following information about your chosen career: nature of the work (what is produced or accomplished), work environment (where the work takes place), qualifications (background), earnings (payment and benefits), and **career outlook** (expected chances for finding employment).

⑥ Write a report documenting the information you find. Be sure to properly cite your sources. Proofread and spell-check the final document for any errors in grammar, spelling, typing, or formatting. Save and close the file.

Figure 11.5
The Bureau of Labor and Statistics can be helpful in researching careers.

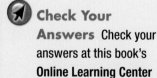 **Reading Check** **Explain** Why is a self-assessment helpful when researching a career?

Section 11.1 After You Read

Review Key Concepts

1. **Describe** the two career clusters that involve multimedia.

2. **List** four types of extended learning opportunities. How are they different?

 **Check Your Answers** Check your answers at this book's **Online Learning Center** through glencoe.com.

Practice Academic Skills

English Language Arts

3. **Predict** With a partner, conduct online research exploring the career outlook for three different multimedia careers over the next five years. Create a presentation to share your findings.

4. **Examine** Using the self-assessment checklists in this section, choose a multimedia career that might interest you. Conduct research and write an essay that summarizes the training, education, and certification requirements that you would still need to pursue for that career.

 **Online Student Manual • glencoe.com**

Go to your Online Student Manual and enter your password to find projects that allow you to practice and apply multimedia skills.

NCTE 8 Use information resources to gather information and create and communicate knowledge.

NCTE 12 Use language to accomplish individual purposes.

SECTION 11.2 Develop Your Multimedia Career

Reading Guide

Before You Read

Get Creative To help you remember the information you read, think of a rhyme for it or set it to music. Your memory device does not have to be carefully crafted, just meaningful to you.

Read to Learn
Key Concepts

- **Examine** the roles of education, training, portfolios, and résumés in preparing for a multimedia career.
- **Evaluate** the importance of transferable employability skills and qualities.
- **Summarize** ways that one can advance in a career.

Main Idea

Preparation is important in getting one's first job in a chosen multimedia career. Employability and career skills then play a critical role in workplace success and advancement.

Content Vocabulary

- ◇ e-portfolio
- ◇ résumé
- ◇ employability skills

Academic Vocabulary

You will find these words in your reading and on your tests. Use the glossary to look up their definitions, if necessary.

- ◆ pursue
- ◆ utilize

Graphic Organizer

As you read, identify five opportunities which can help you advance in your career. Use a tree diagram like the one shown to help you organize your information.

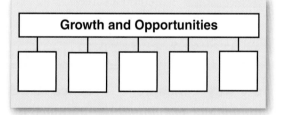
Growth and Opportunities

 Graphic Organizer Go to this book's **Online Learning Center** at glencoe.com to print this graphic organizer.

Academic Standards

 English Language Arts

NCTE 3 Apply strategies to interpret texts.
NCTE 5 Use different writing process elements to communicate effectively.

NCTE 12 Use language to accomplish individual purposes.

NCTE National Council of Teachers of English
NSES National Science Education Standards

NCTM National Council of Teachers of Mathematics
NCSS National Council for the Social Studies

Start Your Career

How can you prepare for and get your first job in multimedia?

Getting your first job in multimedia depends largely on preparation. You must have the appropriate background and an effective way to present your qualifications.

Education and Training

Most careers in multimedia production require education, training, or professional certification after high school. Depending on the career, you might **pursue**, or work toward, studies in trade school, technical school, college, university, or distance-learning courses. For example, a graphic artist might have a degree or certificate in graphic design from a college, art school, or technical school. A computer programmer might have in-person or online training in programming languages. Based on your research, make a plan to get the education and training you need for your chosen career.

Portfolio and Résumé

When you begin your job search, you will need a portfolio and a résumé. A portfolio is a collection of representative pieces that a creative professional can show to potential customers or employers. An **e-portfolio** showcases digital samples of your work. You might create an e-portfolio using Web design, presentation, or multimedia authoring software. An e-portfolio might include (or link to) examples of text, graphics, animation, audio, video, or completed multimedia productions such as Web sites or online ads. Refer to this book's Career Skills Handbook to learn more about building a college and career portfolio.

Your **résumé** includes important information, such as a brief account of your employment qualifications. You might use a résumé to answer a classified ad, provide information not covered by a job application, or let an interesting company know about you and your interest in the organization. A résumé can be organized by job or by skill area.

Activity 11B Create a Résumé

1. Open your word processing software.

2. Format your document with a 1-inch margin. Use a standard font at 10 to 12 pts. (14 pts. for heads). Limit the résumé to one page.

3. Include the information listed in Figure 11.6. If needed, you can make up information that is consistent with the background for your chosen career.

Résumé Content Checklist

- ☑ Personal contact information
- ☑ Career objective
- ☑ Education
- ☑ Work experience
- ☑ Skills
- ☑ Awards and achievements
- ☑ Hobbies and interests (optional)
- ☑ References (optional)

As You Read

Connect What content and information might you include in an e-portfolio?

Academic Focus

English Language Arts

Visualize Information
Format your career plan as a time line. Estimate how long each goal will take to achieve. Write a paragraph that explains why it is important to visualize a career plan

NCTE 5 Use different writing process elements to communicate effectively.

YOU TRY IT

Figure 11.6
Your résumé should include the basic sections shown here, which employers expect to see.

④ Proofread and spell-check the final document for any errors in grammar, spelling, typing, or formatting.

⑤ Save and close the file.

Finding Your First Job

To get a job in multimedia production, you might follow the typical steps shown here. Refer to the Career Skills Handbook in the back of the book for more details.

1. Locate job opportunities, using various resources.

2. Apply for a job, providing a résumé and an introductory cover letter. Cover letters should be specific for each job opportunity.

3. Interview for the job, and follow up after the interview.

4. Evaluate and compare any job offers to find the one that best meets your goals.

Due to the computer-based nature of multimedia jobs, they are more likely to be advertised online than in traditional print publications such as newspapers. Online job sites geared towards multimedia professionals include MultimediaCareers.com, Digital Media Jobs, and Creative Hotlist (see Figure 11.7).

Figure 11.7 ●⟶
Online job sites are a good place to look for job opportunities on the Web. **What are some other resources for finding multimedia-related jobs?**

Job Interviews Many job interviews are conducted on the phone rather than in person. Regardless of how an interview is conducted, you should be completely honest.

Why It's Important

What might happen if you got a job based on false information?

✔ **Reading Check** **Define** What is an e-portfolio?

Succeed in the Workplace

How can you turn a multimedia job into a career?

By improving your skills and taking advantage of growth opportunities, you can advance in your career.

Employability and Career Skills

Employability skills, also called transferable skills, are the general qualities and behaviors of good employees. Some examples include: promptness, making the most productive use of your time, a positive attitude, respect, collaboration and teamwork, and leadership and listening skills. You may get a raise or promotion based on the strength of these skills, which can be transferred between positions and jobs.

Certain basic career skills are specific to success and advancement in multimedia careers.

- Use technical knowledge and skills.
- **Utilize**, or use, technology to create and manipulate information.
- Use critical thinking skills to solve problems creatively.
- Understand roles within teams and systems.

In addition to general career skills and knowledge, each career pathway will require further specific knowledge and skills.

Growth Opportunities

You will encounter various opportunities to grow as an employee in your chosen career. For instance, you might have the chance to attend seminars, continue your education, participate in training, take a leadership role, or work on a team. You should take advantage of these opportunities for growth.

Go Online ACTIVITY
glencoe.com

Cover Letters
Get tips for writing a cover letter and other employment communications at the Online Learning Center. Go to glencoe.com. Choose Activities, then Chapter 11.

Reading Check **Describe** How do employability skills differ from career skills?

Section 11.2 After You Read

Review Key Concepts

1. Summarize the information that should be included on a résumé.

2. List at least three employability skills that can help you advance in your choice of career.

 **Check Your Answers** Check your answers at this book's **Online Learning Center** through glencoe.com.

Practice Academic Skills

English Language Arts

3. **Predict** Write a paragraph in which you identify three types of samples you might find in the e-portfolio of a motion designer. (A motion designer develops motion graphics, commonly combined with audio, for multimedia projects.)

4. **Plan** Create a time line for pursuing your chosen career in multimedia. Include milestones for obtaining the necessary education and training, creating a portfolio, preparing a résumé, and searching for job opportunities. Include a target date for each milestone.

NCTE 3 Apply strategies to interpret texts.

NCTE 5 Use different writing process elements to communicate effectively.

Online Student Manual • glencoe.com

Go to your Online Student Manual and enter your password to find projects that allow you to practice and apply multimedia skills.

Careers & Technology

Leadership Skills

Knowing how to manage people and resources will help you both on and off the job. To be an effective leader, you must have certain qualities.

Qualities of a Leader

Effective leaders share qualities and skills:

- **Communication Skills** Good managers are diplomatic. They avoid offending others, but are direct when giving information.

- **Decision-Making Skills** Managers often have to make unpopular choices. Decision-making is easier when you understand as much as possible about a project, its mission, and the available resources.

- **Relationship Skills** Good leaders learn as much as they can about the responsibilities of colleagues. This knowledge enhances their ability to provide feedback.

- **Trustworthiness** Managing people means motivating and directing them. For these efforts to be successful, people must believe they can trust you. Good leaders are honest, deliver on promises, and do not share information communicated to them privately.

- **Accountability** Good leaders accept responsibility and give credit to those who deserve it.

Organizations can help you develop leadership skills.

Build Leadership Qualities

You can do many things to build and improve your leadership qualities:

- Get involved in classroom or community projects and activities.

- Take business, communications, and management courses. These studies will give you insights into leadership.

- Join organizations that can help you develop leadership skills, such as Business Professionals of America (BPA) and Future Business Leaders of America (FBLA). Participation in these organizations helps to promote development of the skills needed to be successful in the workplace.

Skill Builder

1. **Compare Leadership Qualities** Make a list of leadership qualities. Why are these qualities valuable in leading others? Compare your own skills and characteristics against the list. Which leadership qualities do you still need to build?

2. **Prepare a Presentation** Follow your teacher's instructions to form a team. Each team member should research a different leadership quality. Then work together to build a multimedia presentation about leadership qualities.

Chapter Summary

It is important to plan carefully in order to have a successful career in multimedia production. Becoming familiar with multimedia careers and choosing a suitable career are the first steps. To help you explore and focus on possible careers, the U.S. Department of Education has organized similar careers into broad groups called career clusters. The two career clusters related to multimedia are Information Technology and Arts, Audio/Video (A/V) Technology, and Communications. Extended learning opportunities, such as in-school classes, extracurricular activities, career-based interning, and service experience can help you to choose a multimedia career that is right for you.

Getting your first job in your chosen career takes preparation. This preparation includes building appropriate skills with education, training, and professional certification. It is also important to effectively present your qualifications with a carefully crafted portfolio, résumé, and cover letter. Your employability and career skills are important to your workplace success and advancement.

Vocabulary Review

1. Create a multiple-choice question for each of the content and academic vocabulary words. Each question should contain enough information to help determine the correct answer.

Content Vocabulary

◆ career pathway (p. 323)
◆ career outlook (p. 327)
◆ e-portfolio (p. 327)
◆ résumé (p. 327)
◆ employability skills (p. 328)

Academic Vocabulary

◆ tailor (p. 323)
◆ require (p. 323)
◆ pursue (p. 327)
◆ utilize (p. 329)

Review Key Concepts

2. Identify multimedia career clusters, their pathways, and sample careers.

3. Explain how extended learning opportunities provide insights into careers.

4. Describe how conducting a self-assessment is useful when choosing a career.

5. List aspects of possible career choices that should be researched during career exploration.

6. Examine the roles of education, training, portfolios, and résumés in preparing for a multimedia career.

7. Evaluate the importance of transferable employability skills and qualities.

8. Summarize ways that one can advance in a career.

Critical Thinking

9. **Illustrate** What positive work behaviors enhance employability and job advancement? Use the content in the chapter and the Career Skills Handbook to help you identify at least five behaviors. Then give an example of how each one might help you advance in the workplace. Use a graphic organizer like the one below to organize your information.

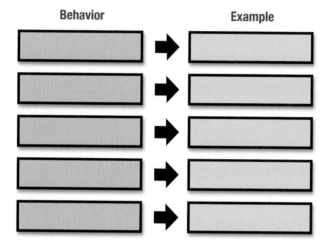

10. **Analyze** Find local career opportunities that are available in the areas of audio/ video technology and communications. Which opportunities would you be most interested in? Explain your answer.

11. **Plan** Choose a multimedia career that you might be interested in pursuing. Then consider the extended learning opportunities discussed in the text. Which of these learning opportunities could you use now to help prepare for your chosen career? Use a time line to illustrate when you could take advantage of these learning opportunities.

12. **Describe** Your friend is interested in the history and evolution of career clusters. She has asked for your help in researching and understanding this topic. With your teacher's permission, use the Internet to research this topic. Write a one-page essay based on your findings.

13. **Explain** Different work industries and career fields use different terminology, often called jargon, or terms that are specific to that industry. For example, the area of computer graphics uses such terminology as vector graphics, dithering, and cropping. Conduct research to find terminology used in the arts, audio/ video technology, and communications cluster of industries. Write at least six terms and their definitions into a graphic organizer such as the one below.

Term	Definition

14. **Compare and Contrast** Visit two job-search Web sites. Examine the features of each site. Then, write a paragraph describing the features the sites have in common and those features which are different. Use bulleted lists where appropriate.

Go Online e-RESOURCES

glencoe.com

Go to the **Online Learning Center** to find additional activities and career resources.

Practice Quizzes Test your knowledge of the material in this chapter.

Career Resources Find out more about careers, including information about résumés, portfolios, and interview and workplace tips.

Academic Connections

NCTE 8 Use information resources to gather information and create and communicate knowledge.

15. Language Arts–Research and Create a Résumé

Employers with job openings often search employment-related Web sites to find electronic résumés that match their needs. An electronic résumé needs to follow the guidelines for a regular résumé.

A. To learn about the different types of résumés, conduct print or online research. Locate at least three different types of résumés and determine which type will work best for you.

B. For your chosen type of résumé, use a table such as this to organize your information. Fill in a description of each component of the résumé. Then add your personal information for each component shown.

C. Use the information in the completed chart to design and create your personal résumé. Edit, proofread, and spell-check your résumé.

COMPONENT	DESCRIPTION	PERSONAL INFORMATION
Identification		
Objective		
Experience		
Education		
References		

Standardized Test Practice

Multiple Choice

Read the paragraph below and then answer the question.

Choosing a career is one of the most important decisions you will ever make because it will affect every aspect of your life. Where you live, your friends and family, and your fitness and health may depend on your career. As you explore a career in multimedia, consider how this information can help you achieve your own career aspirations.

The first step is to ask yourself some questions: What kinds of activities do you like to do? What kind of work do you enjoy? Knowing what you like to do and how your career will fit into a balanced life are important when you are searching for a career.

16. Which statement best summarizes the main idea of the paragraph?

A. A career may affect every aspect of your life.

B. Your health may depend on your career.

C. Multimedia is key to many job opportunities.

D. It might be important to know what you like to do when searching for a career.

Test-Taking Tip Be sure to read all answers, paying attention to words like correct and best. If you are asked to choose the best answer, there may be more than one correct answer from which to choose.

17. Recommend Technology

As head of the interactive media department at a small publishing firm, one of your duties includes staying informed about new technologies in the area of interactive media. You feel that it is time to upgrade some of the technology in your department in order to stay competitive. You decide to research the technologies that have surfaced within the last three years in the area of interactive media and to report your findings and recommendations to your supervisors.

NETS 3c Evaluate and select information sources and digital tools based on the appropriateness to specific tasks.

A. Conduct research into new technologies related to interactive media. Record the name of the technology and a description, and determine whether you would recommend it to your supervisor for purchase for your department.

B. Organize your findings in a table similar to the one shown below.

INTERACTIVE MEDIA TECHNOLOGY		
Technology	Description	Recommendation

18. Give a Presentation to Colleagues

You teach in the graphic design department at the local community college. The college is interested in expanding their offerings in this department and would like to offer classes in the audio/video technology and communications cluster. You have been asked to give a presentation to your department about the feasibility of adding these classes. Your presentation should include information about:

NETS 3d Process data and report results.

- The nature and types of businesses in this cluster, which will allow the college to design classes that will prepare students for a career in this cluster.

- The history and evolution of the various related fields of study in this cluster.

- The cluster's economic base and outlook.

- The interdependence between the technical and artistic sides of this cluster.

Conduct research to decide which classes you would offer and which might not be feasible to add. Then, organize your information and design and create a presentation to give to your colleagues. Be sure to include graphics to enhance the presentation.

19. Identify Leadership Qualities

Follow your teacher's instructions to work with a partner. With your partner, identify and demonstrate leadership skills.

A. Conduct research to create a list of qualities that successful leaders exhibit, such as integrity, communication, and teamwork.

B. With your partner, identify the qualities and provide an example of each quality in action in a multimedia career. Use a graphic organizer such as the one shown to help you organize your information.

C. Work with your partner to create a skit that will demonstrate these leadership skills in action. Decide who will portray the leader and who will portray the team member. Write realistic dialogue for the leader and the team member, and include effective verbal and nonverbal communication skills. Present your skit to the class.

Quality   **Example**

20. Present Employment Opportunities

You have been hired by an employment agency to design a presentation to showcase employment opportunities in the information technology field. They have asked you to focus your research on the area of interactive media.

A. Research and brainstorm ideas for the presentation. Choose five jobs in the area of interactive media that are of personal interest to you. The presentation will consist of seven pages:

- The title page

- A table of contents page that lists five employment opportunities

- One page for a description of each employment opportunity

B. For each employment opportunity, identify the job duties and tasks, as well as the education, job skills, and experience required.

C. Create a storyboard for your presentation. As you create your presentation, keep in mind the elements of art and the principles of visual design. Include the text and information that will appear on each page, as well as descriptions of the graphics you will use.

D. Use presentation software to build a slide show presentation. If possible, include graphics. Edit, proofread, and spell-check your presentation.

NCTE 3 Apply strategies to interpret texts.

NCTE 8 Use information resources to gather information and create and communicate knowledge.

Project 1

NCTE 3 Apply strategies to interpret texts.

Evaluate and Compare Employment Opportunities

English Language Arts It takes skill and practice to evaluate employment opportunities effectively. Taking the time to carefully analyze job opportunities will help to ensure that you choose the right job.

Plan

1. Determine the career pathway, such as visual arts, audio/video technology, or interactive media, in which you would like to find employment.

2. Determine the criteria you will use to evaluate and compare employment opportunities. You might consider criteria such as pay, work schedule, responsibilities, tasks, and commute.

Research

3. Locate newspapers or online employment sites that have job postings in your area of interest. Take notes and be sure to include information regarding the criteria you determined in Step 2.

Create

4. Evaluate and compare the employment opportunities you researched. Create a graphic organizer that displays your evaluation of the employment opportunities.

5. Edit your graphic organizer. Proofread and spell-check the visual for errors.

Project 2

Build a Personal Presentation

NCTE 12 Use language to accomplish individual purposes.

English Language Arts Use your résumé to help promote yourself when trying to get a job. As an applicant for multimedia positions, you can turn your résumé into a multimedia showcase that can be used as part of the portfolio you will be developing in the next project and in the Unit 4 Portfolio Project.

Plan

1. Review and analyze your résumé. Which pieces of it would you want to highlight? Think about how you might use different multimedia elements, including text, graphics, animation, audio, and video, to enhance your résumé and showcase your skills. For example, you might turn your name into a logo.

2. Design a slide show that presents you and your multimedia skills, using the information from your résumé. Be sure to think about consistent elements you will use on all slides.

Create

3. Build your presentation. The first slide should include your name and introductory information, such as how to contact you. Other slides should highlight skills, interests, education, and experience.

Review

4. Edit, proofread, and spell-check your presentation.

Project 3

Develop a Portfolio

English Language Arts A portfolio is a collection of work samples that best demonstrate your skills. When looking for a job in the area of digital and interactive media, an electronic portfolio, or e-portfolio, is an absolute necessity. Prospective employers will want to evaluate the work you have produced.

> **NCTE 5** Use different writing process elements to communicate effectively.

Research

1. Research the role portfolios play in the information technology profession. What do prospective employers expect to learn from a portfolio? What should the portfolio contain? How should the portfolio be delivered?

Create

2. Use the projects you have created in this course to compile a portfolio. Use a table similar to the one below to make sure you include three sample pieces of your work in each of the following areas:

- **Software**—Web design software, presentation software, authoring software, and a variety of utility software.

- **Text**—alignment, lists, text spacing, special formatting, and effects.

- **Graphics**—edited graphics showing dithering, cropping, anti-aliasing, and resizing.

	PIECE 1	PIECE 2	PIECE 3
Software			
Text			
Graphics			
Animation			
Audio & Video			

- **Animation**—frame-based animation, vector animation, rollovers, morphing, 3-D graphics and virtual reality, and 3-D tools.

- **Audio and Video**—streaming audio, audio clips, sound effects, streaming video, and video clips.

Review

3. Share the contents of your portfolio with your teacher and classmates. Ask for their reactions. Do they feel that the samples best show your skills? What changes would they suggest you make to your portfolio?

Revise

4. Based on the feedback from your teacher and classmates, make changes to your portfolio. Proofread and spell-check the contents of your portfolio. You can use this in your Unit 4 Portfolio Project.

Go Online RUBRICS
glencoe.com

Chapter Projects Use the rubrics for these projects to help create and evaluate your work. Go to the **Online Learning Center** at **glencoe.com**. Choose **Rubrics**, then **Chapter 11**.

UNIT 4 Portfolio Project

Create a Digital Portfolio

In this unit, you learned that teamwork is vital when developing multimedia projects. You learned that not only technical skills, but also general employability skills are needed to be successful. In this portfolio project, you will develop a digital portfolio that showcases your skills and talents. Remember that it should draw attention to your ability to be a productive professional in the field of multimedia development.

Project Assignment

In this project, you will:

- Create a digital portfolio that can be implemented as part of a Web site.
- On the home page, list professional information about yourself, including your goals in developing a career in multimedia.
- Create a résumé with a list of your skills, talents, and qualifications. List both multimedia development skills and employability skills.
- Include a page that lists frequently asked questions (and their answers) about you.
- Create a page describing multimedia projects you have developed with links to projects.
- Create at least one graphic and one animation to enhance your site.
- Include a page that emphasizes your role as a team player and the qualities you possess that demonstrate leadership and a positive attitude.

Multimedia Design Skills Behind the Project
Your success in multimedia design will depend on your skills:
- Apply the principles and elements of design.
- Create graphics and animation.
- Properly implement links to external files.
- Demonstrate planning and time-management skills such as project management and storyboard.

Academic Skills Behind the Project
Remember these key academic concepts:

Writing Skills
- Use correct grammar, punctuation, and terminology to write and edit multimedia documents.
- Employ effective verbal and nonverbal communication skills.
- Adapt language for audience, purpose, situation, and intent.

Problem-Solving Skills
- Solve problems and think critically.

English Language Arts

NCTE 4 Use written language to communicate effectively.
NCTE 5 Use different writing process elements to communicate effectively.
NCTE 12 Use language to accomplish individual purposes.

Mathematics

NCTM Problem Solving Apply and adapt a variety of appropriate strategies to solve problems.

STEP 1   Analyze and Plan Your Project

Follow these steps to plan your digital portfolio:

- Develop a list of project goals.

- Describe the target audience and the project's scope.

- Write a mission statement.

STEP 2   Design Your Project

Follow these steps to design your project:

- Create a storyboard.

- Choose a color scheme for the site.

- Choose attractive and readable typefaces and font sizes for the headings and text.

- Create at least one original graphic and one original animation.

STEP 3   Develop Your Project

Follow these steps to develop your project:

- Use the storyboard to create the content.

- Write your résumé. Avoid including personal information.

- Create links for the multimedia project you want to highlight.

- Include a page that explains the value you place on being a team player and the importance of demonstrating leadership and a positive attitude.

STEP 4   Share Your Project

Ask a classmate or trusted adult to review your project.

- Ask for feedback, constructive criticism, and suggestions.

- Encourage your reviewer to ask questions.

STEP 5   Test and Evaluate Your Project

Apply what you have learned about project testing to perform these tasks:

- Write a paragraph describing how you would test your portfolio.

- Use the Portfolio Project Checklist to evaluate your work.

Portfolio Project Checklist

ANALYSIS AND PLANNING

☑ A content plan that includes a mission statement that specifies the site's purpose, goals, and target audience has been written.

☑ A project plan that defines the project's scope has been written.

DESIGN AND DEVELOPMENT

☑ A storyboard has been created that shows the basic layout and contents of the project.

☑ The elements and principles of visual design have been followed.

☑ An appropriate color scheme has been chosen.

☑ All text is complete and clearly and concisely written.

☑ All multimedia elements enhance the site.

☑ Descriptions and links have been included for each project example.

TESTING AND EVALUATION

☑ The testing plan explains that all components will be checked for accuracy, functionality, and consistency.

☑ The project has been reviewed by a classmate or trusted adult and appropriate changes have been made.

 Go Online **RUBRICS**

glencoe.com

Go to this book's **Online Learning Center** at glencoe.com for a rubric you can use to evaluate your final project.

Number and Operations

▶ *Understand numbers, ways of representing numbers, relationships among numbers, and number systems*

Fraction, Decimal, and Percent

A percent is a ratio of a number to 100. To write a percent as a fraction, drop the percent sign, and use the number as the numerator in a fraction with a denominator of 100. Simplify, if possible. For example, $76\% = \frac{76}{100}$, or $\frac{19}{25}$. To write a fraction as a percent, convert it to an equivalent fraction with a denominator of 100. For example, $\frac{3}{4} = \frac{75}{100}$, or 75%. A fraction can be expressed as a percent by first converting the fraction to a decimal (divide the numerator by the denominator) and then converting the decimal to a percent by moving the decimal point two places to the right.

Comparing Numbers on a Number Line

In order to compare and understand the relationship between real numbers in various forms, it is helpful to use a number line. The zero point on a number line is called the origin. The points to the left of the origin are negative, and those to the right are positive. The number line below shows how numbers in fraction, decimal, percent, and integer form can be compared.

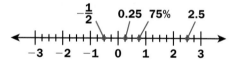

Percents Greater Than 100 and Less Than 1

Percents greater than 100% represent values greater than 1. For example, if the weight of an object is 250% of another, it is 2.5, or $2\frac{1}{2}$, times the weight.

Percents less than 1 represent values less than $\frac{1}{100}$. In other words, 0.1% is one tenth of one percent, which can also be represented in decimal form as 0.001, or in fraction form as $\frac{1}{1,000}$. Similarly, 0.01% is one hundredth of one percent or 0.0001 or $\frac{1}{10,000}$.

Ratio, Rate, and Proportion

A ratio is a comparison of two numbers using division. If a basketball player makes 8 out of 10 free throws, the ratio is written as 8 to 10,

8:10, or $\frac{8}{10}$. Ratios are usually written in simplest form. In simplest form, the ratio 8 out of 10 is 4 to 5, 4:5, or $\frac{4}{5}$. A rate is a ratio of two measurements having different kinds of units—cups per gallon, or miles per hour, for example. When a rate is simplified so that it has a denominator of 1, it is called a unit rate. An example of a unit rate is 9 miles per hour. A proportion is an equation stating that two ratios are equal. $\frac{3}{18} = \frac{13}{78}$ is an example of a proportion. The cross products of a proportion are also equal. $\frac{3}{18} = \frac{13}{78}$ and $3 \times 78 = 18 \times 13$.

Representing Large and Small Numbers

In order to represent large and small numbers, it is important to understand the number system. Our number system is based on 10, and the value of each place is 10 times the value of the place to its right. The value of a digit is the product of a digit and its place value. For instance, in the number 6,400, the 6 has a value of six thousands and the 4 has a value of four hundreds. A place value chart can help you read numbers. In the chart, each group of three digits is called a period. Commas separate the periods: the ones period, the thousands period, the millions period, and so on. Values to the right of the ones period are decimals. By understanding place value you can write very large numbers like 5 billion and more, and very small numbers that are less than 1, like one-tenth.

Scientific Notation

When dealing with very large numbers like 1,500,000, or very small numbers like 0.000015, it is helpful to keep track of their value by writing the numbers in scientific notation. Powers of 10 with positive exponents are used with a decimal between 1 and 10 to express large numbers. The exponent represents the number of places the decimal point is moved to the right. So, 528,000 is written in scientific notation as 5.28×10^5. Powers of 10 with negative exponents are used with a decimal between 1 and 10 to express small numbers. The exponent represents the number of places the decimal point is moved to the left. The number 0.00047 is expressed as 4.7×10^{-4}.

Factor, Multiple, and Prime Factorization

Two or more numbers that are multiplied to form a product are called factors. Divisibility rules can be used to determine whether 2, 3, 4, 5, 6, 8, 9, or 10 are factors of a given number.

Multiples are the products of a given number and various integers.

For example, 8 is a multiple of 4 because $4 \times 2 = 8$. A prime number is a whole number that has exactly two factors: 1 and itself. A composite number is a whole number that has more than two factors. Zero and 1 are neither prime nor composite. A composite number can be expressed as the product of its prime factors. The prime factorization of 40 is $2 \times 2 \times 2 \times 5$, or $2^3 \times 5$. The numbers 2 and 5 are prime numbers.

Integers

A negative number is a number less than zero. Negative numbers like -8, positive numbers like $+6$, and zero are members of the set of integers. Integers can be represented as points on a number line. A set of integers can be written $\{..., -3, -2, -1, 0, 1, 2, 3, ...\}$ where ... means continues indefinitely.

Real, Rational, and Irrational Numbers

The real number system is made up of the sets of rational and irrational numbers. Rational numbers are numbers that can be written in the form $\frac{a}{b}$ where a and b are integers and $b \neq 0$. Examples are 0.45, $\frac{1}{2}$, and $\sqrt{36}$. Irrational numbers are non-repeating, non-terminating decimals. Examples are $\sqrt{71}$, π, and $0.020020002...$.

Complex and Imaginary Numbers

A complex number is a mathematical expression with a real number element and an imaginary number element. Imaginary numbers are multiples of i, the imaginary square root of -1. Complex numbers are represented by $a + bi$, where a and b are real numbers and i represents the imaginary element. When a quadratic equation does not have a real number solution, the solution can be represented by a complex number. Like real numbers, complex numbers can be added, subtracted, multiplied, and divided.

Vectors and Matrices

A matrix is a set of numbers or elements arranged in rows and columns to form a rectangle. The number of rows is represented by m and the number of columns is represented by n. To describe the number of rows and columns in a matrix, list the number of rows first using the format $m \times n$. Matrix A is a 3×3 matrix because it has 3 rows and 3 columns. To name

an element of a matrix, the letter i is used to denote the row and j is used to denote the column, and the element is labeled in the form $a_{i,j}$. In matrix A below, $a_{3,2}$ is 4.

$$\text{Matrix A} = \begin{pmatrix} 1 & 3 & 5 \\ 0 & 6 & 8 \\ 3 & 4 & 5 \end{pmatrix}$$

A vector is a matrix with only one column or row of elements. A transposed column vector, or a column vector turned on its side, is a row vector. In the example below, row vector b' is the transpose of column vector b.

$$b = \begin{pmatrix} 1 \\ 2 \\ 3 \\ 4 \end{pmatrix}$$

$$b = (1 \quad 2 \quad 3 \quad 4)$$

▶ Understand meanings of operations and how they relate to one another

Properties of Addition and Multiplication

Properties are statements that are true for any numbers. For example, $3 + 8$ is the same as $8 + 3$ because each expression equals 11. This illustrates the Commutative Property of Addition. Likewise, $3 \times 8 = 8 \times 3$ illustrates the Commutative Property of Multiplication.

When evaluating expressions, it is often helpful to group or associate the numbers. The Associative Property says that the way in which numbers are grouped when added or multiplied does not change the sum or product. The following properties are also true:

- **Additive Identity Property:** When 0 is added to any number, the sum is the number.

- **Multiplicative Identity Property:** When any number is multiplied by 1, the product is the number.

- **Multiplicative Property of Zero:** When any number is multiplied by 0, the product is 0.

Rational Numbers

A number that can be written as a fraction is called a rational number. Terminating and repeating decimals are rational numbers because both can be written as fractions. Decimals that are neither terminating nor repeating are called irrational numbers because they cannot be written as fractions.

Terminating decimals can be converted to fractions by placing the number (without the decimal point) in the numerator. Count the number of places to the right of the decimal point, and in the denominator, place a 1 followed by a number of zeros equal to the number of places that you counted. The fraction can then be reduced to its simplest form.

Writing a Fraction as a Decimal

Any fraction $\frac{a}{b}$, where $b \neq 0$, can be written as a decimal by dividing the numerator by the denominator. So, $\frac{a}{b} = a \div b$. If the division ends, or terminates, when the remainder is zero, the decimal is a terminating decimal. Not all fractions can be written as terminating decimals. Some have a repeating decimal. A bar indicates that the decimal repeats forever. For example, the fraction $\frac{4}{9}$ can be converted to a repeating decimal, 0.4.

Adding and Subtracting Like Fractions

Fractions with the same denominator are called like fractions. To add like fractions, add the numerators and write the sum over the denominator. To add mixed numbers with like fractions, add the whole numbers and fractions separately, adding the numerators of the fractions, then simplifying if necessary. The rule for subtracting fractions with like denominators is similar to the rule for adding. The numerators can be subtracted and the difference written over the denominator. Mixed numbers are written as improper fractions before subtracting. These same rules apply to adding or subtracting like algebraic fractions. An algebraic fraction is a fraction that contains one or more variables in the numerator or denominator.

Adding and Subtracting Unlike Fractions

Fractions with different denominators are called unlike fractions. The least common multiple of the denominators is used to rename the fractions with a common denominator. After a common denominator is found, the numerators can then be added or subtracted. To add mixed numbers with unlike fractions, rename the mixed numbers as improper fractions. Then find a common denominator, add the numerators, and simplify the answer.

Multiplying Rational Numbers

To multiply fractions, multiply the numerators and multiply the denominators. If the numerators and denominators have common factors, they can be simplified before multiplication.

If the fractions have different signs, then the product will be negative. Mixed numbers can be multiplied in the same manner, after first renaming them as improper fractions. Algebraic fractions may be multiplied using the same method described above.

Dividing Rational Numbers

To divide a number by a rational number (a fraction, for example), multiply the first number by the multiplicative inverse of the second. Two numbers whose product is 1 are called multiplicative inverses, or reciprocals. $\frac{7}{4} \times \frac{4}{7} = 1$. When dividing by a mixed number, first rename it as an improper fraction, and then multiply by its multiplicative inverse.

Adding Integers

To add integers with the same sign, add their absolute values. The sum takes the same sign as the addends. An addend is a number that is added to another number (the augend). The equation $-5 + (-2) = -7$ is an example of adding two integers with the same sign. To add integers with different signs, subtract their absolute values. The sum takes the same sign as the addend with the greater absolute value.

Subtracting Integers

The rules for adding integers are extended to the subtraction of integers. To subtract an integer, add its additive inverse. For example, to find the difference $2 - 5$, add the additive inverse of 5 to 2: $2 + (-5) = -3$. The rule for subtracting integers can be used to solve real-world problems and to evaluate algebraic expressions.

Additive Inverse Property

Two numbers with the same absolute value but different signs are called opposites. For example, −4 and 4 are opposites. An integer and its opposite are also called additive inverses. The Additive Inverse Property says that the sum of any number and its additive inverse is zero. The Commutative, Associative, and Identity Properties also apply to integers. These properties help when adding more than two integers.

Absolute Value

In mathematics, when two integers on a number line are on opposite sides of zero, and they are the same distance from zero, they have the same absolute value. The symbol for absolute value is two vertical bars on either side of the number. For example, $|{-5}| = 5$.

Multiplying Integers

Since multiplication is repeated addition, $3(-7)$ means that -7 is used as an addend 3 times. By the Commutative Property of Multiplication, $3(-7) = -7(3)$. The product of two integers with different signs is always negative. The product of two integers with the same sign is always positive.

Dividing Integers

The quotient of two integers can be found by dividing the numbers using their absolute values. The quotient of two integers with the same sign is positive, and the quotient of two integers with a different sign is negative. $-12 \div (-4) = 3$ and $12 \div (-4) = -3$. The division of integers is used in statistics to find the average, or mean, of a set of data. When finding the mean of a set of numbers, find the sum of the numbers, and then divide by the number in the set.

Adding and Multiplying Vectors and Matrices

In order to add two matrices together, they must have the same number of rows and columns. In matrix addition, the corresponding elements are added to each other. In other words $(a + b)_{ij} = a_{ij} + b_{ij}$. For example,

$$\begin{pmatrix} 1 & 2 \\ 2 & 1 \end{pmatrix} + \begin{pmatrix} 3 & 6 \\ 0 & 1 \end{pmatrix} = \begin{pmatrix} 1+3 & 2+6 \\ 2+0 & 1+1 \end{pmatrix} = \begin{pmatrix} 4 & 8 \\ 2 & 2 \end{pmatrix}$$

Matrix multiplication requires that the number of elements in each row in the first matrix is equal to the number of elements in each column in the second. The elements of the first row of the first matrix are multiplied by the corresponding elements of the first column of the second matrix and then added together to get the first element of the product matrix. To get the second element, the elements in the first row of the first matrix are multiplied by the corresponding elements in the second column of the second matrix then added, and so on, until every row of the first matrix is multiplied by every column of the second. See the example below.

$$\begin{pmatrix} 1 & 2 \\ 3 & 4 \end{pmatrix} \times \begin{pmatrix} 3 & 6 \\ 0 & 1 \end{pmatrix} = \begin{pmatrix} (1 \times 3)+(2 \times 0) & (1 \times 6)+(2 \times 1) \\ (3 \times 3)+(4 \times 0) & (3 \times 6)+(4 \times 1) \end{pmatrix} = \begin{pmatrix} 3 & 8 \\ 9 & 22 \end{pmatrix}$$

Vector addition and multiplication are performed in the same way, but there is only one column and one row.

Permutations and Combinations

Permutations and combinations are used to determine the number of possible outcomes in different situations. An arrangement, listing, or pattern in which order is important is called a permutation. The symbol $P(6, 3)$ represents the number of permutations of 6 things taken 3 at a time. For $P(6, 3)$, there are $6 \times 5 \times 4$ or 120 possible outcomes. An arrangement or listing where order is not important is called a combination. The symbol $C(10, 5)$ represents the number of combinations of 10 things taken 5 at a time. For $C(10, 5)$, there are $(10 \times 9 \times 8 \times 7 \times 6) \div (5 \times 4 \times 3 \times 2 \times 1)$ or 252 possible outcomes.

Powers and Exponents

An expression such as $3 \times 3 \times 3 \times 3$ can be written as a power. A power has two parts, a base and an exponent. $3 \times 3 \times 3 \times 3 = 3^4$. The base is the number that is multiplied (3). The exponent tells how many times the base is used as a factor (4 times). Numbers and variables can be written using exponents. For example, $8 \times 8 \times 8 \times m \times m \times m \times m \times m$ can be expressed $8^3 m^5$. Exponents also can be used with place value to express numbers in expanded form. Using this method, 1,462 can be written as $(1 \times 10^3) + (4 \times 10^2) + (6 \times 10^1) + (2 \times 10^0)$.

Squares and Square Roots

The square root of a number is one of two equal factors of a number. Every positive number has both a positive and a negative square root. For example, since $8 \times 8 = 64$, 8 is a square root of 64. Since $(-8) \times (-8) = 64$, -8 is also a square root of 64. The notation $\sqrt{}$ indicates the positive square root, $-\sqrt{}$ indicates the negative square root, and $\pm\sqrt{}$ indicates both square roots. For example, $\sqrt{81} = 9$, $-\sqrt{49} = -7$, and $\pm\sqrt{4} = \pm2$. The square root of a negative number is an imaginary number because any two factors of a negative number must have different signs, and are therefore not equivalent.

Logarithm

A logarithm is the inverse of exponentiation. The logarithm of a number x in base b is equal to the number n. Therefore, $b^n = x$ and $\log b x = n$. For example, $\log_4(64) = 3$ because $4^3 = 64$. The most commonly used bases for logarithms are 10, the common logarithm; 2, the binary logarithm; and the constant e, the natural logarithm (also called $ln(x)$ instead of $\log_e(x)$). Following is a list of some of the rules of logarithms that are important to understand if you are going to use them.

$$\log_b(xy) = \log_b(x) + \log_b(y)$$
$$\log_b\frac{x}{y} = \log_b(x) - \log_b(y)$$
$$\log_b\frac{1}{x} = -\log_b(x)$$
$$\log_b(x)y = y\log_b(x)$$

▶ Compute fluently and make reasonable estimates

Estimation by Rounding
When rounding numbers, look at the digit to the right of the place to which you are rounding. If the digit is 5 or greater, round up. If it is less than 5, round down. For example, to round 65,137 to the nearest hundred, look at the number in the tens place. Since 3 is less than 5, round down to 65,100. To round the same number to the nearest ten thousandth, look at the number in the thousandths place. Since it is 5, round up to 70,000.

Finding Equivalent Ratios
Equivalent ratios have the same meaning. Just like finding equivalent fractions, to find an equivalent ratio, multiply or divide both sides by the same number. For example, you can multiply 7 by both sides of the ratio 6:8 to get 42:56. Instead, you can also divide both sides of the same ratio by 2 to get 3:4. Find the simplest form of a ratio by dividing to find equivalent ratios until you can't go any further without going into decimals. So, 160:240 in simplest form is 2:3. To write a ratio in the form *1:n,* divide both sides by the left-hand number. In other words, to change 8:20 to *1:n,* divide both sides by 8 to get 1:2.5.

Front-End Estimation
Front-end estimation can be used to quickly estimate sums and differences before adding or subtracting. To use this technique, add or subtract just the digits of the two highest place values, and replace the other place values with zero. This will give you an estimation of the solution of a problem. For example, 93,471 − 22,825 can be changed to 93,000 − 22,000 or 71,000. This estimate can be compared to your final answer to judge its correctness.

Judging Reasonableness
When solving an equation, it is important to check your work by considering how reasonable your answer is. For example, consider the equation $9\frac{3}{4} \times 4\frac{1}{3}$. Since $9\frac{3}{4}$ is between 9 and 10 and $4\frac{1}{3}$ is between 4 and 5, only values that are between 9×4 or 36 and 10×5 or 50 will be reasonable. You can also use front-end estimation,

or you can round and estimate a reasonable answer. In the equation 73×25, you can round and solve to estimate a reasonable answer to be near 70×30 or 2,100.

Algebra

▶ Understand patterns, relations, and functions

Relation
A relation is a generalization comparing sets of ordered pairs for an equation or inequality such as $x = y + 1$ or $x > y$. The first element in each pair, the x values, forms the domain. The second element in each pair, the y values, forms the range.

Function
A function is a special relation in which each member of the domain is paired with exactly one member in the range. Functions may be represented using ordered pairs, tables, or graphs. One way to determine whether a relation is a function is to use the vertical line test. Using an object to represent a vertical line, move the object from left to right across the graph. If, for each value of x in the domain, the object passes through no more than one point on the graph, then the graph represents a function.

Linear and Nonlinear Functions
Linear functions have graphs that are straight lines. These graphs represent constant rates of change. In other words, the slope between any two pairs of points on the graph is the same. Nonlinear functions do not have constant rates of change. The slope changes along these graphs. Therefore, the graphs of nonlinear functions are *not* straight lines. Graphs of curves represent nonlinear functions. The equation for a linear function can be written in the form $y = mx + b$, where m represents the constant rate of change, or the slope. Therefore, you can determine whether a function is linear by looking at the equation. For example, the equation $y = \frac{3}{x}$ is nonlinear because x is in the denominator and the equation cannot be written in the form $y = mx + b$. A nonlinear function does not increase or decrease at a constant rate. You can check this by using a table and finding the increase or decrease in y for each regular increase in x. For example, if for each increase in x by 2, y does not increase or decrease the same amount each time, the function is nonlinear.

Linear Equations in Two Variables

In a linear equation with two variables, such as $y = x - 3$, the variables appear in separate terms and neither variable contains an exponent other than 1. The graphs of all linear equations are straight lines. All points on a line are solutions of the equation that is graphed.

Quadratic and Cubic Functions

A quadratic function is a polynomial equation of the second degree, generally expressed as $ax^2 + bx + c = 0$, where a, b, and c are real numbers and a is not equal to zero. Similarly, a cubic function is a polynomial equation of the third degree, usually expressed as $ax^3 + bx^2 + cx + d = 0$. Quadratic functions can be graphed using an equation or a table of values. For example, to graph $y = 3x^2 + 1$, substitute the values -1, -0.5, 0, 0.5, and 1 for x to yield the point coordinates $(-1, 4)$, $(-0.5, 1.75)$, $(0, 1)$, $(0.5, 1.75)$, and $(1, 4)$. Plot these points on a coordinate grid and connect the points in the form of a parabola. Cubic functions also can be graphed by making a table of values. The points of a cubic function from a curve. There is one point at which the curve changes from opening upward to opening downward, or vice versa, called the point of inflection.

Slope

Slope is the ratio of the rise, or vertical change, to the run, or horizontal change of a line: slope = rise/run. Slope (m) is the same for any two points on a straight line and can be found by using the coordinates of any two points on the line:

$$m = \frac{y_2 - y_1}{x_2 - x_1}, \text{ where } x_2 \neq x_1$$

Asymptotes

An asymptote is a straight line that a curve approaches but never actually meets or crosses. Theoretically, the asymptote meets the curve at infinity. For example, in the function $f(x) = \frac{1}{x}$, two asymptotes are being approached: the line $y = 0$ and $x = 0$. See the graph of the function below.

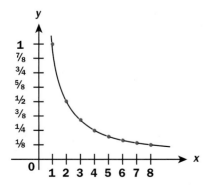

Represent and analyze mathematical situations and structures using algebraic symbols

Variables and Expressions

Algebra is a language of symbols. A variable is a placeholder for a changing value. Any letter, such as x, can be used as a variable. Expressions such as $x + 2$ and $4x$ are algebraic expressions because they represent sums and/or products of variables and numbers. Usually, mathematicians avoid the use of i and e for variables because they have other mathematical meanings ($i = \sqrt{-1}$ and e is used with natural logarithms). To evaluate an algebraic expression, replace the variable or variables with known values, and then solve using order of operations. Translate verbal phrases into algebraic expressions by first defining a variable: Choose a variable and a quantity for the variable to represent. In this way, algebraic expressions can be used to represent real-world situations.

Constant and Coefficient

A constant is a fixed value unlike a variable, which can change. Constants are usually represented by numbers, but they can also be represented by symbols. For example, π is a symbolic representation of the value $3.1415\dots$. A coefficient is a constant by which a variable or other object is multiplied. For example, in the expression $7x^2 + 5x + 9$, the coefficient of x^2 is 7 and the coefficient of x is 5. The number 9 is a constant and not a coefficient.

Monomial and Polynomial

A monomial is a number, a variable, or a product of numbers and/or variables such as 3×4. An algebraic expression that contains one or more monomials is called a polynomial. In a polynomial, there are no terms with variables in the denominator and no terms with variables under a radical sign. Polynomials can be classified by the number of terms contained in the expression. Therefore, a polynomial with two terms is called a binomial ($z^2 - 1$), and a polynomial with three terms is called a trinomial ($2y^3 + 4y^2 - y$). Polynomials also can be classified by their degrees. The degree of a monomial is the sum of the exponents of its variables. The degree of a nonzero constant such as 6 or 10 is 0. The constant 0 has no degree. For example, the monomial $4b^5c^2$ had a degree of 7. The degree of a polynomial is the same as that of the term with the greatest degree. For example, the polynomial $3x^4 - 2y^3 + 4y^2 - y$ has a degree of 4.

Equation

An equation is a mathematical sentence that states that two expressions are equal. The two expressions in an equation are always separated by an equal sign. When solving for a variable in an equation, you must perform the same operations on both sides of the equation in order for the mathematical sentence to remain true.

Solving Equations with Variables

To solve equations with variables on both sides, use the Addition or Subtraction Property of Equality to write an equivalent equation with the variables on the same side. For example, to solve $5x - 8 = 3x$, subtract $3x$ from each side to get $2x - 8 = 0$. Then add 8 to each side to get $2x = 8$. Finally, divide each side by 2 to find that $x = 4$.

Solving Equations with Grouping Symbols

Equations often contain grouping symbols such as parentheses or brackets. The first step in solving these equations is to use the Distributive Property to remove the grouping symbols. For example $5(x + 2) = 25$ can be changed to $5x + 10 = 25$, and then solved to find that $x = 3$.

Some equations have no solution. That is, there is no value of the variable that results in a true sentence. For such an equation, the solution set is called the null or empty set, and is represented by the symbol $\varnothing$ or {}. Other equations may have every number as the solution. An equation that is true for every value of the variable is called the identity.

Inequality

A mathematical sentence that contains the symbols < (less than), > (greater than), ≤ (less than or equal to), or ≥ (greater than or equal to) is called an inequality. For example, the statement that it is legal to drive 55 miles per hour or slower on a stretch of the highway can be shown by the sentence $s \leq 55$. Inequalities with variables are called open sentences. When a variable is replaced with a number, the inequality may be true or false.

Solving Inequalities

Solving an inequality means finding values for the variable that make the inequality true. Just as with equations, when you add or subtract

the same number from each side of an inequality, the inequality remains true. For example, if you add 5 to each side of the inequality $3x < 6$, the resulting inequality $3x + 5 < 11$ is also true. Adding or subtracting the same number from each side of an inequality does not affect the inequality sign. When multiplying or dividing each side of an inequality by the same positive number, the inequality remains true. In such cases, the inequality symbol does not change. When multiplying or dividing each side of an inequality by a negative number, the inequality symbol must be reversed. For example, when dividing each side of the inequality $-4x \geq -8$ by -2, the inequality sign must be changed to ≤ for the resulting inequality, $2x \leq 4$, to be true. Since the solutions to an inequality include all rational numbers satisfying it, inequalities have an infinite number of solutions.

Representing Inequalities on a Number Line

The solutions of inequalities can be graphed on a number line. For example, if the solution of an inequality is $x < 5$, start an arrow at 5 on the number line, and continue the arrow to the left to show all values less than 5 as the solution. Put an open circle at 5 to show that the point 5 is *not* included in the graph. Use a closed circle when graphing solutions that are greater than or equal to, or less than or equal to, a number.

Order of Operations

Solving a problem may involve using more than one operation. The answer can depend on the order in which you do the operations. To make sure that there is just one answer to a series of computations, mathematicians have agreed upon an order in which to do the operations. First simplify within the parentheses, often called graphing symbols, and then evaluate any exponents. Then multiply and divide from left to right, and finally add and subtract from left to right.

Parametric Equations

Given an equation with more than one unknown, a statistician can draw conclusions about those unknown quantities through the use of parameters, independent variables that the statistician already knows something about. For example, you can find the velocity of an object if you make some assumptions about distance and time parameters.

Recursive Equations

In recursive equations, every value is determined by the previous value. You must first plug an initial value into the equation to get the first value, and then you can use the first value to determine the next one, and so on. For example, in order to determine what the population of pigeons will be in New York City in three years, you can use an equation with the birth, death, immigration, and emigration rates of the birds. Input the current population size into the equation to determine next year's population size, then repeat until you have calculated the value for which you are looking.

▶ Use mathematical models to represent and understand quantitative relationships

Solving Systems of Equations

Two or more equations together are called a system of equations. A system of equations can have one solution, no solution, or infinitely many solutions. One method for solving a system of equations is to graph the equations on the same coordinate plane. The coordinates of the point where the graphs intersect is the solution. In other words, the solution of a system is the ordered pair that is a solution of all equations. A more accurate way to solve a system of two equations is by using a method called substitution. Write both equations in terms of y. Replace y in the first equation with the right side of the second equation. Check the solution by graphing. You can solve a system of three equations using matrix algebra.

Graphing Inequalities

To graph an inequality, first graph the related equation, which is the boundary. All points in the shaded region are solutions of the inequality. If an inequality contains the symbol $\leq$ or $\geq$, then use a solid line to indicate that the boundary is included in the graph. If an inequality contains the symbol $<$ or $>$, then use a dashed line to indicate that the boundary is not included in the graph.

▶ Analyze change in various contexts

Rate of Change

A change in one quantity with respect to another quantity is called the rate of change. Rates of change can be described using slope:

$$\text{slope} = \frac{\text{change in } y}{\text{change in } x}$$

You can find rates of change from an equation, a table, or a graph. A special type of linear equation that describes rate of change is called a direct variation. The graph of a direct variation always passes through the origin and represents a proportional situation. In the equation $y = kx$, k is called the constant of variation. It is the slope, or rate of change. As x increases in value, y increases or decreases at a constant rate k, or y varies directly with x. Another way to say this is that y is directly proportional to x. The direct variation $y = kx$ also can be written as $k = \frac{y}{x}$. In this form, you can see that the ratio of y to x is the same for any corresponding values of y and x.

Slope-Intercept Form

Equations written as $y = mx + b$, where m is the slope and b is the y-intercept, are linear equations in slope-intercept form. For example, the graph of $y = 5x - 6$ is a line that has a slope of 5 and crosses the y-axis at $(0, -6)$. Sometimes you must first write an equation in slope-intercept form before finding the slope and y-intercept. For example, the equation $2x + 3y = 15$ can be expressed in slope-intercept form by subtracting $2x$ from each side and then dividing by 3: $y = -\frac{2}{3}x + 5$, revealing a slope of $-\frac{2}{3}$ and a y-intercept of 5. You can use the slope-intercept form of an equation to graph a line easily. Graph the y-intercept and use the slope to find another point on the line, then connect the two points with a line. Analyze characteristics and properties of two- and three-dimensional geometric shapes and develop mathematical arguments about geometric relationships

Geometry

▶ Analyze characteristics and properties of two- and three-dimensional geometric shapes and develop mathematical arguments about geometric relationships

Angles

Two rays that have the same endpoint form an angle. The common endpoint is called the vertex, and the two rays that make up the angle are called the sides of the angle. The most common unit of measure for angles is the degree. Protractors can be used to measure angles or to draw an angle of a given measure. Angles can be classified by their degree measure. Acute angles have measures less than 90° but greater than 0°. Obtuse angles have measures greater than 90° but less than 180°. Right angles have measures of 90°.

Triangles

A triangle is a figure formed by three line segments that intersect only at their endpoints. The sum of the measures of the angles of a triangle is 180°. Triangles can be classified by their angles. An acute triangle contains all acute angles. An obtuse triangle has one obtuse angle. A right triangle has one right angle. Triangles can also be classified by their sides. A scalene triangle has no congruent sides. An isosceles triangle has at least two congruent sides. In an equilateral triangle all sides are congruent.

Quadrilaterals

A quadrilateral is a closed figure with four sides and four vertices. The segments of a quadrilateral intersect only at their endpoints. Quadrilaterals can be separated into two triangles. Since the sum of the interior angles of all triangles totals 180°, the measures of the interior angles of a quadrilateral equal 360°. Quadrilaterals are classified according to their characteristics, and include trapezoids, parallelograms, rectangles, squares, and rhombuses.

Two-Dimensional Figures

A two-dimensional figure exists within a plane and has only the dimensions of length and width. Examples of two-dimensional figures include circles and polygons. Polygons are figures that have three or more angles, including triangles, quadrilaterals, pentagons, hexagons, and many more. The sum of the angles of any polygon totals at least 180° (triangle), and each additional side adds 180° to the measure of the first three angles. The sum of the angles of a quadrilateral, for example, is 360°. The sum of the angles of a pentagon is 540°.

Three-Dimensional Figures

A plane is a two-dimensional flat surface that extends in all directions. Intersecting planes can form the edges and vertices of three-dimensional figures or solids. A polyhedron is a solid with flat surfaces that are polygons. Polyhedrons are composed of faces, edges, and vertices and are differentiated by their shape and by their number of bases. Skew lines are lines that lie in different planes. They are neither intersecting nor parallel.

Congruence

Figures that have the same size and shape are congruent. The parts of congruent triangles that match are called corresponding parts. Congruence statements are used to identify corresponding parts of congruent triangles. When writing a congruence statement, the letters must be written so that corresponding vertices appear in the same order. Corresponding parts can be used to find the measures of angles and sides in a figure that is congruent to a figure with known measures.

Similarity

If two figures have the same shape but not the same size they are called similar figures. For example, the triangles below are similar, so angles A, B, and C have the same measurements as angles D, E, and F, respectively. However, segments AB, BC, and CA do not have the same measurements as segments DE, EF, and FD, but the measures of the sides are proportional.

For example, $\dfrac{\overline{AB}}{\overline{DE}} = \dfrac{\overline{BC}}{\overline{EF}} = \dfrac{\overline{CA}}{\overline{FD}}$.

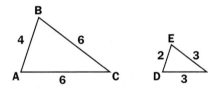

Solid figures are considered to be similar if they have the same shape and their corresponding linear measures are proportional. As with two-dimensional figures, they can be tested for similarity by comparing corresponding measures. If the compared ratios are proportional, then the figures are similar solids. Missing measures of similar solids can also be determined by using proportions.

The Pythagorean Theorem

The sides that are adjacent to a right angle are called legs. The side opposite the right angle is the hypotenuse.

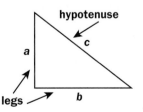

The Pythagorean Theorem describes the relationship between the lengths of the legs a and b and the hypotenuse c. It states that if a triangle is a right triangle, then the square of the length of the hypotenuse is equal to the sum of the squares of the lengths of the legs. In symbols, $c^2 = a^2 + b^2$.

Sine, Cosine, and Tangent Ratios

Trigonometry is the study of the properties of triangles. A trigonometric ratio is a ratio of the lengths of two sides of a right triangle. The most common trigonometric ratios are the sine, cosine, and tangent ratios. These ratios are abbreviated as *sin*, *cos*, and *tan*, respectively.

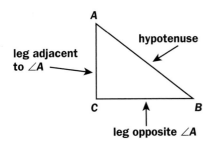

If $\angle A$ is an acute angle of a right triangle, then

$$sin\ \angle A = \frac{\text{measure of leg opposite } \angle A}{\text{measure of hypotenuse}},$$

$$cos\ \angle A = \frac{\text{measure of leg adjacent to } \angle A}{\text{measure of hypotenuse}}, \text{ and}$$

$$tan\ \angle A = \frac{\text{measure of leg opposite } \angle A}{\text{measure of leg adjacent to } \angle A}.$$

▶ Specify locations and describe spatial relationships using coordinate geometry and other representational systems

Polygons

A polygon is a simple, closed figure formed by three or more line segments. The line segments meet only at their endpoints. The points of intersection are called vertices, and the line segments are called sides. Polygons are classified by the number if sides they have. The diagonals of a polygon divide the polygon into triangles. The number of triangles formed is two less than the number of sides. To find the sum of the mea-

sures of the interior angles of any polygon, multiply the number of triangles within the polygon by 180. That is, if n equals the number of sides, then $(n - 2)$ 180 gives the sum of the measures of the polygon's interior angles.

Cartesian Coordinates

In the Cartesian coordinate system, the y-axis extends above and below the origin and the x-axis extends to the right and left of the origin, which is the point at which the x- and y-axes intersect. Numbers below and to the left of the origin are negative. A point graphed on the coordinate grid is said to have an x-coordinate and a y-coordinate. For example, the point $(1,-2)$ has as its x-coordinate the number 1, and has as its y-coordinate the number -2. This point is graphed by locating the position on the grid that is 1 unit to the right of the origin and 2 units below the origin.

The x-axis and the y-axis separate the coordinate plane into four regions, called quadrants. The axes and points located on the axes themselves are not located in any of the quadrants. The quadrants are labeled I to IV, starting in the upper right and proceeding counterclockwise. In quadrant I, both coordinates are positive. In quadrant II, the x-coordinate is negative and the y-coordinate is positive. In quadrant III, both coordinates are negative. In quadrant IV, the x-coordinate is positive and the y-coordinate is negative. A coordinate graph can be used to show algebraic relationships among numbers.

▶ Apply transformations and use symmetry to analyze mathematical situations

Similar Triangles and Indirect Measurement

Triangles that have the same shape but not necessarily the same dimensions are called similar triangles. Similar triangles have corresponding angles and corresponding sides. Arcs are used to show congruent angles. If two triangles are similar, then the corresponding angles have the same measure, and the corresponding sides are proportional. Therefore, to determine the measures of the sides of similar triangles when some measures are known, proportions can be used.

Transformations

A transformation is a movement of a geometric figure. There are several types of transformations. In a translation, also called a slide, a figure is slid from one position to another without turning it. Every point of the original figure is moved the same distance and in the same direction. In a reflection, also called a flip, a figure is flipped over a line to form a mirror image. Every point of the original figure has a corresponding point on the other side of the line of symmetry. In a rotation, also called a turn, a figure is turned around a fixed point. A figure can be rotated 0°–360° clockwise or counterclockwise. A dilation transforms each line to a parallel line whose length is a fixed multiple of the length of the original line to create a similar figure that will be either larger or smaller.

▶ Use visualizations, spatial reasoning, and geometric modeling to solve problems

Two-Dimensional Representations of Three-Dimensional Objects

Three-dimensional objects can be represented in a two-dimensional drawing in order to more easily determine properties such as surface area and volume. When you look at the triangular prism, you can see the orientation of its three dimensions, length, width, and height. Using the drawing and the formulas for surface area and volume, you can easily calculate these properties.

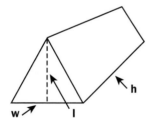

Another way to represent a three-dimensional object in a two-dimensional plane is by using a net, which is the unfolded representation. Imagine cutting the vertices of a box until it is flat then drawing an outline of it. That's a net. Most objects have more than one net, but any one can be measured to determine surface area. Below is a cube and one of its nets.

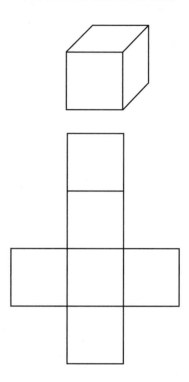

Measurement

▶ Understand measurable attributes of objects and the units, systems, and processes of measurement

Customary System

The customary system is the system of weights and measures used in the United States. The main units of weight are ounces, pounds (1 equal to 16 ounces), and tons (1 equal to 2,000 pounds). Length is typically measured in inches, feet (1 equal to 12 inches), yards (1 equal to 3 feet), and miles (1 equal to 5,280 feet), while area is measured in square feet and acres (1 equal to 43,560 square feet). Liquid is measured in cups, pints (1 equal to 2 cups), quarts (1 equal to 2 pints), and gallons (1 equal to 4 quarts). Finally, temperature is measured in degrees Fahrenheit.

Metric System

The metric system is a decimal system of weights and measurements in which the prefixes of the words for the units of measure indicate the relationships between the different measurements. In this system, the main units of weight, or mass, are grams and kilograms. Length is measured in millimeters, centimeters, meters, and kilometers, and the units of area are square millimeters, centimeters, meters, and kilometers. Liquid is typically measured in milliliters and liters, while temperature is in degrees Celsius.

Selecting Units of Measure

When measuring something, it is important to select the appropriate type and size of unit. For example, in the United States it would be appropriate when describing someone's height to use feet and inches. These units of height or length are good to use because they are in the customary system, and they are of appropriate size. In the customary system, use inches, feet, and miles for lengths and perimeters; square inches, feet, and miles for area and surface area; and cups, pints, quarts, gallons or cubic inches and feet (and less commonly miles) for volume. In the metric system use millimeters, centimeters, meters, and kilometers for lengths and perimeters; square units millimeters, centimeters, meters, and kilometers for area and surface area; and milliliters and liters for volume. Finally, always use degrees to measure angles.

▶ Apply appropriate techniques, tools, and formulas to determine measurements

Precision and Significant Digits

The precision of measurement is the exactness to which a measurement is made. Precision depends on the smallest unit of measure being used, or the precision unit. One way to record a measure is to estimate to the nearest precision unit. A more precise method is to include all of the digits that are actually measured, plus one estimated digit. The digits recorded, called significant digits, indicate the precision of the measurement. There are special rules for determining significant digits. If a number contains a decimal point, the number of significant digits is found by counting from left to right, starting with the first nonzero digit. If the number does not contain a decimal point, the number of significant digits is found by counting the digits from left to right, starting with the first digit and ending with the last nonzero digit.

Surface Area

The amount of material needed to cover the surface of a figure is called the surface area. It can be calculated by finding the area of each face and adding them together. To find the surface area of a rectangular prism, for example, the formula $S = 2lw + 2lh + 2wh$ applies. A cylinder, on the other hand, may be unrolled to reveal two circles and a rectangle. Its surface area can be determined by finding the area of the two circles, $2\pi r^2$, and adding it to the area of the rectangle, $2\pi rh$ (the length of the rectangle is the circumference of one of the circles), or $S = 2\pi r^2 + 2\pi rh$. The surface area of a pyramid is measured in a slightly different way because the sides of a pyramid are triangles that intersect at the vertex. These sides are called lateral faces and the height of each is called the slant height. The sum of their areas is the lateral area of a pyramid. The surface area of a square pyramid is the lateral area $\frac{1}{2}bh$ (area of a lateral face) times 4 (number of lateral faces), plus the area of the base. The surface area of a cone is the area of its circular base (πr^2) plus its lateral area (πrl, where l is the slant height).

Volume

Volume is the measure of space occupied by a solid region. To find the volume of a prism, the area of the base is multiplied by the measure of the height, $V = Bh$. A solid containing several prisms can be broken down into its component prisms. Then the volume of each component can be found and the volumes added. The volume of a cylinder can be determined by finding the area of its circular base, πr^2, and then multiplying by the height of the cylinder. A pyramid has one-third the volume of a prism with the same base and height. To find the volume of a pyramid, multiply the area of the base by the pyramid's height, and then divide by 3. Simply stated, the formula for the volume of a pyramid is $V = \frac{1}{3}bh$. A cone is a three-dimensional figure with one circular base and a curved surface connecting the base and the vertex. The volume of a cone is one-third the volume of a cylinder with the same base area and height. Like a pyramid, the formula for the volume of a cone is $V = \frac{1}{3}bh$. More specifically, the formula is $V = \frac{1}{3}\pi r^2 h$.

Upper and Lower Bounds

Upper and lower bounds have to do with the accuracy of a measurement. When a measurement is given, the degree of accuracy is also stated to tell you what the upper and lower bounds of the measurement are. The upper bound is the largest possible value that a measurement could have had before being rounded down, and the lower bound is the lowest possible value it could have had before being rounded up.

Data Analysis and Probablity

▶ *Formulate questions that can be addressed with data and collect, organize, and display relevant data to answer them*

Histograms

A histogram displays numerical data that have been organized into equal intervals using bars that have the same width and no space between them. While a histogram does not give exact data points, its shape shows the distribution of the data. Histograms also can be used to compare data.

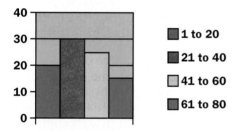

- 1 to 20
- 21 to 40
- 41 to 60
- 61 to 80

Box-and-Whisker Plot

A box-and-whisker plot displays the measures of central tendency and variation. A box is drawn around the quartile values, and whiskers extend from each quartile to the extreme data points. To make a box plot for a set of data, draw a number line that covers the range of data. Find the median, the extremes, and the upper and lower quartiles. Mark these points on the number line with bullets, then draw a box and the whiskers. The length of a whisker or box shows whether the values of the data in that part are concentrated or spread out.

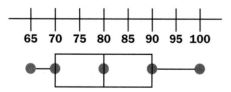

Scatter Plots

A scatter plot is a graph that shows the relationship between two sets of data. In a scatter plot, two sets of data are graphed as ordered

pairs on a coordinate system. Two sets of data can have a positive correlation (as *x* increases, *y* increases), a negative correlation (as *x* increases, *y* decreases), or no correlation (no obvious pattern is shown). Scatter plots can be used to spot trends, draw conclusions, and make predictions about data.

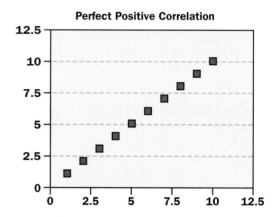

Randomization

The idea of randomization is a very important principle of statistics and the design of experiments. Data must be selected randomly to prevent bias from influencing the results. For example, you want to know the average income of people in your town but you can only use a sample of 100 individuals to make determinations about everyone. If you select 100 individuals who are all doctors, you will have a biased sample. However, if you chose a random sample of 100 people out of the phone book, you are much more likely to accurately represent average income in the town.

Statistics and Parameters

Statistics is a science that involves collecting, analyzing, and presenting data. The data can be collected in various ways—for example through a census or by making physical measurements. The data can then be analyzed by creating summary statistics, which have to do with the distribution of the data sample, including the mean, range, and standard error. They can also be illustrated in tables and graphs, like box-plots, scatter plots, and histograms. The presentation of the data typically involves describing the strength or validity of the data and what they show. For example, an analysis of ancestry of people in a city might tell you something about immigration patterns, unless the data set is very small or biased in some way, in which case it is not likely to be very accurate or useful.

Categorical and Measurement Data

When analyzing data, it is important to understand if the data is qualitative or quantitative. Categorical data is qualitative and measurement, or numerical, data is quantitative. Categorical data describes a quality of something and can be placed into different categories. For example, if you are analyzing the number of students in different grades in a school, each grade is a category. On the other hand, measurement data is continuous, like height, weight, or any other measurable variable. Measurement data can be converted into categorical data if you decide to group the data. Using height as an example, you can group the continuous data set into categories like under 5 feet, 5 feet to 5 feet 5 inches, over 5 feet five inches to 6 feet, and so on.

Univariate and Bivariate Data

In data analysis, a researcher can analyze one variable at a time or look at how multiple variables behave together. Univariate data involves only one variable, for example height in humans. You can measure the height in a population of people then plot the results in a histogram to look at how height is distributed in humans. To summarize univariate data, you can use statistics like the mean, mode, median, range, and standard deviation, which is a measure of variation. When looking at more than one variable at once, you use multivariate data. Bivariate data involves two variables. For example, you can look at height and age in humans together by gathering information on both variables from individuals in a population. You can then plot both variables in a scatter plot, look at how the variables behave in relation to each other, and create an equation that represents the relationship, also called a regression. These equations could help answer questions such as, for example, does height increase with age in humans?

▶ Select and use appropriate statistical methods to analyze data

Measures of Central Tendency

When you have a list of numerical data, it is often helpful to use one or more numbers to represent the whole set. These numbers are called measures of central tendency. Three measures of central tendency are mean, median, and mode. The mean is the sum of the data divided by the number of items in the data set. The median is the middle number of the ordered data (or the mean of the two middle numbers).

The mode is the number or numbers that occur most often. These measures of central tendency allow data to be analyzed and better understood.

Measures of Spread

In statistics, measures of spread or variation are used to describe how data are distributed. The range of a set of data is the difference between the greatest and the least values of the data set. The quartiles are the values that divide the data into four equal parts. The median of data separates the set in half. Similarly, the median of the lower half of a set of data is the lower quartile. The median of the upper half of a set of data is the upper quartile. The interquartile range is the difference between the upper quartile and the lower quartile.

Line of Best Fit

When real-life data are collected, the points graphed usually do not form a straight line, but they may approximate a linear relationship. A line of best fit is a line that lies very close to most of the data points. It can be used to predict data. You also can use the equation of the best-fit line to make predictions.

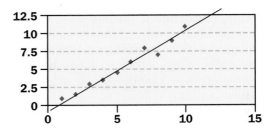

Stem and Leaf Plots

In a stem and leaf plot, numerical data are listed in ascending or descending order. The greatest place value of the data is used for the stems. The next greatest place value forms the leaves. For example, if the least number in a set of data is 8 and the greatest number is 95, draw a vertical line and write the stems from 0 to 9 to the left of the line. Write the leaves from to the right of the line, with the corresponding stem. Next, rearrange the leaves so they are ordered from least to greatest. Then include a key or explanation, such as 1|3 = 13. Notice that the stem-and-leaf plot below is like a histogram turned on its side.

```
0|8
1|3 6
2|5 6 9
3|0 2 7 8
4|0 1 4 7 9
5|1 4 5 8
6|1 3 7
7|5 8
8|2 6
9|5
```
Key: **1|3** = **13**

▶ Develop and evaluate inferences and predictions that are based on data

Sampling Distribution
The sampling distribution of a population is the distribution that would result if you could take an infinite number of samples from the population, average each, and then average the averages. The more normal the distribution of the population, that is, how closely the distribution follows a bell curve, the more likely the sampling distribution will also follow a normal distribution. Furthermore, the larger the sample, the more likely it will accurately represent the entire population. For instance, you are more likely to gain more representative results from a population of 1,000 with a sample of 100 than with a sample of 2.

Validity
In statistics, validity refers to acquiring results that accurately reflect that which is being measured. In other words, it is important when performing statistical analyses, to ensure that the data are valid in that the sample being analyzed represents the population to the best extent possible. Randomization of data and using appropriate sample sizes are two important aspects of making valid inferences about a population.

▶ Understand and apply basic concepts of probability

Complementary, Mutually Exclusive Events
To understand probability theory, it is important to know if two events are mutually exclusive, or complementary: the occurrence of one event automatically implies the non-occurrence of the other. That is, two complementary events cannot both occur. If you roll a pair of dice, the event of rolling 6 and rolling doubles have an outcome in common (3, 3), so they are not mutually exclusive. If you roll (3, 3), you also roll doubles. However, the events of rolling a 9 and rolling doubles are mutually exclusive because they have no outcomes in common. If you roll a 9, you will not also roll doubles.

Independent and Dependent Events
Determining the probability of a series of events requires that you know whether the events are independent or dependent. An independent event has no influence on the occurrence of subsequent events, whereas, a dependent event does influence subsequent events. The chances that a woman's first child will be a girl are $\frac{1}{2}$, and the chances that her second child will be a girl are also $\frac{1}{2}$ because the two events are independent of each other. However, if there are 7 red marbles in a bag of 15 marbles, the chances that the first marble you pick will be red are $\frac{7}{15}$ and if you indeed pick a red marble and remove it, you have reduced the chances of picking another red marble to $\frac{6}{14}$.

Sample Space
The sample space is the group of all possible outcomes for an event. For example, if you are tossing a single six-sided die, the sample space is {1, 2, 3, 4, 5, 6}. Similarly, you can determine the sample space for the possible outcomes of two events. If you are going to toss a coin twice, the sample space is {(heads, heads), (heads, tails), (tails, heads), (tails, tails)}.

Computing the Probability of a Compound Event
If two events are independent, the outcome of one event does not influence the outcome of the second. For example, if a bag contains 2 blue and 3 red marbles, then the probability of selecting a blue marble, replacing it, and then selecting a red marble is $P(A) \times P(B) = \frac{2}{5} \times \frac{3}{5}$ or $\frac{6}{25}$.

If two events are dependent, the outcome of one event affects the outcome of the second. For example, if a bag contains 2 blue and 3 red marbles, then the probability of selecting a blue and then a red marble without replacing the first marble is $P(A) \times P(B$ following $A) = \frac{2}{5} \times \frac{3}{4}$ or $\frac{3}{10}$. Two events that cannot happen at the same time are mutually exclusive. For example, when you roll two number cubes, you cannot roll a sum that is both 5 and even. So, $P(A$ or $B) = \frac{4}{36} + \frac{18}{36}$ or $\frac{11}{18}$.

MAKING CAREER CHOICES

A career differs from a job in that it is a series of progressively more responsible jobs in one field or a related field. You will need to learn some special skills to choose a career and to help you in your job search. Choosing a career and identifying career opportunities require careful thought and preparation.

STEPS TO MAKING A CAREER DECISION

The *Career Plan Project Workbook* is available at this book's Online Learning Center at **glencoe.com**. It provides information and worksheets that can help you develop the essential elements of a career plan. You can use this workbook to explore the three core areas of career decision making: self-assessment, career exploration, and goal setting. Then you can follow step-by-step directions to create your own career plan. These are the five basic steps to making a career decision:

1. Create a self-profile with these headings: lifestyle goals, values, interests, aptitudes, skills and abilities, personality traits, learning styles. Fill in information about yourself.

2. Identify possible career choices based on your self-assessment.

3. Gather information on each choice, including future trends.

4. Evaluate your choices based on your self-assessment.

5. Make your decision.

After you make your decision, create a career plan that explains how you will reach your goal. Include short-term, medium-term, and long-term goals. In making your choices, explore the future opportunities in this field or fields over the next several years. What impact will new technology and automation have on job opportunities in a rapidly evolving workplace environment? Remember, if you plan, you make your own career opportunities.

COLLEGE AND CAREER PORTFOLIO

A college and career portfolio is a collection of information about a person, including documents, projects, and work samples that show a person's skills, talents, and qualifications. It includes information needed for a job search or to apply for college. Turn to the end of this Career Skills Handbook for more information and instructions for creating your own college and career portfolio.

CAREER RESEARCH RESOURCES

In order to gather information on various career opportunities, there are a variety of sources to research:

- **Libraries.** Your school or public library offers books, magazines, pamphlets, videos, and reference materials on careers. The U.S. Department of Labor publishes the *Dictionary of Occupational Titles (DOT)*, which describes about 20,000 jobs and their relationships with data, people, and things; the *Occupational Outlook Handbook (OOH)*, with information on more than 200 occupations; and the *Guide for Occupational Exploration (GOE),* a reference that organizes the world of work into interest areas that are subdivided into work groups and subgroups.

- **The Internet.** The Internet is a primary source of research on any topic. It is especially helpful in researching careers.

- **Career Consultations.** Career consultation, an informational interview with a professional who works in a career that interests you, provides an opportunity to learn about the realities of a career.

- **On-the-Job Experience.** On-the-job experience can be valuable in learning firsthand about a job or career. You can find out if your school has a work-experience program, or look into a company or organization's internship opportunities. Interning gives you direct work experience and often allows you to make valuable contacts.

THE JOB SEARCH

To aid you in your actual job search, there are various sources to explore. You should contact and research all the sources that might produce a job lead, or information about a job. Keep a contact list as you proceed with your search. Some job search resources include:

- **Networking with family, friends, and acquaintances.** This means contacting people you know personally, including school counselors, former employers, and professional people.
- **Cooperative education and work-experience programs.** Many schools have programs in which students work part-time on a job related to one of their classes. Many also offer work-experience programs that are not limited to just one career area, such as marketing.
- **Newspaper ads.** Reading the Help Wanted advertisements in your local papers will provide a source of job leads, as well as teach you about the local job market.
- **Employment agencies.** Most cities have two types of employment agencies, public and private. These employment agencies match workers with jobs. Some private agencies may charge a fee, so be sure to know who is expected to pay the fee and what the fee is.
- **Company personnel offices.** Large and medium-sized companies have personnel offices to handle employment matters, including the hiring of new workers. You can check on job openings by contacting the office by telephone or by scheduling a personal visit.
- **Searching the Internet.** Cyberspace offers multiple opportunities for your job search. Many Web sites provide lists of companies offering employment. There are thousands of career-related Web sites, so find those that have jobs that interest you. Companies that interest you may have a Web site, which may provide information on their benefits and opportunities for employment.

APPLYING FOR A JOB

When you have contacted the sources of job leads and found some jobs that interest you, the next step is to apply for them. You will need to complete application forms, write letters of application, and prepare your own résumé. Before you apply for a job, you will need to have a work permit if you are under the age of 18 in most states. Some state and federal labor laws designate certain jobs as too dangerous for young workers. Laws also limit the number of hours of work allowed during a day, a week, or the school year. You will also need to have proper documentation, such as a green card if you are not a U.S. citizen.

JOB APPLICATION

You can obtain the job application form directly at the place of business, by requesting it in writing, or over the Internet. It is best if you can fill the form out at home, but some businesses require that you fill it out at the place of work.

Fill out the job application forms neatly and accurately, using standard English, the formal style of speaking and writing you learned in school. You must be truthful and pay attention to detail in filling out the form.

PERSONAL FACT SHEET

To be sure that the answers you write on a job or college application form are accurate, make a personal fact sheet before filling out the application:

- Your name, home address, and phone number
- Your Social Security number
- The job you are applying for
- The date you can begin work
- The days and hours you can work
- The pay you want
- Whether or not you have been convicted of a crime
- Your education
- Your previous work experience
- Your birth date

- Your driver's license number if you have one
- Your interests and hobbies, and awards you have won
- Your previous work experience, including dates
- Schools you have attended
- Places you have lived
- Accommodations you may need from the employer
- A list of references—people who will tell an employer that you will do a good job, such as relatives, students, former employers.

LETTERS OF RECOMMENDATION

Letters of recommendation are helpful. You can request teachers, counselors, relatives, and other acquaintances who know you well to write these letters. They should be short, to the point, and give a brief overview of your important accomplishments or projects. The letter should end with a description of your character and work ethic.

LETTER OF APPLICATION

Some employees prefer a letter of application, rather than an application form. This letter is like writing a sales pitch about yourself. You need to tell why you are the best person for the job, what special qualifications you have, and include all the information usually found on an application form. Write the letter in standard English, making certain that it is neat, accurate, and correct.

RÉSUMÉ

The purpose of a résumé is to make an employer want to interview you. A résumé tells prospective employers what you are like and what you can do for them. A good résumé summarizes you at your best in a one- or two-page outline. It should include the following information:

1. **Identification.** Include your name, address, telephone number, and e-mail address.
2. **Objective.** Indicate the type of job you are looking for.
3. **Experience.** List experience related to the specific job for which you are applying. List other work if you have not worked in a related field.
4. **Education.** Include schools attended from high school on, the dates of attendance, and diplomas, degrees, licenses, or certifications earned. A professional certification is a designation earned by a person to assure qualification to perform a job or task. You may also include courses you are taking or have taken that are related to the job you are applying for.
5. **References.** Include up to three references or indicate that they are available. Always ask people ahead of time if they are willing to be listed as references for you.

A résumé that you put online or send by e-mail is called an electronic résumé. Some Web sites allow you to post them on their sites without charge. Employers access these sites to find new employees. Your electronic résumé should follow the guidelines for a print résumé. It needs to be accurate. Stress your skills and sell yourself to prospective employers.

COVER LETTER

If you are going to get the job you want, you need to write a great cover letter to accompany your résumé. Think of a cover letter as an introduction: a piece of paper that conveys a smile, a confident hello, and a nice, firm handshake. The cover letter is the first thing a potential employer sees, and it can make a powerful impression. The following are some tips for creating a cover letter that is professional and gets the attention you want:

- **Keep it short.** Your cover letter should be one page, no more.
- **Make it look professional.** Key your letter on a computer and print it on a laser printer. Use white or buff-colored paper. Key your name, address, phone number, and e-mail address at the top of the page.
- **Explain why you are writing.** Start your letter with one sentence describing where you heard of the opening. "Joan Wright suggested I contact you regarding a position in your marketing department," or "I am writing to apply for the position you advertised in the Sun City Journal."

- **Introduce yourself.** Give a short description of your professional abilities and background. Refer to your attached résumé: "As you will see in the attached résumé, I am an experienced editor with a background in newspapers, magazines, and textbooks." Then highlight one or two specific accomplishments.
- **Sell yourself.** Your cover letter should leave the reader thinking, "This person is exactly who we are looking for." Focus on what you can do for the company. Relate your skills to the skills and responsibilities mentioned in the job listing. If the ad mentions solving problems, relate a problem you solved at school or work. If the ad mentions specific skills or knowledge required, mention your mastery of these in your letter. (Also be sure these skills are included on your résumé.)
- **Provide all requested information.** If the Help Wanted ad asked for "salary requirements" or "salary history," include this information in your cover letter. However, you do not have to give specific numbers. It is okay to say, "My wage is in the range of $10 to $15 per hour." If the employer does not ask for salary information, do not offer any.
- **Ask for an interview.** You have sold yourself, now wrap it up. Be confident, but not pushy. "If I would be an asset to your company, please call me at [insert your phone number]. I am available for an interview at your convenience." Finally, thank the person. "Thank you for your consideration. I look forward to hearing from you soon." Always close with a "Sincerely," followed by your full name and signature.
- **Check for errors.** Read and re-read your letter to make sure each sentence is correctly worded and there are no errors in spelling, punctuation, or grammar. Do not rely on your computer's spell checker or grammar checker. A spell check will not detect if you keyed "tot he" instead of "to the." It is a good idea to have someone else read your letter, too. He or she might notice an error you overlooked.

INTERVIEW

Understanding how to best prepare for and follow up on interviews is critical to your career success. At different times in your life, you may interview with a teacher or professor, a prospective employer, a supervisor, or a promotion or tenure committee. Just as having an excellent résumé is vital for opening the door, interview skills are critical for putting your best foot forward and seizing the opportunity to clearly articulate why you are the best person for the job.

RESEARCH THE COMPANY

Your ability to convince an employer that you understand and are interested in the field you are interviewing to enter is important. Show that you have knowledge about the company and the industry. What products or services does the company offer? How is it doing? What is the competition? Use your research to demonstrate your understanding of the company.

PREPARE QUESTIONS FOR THE INTERVIEWER

Prepare interview questions to ask the interviewer. Some examples include:

- "What would my responsibilities be?"
- "Could you describe my work environment?"
- "What are the chances to move up in the company?"
- "Do you offer training?"
- "What can you tell me about the people who work here?"

DRESS APPROPRIATELY

You will never get a second chance to make a good first impression. Nonverbal communication is 90 percent of communication, so dressing appropriately is of the utmost importance. Wear clothing that is appropriate for the job for which you are applying. In most situations, you will be safe if you wear clean, pressed, conservative business clothes in neutral colors. Pay special attention to grooming. Keep makeup light and wear very little jewelry. Make certain your nails and hair are clean, trimmed, and neat. Do not carry a large purse, backpack, books, or coat. Simply carry a pad of paper, a pen, and extra copies of your résumé and letters of reference.

EXHIBIT GOOD BEHAVIOR

Conduct yourself properly during an interview. Go alone; be courteous and polite to everyone you meet. Relax and focus on your purpose: to make the best possible impression.

- Be on time.
- Be poised and relaxed.
- Avoid nervous habits.
- Avoid littering your speech with verbal clutter such as "you know," "um," and "like."
- Look your interviewer in the eye and speak with confidence.
- Use nonverbal techniques to reinforce your confidence, such as a firm handshake and poised demeanor.
- Convey maturity by exhibiting the ability to tolerate differences of opinion.
- Never call anyone by a first name unless you are asked to do so.
- Know the name, title, and the pronunciation of the interviewer's name.
- Do not sit down until the interviewer does.
- Do not talk too much about your personal life.
- Never bad-mouth your former employers.

BE PREPARED FOR COMMON INTERVIEW QUESTIONS

You can never be sure exactly what will happen at an interview, but you can be prepared for common interview questions. There are some interview questions that are illegal. Interviewers should not ask you about your age, gender, color, race, or religion. Employers should not ask whether you are a parent, married or pregnant, or question your health or disabilities.

Take time to think about your answers now. You might even write them down to clarify your thinking. The key to all interview questions is to be honest, and to be positive. Focus your answers on skills and abilities that apply to the job you are seeking. Practice answering the following questions with a friend:

- "Tell me about yourself."
- "Why do you want to work at this company?"

- "What did you like/dislike about your last job?"
- "What is your biggest accomplishment?"
- "What is your greatest strength?"
- "What is your greatest weakness?"
- "Do you prefer to work with others or on your own?"
- "What are your career goals?" or "Where do you see yourself in five years?"
- "Tell me about a time that you had a lot of work to do in a short time. How did you manage the situation?"
- "Have you ever had to work closely with a person you didn't get along with? How did you handle the situation?"

AFTER THE INTERVIEW

Be sure to thank the interviewer after the interview for his or her time and effort. Do not forget to follow up after the interview. Ask, "What is the next step?" If you are told to call in a few days, wait two or three days before calling back.

If the interview went well, the employer may call you to offer you the job. Find out the terms of the job offer, including job title and pay. Decide whether you want the job. If you decide not to accept the job, write a letter of rejection. Be courteous and thank the person for the opportunity and the offer. You may wish to give a brief general reason for not accepting the job. Leave the door open for possible employment in the future.

FOLLOW UP WITH A LETTER

Write a thank-you letter as soon as the interview is over. This shows your good manners, interest, and enthusiasm for the job. It also shows that you are organized. Make the letter neat and courteous. Thank the interviewer. Sell yourself again.

ACCEPTING A NEW JOB

If you decide to take the job, write a letter of acceptance. The letter should include some words of appreciation for the opportunity, written acceptance of the job offer, the terms of employment (salary, hours, benefits), and the starting date. Make sure the letter is neat and correct.

◕ STARTING A NEW JOB

Your first day of work will be busy. Determine what the dress code is and dress appropriately. Learn to do each task assigned properly. Ask for help when you need it. Learn the rules and regulations of the workplace.

You will do some paperwork on your first day. Bring your personal fact sheet with you. You will need to fill out some forms. Form W-4 tells your employer how much money to withhold for taxes. You may also need to fill out Form I-9. This shows that you are allowed to work in the United States. You will need your Social Security number and proof that you are allowed to work in the United States. You can bring your U.S. passport, your Certificate of Naturalization, or your Certificate of U.S. Citizenship. If you are not a permanent resident of the United States, bring your green card. If you are a resident of the United States, you will need to bring your work permit on your first day. If you are under the age of 16 in some states, you need a different kind of work permit.

You might be requested to take a drug test as a requirement for employment in some states. This could be for the safety of you and your coworkers, especially when working with machinery or other equipment.

EMPLOYABILITY SKILLS

You will need employability skills to succeed in a rapidly evolving workplace environment. These skills include personal and interpersonal skills, such as functioning effectively as part of a team and demonstrating leadership skills, no matter what position you are in. There are also certain qualities and behaviors that are needed to be a good employee.

- Attend work regularly.
- Be prompt.
- Make the most productive use of your time.
- Be cooperative, responsible, and honest.
- Obey company rules.
- Have a positive attitude.
- Show enthusiasm for and pride in your work.
- Tolerate differences.
- Be open-minded.
- Show respect.

- Be flexible.
- Take initiative.
- Be willing to learn new skills.
- Listen attentively.
- Use an appropriate voice.
- Demonstrate planning and time-management skills.
- Keep your work environment clean and safe.
- Understand the legal and ethical responsibilities related to your job.
- Understand the relationship between health and achievement.
- Understand and avoid the personal and occupational implications of substance abuse.

LEAVING A JOB

If you are considering leaving your job or are being laid off, you are facing one of the most difficult aspects in your career. The first step in resigning is to prepare a short resignation letter to offer your supervisor at the conclusion of the meeting you set up with him or her. Keep the letter short and to the point. Express your appreciation for the opportunity you had with the company. Do not try to list all that was wrong with the job.

You want to leave on good terms. Do not forget to ask for a reference. Do not talk about your employer or any of your coworkers. Do not talk negatively about your employer when you apply for a new job.

If you are being laid off or face downsizing, it can make you feel angry or depressed. Try to view it as a career-change opportunity. If possible, negotiate a good severance package. Find out about any benefits you may be entitled to. Perhaps the company will offer job-search services or consultation for finding new employment.

◕ TAKE ACTION!

It is time for action. Remember the networking and contact lists you created when you searched for this job. Reach out for support from friends, family, and other acquaintances. Consider joining a job-search club. Assess your skills. Upgrade them if necessary. Examine your attitude and your career choices. Decide the direction you wish to take and move on!

BUILD YOUR COLLEGE AND CAREER PORTFOLIO

A college and career portfolio is a collection of information about a person, including documents, projects, and work samples that showcase a person's academic and professional skills, talents, accomplishments, and qualifications. It includes the information needed for a job search or for applying for college. Your portfolio can be a paper portfolio in a folder, a digital portfolio with electronic files, or a combination of both. You can use your college and career portfolio throughout your life to keep track of your academic and career goals and accomplishments.

- **Personal Fact Sheet** When you apply for a job, you will probably fill out an application that asks for information that may not be on your résumé. For that reason you should include a personal fact sheet in your college and career portfolio. Include all of the items listed in the "Résumé" section earlier in this handbook.

- **Evaluate Yourself** The information you know about yourself can help you choose a career that is right for you. Update your self evaluation periodically to make sure you are on the right path.

- **Conduct Career Research** Create a section for your portfolio called Career Research. Include information about career clusters and careers that interest you and sources of information you find helpful. Also include notes from career interviews and career evaluations. Update the Career Research section of your portfolio as you continue to explore your career options.

- **Prepare a Career Plan** After you have made a career decision, you can make a career plan. Create a section for your portfolio called career plan. Your first step in making your career plan is setting a career goal. Then you can set the short-term goals, medium-term goals, and long-term goals that will lead you to your career goal. Include goals related to education or training and other experiential learning. Review, update, or create new career plans as you continue to explore your career options.

- **Résumé and Cover Letter** Your college and career portfolio should include your résumé and a sample cover letter that you can use when following up job leads. When you find a job that interests you, note the qualifications required. Then customize your cover letter and résumé so that they are tailored to the job. Relate the skills you have to the skills required for the job.

- **Develop References** You should supply references when you apply for a job. You may also need them when applying for college. Include a list of your references in your college and career portfolio. Include each person's name, title and company, address, phone number, and e-mail address. If your references will provide written letters of reference, include copies in your portfolio. People to ask include former managers, teachers, counselors, or other trusted adults in the community who can comment on your reliability and attitude.

- **Showcase Your Technology Skills** The best way to show an employer what you know about technology is by demonstrating your technology skills! As you research the career that interests you, take note of the hardware, software, and other technology tools that are current in the field. Then, learn to use the technologies and include examples that show your mastery of these tools in your college and career portfolio. Include a list of hardware and software that you know how to use.

- **Awards, Honors, and Certifications** If you have received awards or honors, include any relevant information about them in your college and career portfolio. Also, if you have any licenses or certifications related to your continuing education or job search, also include these in your portfolio.

Career Skills Handbook

REVIEW KEY CONCEPTS

1. What are the five steps to making a career decision?

2. What three types of goals should a career plan include?

3. Why is a personal fact sheet useful?

4. What are employability skills?

5. What is the role of professional certifications in a career search?

6. What is the role of a career and college portfolio?

7. What are the functions of résumés and portfolios?

8. Why is it important to demonstrate leadership skills?

9. What are five positive work qualities?

10. What are three questions you should be prepared to answer in a job interview?

CRITICAL THINKING

11. Compare and contrast the role of a résumé and a cover letter.

12. Analyze why your career choice might change as you get older.

13. Predict the consequences of choosing a career that conflicts with your personal values.

14. Evaluate how tracking employment trends and technology trends can help you manage your own career.

15. Explain why you think it is important to think critically, demonstrate strong communication skills, and function effectively as part of a team in order to be successful in the workplace.

16. Analyze the importance of time management and project management skills in your chosen career field. Explain your answer.

CHALLENGE YOURSELF!

17. Imagine that you have been asked to work on a project team either at school or where you work.

    - Think about the leadership and team-work skills that you would need to be a successful member of the project team.

    - Demonstrate your knowledge of leadership and teamwork skills by creating a checklist that outlines what these skills are.

    - Work with a partner to identify how you would demonstrate these skills and behaviors in a work or school environment. Relate the skills to the "Employability Skills" section elsewhere in this handbook. For example, offering to perform a task that another team member cannot complete may demonstrate initiative and support for a fellow team member.

18. Research careers of personal interest to you. Look at career Web sites to find job opportunities and accompanying duties.

    - Find out what type of education, certification, job training, and experience are required to meet your career goals.

    - Create a five-year plan that breaks down your goals.

    - What do you need to do now in order to meet your goals? What will you need to do next year? How will you assess your progress?

Go Online e-RESOURCES
glencoe.com

Go to the **Online Learning Center** to find career resources, including information about résumés, portfolios, and interview and workplace tips. Use the *Career Plan Project Workbook* to help you create a career plan.

How to Use This Glossary

- Content vocabulary terms in this glossary are words that relate to this book's content. They are **highlighted yellow** in your text.

- Words in this glossary that are boldfaced blue are academic vocabulary terms. They help you understand your school subjects and are used on tests. They are **boldfaced blue** in your text.

- Some of the vocabulary words in this glossary include pronunciation symbols to help you pronounce the words.

Pronunciation Key

a . . . .at	ô . . . .fork, all	th . . .thin
ā . . . .ape	oo . . .wood, put	th . . .this
ä . . . .father	o͞o . . .fool	zh . . .treasure
e . . . .end	oi . . .oil	ə . . . .ago, taken, pencil, lemon, circus
ē . . . .me	ou . . .out	
i . . . .it	u . . . .up	' . . . .indicates primary stress (symbol in front of and *above* letter)
ī . . . .ice	ū . . . .use	
o . . . .hot	ü . . . .rule	ˌ . . . .indicates secondary stress (symbol in front of and *below* letter)
ō . . . .hope	u̱ . . . .pull	
ȯ . . . .saw	ŋ . . . .sing	

A

acceptable use policy (AUP) A policy used by organizations such as schools and businesses to regulate online use. (p. 52)

access Retrieve. (p. 33)

accessibility (ik-ˌse-sə-'bi-lə-tē) The quality that enables people with different needs to access and use multimedia resources. (p. 117)

accurate Free from error. (p. 117)

acquire To get. (p. 321)

adequate Sufficient. (p. 242)

alignment (ə-'līn-mənt) The position of text on a page such as left, right, or center. (p. 180)

alpha test Testing used to check that an application runs correctly, is free of errors, and is easy for the audience to use. (p. 117)

analog A mechanism which represents data by continuously variable physical quantities. (p. 233)

analyze To determine the nature of something. (p. 101)

animation (ˌa-nə-'mā-shən) The representation of motion in graphics or text. (p. 8)

application software Commonly referred to as an application, software used to perform specific tasks on a computer. (p. 77)

attribute A descriptive property or characteristic of an object or image. (p. 203)

audio ('ȯ'dē-ˌō) Live, streamed, or recorded sound. (p. 8)

audio card Also called a sound card, a circuit board that processes sound and sends it to a computer's speakers. (p. 8, 242)

auditory Experienced through hearing. (p. 258)

automatic Programmed to occur with minimal human interaction. (p. 215)

B

back end The part of an application that processes data and makes production work. (p. 293)

balance The arrangement of elements so that no one part overpowers any other part. (p. 139)

bandwidth The amount of data that can be transmitted to the receiver in a given amount of time. (p. 236)

banner ad A type of advertisement that, when clicked, navigates to the sponsor's home page. (p. 167)

batch processing A process that applies a particular action to multiple files automatically. (p. 262)

benefit Advantage. (p. 323)

bitmapped graphic Also known as a raster graphic, or simply a bitmap, an image made up of tiny dots, or pixels. (p. 199)

Boolean search (ˈbü-lē-ən ˈsərch) A type of search that combines keywords in specific ways to locate specific information. (p. 46)

buffer To hold a file in a computer's memory before playback begins. (p. 263)

bug An error in the code. (p. 295)

C

camcorder A mobile electronics device combining a video camera and a video recorder. (p. 267)

canvas The area where a video is displayed. (p. 262)

capacity Capability. (p. 74)

career pathway An area of concentration within a career cluster. (p. 315)

central processing unit (CPU) The brain of a computer, on which all of the internal parts rely; also called processor. (p. 71)

channel A stream of audio. (p. 234)

citation A short note that acknowledges the source of material. (p. 55)

client (1) An individual computer that is part of a network. (p. 81) (2) The group or person who pays for and publishes a multimedia production. (p. 290)

clip A segment of a longer video recording, or any relatively short video. (p. 259)

CMYK color model A subtractive color model consisting of cyan, magenta, yellow, and black; used mainly for print deliverables. (p. 137)

codec (ˈkōd-ˌək) Short for compression/decompression; the means of compressing and decompressing data. (p. 236)

collaboration Working together. (p. 49)

color The appearance of objects and light sources as described by hue, tint, and brightness. (p. 136)

color model The model used to create color. (p. 206)

color theory A standard set of guidelines about using color. (p. 136)

common Shared. (p. 177)

communicate To transmit information and express ideas. (p. 33, 301)

complementary color Color that is similar in hue and intensity to another color. (p. 137)

comprehensive Thorough. (p. 99)

comps Short for comprehensive artwork or composite design; illustrates the site's proposed visual design. (p. 301)

computer An electronic device that processes data. (p. 69)

computer-generated imagery (CGI) Three-dimensional special effects applied to computer graphics. (p. 213)

consider To think about carefully. (p. 176)

contrasting color Colors which are obviously distinct from each other. (p. 137)

convert To change the form of. (p. 82)

cooperative experience An agreement with a local business to hire students to perform jobs that use knowledge and skills taught in their classes, also called work-based experience. (p. 21)

copyright A law that asserts that only the copyright's owner has the right to sell the work or allow someone else to sell it. (p. 54)

crucial Extremely important. (p. 261)

curricular experience Real-world skills gained through class content; experience gained from classroom projects and activities. (p. 20)

cyberbullying Repeated harassment of a teenager by another teenager using Internet chat rooms, text messages, social networking sites, or other digital technology such as cell phones. (p. 53)

D

debug To correct any errors. (p. 295)

deliverable The final format a multimedia project will take; the actual multimedia elements a project team will submit. (p. 104)

demographic Statistical data about a population. (p. 297)

demonstrate To illustrate and explain. (p. 13)

developer The organization or department enlisted by the client to create a multimedia project. (p. 293)

device A piece of equipment. (p. 297)

distinct Distinguishable to the eye as being separate. (p. 204)

distort To twist to exaggerate proportions. (p. 140)

diverse Differing. (p. 70)

domain name Part of a URL that identifies the entity (such as a university, individual, or business) that sponsors the Web site. (p. 41)

E

edit To revise and correct. (p. 118)

element A component. (p. 7)

emphasis The principle of visual design that makes one part of a work dominant over the other parts. (p. 140)

employability skill The general qualities and behaviors of good employees. (p. 323)

enable To allow. (p. 81)

ensure To guarantee. (p. 7)

e-portfolio A showcase of digital samples of your work. (p. 321)

ethics Values for human conduct concerning right and wrong or good and bad behavior. (p. 52)

evaluate To study and judge. (p. 150)

evaluation The process of judging how effective a multimedia project is. (p. 119)

evident Capable of being seen. (p. 144)

exemplary Model. (p. 293)

extended learning opportunity An opportunity that connects what students learn in school to what they hope to do in their career. (p. 20)

extracurricular activity An activity that students do outside of school. (p. 21)

F

file compression A method of saving a file in a smaller format. (p. 201)

file format The way a document is saved, which determines the programs and operating systems that can open it. (p. 172)

flexible Capable of changing to meet more than one purpose. (p. 111)

focal point The element that first attracts the attention of the viewer. (p. 135)

focus Emphasis. (p. 20)

font A family of letters, numbers, and other symbols that share a consistent style. (p. 176)

footage The raw scenes from a video camera, prior to editing. (p. 270)

form The shape and structure of something. (p. 134)

frame A single still image in a video or animation. (p. 258)

frame rate The speed at which frames are displayed, measured in frames per second (fps). (p. 258)

Glossary

frame-by-frame animation Animation that uses the same principles as live video by simulating motion through a series of many frames showing tiny changes in position. (p. 215)

front end The visible part of an application, with which the user interacts. (p. 293)

fundamental Essential. (p. 145)

G

generate To bring into existance. (p. 258)

goal Objective. (p. 293)

graphic A drawing, chart, diagram, painting, picture, or photograph shared in a digital format. (p. 8)

graphical user interface (GUI) ('gü-ē) The display that allows users to interact with a computer by clicking the mouse or using a keyboard. (p. 76)

graphics tablet A tool that lets users create sketches and drawings for display on a computer monitor. (p. 72)

guideline A rule or principle that provides advice for appropriate behavior. (p. 183)

H

hardware The physical components of a computer. (p. 33)

harmony The principle of art that creates unity by stressing the similarities of separate but related parts. (p. 140)

hue The name of a color. (p. 136)

Hypertext Transfer Protocol (HTTP) ('hī-pər-ˌtekst 'prō-tə- kȯl) A protocol used to transfer files from a Web server to a Web browser. (p. 39)

I

implementation The project stage in which the finished project is delivered to the audience; sometimes called "roll-out." (p. 119)

incorporate Include. (p. 171)

intensity The brightness or dullness of a color. (p. 136)

input device A tool for entering data into a computer. (p. 72)

interact Act together. (p. 14)

interactive media Media that allows active participation by the user. (p. 7)

Internet Hardware, such as computers and cables, that is connected to create a massive worldwide network. (p. 33)

Internet service provider (ISP) A business that allows its users to access the Internet through the provided network. (p. 34)

internship A temporary paid or unpaid position that involves direct work experience in a career field. (p. 21)

J

job shadowing A process that involves following a worker on the job for a short time. (p. 21)

K

kerning The amount of space between a specific pair of characters. (p. 181)

keyword An important word related to the specific topic you are trying to locate. (p. 46)

L

layout The arrangement of text and graphics on each page or display. (p. 144)

line The path of a moving point through space. (p. 134)

local area network (LAN) A network that connects computers in a single location, such as a department within a company. (p. 81)

M

maintenance The regular care needed to keep a multimedia production up-to-date and working properly. (p. 119)

media Multiple means of conveying information; the plural of medium. (p. 7)

medium Any means of conveying information. (p. 7)

minimize To keep to a minimum. (p. 206)

mission statement A brief statement that describes the purpose and audience of a multimedia project. (p. 103)

mock-up A working model of a multimedia project's designs and navigation elements. (p. 113)

multimedia The integration of interactive elements such as text, graphics, animation, audio, and video using computer technology. (p. 7)

N

native file format The default format in which a file is saved. (p. 200)

navigation scheme The plan that determines how the components of a multimedia project relate to each other. (p. 108)

netiquette General guidelines for online users. (p. 53)

network A system that allows computers to connect and communicate. (p. 33)

network interface card (NIC) A circuit board or PC card that allows a client computer to connect to a network. (p. 82)

network operating system (NOS) An operating system with special functions for linking computers and other devices in LANs. (p. 82)

O

objective One of the items that must be completed to meet a project's goals. (p. 101)

open source Published software that the public can freely copy, modify, and distribute. (p. 169)

operating system (OS) A program that acts as an interface between the hardware, the user, and all of the software programs on a computer. (p. 76)

orientation Arrangement and alignment. (p. 145)

output device A tool that lets users examine the results of processed data. (p. 73)

P

pattern Two-dimentional decorative affect achieved through the repetition of colors, lines, shapes, or textures. (p. 140)

peer review An informal editing process in which team members review and critique each other's work. (p. 150)

perspective A graphic system that creates the illusion of depth and volume on a two-dimensional surface. (p. 136)

pixel A single point in a graphic image, an abbreviation for **pic**ture **el**ements. (p. 198)

plug-in Software that works with a Web browser to play a particular file format, such as an audio or video file. (p. 40)

podcast An audio or video recording of a broadcast that is distributed via the Web. (p. 50)

point One seventy-second of an inch. (p. 178)

potential Possible. (p. 297)

presentation A sequence of slides that usually incorporates multimedia elements; a visual display. (p. 11)

principle A rule or code of conduct. (p. 230)

print publication A document that can be printed. (p. 11)

professional Someone who engages in an activity as an occupation. (p. 239)

project plan A plan that defines the purpose, audience, technical needs, and design needs of a multimedia project. (p. 101)

project team A team created for a particular purpose and time period. (p. 293)

propaganda Facts, ideas, and opinions that are used in a misleading way to promote a cause. (p. 54)

proportion The principle of visual design concerned with the size relationship of one component to another. (p. 140)

proposal A formal outline of the work according to a stated schedule. (p. 290)

Glossary

Glossary

protocol A set of rules and procedures specifying how data needs to be formatted and transmitted between computer systems. (p. 35)

prototype A sample version or model of a product design and navigation elements. (p. 293)

proprietary Exclusive use of something. (p. 233)

pursue Work toward. (p. 321)

R

raster graphic ('ras-tər 'gra-fik) A graphic made of pixels, also called a bitmap. (p. 198)

real time A signal that is transmitted live, without edits or delays. (p. 260)

require To demand as necessary or essential. (p. 315)

resolution The number of pixels per inch (ppi) of a bitmap. (p. 201)

résumé A brief, written account of employment qualifications. (p. 321)

retrieve To locate and bring back. (p. 40)

RGB color model An additive color model consisting of red, green, and blue, mainly used for onscreen displays. (p. 136)

rich media Interactive multimedia productions that require powerful technology for proper delivery, such as streaming audio and video. (p. 7)

role A function or the part performed. (p. 167)

rollover A small animation consisting of two or three images that switch when the cursor rolls over a navigation button or other onscreen element. (p. 215)

router A special hardware device used to join local area networks (LANs). (p. 82)

S

sample size The number of bits of data in an audio sample, usually 8 or 16 bits. (p. 234)

sampling Recording fragments of a continuous event, such as sound, to reproduce it. (p. 234)

sampling rate The number of times per second a recording device samples sound waves. (p. 234)

sans serif (sanz-'ser-əf) A font that lacks special adornment at the end of letters or numbers. (p. 176)

scope The set of features and content a multimedia project will include given the available resources. (p. 104)

search engine An application that locates information about Web pages and then stores this information in searchable databases that can be accessed with a browser. (p. 45)

secure Free from risk or loss. (p. 268)

serif ('ser-əf) A font with decorative lines or curves on the ends of most letters. (p. 176)

server A powerful central computer that manages files and services on a network. (p. 81)

service learning An extended learning opportunity in which you do volunteer work related to career goals. (p. 21)

shape A two-dimensional object created by joining the points of lines. (p. 134)

significant Considerable. (p. 19)

simulation A computer-based model of a real-life situation. (p. 14)

software A program that translates a user's commands into instructions a computer can process. (p. 76)

sound effect An artificially created or enhanced sound used to achieve an effect, without speech or music, in a presentation. (p. 229)

source code The programming instructions and commands for a Web site. (p. 303)

space The real or implied area between, around, above, below, or within objects. (p. 134)

specific Particular. (p. 109)

speech synthesis A computer program used to articulate human speech. (p. 242)

standard image format A format that is supported by most graphics applications. (p. 200)

storyboard A visual representation of a multimedia project. (p. 112)

streaming media A downloading process that shortens the user's wait time by breaking the transmission into small pieces. (p. 40)

streaming video A way of transferring data so that a browser starts to display the video before the entire file has been transmitted. (p. 40, 262)

suit To be appropriate. (p. 302)

supplement To complete or add to. (p. 321)

symmetry Balanced proportions. (p. 139)

T

tag A code that instructs a browser how to display a Web page. (p. 303)

tailor To adapt to fit. (p. 315)

target audience The group of people who will use or view a multimedia production. (p. 102)

team A group of people organized to work together in an activity. (p. 293)

teamwork To collaborate with others on a common goal such as the completion of a multimedia project. (p. 293)

text Consisting of written words, numbers, or symbols. (p. 7)

text editor A program for modifying plain text files and to create XHTML documents. (p. 170)

text format The appearance of text: font, point size, spacing, and so forth. (p. 171)

text message A brief electronic message between mobile devices. (p. 168)

texture The surface quality or characteristic that you can see or feel. (p. 137)

tracking The amount of space between characters. (p. 181)

trademark A name, symbol, or other feature that identifies a product with a specific owner. (p. 54)

tutorial A computer application that trains or teaches content or skills. (p. 13)

tweening The animation process of generating transitional frames between two keyframes. (p. 215)

typeface A design for a set of characters such as letters, numbers, and punctuation marks. (p. 176)

typography (tī-ˈpä-grə-fē) The style, arrangement, and appearance of text. (p. 176)

U

uniform resource locator (URL) A unique address that enables a browser to locate specific page files on the Web. (p. 41)

unique (yu̇-ˈnēk) One-of-a-kind. (p. 41)

unity A combination of parts to make one. (p. 140)

usability test An assessment by untrained professionals to see how easy a product is to use. (p. 293)

utilize Use. (p. 323)

V

value The lightness or darkness of a color. (p. 136)

vector graphic An image drawn in lines, curves, and shapes defined by mathematical equations. (p. 199)

via By way of. (p. 212)

video Live or recorded moving images. (p. 8)

video capture card A circuit board that converts analog video, such as tape from a VCR or analog camcorder, to digital format. (p. 268)

video game A software program combining multimedia elements designed primarily for entertainment. (p. 14)

video tuner card A card that allows a computer to receive cable, aerial, or satellite television signals. (p. 268)

virtual reality A simulation, which often uses 3D graphics and animation, that lets you interact with an artificial environment by moving around in it and manipulating simulated objects. (p. 213)

Glossary

vision Concept or mental image. (p. 293)

visual design The process of planning, arranging, and integrating visual elements to address a purpose. (p. 133)

vlog Video blog, a blog that mainly publishes videos clips. (p. 259)

voice recognition An input device for a computer that recognizes the human voice. (p. 242)

voice-over Narration over all or part of a presentation. (p. 229)

W

Web browser Software that locates and displays Web pages on a user's computer screen. (p. 38)

Web page The basic component of the Web, a single file within a Web site that has a unique name. (p. 38)

Web site A group of related and interlinked XHTML files organized around a common topic. (p. 38)

Web site authoring software A sophisticated application package that some Web developers use to create Web sites. Also known as Web site development application. (p. 303)

Webcam A low-end digital camera that broadcasts real-time video. (p. 267)

Webcasting Broadcasting audio and video using the Web. (p. 260)

wide area network (WAN) A network that connects computers across a wider geographical area than a local area network (LAN). (p. 81)

wireframe model Mathematical representation that lets you visualize the entire 3D structure of an object. (p. 213)

World Wide Web A software system of linked files that may contain text, graphics, audio, video, or animation that is used on the Internet. (p. 33)

INDEX

+ (Boolean operator), 74
− (Boolean operator), 74
/ (forward slash), 94
<, > (angle brackets), 93

A

Absolute value, 338
Acceptable use policy (AUP), 52
Acceptance of job, 355
Accessibility, 117, 122
  of audio, 232
  of PDFs, 172
  Section 508 standards for, 149
  of video, 258
  and visual design, 148
  of Web sites, 302
Accountability, 326
Active listening, 289
Addition, 337–339
Additive inverse property, 338
Advertising, online, 167
AIFF files, 232
Alerts, audio, 229
Algebra, 340–343
Alignment, text, 180
Alpha test, 117, 118
Analog audio recordings, 233
Analysis and planning stage,
  101–103, 297–298
Analyzing audio, 239
Angles, 343–344
Animation, 8, 211–217
  appropriate use of, 212
  development of, 302
  editing, 215–217
  file formats for, 214
  Internet sources of, 211
  software for, 214
  of text, 180
  three-dimensional, 213
  two-dimensional, 212–213
  types of, 212
  using, 211
Appearance, for job interview,
  354
Application letters, 353
Application software
  (applications), 77

Applications, job, 352–354
Artists, 22
Arts, audio/video (A/V) technology, and communica-
  tions career cluster, 317
Aspect ratio, 204
Asymptotes, 341
AU files, 232
Audacity, 240
Audience, 31, 102, 299
Audio, 8, 229–245
  accessibility issues with, 232
  adding sound effects,
    244–245
  development of, 302
  editing software for, 239–242
  file formats for, 232, 233
  file size for, 235–236
  forms of, 229
  hardware for, 242–244
  locating files online, 230
  project requirements for,
    298
  role of, in multimedia, 231
  sound quality, 233–234
  working with, 238–239
Audio cards, 242
Audio effects, 8
Audio software, 77
Audio specialists, 22, 294,
  318
Authoring software, 171, 303
AVI files, 264
Awards, in college and career
  portfolio, 357

B

Back end, 293
Back-end developer roles,
  294, 319
Background, 135
Balance, 138, 139, 144
Bandwidth, 236
Banner ads, 167
Batch processing, 271
Behavior, in job interviews,
  355
Beta test/review, 118

Bitmaps, 199
Bivariate data, 349
Blogs, 49
Blue-ray discs (BDs), 74
BMP file format, 200
Bold type, 179, 184
Boolean searches, 46–47
Box-and-whisker plots, 348
Brainstorming, 144
Brightness, 204
Broadband connections, 34
Broadcasts, video, 260
Browsers, 299
Budget, project, 104
Buffering, 263
Bugs, 294

C

Camcorders, 267
Cameras, 267
Canvas, video, 262
Canvas size, video, 262
Capture cards, 268
Capturing video, 262
Career clusters, 19, 317
Career consultations, 351
Career outlook, 321
Career plan, 351, 357
Career Plan Project Workbook,
  351
Career planning, 19
Career research, 351, 357
Career skills, 351–358
  accepting a new job, 355
  action plan, 356
  after-interview activities, 355
  applying for a job, 352–354
  career research, 351
  college and career portfolio,
    351, 357
  employability skills, 356
  job interviews, 354–355
  job search, 352
  leaving a job, 356
  making career decisions, 351
  starting a new job, 356
Career-based learning
  experiences, 21, 319

D

Index

Index

Index

Index

CREDITS

SCREEN CAPTURE CREDITS

Microsoft product screen shots reprinted with permission from Microsoft Corporation.

Adobe product screen shots reprinted with permission from Adobe Systems Incorporated.

Microsoft Office Word 2007, © 2007, **7**, **191**; National Aeronautics and Space Administration (NASA), **8**, **57**; Microsoft Office PowerPoint 2007, © 2007, **12**, **63**, **147**, **211**; © 1999–2009 Google, **11**, **45**, **47**, **49**; Glencoe/ McGraw-Hill © 2009, **13**; © 2009 Yahoo! Inc. All rights reserved, **36**, **111**, **257**; Bing, © 2009, Microsoft, **39**; Mozilla Firefox, **40**, **299**; © 2009 CNN Cable News Network, **50**; © 2009 Quickwebco.nz, **52**; © 1995–2008 The Writing Lab, The OWL at Purdue, the English Department, and Purdue University. All rights reserved, **56**, **58**; © Wikimedia Foundation, Inc., **61**; Microsoft Clip Art © 2009 MS Clip Art, Microsoft Corporation, all rights reserved, **72–74**, **121**, **139**; Microsoft Windows Vista, © 2007 Microsoft Corporation, **76**, **83–84**; Apple iPhone © 2009 Apple Inc., **76**; PBS Sprout © 2005–2009, Children's Network, LLC, **101**; © 1994–1999 FIFA, **114**; © 2009 Interior Design Services, Inc., **134**; © 2007 Discovery Communications LLC, **136**; Museum of Neon Art, **141**; HighSchoolSports.net, **150**; Technorati.com, **167**; © 1983–2007 Apple Inc., **168**; © 2009 Adobe Systems Incorporated, **169**, **177**, **271**; Adobe Dreamweaver, © 2009, **170**; Adobe InDesign, © 2009, **171**; Microsoft Internet Explorer, copyright © 2009 Microsoft Corporation, **174**; Adobe Photoshop, copyright © 1990–2007 Adobe Systems Incorporated, **202**, **208–209**; Adobe Flash, copyright © 1990–2007 Adobe Systems Incorporated, **216–217**; © 2009 Extensis, a division of Celartem, Inc., **218**; © 2001–2009 Listen.com, a subsidiary of RealNetworks, **230**; Apple QuickTime, © 2009, **236**; Audacity, © 2009, **240–241**, **244–245**; © 1994–2008 by Encyclopædia Britannica, Inc., **259**; Smithsonian Institution, **263**; © 1996–2009 EarthCam, Inc., All rights reserved, **267**; Microsoft Windows MovieMaker © 2007, **269**; © 2009 March of Dimes Foundation, All rights reserved, **297**; Safari, © 2007–2008 Apple Inc. All rights reserved, **299**; U.S. Bureau of Labor Statistics, **321**; © 2006 Multimedia Careers.com, All rights reserved, **324**; © 2009 FBLA-PBL. All rights reserved, **326**.

IMAGE CREDITS

Cover(c) Matt Carr/Getty Images; (lc) Mike Kemp/Getty Images; (rc) Peter Dazeley/Getty Images; (l) Rolf Bruderer/Corbis; (r) Tom Carter/Photolibrary; **2–3** Juice Images/Corbis; **4–5** Juice Images/Corbis; **14** Tom Fox/ Dallas Morning News/Corbis; **22** DreamPictures/VStock/Getty Images; **30–31** Laurence Mouton/PhotoAlto/ Corbis; **38** Rolf Bruderer/Masterfile; **51** Andersen Ross/Gettyimages; **66–67** Ken Chernus/Getty Images; **79** Edward Bock/Corbis; **94–95** Thinkstock Images/Getty Images; **96–97** AFP/Getty Images; **120** McGraw-Hill Companies Inc.; **122** Kim Kulish/Corbis; **130–131** Ableimages/Getty Images; **152** Masterfile; **162-163** Tim Pannell/Corbis; **164–165** Ronnie Kaufman; **174** Hein van den Heuvel/Corbis; **186** Masterfile; **194–195** Masterfile; **197** The McGraw-Hill Companies Inc.; **204** Royalty-Free/Corbis; **226–227** Jim Craigmyle/Corbis; **229** Masterfile; **243**(l) Microsoft Corp.; **243**(r) Royalty-Free/Corbis/Microsoft; **246** Image Source/Corbis; **254–255** Thierry Dosogne/Getty Images; **261** Masterfile; **284–285** Justin Guariglia/Corbis; **286–287** Masterfile; **306** Masterfile; **314–315** Ben & Marcos Welsh/Age Fotostock; **319** Reggie Casagrande/Getty Images.